D1155027

RHETORIC AND PEDAGOGY
ITS HISTORY, PHILOSOPHY, AND PRACTICE

Essays in Honor of James J. Murphy

RHETORIC AND PEDAGOGY
ITS HISTORY, PHILOSOPHY, AND PRACTICE

Essays in Honor of James J. Murphy

Edited by

Winifred Bryan Horner
Texas Christian University

Michael Leff
Northwestern University

 LAWRENCE ERLBAUM ASSOCIATES, PUBLISHERS
1995   Mahwah, New Jersey   Hove, UK

Lawrence Erlbaum Associates, Inc., Publishers
10 Industrial Avenue
Mahwah, New Jersey 07430

Library of Congress Cataloging-in-Publication Data

Rhetoric and pedagogy : its history, philosophy, and practice : essays
in honor of James J. Murphy / edited by Winifred Bryan Horner,
Michael Leff.
    p.   cm.
   Includes bibliographical references and index.
   ISBN 0-8058-1821-9. — ISBN 0-8058-1822-7 (pbk.)
   1. Murphy, James Jerome. 2. Rhetoric. 3. Rhetoric—Study and
teaching. I. Horner, Winifred Bryan. II. Leff, Michael C.
PN175.R39 1995
808—dc20   95-9848
                                             CIP

Books published by Lawrence Erlbaum Associates are printed on acid-free
paper, and their bindings are chosen for strength and durability.

James J. Murphy

Contents

PART II   RENAISSANCE TEXTBOOKS
AND RHETORICAL EDUCATION

PART III   CONTINUITY AND CHANGE IN
18TH-CENTURY RHETORICAL EDUCATION

Preface

This book is a celebration of James J. Murphy's long career as teacher and scholar, a career that gives no indication of abating as attested by the "works in progress" at the end of his bibliography.

Many of the contributors to this book actually had the privilege of sitting in his classroom at the universities where he taught. The quality of their work and their status in the profession are evidence of his influence and his skill. At his own university, The University of California, Davis, he served briefly as vice chancellor for Student Affairs and associate dean of the College of Letters and Science. He also served two terms as chair of his own department, one of the few rhetoric departments in the United States. But his teaching extends far beyond his own university. Through his many publications, which have appeared in journals as diverse as the *British Library Occasional Papers*, *Studi Medievali*, *Rhetorica*, *Poetica*, the *American Benedictine Review*, *Arts Liberaux et Philosophie au Moyen Age*, as well as in all of the major communications journals in the United States, he has reached out to students and scholars all over the world. Every student of rhetoric knows and has learned from his work. He functions as a master teacher instructing and inspiring scholars far beyond the walls of his own classroom. Finally, he has never seen his work as excluding pedagogy, or theory as separate from practice, or research as outside the realm of teaching.

In addition to his wide influence as a teacher, or perhaps as part of it, Professor Murphy has for years obtained funds to bring together scholars interested in the history of rhetoric at a number of conferences he organized. He has functioned as a great facilitator in gathering together scholars from the United States, Europe, and Asia who shared a common interest in the history of rhetoric—to exchange ideas, to disseminate their work, and just to talk across cultures, gender, and

borders. He has organized major conferences on such assorted subjects as medieval bibliography, medieval studies, rhetoric and literature, medieval grammar,
the trivium, and the 12th century. Out of the interest and excitement generated
at these initial meetings, a number of annual conventions have developed. In
addition, almost every conference has generated at least one book. He was one
of the founders and president of the International Society for the History of
Rhetoric and the originator and first editor of that organization's journal, *Rhetorica*. His most recent enterprise has been the establishment of the Hermagoras
Press, an increasingly important vehicle for the publication of books on rhetoric.

James J. Murphy has proven to be a man of vision who has helped us all to
see that vision through his eyes. When rhetoric was a quaint old-fashioned word
in English departments, members interested in its history often had to work in
an unfriendly and nonsupportive academic atmosphere. From the beginning, he
reached out to encourage scholars to pursue that interest. No one now questions
the importance of rhetoric, and English departments have joined scholars in
classics, history, philosophy, and speech in pursuing research in the history of
rhetoric.

Each of the authors represented in this volume is indebted to James J. Murphy
in one way or another. Finally, the scholars in this book, through their words on
these pages, are paying their tribute to a superb teacher, a world-renowned scholar,
a good friend, and a fine human being.

—Winifred Bryan Horner

Bibliography

Books

(With Richard Katula) ed. *A Synoptic History of Classical Rhetoric*. Second edition. Davis, CA: Hermagoras Press, 1994.

Peter Ramus's Attack on Cicero: Text and Translation of Ramus's Brutinae questiones. Ed. with Introduction by *James J. Murphy*. Translation by Carole Newlands. Davis, CA: Hermagoras Press, 1992.

Murphy, James J. (ed. and contributor). *A Short History of Writing Instruction from Ancient Greece to Twentieth-Century America*. Davis, CA: Hermagoras Press, 1990.

———. *Medieval Rhetoric: A Select Bibliography*. Second edition. University of Toronto Press, 1989.

———. *Quintilian on the Teaching of Speaking and Writing: Translations from Books One, Two, and Ten of the Institutio oratoria*. Southern Illinois University Press, 1987.

———, Jon M. Ericson, and Raymond Zeuschner. *The Debater's Guide*. Southern Illinois University Press. Revised edition, 1987.

——— and Carole Newlands. *Arguments in Rhetoric Against Quintilian*. Translation of *Rhetoricae distinctiones in Quintilianum* (1549) of Pierre de la Ramée. With Introduction and Latin text on facing pages. Northern Illinois University Press, 1986.

———. (ed. and Introduction). *Renaissance Rhetoric: Key Texts, A.D. 1479–1602. A Microfiche Collection of Important Texts from the Bodleian Library, Oxford*. Oxford and New York: Microforms International, 1986.

La retórica en la edad media: Historia del la retórica desde San Agustin hasta el Renacimiento. Traducción de Guillermo Hirata Vaquera. Mexico City: Fondo de Cultura Económica, 1986.

La retorica nel medioevo: Una storia della teorie retoriche da s. Agostino al Renascimento. Trad. Vincenzo Licitra. Napoli: Liguori Editore, 1983.

Murphy, James J. *Demosthenes on the Crown*. Davis, California: Hermagoras Press, 1983.

———. (ed.). *A Synoptic History of Classical Rhetoric*. Davis, California: Hermagoras Press, 1983.

———. (ed.). *Renaissance Eloquence: Studies in the Theory and Practice of Renaissance Rhetoric*. University of California Press, 1983.

———. (ed.). *The Rhetorical Tradition and Modern Writing*. Modern Language Association, 1982.

————. *Rhetoric in the Middle Ages: A History of Rhetorical Theory from Saint Augustine to the Renaissance*. University of California Press, 1981.

————. *Renaissance Rhetoric: A Short-Title Catalogue of Works on Rhetorical Theory from the Beginning of Printing to A.D. 1700, with Special Attention to the Holdings of the Bodleian Library, Oxford. With a Select Basic Bibliography of Secondary Works on Renaissance Rhetoric*. Garland, 1981.

————. (ed. and contributor). *Medieval Eloquence: Studies in the Theory and Practice of Medieval Rhetoric*. University of California Press, 1978.

————. *Rhetoric in the Middle Ages: A History of Rhetorical Theory from Saint Augustine to the Renaissance*. University of California Press, 1974.

————. (ed.). *A Synoptic History of Classical Rhetoric*. Random House, 1972.

————. (ed. and translator). *Three Medieval Rhetorical Arts*. University of California Press, 1971.

————. *Medieval Rhetoric: A Select Bibliography*. University of Toronto Press, 1971.

————. (ed.). *Demosthenes on the Crown*. Random House, 1967.

———— and Peter G. Kontos (eds.). *Teaching Urban Youth*. John Wiley, 1967.

————. (ed.). *Quintilian on the Early Education of the Citizen-Orator*. Bobbs Merrill: Library of Liberal Arts, 1966.

———— and Jon M. Ericson. *The Debaters Guide*. Bobbs Merrill, 1961.

Articles

"The Discourse of the Future: Toward an Understanding of Medieval Literary Theory." In Keith Busby and Norris J. Lacy, eds., *Conjunctures: Studies in Honor of Douglas Kelly*. Amsterdam-Atlanta: Editions Rodopi B.V., 1994.

"Early Christianity as a Persuasive Campaign: Evidence from the Acts of the Apostles and the Letters of Paul." In Stanley E. Porter and Thomas H. Olbricht, eds., *Rhetoric and the New Testament: Essays from the 1992 Heidelberg Conference. Journal for the Study of the New Testament, Supplement 90*. Sheffield: Sheffield Academic Press, 1993.

"Quintilian's Influence on the Teaching of Speaking and Writing in the Middle Ages and Renaissance." In *Oral and Written Communication: Historical Approaches*, ed. Richard Leo Enos. *Written Communication Annual, Volume 4*. Newbury Park: Sage Publications, 1990.

"Roman Writing Instruction as Described by Quintilian." In *A Short History of Writing Instruction*, ed. *James J. Murphy*. Davis, CA: Hermagoras Press, 1990.

"*Topos* and *Figura*: Cause and Effect?" In *De Ortu Grammaticae: Studies in Medieval Grammar and Linguistic Theory in Memory of Jan Pinborg*, eds. G. L. Bursill-Hall, Sten Ebbesen, and Konrad Koerner. Amsterdam: John Benjamins, 1990.

Articles

Murphy, James J. "The Double Revolution of the First Rhetorical Textbook Published in England: The *Margarita eloquentiae* of Guilielmus Traversagnus (1479)." *Texte: revue de critique et de théorie littéraire*, 1989.

————. "The Middle Ages" (with Martin Camargo). In *The Present State of Scholarship in Historical and Contemporary Rhetoric*, second edition, ed. Winifred B. Horner. University of Missouri Press, 1990.

————. "Western Rhetoric." In *Dictionary of the Middle Ages*, ed. Joseph R. Strayer. New York: Charles Scribner's Sons for the American Council of Learned Societies, Volume 10, 1982–1989.

————. "Ciceronian Influences in Latin Rhetorical Compendia of the Fifteenth Century." In *Acta Conventus Neo-Latini Guelpherbytani: Proceedings of the Sixth International Congress of Neo-Latin Studies*, ed. Stella P. Revard, Fidel Radle, and Mario A. Di Cesare. Binghamton, New York. Medieval and Renaissance Texts and Studies, 1988.

————. "The Computer Search as a Guide to Subject Cataloging of Incunabula." In *Bibliography and the Study of Fifteenth Century Civilization*. British Library Occasional Papers 5. London: The British Library, 1987.

————. "Rhetoric in the Earliest Years of Printing, 1465–1500." *Quarterly Journal of Speech* 70, 1984.

————. "One Thousand Neglected Authors: The Scope and Importance of Renaissance Rhetoric." In *Renaissance Eloquence*, 1983.

————. "The Middle Ages." In *The Present State of Scholarship in Historical and Contemporary Rhetoric*, ed. Winifred B. Horner. University of Missouri Press, 1983.

————. "The Historiography of Rhetoric: Challenges and Opportunities." *Rhetorica*, 1(1), (Inaugural issue), 1983.

————. "Rhetorical History as a Guide to the Salvation of American Reading and Writing: A Plea for Curricular Courage." In *James J. Murphy*(ed.), *The Rhetorical Tradition and Modern Writing*. Modern Language Association, 1982.

———— and D. Thomson. "Dictamen as a Developed Genre: The Fourteenth Century 'Brevis doctrine dictaminus' of Ventura da Bergamo." *Studi Medievali* 3a Serie, 23, 1982.

————. "Poetry without Genre: The Metapoetics of the Middle Ages." *Poetica* (Tokyo, Japan) 11. (Title page 1979 and 1980).

————. "The teaching of Latin as a Second Language in the 12th Century." *Historiographia Linguistica* II, 1980.

————. "Rhetoric and dialectic in *Owl and the Nightingale*." In *James J. Murphy* (ed.), *Medieval Eloquence: Studies in the Theory and Practice of Medieval Rhetoric*. University of California Press, 1978.

————. "Demosthenes." In *Encyclopedia Britannica*, Fifteenth Edition, 1974.

————. "The Five Hazards of Education." *Phi Kappa Phi Journal* 54, 1974.

————. "Caxton's Two Choices: 'Modern' and 'Medieval' rhetoric in Traversagni's *Nova Rhetorica* and the anonymous *Court of Sapience*." *Medievalia et Humanistica*, New Series, 3, 1972.

————. "The metarhetorics of Plato, Augustine, and McLuhan: A Pointing Essay." *Philosophy and Rhetoric 4*, 1971.

————. "Alberic of Monte Cassino: Father of the Medieval *Ars Dictaminis*." *American Benedictine Review*, No. 2, 22, 1971.

————. "The rhetorical lore of the *eras* in Byhrtferth's *Manual*." In *Philological Essays: Studies in Old and Middle English Language and Literature*, ed. James L. Rosier. The Hague: Mouton, 1970.

————. "Mistitling and Other Problems in the Field of Renaissance Rhetorical Scholarship." *Quarterly Journal of Speech* 55, 1969.

————. "The Scholastic Condemnation of Rhetoric in the Commentary of Giles of Rome on the Rhetoric of Aristotle." In *Arts Liberaux et Philosophie au Moyen Age* (Montréal et Paris), 1969.

Sharp, H. and *James J. Murphy*. "Forensic Activities in the West: 1957–1968." *Western Speech* No. 4, 32, 1968.

Murphy, James J. "Today's Rhetoric: The Searches for Analogy." *Quarterly Journal of Speech* 54, 1968.

————. "Saint Augustine and Rabanus Maurus: The Genesis of Medieval Rhetoric." *Western Speech*, No. 2, 31, 1967.

————. "Cicero's Rhetoric in the Middle Ages." *Quarterly Journal of Speech* 53, 1967.

————. "Literary Implications of Instruction in the Verbal Arts in Fourteenth Century England." *Leeds Studies in English*, New Series, 1, 1967.

————. "The Four Faces of Rhetoric: A Progress Report." *College Composition and Communication*, 1966.

————. "A Fifteenth Century Treatise on Prose Style." *Newberry Library Bulletin* 6, 1966.

————. "Aristotle's Rhetoric in the Middle Ages." *Quarterly Journal of Speech* 52, 1966.

————. "Rhetoric in Fourteenth Century Oxford." *Medium Aevum* 34, 1965.

————. "Two Medieval Textbooks in Debate." *Journal of the American Forensic Association* 1, 1964.

————. "A new look at Chaucer and the Rhetoricians." *Review of English Studies*, New Series 15, 1964.

————. "Modern Elements in Medieval Rhetoric." *Western Speech* 28, 1964.

————. "The Medieval Arts of Discourse: An Introductory Bibliography." *Speech Monographs* 24, 1962.

————. "John Gower's *Confessio Amantis* and the First Discussion of Rhetoric in the English Language." *Philological Quarterly* 51, 1962.

————. "The Arts of Discourse, 1050–1400." *Medieval Studies* 23, 1961.

————. "Speech and Drama at Stanford." *Western Speech*, 1961.

————. "The Earliest Teaching of Rhetoric at Oxford." *Speech Monographs* 27, 1960.

————. "Saint Augustine and the Debate About a Christian Rhetoric." *Quarterly Journal of Speech* 46, 1960.

———— and J. R. East. "Forensic Activities in the West." *Western Speech*, Fall 1958.

————. "Saint Augustine and the Christianization of Rhetoric." *Western Speech* 21, 1958.

————. Curriculum Committees to Plan Forensic Activities." *Western Speech*, January 1954.

Wilson, R. B. and *J. J. Murphy*. "The Interschool Curriculum." *Southern Speech Journal*, December 1953.

In Press

"The School 'Arts' of Poetry and Prose." In *The Cambridge History of Literary Criticism*, Vol. 2: *The Middle Ages*, ed. Alastair Minnis. Cambridge University Press.

"Preaching." In *The Blackwell Encyclopedia of Medieval, Renaissance and Reformation Christian Thought*, ed. Alister McGrath. Oxford: Blackwell Publishers.

"Antonio Nebrija in the European Rhetorical Tradition." In *Coloquio Humanista: Antonio Nebrija, Edad Media y Renacimiento*, ed. Carmen Codoner. University of Salamanca.

"Rhetoric." In *Medieval Latin Studies: An Introduction and Bibliographical Guide*, ed. Frank A. C. Mantello and George Rigg. Catholic University of America Press.

"Rhetoric." In *An Anthology of Medieval Latin*, ed. Frank A. C. Mantello and George Rigg. Catholic University of America Press.

In Progress

Rhetoric in the Early Renaissance. With an Annotated Catalogue of Rhetorical Works Printed to A.D. 1500.

(With Lawrence Green). Second Edition of *Renaissance Rhetoric: A Short-title Catalogue* (1981).

Introduction: James J. Murphy and the Rhetorical Tradition

Beth S. Bennett
University of Alabama

Michael Leff
Northwestern University

In his review of *Rhetoric in the Middle Ages*, certainly the most ambitious and probably the most influential of Jerry Murphy's books, Judson Boyce Allen concludes with this assessment:

> It is good, therefore, to have in Murphy's book a history of medieval rhetoric which not only provides, as any good reference book should, a well-annotated description of the present state of the art; but which also makes it possible, and necessary, to raise the questions which must be the basis for future and better understanding. For many years now Murphy has been insisting, with enthusiasm and persistence, that rhetoric is important. The spate of recent published studies, and of many others in progress, is witness that he is right. In a field so currently active, and whose primary documentation remains so substantially in manuscript, one must be especially grateful for a book which attempts to be comprehensive before it is possible to be fully conclusive.[1]

A striking feature of this passage is the way the focus shifts, comfortably and naturally, from the book, to the person of the author, and then back to the book. Murphy and his work, it would seem, are so closely connected in Allen's mind that he cannot easily separate them, and an assessment of one leads to an assessment of the other. In this case, the association is probably unconscious, but it also is entirely appropriate. For two generations, students of the history of rhetoric have viewed

---

[1] Judson Boyce Allen, Review, *Speculum*, 52 (1977), 414.

Jerry Murphy as a scholar, a writer, and an editor who is at the same time an advocate, a facilitator, and an organizer. His career has intertwined the production and promotion of scholarship so thoroughly that it defies the isolation and specialization of modern scholarship and recalls the "international humanism" that Kees Meerhoff describes (this volume, chapter 13).

Consequently, although our quotation from Judson Allen properly refers to only one of Murphy's works, the comments about the part seem to shed light on the whole, and the quotation provides an appropriate text for this introduction. In the spirit of the medieval rhetoricians, whom Murphy has studied with such care, we can divide our text into three themes that it implies: (a) Murphy and his work are ahead of their time; (b) Murphy not only studies rhetoric but also uses it to promote a communal effort; and (c) Murphy adopts a comprehensive view that opens an old tradition to future inquiry. Each of these themes deserves attention if we are to make a fair appraisal of Murphy's contribution to rhetorical scholarship.

The first theme requires special emphasis, because those of us who stand on the other side of the 20th-century revival of rhetoric may not appreciate how recently or dramatically attitudes have changed. Thirty years ago anyone professing a serious interest in rhetoric could expect to be greeted by bewildered silence or summary dismissal. Writing in 1963, George Kennedy, another pioneer in the field, introduced his *The Art of Persuasion in Greece* with this trenchant comment about the diminished status of the subject he was investigating: "One of the principal interests of the Greeks was rhetoric. Classicists admit the fact, deplore it, and forget it."[2] And outside the domain of classics, where humanists found less obdurate evidence of past interest in rhetoric, the prospects were even more dismal; rhetoric seemed so trivial that it hardly required an effort to forget or deplore it. In this environment, persistent and enthusiastic assertions about the importance of rhetoric were unconventional and hazardous, and Murphy's effort to put rhetoric on the map placed him outside and ahead of the prevailing academic zeitgeist.

Nowadays, of course, events have passed far beyond Murphy's original expectations. The issue is no longer whether rhetoric belongs on the map, but how much territory it ought to cover and how much its influence should force us to reconfigure traditional boundaries. From this perspective, Murphy might emerge as a venerable and rather conservative figure, committed to the traditional project of writing period histories and developing the scholarly apparatus needed to refine them. But a judgment of this kind would be far too simple. At the least, it would require historical amnesia; we would have to forget the point from which Murphy started, the resistance he encountered, and the considerable impulse he lent to the forward movement of rhetorical studies during a formative period. More important, however, Murphy's work, when viewed as a whole,

[2]George Kennedy, *The Art of Persuasion in Greece* (Princeton University Press, 1963), 3.

reveals a relentlessly progressive tendency—a tendency to find new connections and open new avenues for inquiry. This characteristic emerges when we turn to the second and third themes implied in our text.

John Ward (this volume, chapter 7) compares Jerry Murphy with the 15th-century humanist Guarino da Varona. Like Guarino, Ward tells us, Murphy has inspired teachers for many generations, served as a great facilitator and promoter of the discipline, and "combined a deep concern for the classical sources of rhetorical theory with more modern didactic and practical preoccupations." This judgment rests upon very firm ground; in fact, it is difficult to think of anyone now living who has done more to sustain a community of scholars devoted to the study and teaching of the history of rhetoric. Murphy has not only persistently argued for and demonstrated the importance of rhetoric in his own work; he has also displayed enormous energy and skill in bringing scholars together across disciplinary and national boundaries and in developing opportunities for them to work together.

As all of the contributors to this volume can testify, Jerry Murphy has played an indispensable role in the formation and development of the International Society for the History of Rhetoric. He was one of a small group of international scholars—and the only American representative—who planned the inaugural meeting of that society in 1977, and he was elected its second president. During the early years of the society, his energy, administrative skill, and international contacts were essential to its growth and success. It was largely through his instigation that the society's journal, *Rhetorica*, came into being, and during his term as its first editor, the journal won two major awards and established itself as a primary venue for the publication of research in the history of rhetoric.

Equally important has been Murphy's activity as an organizer of conferences devoted to rhetoric and the language arts. Among the more prominent of these meetings were the Conference on Medieval Rhetoric held at Western Michigan University in 1974, the Conference on Medieval Grammar held at the University of California–Davis in 1976, and the Newberry Library Conference on Rhetoric in the Renaissance held in 1979. From the first and last of these conferences, Murphy edited the companion volumes *Medieval Eloquence: Studies in the Theory and Practice of Medieval Rhetoric* (1978) and *Renaissance Eloquence: Studies in the Theory and Practice of Renaissance Rhetoric* (1983). These two volumes incorporate essays by more than two dozen scholars, representing many countries and virtually every discipline in the humanities. The individual essays each present a specialist's account of some aspect of rhetoric during this long period, and when taken together, the two volumes offer an unparalleled view of the history of Western rhetoric from the end of the Roman Empire to the 16th century.

Remarkably, the range of Murphy's interests and energy extends beyond his effort to integrate specialized and general perspectives on the history of rhetoric. As Ward has observed, Murphy has also labored to sustain a connection between the historical tradition and "modern didactic and practical preoccupations." Maintaining an active role in such organizations as the Modern Language Association, the Speech Communication Association, and the Conference on College Composition and Communication, Murphy has authored articles, sponsored conferences, and edited books designed to stimulate cooperative work among members of these sometimes artificially separated groups and to encourage a renewed interest in the tradition among all teachers of the language arts. Again his efforts have achieved their most durable form in edited volumes that coordinate the work of many scholars, and his *The Rhetorical Tradition and Modern Writing* (1982) and *A Short History of Writing Instruction* (1990) testify to the persistence and effectiveness of his attempt to hold historical scholarship and current pragmatic interests in a useful relationship to one another.

This catalogue of Murphy's achievements as an organizer and facilitator (and we would emphasize that it is only a partial listing) surely demonstrates the breadth and range of his commitments. But amidst this diversity, we also find a pattern of balance and integration. Murphy has actively promoted rhetorical scholarship within professional groups devoted to historical studies; at the same time he has actively promoted historical studies within organizations devoted to rhetoric and composition. This strong presence in the two worlds of academic rhetoric—the worlds of the scholarly historian and of the practicing teacher—marks his distinctive achievement. Working quietly against the grain of a specialized culture, Murphy has opened a conduit between historical scholarship and the classroom. The diversity of his career finds unity in his mission as a teacher of rhetoric and as an architect of a community of teachers.

Even Murphy's work in the area of his most intense specialization—medieval rhetoric—reveals the synthetic and practical instincts of a good teacher. To appreciate this point, we once again need to shift our perspective back three decades and consider the situation of a teacher assigned the task of introducing students to medieval rhetoric or of a student interested in beginning a study of the subject. The resources then available were woefully insufficient. Only a handful of the primary texts had been translated into English; no adequate bibliography existed; and the secondary literature consisted of a smattering of scholarly articles, many of them intelligible only to trained medievalists, and a single survey history (Baldwin's *Medieval Rhetoric and Poetic*)—a book thoroughly marred by the author's all too obvious disdain for his subject.

When his scholarship is judged against this background, we can appreciate how Murphy's work systematically covers the gaps in the pedagogical apparatus. His *Three Medieval Rhetorical Arts* (1971) presents translations (one by his own hand) of typical treatises belonging to each of the distinctively medieval genres of rhetorical instruction. His *Medieval Rhetoric: A Select Bibliography* (first published in 1971, with a revised and greatly expanded second edition published in 1989) offers a guide to the literature thorough enough for professional scholars but organized and indexed in way that made it useful for a beginner—even including a "Basic Library" of 40 books "useful for initiating study."[3] His *Rhetoric in the Middle Ages* (1974) finally gives us an account of the whole period that is well informed, sympathetic to the subject, and accessible to a general reader. And those who wish to sample the secondary literature beyond this text can find easy access through the essays collected in *Medieval Eloquence* (1978). Each of these books, of course, stands as an independent contribution to the scholarship, and only one of them—the collection of translations—seems addressed primarily to students rather than to professional scholars. Nevertheless, both the sequence and the format of these works surely indicate that Murphy's scholarship moves along the lines suggested by pedagogical concerns and that this interaction unifies and invigorates both sides of the project. In any event, all of us who now teach medieval rhetoric, whether as a separate subject or as part of a broader survey, are deeply in Murphy's debt; his scholarship has provided the equipment that we need in a form that our students can use.

The third and final theme that we identified in Judson Allen's text is that Murphy sustains a perspective that is both comprehensive and open. This is the most complex of the three themes, and in order to explicate it, we need to move from a general consideration of the man and his work to more concrete ground. For this purpose, we return to the specific referent for Allen's comments, *Rhetoric in the Middle Ages*, and we now offer a rather detailed account of the book's objectives and significance. In doing so, however, we remain mindful of the points we raised earlier and treat the book as a microcosm intimately connected with the whole of Murphy's career. In particular, we want to stress the link between historical research and pedagogy that we have noted as a general characteristic of Murphy's work and as the unifying thread running through his diverse activities. In fact, our analysis largely consists in an effort to explicate Jeanne Krochalis' judgment that *Rhetoric in the Middle Ages* "is a book about teachers of rhetoric by a teacher of rhetoric."[4] This analysis depends on a comparison between Murphy's book and the earlier scholarship on the subject.

The modern study of medieval rhetoric began in the second half of the 19th century when scholars discovered, catalogued, and edited certain Latin texts that resisted typical literary classification and shared some "rhetorical" features. These texts, when grouped by genre, served as evidence that the Middle Ages had produced three new (i.e., nonclassical) preceptive arts of composition—*ars dictaminis* (the art of letter writing), *ars poetica* (the art of poetic composition), and *ars praedicandi* (the art of preaching). The first collection was Rockinger's (1863) *Briefsteller und Formelbucher* (letter-writing manuals and model letters from the 11th to the 14th centuries); it was followed by Thurot's (1868) *notices et extraits* (studies, lists, and textual excerpts of medieval grammatical doctrines), and Faral's (1924) collection in *Les artes poetiques* (six major treatises on poetic composition

---

[3] J. J. Murphy, *Medieval Rhetoric: A Select Bibliography*, 2nd ed. (Toronto: University of Toronto Press, 1989), 176.

[4] Jean Krochalis, Review, *Journal of English and Germanic Philology*, 76 (1977), 445.

from the 12th and 13th centuries). Work in the area of medieval preaching developed somewhat later, but after the publication of Owst's *Preaching in Medieval England* (1926), Caplan (1934) and Charland (1936) drew up listings that, taken together, included more than 300 treatises of *artes praedicandi*.[5]

The first attempt to synthesize some of these materials into a general history appeared in Charles Baldwin's *Medieval Rhetoric and Poetic*.[6] But, as we have already noted, Baldwin's was a history with an attitude, and Judson Allen accurately describes it as "a survey of great books by a man who disapproved of too much of his subject to understand it properly."[7] The source of this disapproval emerges in the opening chapter, where Baldwin divides the art of rhetoric into two neatly opposed conceptions: (a) giving effectiveness to truth, which he calls Aristotelian, and (b) giving effectiveness to the speaker, which he calls sophistic.[8] Sophistic, he claims, is historically typical and constantly threatens to reduce rhetoric to mere display or style—technique devoid of substance or the power of conception. Baldwin attributes this sharp dichotomy between the truth and the speaker and between content and style to classical Greek sources, but his formulation has a distinctively modern ring. In any event, it is certainly not a medieval perspective.

This modern idealization of a classical norm for rhetoric almost necessarily alienates Baldwin from most of the material he investigates. It is not surprising, then, that the book tells a tale of progressive degeneration and fragmentation, with rhetoric sinking ever deeper into the sophistic mire of empty words. Medieval rhetoric, on his account, gradually lost its proper identity, first becoming blurred with grammar and then surpassed by dialectic. He repeatedly notes and deplores a tendency to equate rhetoric with ornamentation, and by the 12th century, he asserts, *rhetorica* was at a standstill; by the 13th century, it no longer sustained any connection with the genuine classical function of composition. The concern for *inventio* had passed entirely into the domain of dialectic, and "that," he concludes, "may explain why there was no medieval rhetorician who really advanced the subject."[9]

A more sympathetic and better balanced account of medieval rhetoric would have to await scholarship less constrained by the brittle and defensive categories that inform modernist views of rhetoric. One such alternative appeared in 1942 with the publication of Richard McKeon's essay "Rhetoric in the Middle Ages."

---

[5]For the complete references to the works cited here and a more detailed account of the developments summarized briefly in this paragraph, see Murphy, "The Middle Ages," in W. B. Horner, *The Present State of Scholarship in Historical Rhetoric* (Columbia, MO: University of Missouri Press, 1983), 40–43.

[6]Charles Baldwin, *Medieval Rhetoric and Poetic (1400) Interpreted from Representative Works* (New York: Macmillan, 1928).

[7]Allen, *Speculum*, 414.

[8]Baldwin, *Medieval Rhetoric and Poetic*, 2–7.

[9]Baldwin, *Medieval Rhetoric and Poetic*, 182.

The essay, in fact, was part of McKeon's "constant battle against the nonrhetorical suppositions that often dominated the scene of his own philosophical activity."[10] McKeon sought to construct a contemporary philosophy that stressed rather than discounted the role of language and grounded argument, and to this end, he sought to rehabilitate certain historical connections between rhetoric and philosophy. In undertaking this task, he needed to overturn the then-existing disciplinary histories, centered on rhetoric as a discrete verbal art, and explore more general relations between rhetorical concepts and philosophical developments. "Rhetoric in the Middle Ages" is a specific and important effort to advance this project, though it is often interpreted more narrowly as a narrative history of medieval rhetoric.

The essay begins with an extended discussion of the inadequacy of existing histories of rhetoric and of the particular difficulties posed by the medieval period. In general, McKeon argues that histories of rhetoric have treated rhetoric simply as a verbal discipline, "the art of speaking well," applied either to forensic and political or to poetic and literary criticism.[11] This perspective, he maintains, yields a rather narrow and fixed conception of the rhetoric that "is usually found to have little or no history" (93). By contrast, McKeon seeks to write a history of rhetoric that considers how medieval rhetoricians conceived the subject matter and purposes of the art and how differences of conception reflected and influenced the intellectual milieu.

What follows from this redirected effort is less a history of rhetoric than what Mitchell describes as a tracing "of medieval culture and its legacy to the Renaissance as a cycle of arts and sciences which derives from rhetorical terms of art fixed by Cicero."[12] McKeon's argument proceeds through a complex set of overlapping categories charted largely through differing conceptions of the scope and nature of logic. He locates three lines of medieval intellectual development that were strongly influenced by Ciceronian rhetoric in their initial stages: the first, the rhetorical tradition based directly on the works of Cicero and Quintilian; the second, a philosophical-theological tradition, essentially Augustine's neo-Platonism; and the third, a logical tradition, scholasticism, which was called Aristotelian and was popularized by Boethius (94). Next, McKeon outlines the development of these traditions over four periods indicated by the history of logic. The early period is marked by elementary treatises or handbooks that contain sections on dialectic (e.g., Martianus Capella, Cassiodorus, and Isidore of Seville). The second period, beginning near the end of the 10th century, is identified as

[10]Douglass Mitchell, "Richard McKeon's Conception of Rhetoric and the Philosophy of Culture," *Rhetorica*, 6 (1988), 395.

[11]Richard McKeon, "Rhetoric in the Middle Ages," in *The Rhetoric of Western Thought*, ed. J. L. Golden et al. (Dubuque, IA: Kendell Hunt, 1989), 92. This is a reprint of the original essay that appeared in *Speculum*, 17 (1942), 1–32. All subsequent page references to the essay are indicated in the text and are based on the reprinted version in Golden.

[12]Mitchell, *Rhetorica*, 400.

the "Old Logic," during which Boethius' writings and translations dominated. Next came the "New Logic," a period spanning the later 12th through most of the 13th centuries, in which translations of previously unknown parts of Aristotle's *Organon* appear in western Europe. The last period, the 14th century, is determined primarily by the *summulae* of Peter of Spain, Lambert of Auxerre, and William of Shyreswood (96–97).

Putting together these three intellectual developments and the four periods in the development of medieval logic, McKeon sees rhetoric transforming itself in three directions: (a) as an art of logic, subordinated to it because it is concerned with hypotheses or specific subjects; (b) as an art of stating truths certified by theology, expanding the methods of Scriptural interpretation and of the interpretation of discordant religious opinion; and (c) as a simple art of words, which flourished from the 11th century into the Renaissance (99–102). This third category roughly corresponds to the "sophistic" rhetoric that Baldwin finds typical of the disciplinary history of the subject, and McKeon characterizes it in these words:

> This tradition of rhetoric took form . . . not in controversy but in a vast number of textbooks which grew in three distinct groups, differentiated according to subject matters once treated by rhetoric but now concerned with verbal forms employed in those three fields in lieu of direct treatment of the subject matter. (110)

The three genres, of course, are *dictamen*, the art of poetic composition, and the art of preaching. These are the main constituents in the conventional history of later medieval rhetoric, but McKeon has little to say about them.

McKeon's inattention to this tradition is consistent with his effort to uproot the conventional disciplinary histories of medieval rhetoric and open matters to broader philosophical concerns. In this respect, he works directly against the spirit of Baldwin's book and its tendency to minimize the significance of medieval rhetoric. Nevertheless, McKeon's enlarged perspective encompasses and tacitly accepts Baldwin's skepticism about disciplinary history. While Baldwin denounces this history as a regression, McKeon steps around it. And thus his rehabilitation of medieval rhetoric implies much the same story of disciplinary fragmentation and disunity. Medieval rhetoric is important for McKeon, but "if rhetoric is defined in terms of a single subject matter—such as style or literature or discourse—it has no history during the Middle Ages" (113).

McKeon's essay displays great erudition (though often it is more easily admired than understood), and there is no doubt that his project has done much to stimulate fresh thought about rhetoric and its history and has served as a major source of the contemporary revival of rhetorical studies. Unfortunately, however, his summary judgment about disciplinary rhetoric in the Middle Ages was often extracted from its context and used (ironically enough) to support Baldwin's story of fragmentation and regression. Thus, at the time Murphy composed *Rheto-*

ric in the Middle Ages, interest in the medieval phase of preceptive rhetoric seemed blocked in both directions: Traditionalists, following Baldwin as reinforced through a misreading of McKeon, regarded this history as retrograde; revisionists, following a better informed reading of McKeon, regarded it as a trivial aspect of a broader, much more important development. Murphy's achievement was to work through this blockage and formulate a new approach, closer to the disciplinary ground than McKeon's revisionism, but more comprehensive and fluid than Baldwin's traditionalism.

Rhetoric in the Middle Ages, like most of Murphy's writings, proceeds directly to the subject at hand. Murphy presents a history that is not encumbered by abstract theoretical reflection or detailed commentary on and argument with other scholars. Partially for this reason, the book is accessible to general readers and is, as Charlotte Stern has noted, a model of lucidity and organizational coherence.[13] At the same time, however, this simple and direct style belies the difficulty of Murphy's task, and a reader unaware of the troubled history of the scholarship is unlikely to appreciate the strategic agility needed to maintain the clarity at the surface of the text. In fact, however, the argument of the book embeds two subtle and closely linked interpretative moves. The first works toward diversity through an expanded and flexible perspective on the rhetorical tradition. The second works toward unity by locating a common ground for the tradition. Taken together, the two sustain the principle of unity in diversity, a characteristic of all Murphy's work and one that he announces unobtrusively in the page opposite the table of contents in *Rhetoric in the Middle Ages.* There Murphy places a quotation from Cicero's *De oratore*: "All eloquence is one . . . regardless of the regions of discourse it is diverted into."

Almost a decade after publication of *Rhetoric in the Middle Ages,* Murphy wrote this summary description of his work:

> *Rhetoric in the Middle Ages* argues that Greek and Roman rhetoric was committed to the discovery of precepts that could be used to plan and present future discourse. . . . Roman education, built around rhetorical preparation for civic life, systematically applied the Isocratean trilogy of talent, education, and practice to devise a complex training program of great efficiency. Both grammatical and rhetorical precepts were employed. This educational program outlasted the culture that gave it birth, transmitting Roman educational practices directly into the middle ages. Early medieval writers like Saint Augustine defended the values of Roman rhetorical training in the face of Christian distrust of pagan ideas, and the so-called encyclopediasts . . . digested basic rhetorical doctrines as part of their surveys of ancient learning. Thus men of the high middle ages . . . inherited both a respect for Roman learning and a set of texts (mainly Ciceronian) presenting its theory. Commentary writers of the 12th and 13th centuries further popularized these ideas. Medieval rhetoric to a great extent then became a series of adaptations of Ciceronian rhetoric

---

[13]Charlotte Stern, Review, *Romance Philology,* 30 (1977), 665.

to particular needs of the times, with applications to problems of letter-writing, verse-writing, and preaching.[14]

Each of his two major interpretative strategies are indicated in this passage, but its most prominent feature is the sweep of the narrative concerning the tradition from classical Greek origins through the Middle Ages. The phases in this narrative and their sequence correspond closely to Baldwin's account, but the perspective has changed decisively. For Murphy, the tradition is no longer conceived as a fixed, inflexible standard established for all time by classical authority. Instead, he uses Aristotle's "leaden rule," a standard that bends and adjusts in conformity with the material under examination. A living tradition necessarily changes under the pressure of time and circumstance, and so medieval alterations in the scope, purposes, and applications of classical doctrine are evidence not of degeneration but of healthy, pragmatic adjustment.[15]

But if a tradition is constantly changing and altering its configuration, how can it sustain an identity over time? This question is especially pressing in the case of medieval rhetoric, because the *artes* of the High Middle Ages diversify and reconfigure their classical antecedents so dramatically that their continuity with the tradition is not at all obvious. Murphy's answer to this problem is consistent with his position as a teacher of rhetoric. The common thread he finds in the development from Isocrates to Thomas Merke is the teaching of rhetoric as a preceptive art. The preceptive lore changes its specific content and purpose as time and circumstances change, but the activity of teaching persists; and if the books written for and by teachers reflect the needs of differing social and cultural environments, they also testify to the common experience of composition teachers in all ages. It is precisely this common ground that allows Murphy to conclude his history of medieval rhetoric by returning to the Ciceronian adage with which it began:

> Underlying every medieval rhetorical treatise, whatever its genre, is the assumption that the communication process can be analyzed, its principles abstracted, and methods of procedure written down to be used by others. This is the essence of

---

[14]Murphy, "The Middle Ages," 49.

[15]This point about tradition as an adjustment of old resources to new conditions has general application, and Murphy has invoked it not only as a way of understanding medieval rhetoric, but also as a strategy for encountering problems in rhetorical pedagogy. He has consistently argued that good composition teaching requires a combination of historical understanding of the art and accommodation to immediate, pragmatic concerns. In one essay, he expressed this point through a striking analogy: "Consider just one example of old principles reshaped to fit modern needs: when the internal combustion engine made motor cars possible, the cars used regular carriage wheels. The vibration ruined the delicately constructed engines, so Charles Goodyear invented the pneumatic tire to fit that ancient invention, the wheel. The wheel had existed for thousands of years, but the motorcar wheel had to be rethought and replanned to meet modern needs." *The Rhetorical Tradition and Modern Writing* (New York: Modern Language Association, 1982), 10.

rhetoric. This commonality makes it possible for the modern observer to understand the basic agreement among the various genres despite the apparently bewildering array of writers, books, and subjects. The *dictator*, the grammar master, and preaching theorist of the middle ages all would agree with the dictum of Cicero . . . that "Eloquence is one . . . regardless of the regions of discourse it is diverted into."[16]

Thus, by grounding his study in the evolving development of rhetorical pedagogy, Murphy achieves a perspective that was at once comprehensive and open. His position, of course, was not without its hazards and limitations. Most obviously, as Allen noted, Murphy's synthetic narrative appears before all of the evidence has been gathered. Much of the basic research in medieval rhetoric has yet to be done. We still do not have a complete inventory of rhetorical texts produced during the period, and many of the most important works remain unedited and inadequately studied. Thus, Murphy is open to the charge that his whole effort is premature; and because of the sweep of his history, specialists inevitably find that parts of it are incomplete and some of the details inadequate. Yet experience over the two decades since the publication of *Rhetoric in the Middle Ages* vindicates Murphy's effort. Rather than closing or distorting understanding of medieval rhetoric, the book has functioned as a stimulus to further research. Murphy's purpose was to provide a first step toward more systematic and energetic study of the period, and whatever the liabilities of the book in detail, it has provided an extremely useful introduction for the beginning student and a framework that specialists have been able to use, alter, or resist as a context for their work.

More generally, we might say that labeling Murphy's perspective as comprehensive involves something of a paradox. The history of rhetoric is a complex and equivocal subject, and an effort to achieve comprehensiveness in one sense almost automatically leads to a narrowing in another sense. Thus, Murphy can sustain the breadth and balance of his account of preceptive rhetoric only by focusing on the pedagogical tradition and marginalizing other perspectives on rhetoric. Some scholars, such as McKeon, quite legitimately focus on the philosophical significance of rhetoric and its role in the intellectual life of the period. Still others, for equally good reason, deemphasize the preceptive treatises and concentrate on rhetoric-in-use—on the literary and political practice of the art. These alternative perspectives yield significantly different versions of rhetoric and its medieval history. Thus, to be accurate, we should say that Murphy offers a comprehensive approach to one version of the story, and that we need to remain mindful of other possible and useful versions.

In the years since publication of *Rhetoric in the Middle Ages*, controversy about the conception of rhetoric, its history, and its relationship to other arts and activities has become increasingly intense. This controversy has roots that go

---

[16]Murphy, *Rhetoric in the Middle Ages: A History of Rhetorical Theory from Saint Augustine to the Renaissance* (Berkeley: University of California Press, 1974), 363.

back to the origin of the tradition, and there is no reason to believe that the current round will be resolved quickly or definitively. But in the midst of this and other disputes occasioned by the revival of rhetoric, we can appreciate *Rhetoric in the Middle Ages* as an important contribution to this revival and as a humane account of teachers of rhetoric by a teacher of rhetoric. At the very least, Jerry Murphy has taught his colleagues an important lesson: The teaching of composition has a complex and interesting history—a history that constantly changes but that preserves its identity in the very work we do in our classrooms. It is a history worth studying.

The 18 chapters that follow in this volume, written by Jerry Murphy's colleagues, friends, and students, honor his contribution to rhetorical studies and offer further evidence of the richness and complexity of the tradition he has done so much to preserve and advance. The chapters are divided into four main sections. The first three maintain a chronological sequence from the classical and medieval eras, to the Renaissance, and then to the 18th century. Each of these chapters develops a theme directly related to rhetorical pedagogy. The fourth and final section deals with issues of somewhat broader scope and addresses some of the relationships among rhetoric, pedagogy, and cultural history in the period from the Renaissance to the present.

Although the historical sweep of these chapters indicates something of the breadth and diversity of the rhetorical tradition, it is also possible to read across the chapters and locate a number of persistent themes and controversies. In fact, all of the chapters have some bearing on one or more of these three fundamental issues: (a) the transmission and reception of doctrine through the tradition; (b) the status of rhetoric as a discipline and its relationship to other disciplines and activities; and (c) the relative importance of precepts and examples in rhetorical pedagogy. To help guide the reader through the book, we want to note the appearance of these issues in various essays and indicate some of the prominent areas of controversy that persist in the tradition.

The problem of understanding the transmission and reception of rhetorical doctrine always has been a key issue in the historiography of rhetoric. Several of the chapters collected in this volume suggest that the dimensions of this issue have been sharpened and refined in ways that go well beyond conventional documentation of sources and influences. George Kennedy suggests that the attitude toward authority is a key element in the transmission process, and he notes two different ways of conceiving the authority of the tradition. One locates this authority in relation to a particular author or set of authors who have achieved canonical status. The other invests authority in a general or universal system that is not the property of any specific person. Kennedy argues that the second view prevailed in the early Middle Ages. John Ward's study of Guarino da Verona indicates the opposite tendency, for, on Ward's account, Guarino regarded Cicero's text as so authoritative that he was content to comment on Cicero rather than produce an independent rhetoric. Perhaps more important, Guarino made no attempt to "read through the cover" of text to discover abstract unities but instead, in effect, let the classical text speak for itself. This personal or dialogical relation with classical authority is, for Ward, a distinctive mark of Renaissance culture and specifies a crucial difference between Guarino and the medieval commentary writers.

S. Michael Halloran's essay raises another aspect of this issue of authority, one that bears on interpretative controversy among contemporary historians of rhetoric. It is a widely accepted convention that the "new rhetoricians" of late 18th-century Britain systematically rejected the authority of the classical rhetoricians. Halloran, however, maintains that the situation is actually more complex and subtle. By studying the appropriation of Quintilian by two of the "new rhetoricians"—Hugh Blair and Jonathan Witherspoon—Halloran discovers that neither rejected classical authority in its entirety, and that there exists a significant difference between them in their use of Quintilian. This difference, he concludes, can be explained only by understanding their specific situations and purposes. Thus a global judgment on this matter is suspect, and historians must hedge their generalizations about periods by attending carefully to differing circumstances and interests within the same era.

The appropriation of and resistance to authority, then, emerges as an important theme in this volume. Yet this is only one of the problems connected with the transmission and reception of doctrine, as three other studies reveal. Don Abbott argues that Diego Valades, the first American to author a rhetoric, blended traditional lore with his experience preaching to the Indians and produced a rhetoric that reflected a significant interaction between native American and European cultures. Lawrence Green studies the history of the interpretation of the enthymeme and reveals the way that conflations, distortions, and misinterpretations have stubbornly persisted and hampered efforts to apply this important concept to contemporary pedagogy. Tom Conley presents evidence of a lively interplay between Greek and Western rhetorical doctrine during the late Renaissance and early modern period, and he argues that this exchange between the two cultures should receive greater attention.

A second general theme concerns conceptions of the nature and status of rhetoric and its relation to other domains of learning or activity. Because a substantial number of chapters treat this theme, it is convenient to subdivide them between those primarily concerned with rhetoric's placement in respect to other academic or intellectual pursuits and those primarily concerned with its placement in terms of the social or cultural milieu. This division is somewhat arbitrary, for the two sets of issues and interests clearly overlap; but it does seem to reflect a general difference in orientation.

Gaines, Dietz Moss, Wallace, and Vickers all deal with the academic or intellectual status of rhetoric. In his study of *De oratore*, book 1, Robert Gaines attempts to demonstrate that Cicero articulated a reasonably clear and well-argued response to the philosophical critique of rhetoric. The key to Gaines's analysis is what he calls Cicero's "knowledge doctrine": the requirement that the orator must have knowledge of the subject under discussion. This doctrine, Gaines contends, allows Cicero to argue that the practitioner of the art of rhetoric holds a position superior to that of the philosopher, because the orator must have philosophical knowledge to attain the goal of eloquence, but philosophical knowledge in itself cannot produce eloquence. From this perspective, rhetoric is the capstone of the liberal arts—the art that directs and synthesizes all the other arts.

Jean Dietz Moss and William Wallace analyze the works of two late 16th-century Aristotelians who argue for a more restricted and specific placement of rhetoric. Both Ludovico Carbone and Antonio Riccobono regard rhetoric as a faculty for arguing both sides of an issue and seek to demarcate it clearly within a system of the arts. For these Aristotelians, rhetoric must have a limited range of independent operation and a coherent preceptive doctrine. As Dietz Moss and Wallace explain it, then, Carbone and Riccobono consider rhetoric as one of the arts (specifically, the art of persuasion) but not as the master art.

In her chapter, Dietz Moss notes an affinity between Carbone's effort to explain the coherence of rhetoric and Brian Vicker's effort to combat the contemporary expansion of rhetoric beyond any coherent limitation. In this volume, Vickers again makes his case against the Deconstructionists and their effort to subsume or appropriate rhetoric. Although Vickers acknowledges that rhetoric is a broad and mutable concept, he maintains that it does have some limits, and the Deconstructionists stretch well beyond them. Their program would separate persuasion from rhetoric and treat rhetoric as self-contained, intralinguistic action effected through tropes and figures. For Vickers, this position thoroughly upends the rhetorical tradition, which treats verbal action in terms of its impact on others and regards the tropes and figures as instruments of persuasion. Hence, he concludes that Deconstruction and rhetoric are incompatible, and rhetoricians ought to resist Deconstructionist claims to generate a "rhetoric" of writing and reading. Clearly, Vickers' chapter also bears on the theme of appropriation of and resistance to tradition and can be read as a contemporary instance of the historical issues raised by Kennedy, Ward, and Halloran.

The chapters by Schoeck, Plett, and Streuver stress the placement of rhetoric within a particular social and cultural context. Schoeck examines the activities in and around the 16th-century English Inns of Court, the training ground for lawyers, and he finds the connection between law, literature, and rhetoric so intimate that it is best described by the image of the Borromeo Rings—three rings so interlocked that one can be detached only by breaking one of the other two. Schoeck favorably contrasts this interactivity among the arts with the contemporary tendency toward specialized education.

Plett identifies three different types of rhetoric in Shakespeare's plays: a rhetoric of good order, where the words appropriately and candidly match the subject; a rhetoric of dissimulation, in which a speaker effects a separation between the words and a subject; and a rhetoric of denial, where speakers deliberately place themselves outside the social order. Plett correlates these three types of rhetoric with different cultural paradigms that emerge during the Renaissance: the humanist (connected with good order), the rationalist (connected with dissimulation), and the courtly (connected with denial). Hence, Plett concludes that conceptions of rhetoric can serve as indicators of major cultural developments.

Steuver stresses the affinities between rhetoric and medicine in late Renaissance and early modern Europe. Both were "low sciences" based on "shaky empirical" grounds, and both operated on a case basis through pro and contra argumentation rather than through invariable, abstract principles. Both also had to deal with the passions. Developments beginning in the 17th century, however, directed philosophy and science toward more abstract and more purely physical conceptions of the passions and displaced casuistic method and pro and contra argument. Thus, the advent of modern culture powerfully affected both rhetoric and medicine.

Camargo's chapter nicely straddles the line between our subdivisions of this category, because he shows how cultural and social conditions influence academic alignments of the arts. In comparing the teaching of composition at Oxford and Bologna during the late Middle Ages, Camargo finds reasonably clear differences that correspond to local interests. At Bologna, where legal studies were especially prominent, grammar was subordinated to rhetoric. At Oxford, where law was relatively less important than literature, grammar subsumed rhetoric. These local differences, Camargo notes, help explain why no distinctively medieval synthesis of rhetoric appeared during the Middle Ages. Echoing one of Murphy's sentiments, however, he sees medieval diversity not as a sign of the fragmentation of classical rhetoric but as a pragmatic adaptation that permitted a synthesis appropriate for a particular time and place.

Finally, four chapters in this volume deal with the role of examples in rhetorical pedagogy. Jerzy Axer, in his study of Cicero's oratorical texts, argues that it is a bootless task to attempt to reconstruct the spoken versions of his speeches from their published versions. Instead, he proposes to concentrate on the published text as a form of written composition that creates the fiction of an oral situation. Furthermore, consistent with the views of several other Ciceronian scholars, Axer maintains that the published texts were designed primarily for pedagogical purposes—for use as models in teaching rhetoric.

If this was indeed Cicero's purpose, then he succeeded beyond all reasonable expectation. For two millennia, his speeches have remained models in the teaching of eloquence, and during the Renaissance, when Cicero's authority reached its apogee, the speeches sometimes displaced his own (and all other) preceptive works as the major source for pedagogy. In his chapter on international humanism, Kees Meerhoff explains that for 16th-century educators such as Johann Sturm, Bartholmaeus Latomus, and James Omphalius, theory was a tool for achieving eloquence and not something to be pursued for its own sake. The careful analysis and imitation of classical texts was to form the basis for reading and composition, and this kind of study had priority over abstract theory.

In her account of what she calls "a minor skirmish" between two 18th-century French educators, Barbara Warnick offers a vivid case study of the conflict between an inductive rhetorical pedagogy based on exemplars and a pedagogy based on fixed precepts. On one side was Charles Rollin, who sought to reform and modernize the rhetoric curriculum by allowing instruction in the vernacular and emphasizing models over theoretical precepts as the means to instill good taste. On the other side, Balthazar Gibert maintained that Rollin's proposed reform would corrupt taste, which ought to rest upon fixed principles. Rollin, Warnick reports, won the skirmish both in the eyes of his colleagues and in historical judgment.

Finally, Marjorie Woods introduces a novel and important aspect of this issue in her reassessment of Geoffrey of Vinsauf's *Poetria nova.* Following the remarks made by the medieval commentators on this work, Woods argues that Geoffrey composes the treatise so that it exemplifies the precepts it presents. This organic connection between "text and teaching" applies not simply to isolated passages but also to the structure of the whole, which develops and illustrates the metaphoric connections among its precepts. Woods contrasts the stress on analytical order that characterizes classical and modern textbooks with the emphasis on the process of putting things together through imaginative associations that characterizes the medieval rhetorical textbook. And the text itself is made to embody such associations.

Geoffrey's *Poetria nova,* as Woods describes it, offers a striking contrast in both matter and manner to Ludovico Carbone's *De arte dicendi,* as Dietz Moss describes that work. Geoffrey attempts to teach a practice; Carbone attempts to achieve theoretical clarity. Geoffrey seeks to encourage imaginative associations; Carbone uses a disputational method to divide things into distinct logical categories. Geoffrey strives to embody the eloquence he teaches; Carbone stands back from his subject, declaring in his preface that he will not "attempt to be eloquent, but to use a simple style of writing, with no ornament or emotional appeals." Woods and Dietz Moss tell us that both authors succeeded in accomplishing their ends, and the contrast between them illustrates how the teacher's conception of rhetoric shapes the way that rhetoric is taught.

In writing this brief synopsis of the book, we have not attempted to attain the eloquence of Geoffrey or the logical clarity of Carbone. Nevertheless, we do have a rhetorical purpose. However inadequate or inelegant our effort to group chapters and themes, we hope that it at least illustrates the value of reading across as well as through the chapters of the book. Despite the diversity of authors and periods represented in the book, we believe that it articulates themes and concerns common to all the contributors and to the rhetorical tradition. If the book does maintain this sense of unity in diversity, then it appropriately reflects the character and work of the man to whom we dedicate it.

THEORY AND PEDAGOGY IN THE CLASSICAL AND MEDIEVAL TRADITIONS

Chapter 1

Aristotle's Enthymeme
and the Imperfect Syllogism

Lawrence D. Green
University of Southern California

In the past decade several scholars have pointed out a range of meanings for the term *enthymeme* and so provided a cautionary tale for those who would speak naively about Aristotle's enthymeme.[1] It would be nice to think that no one will ever again make the mistake of thinking that Aristotle's enthymeme is a rigidly deductive form of inferential reasoning. But this error has been corrected before, and the correction has been ignored before.[2] As early as the Renaissance, for example, the grand Greek Thesaurus from the Estienne press listed numerous meanings for the term ἐνθύμημα, understood as an *animi conceptus, sensum*

---

[1] See Thomas M. Conley, "The Enthymeme in Perspective," *Quarterly Journal of Speech* 70 (1984): 168–187; Jürgen Sprute, *Die Enthymemtheorie der aristotelischen Rhetoric* (Göttingen: Vandenhoeck & Ruprecht, 1982); and, earlier, Wayne N. Thompson, *Aristotle's Deduction and Induction: Introductory Analysis and Synthesis* (Amsterdam: Rodopi, 1975), 72–77. For recent discussions of some of the issues addressed in this chapter see Carol Poster, "A Historicist Recontextualization of the Enthymeme," *Rhetoric Society Quarterly* 22 (1992): 1–24, and Myles F. Burnyeat, "Enthymeme: Aristotle on the Logic of Persuasion," *Aristotle's "Rhetoric": Philosophical Essays*, ed. David J. Furley and Alexander Nehamas (Princeton: Princeton University Press, 1994), 3–55, which appeared too late to use in the preparation of this chapter.

[2] See, for example, *Animadversiones variorum criticae et exegeticae in Aristotelis de rhetorica libros tres* (Oxford: Clarendon Press, 1820) 37: "Non haec est enthymematis, quasi mutili syllogismi, nota propria, ut media proposito, qua argumentum assumitur, fere desit: quanquam enthymema vulgo ita definiunt." But the authors then go on to declare "Enthymema igitur est syllogismus non accurate expressus, sed accommodate ad dictionem oratoriam" (38).

vel sensus.[3] After 1572 the Greek Thesaurus was widely available, and most commentators on the classics had recourse to it. But despite the wide use of this readily available resource, the most common way to speak about the details of Aristotle's enthymeme continued to be in terms of deductive inferential proceeding, and the other meanings all dropped by the wayside.

In the present chapter I wish to address the longevity of this misperception of Aristotle's enthymeme as both a reductive and a rigidly deductive proceeding—to address not so much the history of this misperception as its power to endure, even in the face of contradiction and correction. Eugene E. Ryan's current theory of rhetorical argumentation, in which Aristotle's orator need only fill in the blanks in one of a variety of topical templates, is one recent form; and William M. A. Grimaldi's view of the enthymeme as a deductive nexus of *ethos, pathos*, and *pragma* can be seen in this tradition as well.[4] My concern here is with the extreme version of this position, that is, with the view of the enthymeme as an incomplete or imperfect syllogism, a syllogism that need not be truncated but that usually is truncated for rhetorical reasons. This view is supposedly discredited today; but it has been discredited repeatedly since the Renaissance, and yet it is still with us. My principal interest is in the longevity of this view and I focus on that position, not to batter a straw man but, rather, to confront—in its historically most enduring form—the willingness, and even the determination, to understand the enthymeme as a mechanistic and deductive formula.[5]

---

[3]Henri Estienne (Henricus Stephanus, 1531–1598), ed., *Thesaurus graecae linguae*, 5 vols. (Paris, 1572). The meanings under the heading ἐνθύμημα include *recordatio, commentum, cogitamentum, sententia quae e contrariis conficiatur, acrius epicheremate*, and *memorabile inventum*, and the entry cites a broad range of classical sources, including Aristotle's *Rhetoric*.

[4]Eugene E. Ryan, *Aristotle's Theory of Rhetorical Argumentation* (Montreal: Les Editions Bellarmin, 1984); William M. A. Grimaldi, S. J., *Studies in the Philosophy of Aristotle's "Rhetoric"* (Wiesbaden: Franz Steiner, 1972); and Grimaldi's two *Commentaries* on books 1 and 2 of the *Rhetoric* (New York: Fordham University Press, 1980, 1988). In this tradition see also Paul D. Brandes, *A History of Aristotle's "Rhetoric" with a Bibliography of Early Printings* (Metuchen, NJ: Scarecrow Press, 1989) 178–207.

[5]This enduring misperception has implications for that branch of modern composition pedagogy in the United States that seeks to use a so-called structural enthymeme. This structural enthymeme is a thoroughly modern pedagogical device that brings together a number of rhetorical perceptions found in Aristotle and in other early writers. But just as Aristotle's enthymeme is misperceived as a reductive and mechanistic formula, so also the modern structural enthymeme is misperceived as such. Those in modern composition who are unconvinced about the utility of the structural enthymeme see it as a mechanistic device that shares all the debilities of formal syllogistic and thus falsifies a student's understanding of persuasive writing. On the other hand, those who have worked with this structural enthymeme claim that it provides a useful kind of shorthand for focusing a student's attention on the principal dynamics of persuasion that Aristotle discusses in the *Rhetoric*. See, for example, Linda Bensel-Meyers, *Rhetoric for Academic Reasoning* (New York: HarperCollins, 1992) 124–128, 167–173, 210; Wayne C. Booth and Marshall W. Gregory, *The Harper and Row Rhetoric: Writing as Thinking, Thinking as Writing*, 2nd ed. (New York: HarperCollins, 1991) 24–29; John T. Gage, "A General Theory of the Enthymeme for Advanced Composition," *Teaching Advanced Composition* ed. Katherine H. Adams and John L. Adams (Portsmouth, NH: Heinemann, 1991)

PART ONE

There are several places in the *Rhetoric* where Aristotle could be understood as referring to the enthymeme as a truncated syllogism (notably at 1.2, 1357ª16ff and again at 2.22, 95ᵇ24ff). Indeed, the most recent English interpreter of the *Rhetoric* notes that Aristotle's statement at 1.2, 1357ª16 "became in postclassical times the authority for defining an enthymeme as a syllogism in which one or more propositions are not expressed."[6] But this postclassical reading is itself the product of earlier ways of thinking that did not originate with the *Rhetoric* proper. That treatise all but disappeared from sight for 15 centuries following Aristotle's death, and during much of that time scholars devoted themselves instead to Aristotle's analytical treatises. When the *Rhetoric* finally reemerged, the understandings about the enthymeme that were read back into the text had less to do with rhetoric and more to do with contemporary understandings about logic.

Thus the starting point for the following discussion is not Aristotle's *Rhetoric* but instead his analytical works and the problems they pose. Even so, the story is not simple. In Aristotle's single reference to the enthymeme in the *Prior Analytics* at 2.27, 70ª10, he calls the enthymeme "a syllogism from probabilities or signs" (ἐνθύμημα δὲ ἐστι συλλογισμὸς ἐξ εἰκότων ἢ σημείων). But in the centuries after the rediscovery of the lost Aristotelian corpus,[7] a consensus slowly emerged that what Aristotle really had in mind in this passage was an imperfect syllogism—συλλογισμὸς ἀτελής. In the succeeding centuries this gloss ἀτελής was interpolated into a few of the manuscripts of the *Prior Analytics*, although the particular steps in the process remain obscure. In 3rd-century Alexandria, the Peripatetic commentator Alexander of Aphrodisias offers a careful discussion of imperfect syllogisms in Aristotle's *Prior Analytics*, but he is concerned almost exclusively with Aristotelian procedures for the conversion of premises and the reduction of second and third figure syllogisms to the perfect syllogisms of the first figure. Alexander uses the term ἀτελής throughout this discussion, but he

---

161–178; John T. Gage, *The Shape of Reason: Argumentative Writing in College*, 2nd ed. (New York: Macmillan, 1991) 144–162; Maxine C. Hairston, "Bringing Aristotle's Enthymeme into the Composition Classroom," *Rhetoric and Praxis: The Contribution of Classical Rhetoric to Practical Reasoning* ed. Jean Dietz Moss (Washington, DC: Catholic University of America Press, 1986) 59–77; William A. Wallace, *"Aitia:* Causal Reasoning in Composition and Rhetoric," in Moss, *Rhetoric and Praxis* 107–133, especially 131–132; Lawrence D. Green, "Enthymemic Invention and Structural Prediction," *College English* 41 (1980): 623–634.

[6]George Kennedy, *Aristotle. "On Rhetoric": A Theory of Civic Discourse, Newly Translated with Introduction, Notes, and Appendixes* (New York: Oxford University Press, 1991) 297.

[7]The eclipse of the Aristotelian school started to reverse only after 86 B.C. with the editorial work by Andronicus of Rhodes. For a review of this revival, and the start of the commentary tradition, see Hans B. Gotschalk, "The Earliest Aristotelian Commentators," *Aristotle Transformed: The Ancient Commentators and Their Influence*, ed. Richard Sorabji (Ithaca: Cornell University Press, 1990) 55–81, revised from "Aristotelian Philosophy in the Roman World from the Time of Cicero to the End of the Second Century A.D.," *Aufstieg und Niedergang der römischen Welt*, ed. Wolfgang Haase, II (Berlin: Walter de Gruyter, 1987) 36:2, 1079–1174.

does not suggest that imperfect syllogisms have anything to do with Aristotle's enthymeme.[8] The reverse is true of Alexander's massive commentary on Aristotle's *Topics*, in which Alexander does discuss enthymemes but does not use the word ἀτελής in connection with them. Here Alexander examines the notion of syllogisms that are missing a premise, but the term he uses is μονοληημμάτους συλλογισμούς, a term that he carefully attributes to the newer Stoic logic rather than the older Aristotelian logic; and Alexander is critical in general here of Stoic syllogistic. Later in this same discussion he explains that Aristotle's enthymeme requires that an auditor supply a missing premise, and that enthymemes of this sort are properly called rhetorical syllogisms (ῥητορικοι συλλογισμοί), because they are not really syllogisms at all in Aristotle's sense. The perfection or imperfection of rhetorical syllogisms is not an issue for Alexander, and the word ἀτελής does not appear in his discussion.[9]

Alexander differentiates between Aristotelian and Stoic understandings of what constitutes a syllogism but points out that a rhetorician with a compliant audience might be able to understand an Aristotelian enthymeme in terms of a Stoic syllogism. But two centuries later in Alexandria, these uses are no longer distinct, and the careful attribution to the Stoics no longer obtains. The Neoplatonist Ammonius explains in his commentary on Aristotle's *Prior Analytics* that rhetoricians use a syllogism that has but one premise (μονολήμματος) and that such a syllogism is imperfect ἀτελής.[10] Ammonius repeats the same argument in his commentary on Porphyry's *Isogoge*, this time introducing the phrase συλλογισμὸς ἀτελής,[11] thus making it easier for subsequent readers to understand *imperfection* as *truncation*. Ammonius's commentary of Porphyry may have had even more influence than his commentary on the *Prior Analytics*, because Porphyry's *Isogoge* was used routinely as an introduction to Aristotle's logical works for over a thousand years, and Ammonius's commentary on Porphyry was widely available.[12] Subsequent commentators in the later Byzantine tradition continued to look at the

---

[8]Alexander of Aphrodisias (ca. A.D. 200), *In analyticorum priorum librum I commentarium*, in *Commentaria in Aristotelem Graeca*, ed. Maximilian Wallies, vol. 2, part 1 (Berlin: George Reimer, 1883) 23.17–24.18. Cited hereafter as *CAG*.

[9]Alexander, *In topicorum libros octo commentaria*, *CAG* 2:2, ed. Maximilian Wallies (1891), 8.17, 9.9. The word μονολήμματο is also used by Chrysippus and by Antipater, *Stoic* 2.84, suggesting a Stoic rather than Peripatetic background.

[10]Ammonius Hermeiou (435/445–517/526), *In analyticorum priororum librum I commentarium*, *CAG* 4:6, ed. Maximilian Wallies (1899), 27.14–20 at *APr* 24ᵇ18.

[11]Ammonius, *In Porphyrii isagogen*, *CAG* 4:3, ed. Adolf Busse (1891) 8.8.

[12]The Aristotelian logical studies by Ammonius and his students (notably Philoponus) were central to the work by Byzantine scholars and, through Boethius, a contemporary of Philoponus, to scholars in the Latin West; see Sten Ebbesen, "Philoponus, 'Alexander' and the Origins of Medieval Logic," in Sorabji, *Aristotle Transformed* 445–461, 451–452. There survive numerous manuscripts of Ammonius's *In Porphirii isagogen*, and many editions were printed during the Renaissance (*CAG* 4:3, xl–xlii). Greek editions were printed in Venice (1500), and twice again in Venice (1545). Latin translations were printed in Venice (1504), Lyon (1547), Venice (1559), and Venice (1581). There were also editions in Arabic and Syriac.

enthymeme as a truncated syllogism, although these later commentators were not concerned directly with the analytical treatises. An anonymous scholiast on Hermogenes' *On Invention* specifies that enthymemes are syllogisms that are ἀτελής and discusses enthymemes using a conflation of Stoic and Peripatetic terminology.[13] An anonymous commentator on the *Rhetoric*, possibly as late as the 12th century, specifies that a syllogism always has two premises, whereas an enthymeme has only one;[14] and in a discussion (at 2.22, 1395ᵇ23) he asserts that an enthymeme is indeed a συλλογισμὸς ἀτελής.[15] Numerous prolegomena and scholia to Hermogenes carry the phrase συλλογισμὸς ἀτελής down through the 12th century and later.[16]

Given the prevalence of this way of thinking, it is not surprising that the ἀτελής gloss crept into the text of the *Prior Analytics* (although never into the text of the *Rhetoric*). The Greek commentators were not shy about such emendations.[17] Of the six oldest manuscripts that provided the text for the modern editions of the *Prior Analytics*, two offered the reading συλλογισμὸς ἀτελής at 2.27, 70ᵃ10, and both manuscripts, in different ways, date from later than the 12th century.[18] Most of codex Coislinianus 330 dates from the 11th century, but the manuscript has major lacunae, including the locus at *Prior Analytics* 2.27; and those lacunae were supplied by a hand from the 12th or 13th century; and those lacunae were supplied by a hand from the 12th or 13th century. Similarly, most of codex Ambrosianus L 93 sup. (490) dates from the 9th century, but the folios that include the present locus have been supplied by an imitator writing in the 15th century. There is no need to postulate a line of textual descent

---

[13]Christian Walz, *Rhetores Graeci* 7:2 (Stuttgart and Tübingen: J. G. Cotta, 1832–1836) ἀτελής at 762.11, 763.9; λῆμμα and πρότασίς at 763.27.

[14]Anonymous, *In artem rhetoricam commentarium, CAG* 21:2, ed. Hugo Rabe (1896) 2.26–27: τοῦ γὰρ συλλογισμοῦ ὄντος ἐκ δύο προτάσεων τὸ ἐνθύμημα ἔχει μίαν. Robert Browning suggests that the author might have been Michael of Ephesus, which, if true, would fix the date of the commentary in the early 12th century in Byzantium; "An Unpublished Funeral Oration on Anna Comnena," in Sorabji, *Aristotle Transformed*, 393–406; reprinted from *Proceedings of the Cambridge Philological Society*, n.s. 8 (1962): 1–12. The anonymous Greek commentary was printed in Paris, 1539.

[15]*CAG* 21:2, 130.17.

[16]See Thomas M. Conley, "Notes on the Byzantine Reception of the Peripatetic Tradition in Rhetoric," *Peripatetic Rhetoric After Aristotle: Rutgers University Studies in Classical Humanities*, vol. 6, ed. William W. Fortenbaugh and David C. Mirhady (New Brunswick, NJ: Transaction Publishers, 1994), 217–242; in particular, Conley's references to the use of ἀτελής in *Prolegomenon sylloge* 234.5 (from MS Par. gr. 3032, 10th or 11th century), 240.24f, and 324.15f, (from MS Ambr. 290, 14th century).

[17]In one passage, for example, the anonymous commentator on the *Rhetoric* explains that Aristotle meant to write one thing but mistakenly wrote another, so the commentator would supply instead what Aristotle meant to write: οὕτω μὲν ὁ φιλόσοφος γράφεσθαι βούλεται τὸ ῥητόν· γράφεται δὲ καί οὕτως (*CAG* 21:2, 41.18–19). I thank Thomas Conley, personal communication, for pointing out this reference.

[18]The standard histories are W. D. Ross, *Analytica Priora et Posteriora* (Oxford: Clarendon Press, 1964); and L. Minio-Paluello, *Aristoteles Latinus III:1–4; Analytica Priora* (Bruges-Paris: Desclée de Brouwer, 1962). For MS Ambr. L 93 sup. (490), see now Mark F. Williams, *Studies in the Manuscript Tradition of Aristotle's Analytica* (Königstein/Ts.: Hain, 1984).

from some original scribal error for the insertion of the word ἀτελής, because there appears to be a continuing cultural interest in seeing the enthymeme in Aristotle's *Prior Analytics* as an imperfect or incomplete or truncated syllogism.

Modern editors of the *Prior Analytics* regularly reject the word ἀτελής at 2.27, 70[a]10, because the very oldest manuscripts do not have the word and it appears to have been introduced later than the 12th century.[19] But even assuming that the rejection by modern editors is correct, there still seems to be an irresistible impulse for editors and interpreters to understand the now purified line as though the offending word were still present. Those who find it convenient to understand Aristotle's enthymeme as an imperfect syllogism continue to do so, viewing it as syllogistically imperfect, truncated for rhetorical reasons, or both. The problem is not at all confined to students of the *Rhetoric*, as is shown by one widely used and representative modern translation of the *Prior Analytics*. Aristotle explains that it is possible to suppress a premise and still have a syllogism (in Aristotle's example, "Pittacus is high-minded, because those who love honour are high-minded, and Pittacus loves honour"); the translator here notes that although Aristotle says "syllogism" he strictly means *enthymeme*.[20] The translator thus rejects the word ἀτελής—with the combined senses of syllogistic imperfection and rhetorical truncation—and at the same time he retains the force of the word.

This misperception of the enthymeme has a power to endure and prosper, even among those who have supposedly corrected it, and its occurrence in the modern period is only the latest in a continuing series. The modern instance repeats what happened in the Renaissance when this problem with the *Prior Analytics* was first addressed in a substantial manner. In 1584 Giulio Pace published a fresh Greek edition and Latin translation of the *Prior Analytics*, and in a marginal note at 2.27 he scathingly observes that the most commonly used manuscripts inexcusably added the word ἀτελής, or "imperfect."[21] In his extensive commentary on the *Prior Analytics* in 1597, Pace offers nine arguments against the offending word.[22]

---

[19]Not only the word but even the status of the entire line is uncertain, and various editors have moved the line around in the text seeking a better context for it. W. D. Ross, for example, displaces it by 10 lines so that it initiates Aristotle's earlier discussion that distinguishes probabilities from signs. Changing the context for Aristotle's statement obviously affects any critical understanding about his enthymeme. The criteria for accepting or rejecting the readings of MS Coisl. 330 are not always clear. In this same line, Ross rejects the reading of ἀτελής from MS Coisl. 330 but accepts the codex reading of δὲ over the reading of μὲν οὖν received from the principal manuscripts he usually follows, and at the same time he rejects the Paris reading of ἢ καὶ in favor of the simpler ἢ of the principal manuscripts. See Ross's critical apparatus, along with L. Minio-Paluello's more recent appendices to Ross's edition.

[20]Hugh Tredennick, *Aristotle: Prior Analytics* (London: Heinemann, 1938; Cambridge: Harvard University Press, 1973) 525n, at *APr* 70[a]24.

[21]Giulio Pace (Iulius Pacius, 1550–1635), *Aristotelis peripateticorum principis organum* (Geneva, 1584): "Vulgati codices male hic adiuunt ἀτελής, *imperfectus*." My text is the Frankfurt edition of 1597, which adds the marginal note "vide nostrum commentarium."

[22]Pace's complete argument concerning the word ἀτελής is found in his *In Porphyrii isagogen et Aristotelis organum, commentarius analyticus* (Frankfurt, 1597) 263–265, published at the same time as the second edition of his *Aristotelis organum*.

1. According to Aristotle, perfection in syllogisms depends not on the number of propositions but only on the probative force (*vim probandi*) of a syllogism, and syllogisms are imperfect until they have been resolved into perfect first figure syllogisms.

2. Four Greek manuscripts lack the word ἀτελής, and even those contemporary professors who themselves prefer to think of the enthymeme as an imperfect syllogism do not attribute the word ἀτελής to Aristotle.[23]

3. The Greek commentators, including Philoponus, do not recognize the word; and even Alexander of Aphrodisias himself does not refer to a formally incomplete syllogism as an enthymeme but, rather, as a syllogism that is μονολήμματος, that is, "with but one premise."[24]

4. Aristotle himself says that an orator is still using an enthymeme even if he offers both premises.

5. Aristotle says in the *Rhetoric* that enthymemes "often" have fewer parts than do syllogisms.[25] But "often" means "not always" (*non perpetuo*), and thus the number of formal parts cannot provide the differentia needed for a definition of the enthymeme.

6. In this problematic locus at 2.27, Aristotle resolves several enthymemes into syllogistic figures by using both premises, so formal completeness must be irrelevant to the definition.

7. Even Aristotle's own words prove that ἀτελής is impossible; the enthymeme is drawn "from probabilities or signs" (*ex verisimilibus, vel signis*), not from "a probability or a sign" (*non, ex verisimili, vel signo*). Aristotle's use of the plural here is impossible without recourse to two premises.

8. As for the unspoken propositions of an enthymeme somehow being supplied by the auditor (*in mente, et in animo*), Aristotle disposes of that possibility in *Posterior Analytics* 1.10.7, where he allows an auditor to supply one, two, or no premises for a syllogism.

9. Aristotle distinguishes the enthymeme from the induction and the example, both of which do in fact use but one proposition. People are commonly confused

---

[23]Pace has in mind the professors at Louvain, and he then adds Rudolph Agricola, who seems to make a sympathetic statement about Aristotle's enthymeme in *De inventione dialectica* (Cologne, 1539; Nieukoop: De Graaf, 1967) 2.18. But Agricola's own commentator does not appear to agree with Pace's reading of Agricola; see 274–275.

[24]Joannes Philoponus (ca. 490–570s) was the literary executor for his master Ammonius, and especially for the logical works. The commentary on the *Prior Analytics*, which is possibly by Philoponus, is silent on the matter of ἀτελής at *APr* 2.27. Although Pace seems to suggest an active rejection, Philoponus may still have agreed with his master; *In analytica priora commentaria, CAG* 13:2, ed. Maximilian Wallies (1905) 481.19. For Alexander, see the earlier discussion on *In topica; CAG* 2:2, 8.17.

[25]This is the same contested phrase at *Rhetorica* 1.2, 1357[a]16ff to which Kennedy refers; see earlier discussion.

and mistakenly call these forms enthymemes. Their single propositions are drawn from causes, or examples, or definitions, or other commonplaces, but because they are not drawn from probabilities or signs, Aristotle was scrupulous in not calling them enthymemes.

Giulio Pace was particularly exercised by the state of contemporary Aristotelian commentary on this issue; most scholars had already agreed that the enthymeme was an imperfect syllogism, and the principal debate was over the nature of its imperfection. Philip Melancthon and others argued that an enthymeme was formed when the major or minor premise was missing. George Pachymeres argued in his *Epitome logices* (1545) that it was only an enthymeme when the major premise was suppressed, and otherwise it was a syllogism.[26] It might have seemed that, whatever the worth of Pace's individual arguments about ἀτελής, the fact that a major commentator had managed to marshal as many as nine of them might have given pause to subsequent editors of the *Prior Analytics*. And yet, Pace's thorough discrediting of ἀτελής had at best a mixed reception during the Renaissance. The authoritative Sylburg edition of Aristotle (Frankfurt, 1585) and the great Casaubon edition (Lyon, 1590) both claim to have consulted Pace scrupulously; yet both include the supposedly offending word ἀτελής, and neither edition even bothers to acknowledge the emendation by Pace in 1584. Isaac Casaubon's massive edition of the Opera in 1590 lists Pace's edition and translation of the *Organon* among the works consulted.[27] But at *Prior Analytics* 2.27, Casaubon, without explanation, accepts Nicholas Grouchy's reading of συλλογισμὸς ἀτελής, along with Grouchy's translation: "Est igitur Enthymema ratiocinatio imperfecta ex verisimilibus vel signis."[28] Friedrich Sylburg's edition of the *Organon* was printed two years after Pace's edition, and by the same press (Andreas Wechel at Frankfurt) that would soon bring out Pace's second edition. Sylburg explicitly claims that he has consulted Pace at every point, and that each divergent reading has been scrupulously noted, along with Pace's findings from the manuscripts.[29] Yet, despite numerous references to Pace's emendations

[26]George Pachymeres (Georgius Pachymerius), *Epitome logices Aristotelis* (Oxford, 1666) 112: "Enthymema vero est Syllogismo persimile, in eo tamen discrepat, quod Syllogismus duabus e Propositionibus est conflatus, vet si ex unica tantum, ex majore, Enthymema autem ex una eaque minore ut diximus."

[27]Isaac Casaubon, ed., *Operum Aristotelis* (Lyons, 1590) Index fol. ii^v: "Iulius Pacius Arist. organum transtulit, & multis notis illustrauit."

[28]Casaubon, *Operum* 75. Grouchy's text and translation were based on the earlier work by Joachim Périon; see sig. [xi^v]. Pace himself reedited the later edition of Casaubon (Geneva, 1595) and silently substituted both his own edition and his own translation of the Organon.

[29]Friedrich Sylburg, ed., *Aristotelis opera quae exstant* (Frankfurt, 1587) 468: "Adnotatio eorum in quibus Isingriniana & Paciana editio a nostra discrepat. His intermista sunt quae Pacius partim ex aliis codicibus, partim e manu scripto adnotavit. Addita etiam nonnulla ex Camotiana editione, & alia Veneta vetustiore; nec non ex doctissimorum virorum animadversionibus."

throughout the *Prior Analytics*, Sylburg makes no reference whatsoever to Pace's excision of ἀτελής at 2.27, and the phrase συλλογισμὸς ἀτελής appears intact.

If there is an explanation for all this, it has less to do with philological squabbling over authoritative codices, and a great deal to do with the predisposition to view Aristotle's enthymeme in the context of deductive syllogistic rather than in the context of rhetoric. We must look, I think, for a more deeply rooted philosophical disposition, one that accounts for the incredibly fertile ground in which this misperception continues to sprout, generation after generation. I suggest instead a different line of inheritance. This line of inheritance starts, not with enthymemes, but with syllogisms, and not with the Peripatetics, but with the Stoics.

PART TWO

Jonathan Barnes argued some years ago that the syllogistic enterprise of the *Prior Analytics* represented an intellectual dead end for Aristotle; he had an interesting if limited analytical device, but he never tried to do anything further with it, and he soon went back to his real work.[30] Perhaps so, but it is certainly the case that after the death of Aristotle, Peripatetic logic lost the initiative to Stoic logic, to the logic of Zeno and Chryssipus. Diogenes Laertius, in fact, declared that if the gods used logic, it would be the logic of Chrysippus.[31] The larger Stoic philosophy seems to have had much more to offer people of the ancient world than did the disparate investigations of Aristotle, and within 80 years of the death of Aristotle the Athenians erected a statue not of Aristotle but of Zeno the Stoic—although presumably not merely for his contributions to logic.[32] One powerful attraction of Stoicism was its reputation for internal unity and consistency.[33] Man's moral nature was intimately connected with the certainties of the physical world, and both were inextricably linked with logic. Each of these could be studied in terms of its own active principle—the *logos* of ethics, the *logos* of physics, and the *logos* of logic (that is, dialectic)—and these three coequal branches of Stoic philosophy were unified as aspects of the one single *logos* that governed the universe.[34] For the

---

[30]Barnes concludes that Aristotle's "syllogistic is a small and relatively insignificant part of logic," rigorous and elegant but useless for science and math; see "Proof and the Syllogism," *Aristotle on Science: The Posterior Analytics. Proceedings of the Eighth Symposium Aristotelicum*, ed. Enrico Berti (Padua: Editrice Antenore, 1981) 17–59, 19. For a critique of Barnes, see Michael Frerejohn, *The Origins of Aristotelian Science* (New Haven: Yale University Press, 1991) 15–37, 140n, 141n, 143n.

[31]Diogenes Laertius 7.180.

[32]Diogenes Laertius 7.6.

[33]I. G. Kidd, "Stoic Intermediates and the End for Man," *Problems in Stoicism*, ed. A. A. Long (London: Athlone Press, 1971) 157.

[34]For a summary statement, see Marcia L. Colish, *The Stoic Tradition from Antiquity to the Early Middle Ages*, 2 vols. (Leiden: E. J. Brill, 1985) 1:7–60. See also A. A. Long, *Hellenistic Philosophy: Stoics, Epicureans, Sceptics*, 2nd ed. (Berkeley: University of California Press, 1986) 107–231.

Stoics, ethical failures occur when men become alienated from the natural world and so make faulty assumptions or draw invalid inferences.[35] Thus Diogenes Laertius reports the Stoic maxim: "Only the sage is a true logician."[36]

There are many similarities, differences, and crossovers between Aristotelian and Stoic syllogistic. For the purposes of the present discussion the differences matter most. There are three principal differences, and each requires clarification. First, Aristotelian syllogistic is concerned with terms and their relations within a categorical matrix, whereas Stoic syllogistic is concerned with propositions in hypothetical schemes of inference. Second, Aristotle's syllogistic is strictly limited to three terms, no more nor less, so that the number of possible syllogisms is finite, whereas Stoic logic has no such restrictions on the number of propositions. Third, Aristotle's syllogistic is categorical and does not depend upon the construction of *if . . . , then . . . .* It is not deductive and it advances no claims to new truths, whereas Stoic syllogistic characteristically appears in the inferential form *if . . . , then . . . ,* followed by a truth claim, leading to a new claim.[37]

Despite the similarities, crossovers, and even confusions between the two kinds of syllogistic, those hellenistic philosophers who were most intimate with the two kinds saw them as operating in very different philosophical systems.[38] The basic form of Aristotelian syllogism as developed in the *Prior Analytics* 4–6 adopts an argumentative form, as in the following:

(1) A is said of every B, and B is said of every C;
(2) thus A necessarily is said of every C.

Aristotle permits three variations of this basic argumentative form, and each variation alters statement (1). The first replaces one or both uses of *every* with *some*. The second negates one or both of the verbs. The third alters the position of the repeated term, that is, the term in (1) that does not appear in (2). The result of these conditions is that there is a finite number of syllogistic forms, determined by manipulating a finite number of categorical terms and relations, which can be manipulated only within a matrix of established positions (apodeictic and conditional syllogisms add two more kinds of variation but finally only enlarge the matrix). Although it is still unclear whether Aristotle here actually

---

[35]A. A. Long, "Language and Thought in Stoicism," in Long, *Problems in Stoicism*, 104.

[36]Diogenes Laertius 7.83: διαλεκτικὸν μόνον εἶναι τὸν σοφόν.

[37]Michael Frede examines "the possibility that the validity of an argument was thought to be due to a real relation that holds between the facts referred to in the argument, if the premises are true," in his essay "Stoic vs. Aristotelian Syllogistic" in Michael Frede, *Essays in Ancient Philosophy* (Minneapolis: University of Minnesota Press, 1987) 104, reprinted from *Archiv für Geschichte der Philosophie* 56:1 (Berlin: Walter de Gruyter, 1956). Some later Stoic thinkers held that their syllogistic was merely formal.

[38]Frede, "Stoic vs. Aristotelian Syllogistic" 99–124. See also Ian Mueller, "Stoic and Peripatetic Logic," *Journal of Philosophy* 51 (1969): 173–187.

has a term logic with true variables, as we would understand that today, it is nevertheless clear that the famous example of a syllogism (*Socrates is a man, all men are mortal, . . .*) is not at all Aristotelian. *Socrates* is not a category that can be introduced with the word *every* or with the word *some*; it is instead a particular, and Aristotle's discussion in book 1 of the *Prior Analytics* disallows particulars (although book 2 seems to allow a more expansive notion of the use of terms). Moreover, although it is certainly possible to reformulate Aristotle's syllogism into an *if . . . , then . . .* construction, this reformulation is not really part of the Aristotelian approach and it changes nothing. Statement (1) deals with a categorical world in which things in fact belong in the category in which they are said to belong, and it is a static world, in which universal statements can be made. Finally, it is this same static world that justifies the lengthy procedures in book 2 of the *Prior Analytics* where Aristotle demonstrates how to construct a repeatable "middle" term for statement (1). It is in this static sense that Aristotle's syllogistic is not at all deductive, because he does not use statement (1) to infer (2). Instead he takes as a given one of the categorical terms in (1) and also takes as a given one of the terms in (2); only then does he look for ways to connect them.

Stoic propositional logic, on the other hand, occupied a philosophical world of contingency and flux, a world without fixed essences and without an unchanging structure among those essences. The Stoic propositions identify concrete individual phenomena and then focus on the changing relations among those individuations, and in this respect Stoic logic is compatible with Stoic physics.[39] One of the basic Stoic arguments takes the following form

(3) If p, then q;

(4) but p; therefore q.

Here the *if . . . , then . . .* construction is not simply formal. Statement (3) first postulates a world in which, for the purposes of this particular argument, the individuation *p* does in fact entail the individuation *q*. Statement (4) specifies a fact within that world at this particular moment and deduces a new fact that was previously only a formal possibility. Thus, in the simple school text example, *If it is light, it is day; but it is light; therefore it is day.* Or, to toy with a noncanonical example, *If Socrates is a man, then he is mortal; but Socrates is a man; therefore he is mortal.* According to Stoic thinking, this argument does not rely upon a prior universal statement (spoken or unspoken) about the changeless relations between essential humanity and essential mortality. Instead, the adequacy of (4) is assured by the hypothetical postulation of (3).

There are other distinctions between Aristotelian and Stoic syllogistic. Stoic logicians recognized at least five different principal types of syllogism: condi-

---

[39]Colish, *Stoic Tradition* 1:54–55.

tional (as in the preceding), conjunctive, disjunctive, causal, and probable. Moreover, propositions could be combined and embedded.[40] In statement (3), for
example, the proposition p could itself be yet another entire argument of the
form *if p, then q*. Because there was no systematic limit on the number of
propositions or on the number of resultant syllogisms, Stoic syllogistic was much
more flexible and powerful than Aristotelian syllogistic. The fact that one was
a propositional logic and the other a term-logic seems not to have been the crucial
distinction, because there are ways in which the two could be made to seem
complementary to one another. But at the time neither school seems to have
regarded the other as complementary, and each seems to have rejected the other's
claim to having any syllogistic whatsoever.[41] Rather than being a simple turf
war, this rejection was rooted in an opposition of underlying philosophies; one
viewed a world of changing relations among particulars, and the other viewed a
world of changeless relations among categories. There were, nevertheless, later
Peripatetics who tried to recover the initiative from the Stoics, claiming that these
complex logical innovations had their roots in Aristotle's conditional syllogism,
and that his followers Theophrastus and Eudemus had both developed something
like hypothetical syllogisms.[42] These claims are generally recognized as rearguard
actions; they underscore the vitality of the new directions but suggest how easily
writers in the classical world might slide from one system into the other.

One such writer was Cicero, whose own relations to Stoic and Peripatetic
philosophy were always ambiguous and yet whose writings provided one of the
most important conduits of Stoic thinking for later centuries.[43] Cicero rejects
Stoic rhetorical theory, or at least Stoic rhetorical theory as it existed by Cicero's
time, as being too spare, too austere, too didactic, and too uninterested in moving
the passions.[44] And yet, at many points, Cicero seems uncertain about the distinctions between Stoic and Peripatetic thinking. In his treatise on the *Topics*, in
particular, Cicero begins by claiming he would explain Aristotle's lengthy and
diffuse treatise on this subject, but finally does nothing of the kind, and instead

---

[40]By contrast, as Benson Mates observes, "it is obvious that the result of substituting sentences
for the variables in an Aristotelian syllogism will always be nonsensical"; Benson Mates, *Stoic Logic*
(Berkeley: University of California Press, 1953) 3n.

[41]Frede, "Stoic vs. Aristotelian Syllogistic" 99ff.

[42]Henry Chadwick, *Boethius: The Consolations of Music, Logic, Theology, and Philosophy*
(Oxford: Clarendon Press, 1981) 167.

[43]Colish reviews Cicero's tortured relations, and subsequent commentators' tortured efforts to
make sense of those relations, in her detailed chapter on Cicero in *Stoic Tradition* 1:61–158.

[44]The passages in Cicero's mature rhetorical works are numerous and extensive, for instance,
Orator 24.81, 26.91–28.96; *De oratore* 3.10.37, 3.21.91, 3.25.96–3.27.108, 3.37.149–3.61.227; *De
partitione oratoriae* 6.19–6.22. See, in particular, Colish's discussion of Cicero's rhetorical theory,
Stoic Tradition 1:79–89. For a more complex view of Stoic rhetoric than that presented by Cicero,
see Karl Barwick, *Problem der Stoischen Sprachlehre und Rhetorik*, Abhandlungen der Sächsischen
Akademie der Wissenschaften zu Leipzig 49:3 (Berlin: Akademie Verlag, 1957).

offers a version of the topics that is difficult to reconcile with Aristotle's.[45] In the midst of his own *Topics* Cicero offers a discussion of enthymemes, introduced under the topic of consequents, antecedents, and oppositions (*Topica* 13.53ff). Cicero provides seven different forms of syllogisms, and they are all forms of the five basic hypothetical propositional syllogisms that are at the heart of Stoic logic.[46] According to Cicero, these syllogisms are the same forms of reasoning that philosophers use, that poets use, that in fact everybody uses. But when orators use them, they are called ενθυμήματα; and an enthymeme is best understood as a very concise and pointed form of reasoning from contraries (*Topica* 13.55). Cicero's third enthymeme illustrates what he has in mind: "either this or that; but this; therefore not that" (*Aut hoc aut illud; hoc autem; non igitur illud. Topica* 15.56). This enthymeme is not at all Aristotelian. It is, instead, the fourth principal Stoic syllogism, which we can read as *either p or q; but p; therefore not q.*[47]

Cicero apparently learned his syllogistic from Stoic teachers; his early teacher Diodotus the Stoic later became very close to Cicero, living with him and dying as a member of his household. Perhaps Cicero's knowledge of Aristotelian syllogistic was filtered through these same Stoic teachers, although such a specific source is hardly necessary. As early as *De inventione*, Cicero indicated his confusion about Peripatetic syllogistic, attributing to Aristotle a five-part syllogism (*De inv.* 1.35.61; but this might even prove to be a three-part syllogism!), and then apparently a four-part syllogism (*De inv.* 1.39.70), before finally offering as a syllogism, *If it is daytime, it is light* (*De inv.* 1.46.86), that is, the same first Stoic syllogism which Cicero will later present in the *Topics*. Much the same conflation of ideas is found in a compressed form in *Rhetorica ad Herennium* at 2.18.28, suggesting that the uncertainty about syllogistic was widespread. Nowhere in Cicero's *De inventione* do we find any mention of enthymemes. But at 1.36.62ff,

---

[45]There is some question whether Cicero thinks he is summarizing Aristotle, in which case he is seriously confused, or simply discussing a subject on which Aristotle has also written. The opening sections of his *Topics* are ambiguous on this subject, and commentators often clarify the issue by a phrase in one of Cicero's letters to the ostensible addressee of the *Topics*: "institui Topica Aristotelea conscribere" (*Ad fam.* 2.7.19). W. G. Williams translates this phrase as "I set about writing a summary of the *Topics* of Aristotle"; W. G. Williams, *Cicero: Letters to His Friends* (London: William Heinemann, 1928). Eleonore Stump argues that the phrase instead should be translated "I began to write about Aristotelian Topics"; see Eleonore Stump, *Boethius's "De topicis differentiis": Translated, with Notes and Essays on the Text* (Ithaca: Cornell University Press, 1978) 20–21.

[46]H. M. Hubbell views the first five of Cicero's seven argumentative forms as a restatement of the Stoic five syllogisms, whereas the sixth and seventh merely repeat the third; H. M. Hubbell, *Cicero: Topica* (London: Heinemann, 1949) 422–423. But in Colish's view, Cicero lists only the first four Stoic hypotheticals, and the remaining three forms either vary or negate the first, third, and fourth; Colish, *Stoic Tradition* 1:84.

[47]Cicero's Latin and the Greek of Diogenes Laertius 7.81 read as translations of one another. Sextus Empiricus provides much the same in *Pyrrhoneae hypotyposes* 2.157.

we find the fullest early discussion of why orators might suppress parts of a syllogism, and it is to this discussion that later commentators continually turned.[48]

Marcia Colish has suggested that "Cicero's conflation of the Stoic hypothetical syllogism with the Aristotelian enthymeme may be seen either as a reflection of post-Aristotelian eclecticism within the Peripatetic school, as an act of misinformed or partisan doxography on Cicero's part, or as an inspired association of two doctrines which in fact work quite well together."[49] Cicero makes it clear late in his career that—whether he is eclectic, confused, or inspired—he sees no reason for the orator to choose between Aristotelian and Stoic logic; they are more or less interchangeable.[50] But if the two doctrines do in fact work well together, they do so at a cost to understanding what Aristotle might have had in mind. Less debatable is the fact that at Rome, from 250 B.C. to A.D. 100, there was a gradual loss of distinction among the several philosophical schools at the elementary level of education.[51] Even at the higher levels of education, the competing schools of Platonic, Peripatetic, Epicurean, and Stoic philosophy slowly coalesced, with the two former sects absorbing those doctrines of the latter two that had become part of the common intellectual understanding among the educated.

PART THREE

By the 6th century the canonical authors were Plato and Aristotle, and such Stoic teaching as survived in the work of Boethius (ca. 480–525/526) was viewed primarily in terms of the thinking of the two major schools.[52] But to put it this way is to obscure the amount of Stoic thinking that actually did survive and the extent to which it affected later understandings of Aristotle. Boethius himself was both a translator of and a commentator on Aristotle's works,[53] and although not actually dismissive of Stoic logic,[54] he certainly saw Stoic logic in terms of

---

[48]See, for example, the often cited discussions in Quintilian 5.10.1ff and 5.14.5ff. It is not clear whom Quintilian has in mind when he reports the views of certain Peripatetics.

[49]Colish, *Stoic Tradition* 1:84–85.

[50]Cicero *Orator* 32.115: "Ego eum censeo qui eloquentiae laude ducatur non esse earum rerum omnino rudem sed vel illa antiqua vel hac Chrysippi disciplina institutum."

[51]See Sten Ebbesen, "Ancient Scholastic Logic as the Source of Medieval Scholastic Logic," *The Cambridge History of Later Medieval Philosophy: From the Rediscovery of Aristotle to the Disintegration of Scholasticism, 1100–1600*, ed. Norman Kretzmann, Anthony Kenny, Jan Pinborg, and Eleonore Stump (Cambridge: Cambridge University Press, 1982) 101–127, 103; cited as *CHLMP*.

[52]Colish, *Stoic Tradition* 2:266–290, 2:267.

[53]James Shiel, "Boethius' Commentaries on Aristotle," in Sorabji, *Aristotle Transformed* 349–372, revised from *Medieval and Renaissance Studies* 4 (1958): 217–244. Sten Ebbesen, "Boethius as an Aristotelian Commentator," in Sorabji, *Aristotle Transformed* 373–391, reprinted from "Boethius as an Aristotelian Scholar," *Aristoteles: Werk und Wirkung*, vol. 2, ed. Jürgen Wiesner (Berlin: Walter de Gruyter, 1987).

[54]Jonathan Barnes argues that Boethius knew Stoic logic but generally dismissed it and saw no reason to expound it; see "Boethius and the Study of Logic," in Margaret Gibson, ed., *Boethius: His Life, Thought and Influence* (Oxford: Basil Blackwell, 1981) 73–89, 83. Colish contests Barnes's view; Colish, *Stoic Tradition* 2:269n.

Peripatetic logic. In his treatise *De hypotheticis syllogismis* he appropriates the Stoic hypothetical conditional syllogism *if p, then q; but p; therefore q* and converts it into a three-term Aristotelian categorical syllogism: *If A, then B; if B, then C; but if A, therefore C.*[55] Lost here are the philosophical underpinnings that distinguished the Peripatetic and Stoic enterprises in logic, and, indeed, Boethius is so out of sympathy with the Stoic thinking that he all but ignores the remaining four Stoic syllogistic forms to focus on the one that was most easily appropriated for the Aristotelian syllogism.

When Boethius turned to Cicero's *Topics*, in which Cicero had offered his own very uncertain blend of Peripatetic enthymemes and Stoic syllogisms, he reformulated Cicero's *Topics* as thoroughly as Cicero had reformulated Aristotle's discussion of topics. We are familiar today with the enormous impact of Boethius' *De topicis differentiis* during the later Middle Ages and the early Renaissance. But prior to the 15th century, the more widely reproduced and read treatise was Boethius' commentary on Cicero's *Topics*. Early in that commentary Boethius explains that "every argument is expressed by a syllogism or an enthymeme. But an enthymeme is an incomplete syllogism, some of whose parts are omitted either for the sake of brevity or because they are already known, and so argumentation of this sort also does not fall outside the genus of syllogism."[56]

When Boethius comes to the analysis of Cicero's syllogisms—and those are Stoic hypothetical syllogisms, not Peripatetic categorical syllogisms—he does not strictly follow Cicero's conflation of the terms *syllogism* and *enthymeme*. In Cicero's *Topics* the statement that explicitly conflates those two terms is placed after his discussion of the third Stoic hypothetical syllogism (*Topica* 14.56), although the point Cicero makes there simply repeats his earlier discussion about all seven syllogisms being understood as enthymemes (*Topica* 13.55). But Boethius instead understands Cicero's general statement as a local statement that applies only to the third Stoic hypothetical syllogism, and then Boethius has to try to make sense of this reading. According to Boethius, Cicero's third syllogism negates a conjunction of things and then joins another negation to the first. Such a syllogism is already dealing in contraries, and if the contrariety is expressed concisely, it will provide an enthymeme: "From these, Cicero says, enthymemes arise which are inferred from contraries" and "these are called enthymemes because the things discovered, which are concisely deduced from contraries, are especially pointed."[57]

Boethius' discussion of the double negation of conjunctions in enthymemes reads very much like first-year algebra. Boethius explicitly says we should reduce the argumentative form to a syllogism, namely, to a syllogism from incompatibles, from which enthymemes generally arise.[58] Boethius goes even further than this

---

[55]Colish, *Stoic Tradition* 2:278.

[56]Eleonore Stump, *Boethius's "In Ciceronis Topica": Translated, with Notes and an Introduction* (Ithaca: Cornell University Press, 1988) 31–32.

[57]Stump, *Boethius's "In Ciceronis Topica"* 149; compare 152.

[58]Stump, *Boethius's "In Ciceronis Topica"* 150.

in his treatise *De topicis differentiis*, in part because he is no longer constrained merely to elucidate Cicero:

> An enthymeme is an imperfect syllogism, that is, discourse in which the precipitous conclusion is derived without all the propositions having been laid down beforehand . . . So since an enthymeme argues from universals to particulars which are to be proved, it is, as it were, similar to a syllogism; but because it does not use all the propositions appropriate to a syllogism, it deviates from the definition of a syllogism and so is called an imperfect syllogism.[59]

Thus the enthymeme is a substitute for the syllogism and is derived from it.

In the Latin West, from the late 11th century onward, Boethius' formulations had a telling impact on logical distinctions, even after the full program of his *De topicis differentiis* had been left behind.[60] Garlandus Compotista, for example, devotes book 4 of his *Dialectica* to a discussion of Boethius' *De topicis differentiis*, but when Garlandus tries to explicate the enthymeme he falls back on Boethius' *De syllogismis categoricis* for his discussion of complete and incomplete arguments.[61] And Peter Abelard, who follows Boethius very closely in associating enthymemes with hypothetical syllogisms, even extends the notion of imperfection, so that just as the enthymeme is an incomplete syllogism, so the example is an incomplete induction.[62]

Peter of Spain, in the 13th century, offers a particularly strong version of Boethius' views on the enthymeme in his *Tractatus*. It is a view that hopelessly conflates Aristotelian syllogistic with the Stoic aspects of Cicero's and Boethius' syllogistic:

> It is important to know that every enthymeme must be reduced to a syllogism. Consequently, in every enthymeme there are three terms, as in a syllogism. Two of these terms are used in the conclusion and are the extremes; the other is the middle (*medium*) and is never used in the conclusion. One of the extremes is taken twice in an enthymeme, the other once. In accordance with the requirement of the

---

[59]Stump, *Boethius's "De topicis differentiis"* 45.

[60]There is little sign of Boethius's syllogistic studies or Aristotle's analytical and topical treatises before the 11th century. See Mark W. Sullivan, *Apuleian Logic: The Nature, Sources, and Influences of Apuleius's "Peri Hermeneias"* (Amsterdam: North-Holland, 1967) 190–191, 203–204. Sullivan also explores the hypothesis that Boethius himself drew upon Apuleius for understanding Aristotle's *Prior Analytics*; see 210–227. See also Martin M. Tweedale, "Logic (i): From the Late Eleventh Century to the Time of Abelard," *A History of Twelfth-Century Western Philosophy*, ed. Peter Dronke (Cambridge: Cambridge University Press, 1988) 196–226.

[61]Osmund Lewry, O. P., "Boethian Logic in the Medieval West," in Gibson, *Boethius* 90–134, 99. See also Eleonore Stump, "Topics: Their Development and Absorption Into Consequences," in *CHLMP*, 273–299, 275–281.

[62]Peter Abelard (Petrus Abaelardus, 1079–1142), *Dialectica*, ed. L. M. de Rijk (Assen: Van Gorcum, 1956) *Tractatus Tertius, Topica*, 464: "Si vero consequentiam praeponam, hypotheticum quoque enthymema erit propter eam, sicut syllogismus, quamvis necessitatem quam syllogismus habet, non teneat. Sicut ergo enthymema imperfectus est syllogismus, sic exemplum imperfecta inductio dicitur."

[syllogistic] mood, one must make a universal proposition out of the extreme that is taken once and the middle (*medium*), and in this way a syllogism will be produced.[63]

This might at first seem like simple Aristotelian commentary, but it is not. Peter does not use the word *medium* to refer to the distributed middle term of an Aristotelian syllogism but instead to signify a topically differentiated relationship that obtains between the middle term and one of the extremes.[64] Thus what had started in Boethius' commentary as an attempt to make sense of Cicero's Stoic syllogisms became in Boethius' *De topicis differentiis* a procedure for inventing Stoic enthymemes. But by the time of Peter of Spain this heuristic procedure was little more than a logical and analytical procedure for checking the validity of enthymemes by reconstructing middle terms and by casting them into the form of Aristotelian syllogisms. And Peter is not at all unusual; Walter Burley and a host of others say much the same thing.[65] By the 13th century, the doctrine of the truncated syllogism is so secure that Giles of Rome can work from a manuscript of Aristotle's *Prior Analytics* that clearly does not have the challenged word ἀτελής; and yet his larger discussion still comes out at the same place.[66] So also in the early 15th century, with Lorenzo Valla's wide-ranging *Retractio totius dialectice cum fundamentis universe philosophie*.[67] With the introduction of print in the late 15th century, what appears to be conflicting evidence in fact confirms the story. John Argyropulus, one of the Byzantines who came to Italy, translates Aristotle with no trace of the offending word ἀτελής, whereas the first edition of Aristotle from the Aldine press does indeed include the offending

---

[63]Peter of Spain (Petrus Hispanus, 1205–1276), *Tractatus*, in *The Cambridge Translations of Medieval Philosophical Texts: Volume One, Logic and the Philosophy of Language*, ed. Norman Kretzmann and Eleonore Stump (Cambridge: Cambridge University Press, 1988) 227.

[64]Stump, *Boethius's "De topicis differentiis"* 234.

[65]Walter Burley (Burleigh, 1275–1344/1345), *De puritate artis logicae tractatus longior*, ed. Philotheus Boehner (St. Bonaventure, NY: Franciscan Institute, 1955) *Capitulum II: De modo arguendi enthymematice in conditionalibus*, 66–79, where Burley defines the enthymeme as a "syllogismus curtatus" (66). For discussions of Burley and others, see Niels Jørgen Green-Pedersen, *The Tradition of the Topics in the Middle Ages: The Commentaries on Aristotle's and Boethius' "Topics"* (Munich: Philosophia Verlag, 1984), especially 309–313. The position is so common for medieval logic that, in the modern period, Alexander Broadie can declare that "an enthymeme is an inference one of whose premises is unstated"; Alexander Broadie, *Introduction to Medieval Logic* (Oxford: Clarendon Press, 1987) 60.

[66]Giles of Rome (Aegidius Romanus, Egidio Colonna, ca. 1243/1247–1316), *In libros priorum analeticorum expositio* (Venice, 1516) 81ᵛ–82ʳ. So, also, John Buridan (Johannes Buridanus, ca. 1300–ca. 1360), who had all the relevant Aristotelian treatises to hand, supports the medieval consensus through careful distinctions: "Sed minor patet, quia licet inductio, exemplum et enthymema non sunt perfectae argumentationes, tamen sunt bene perfectae argumentationes dialecticae"; *Quaestiones topicorum* I. qu. 16, in MS Munich, Bayr. St. B., clm. 12707, ff. 110ᵛb–111ʳa, ed. Green-Pedersen, 372.

[67]Lorenzo Valla (1407–1457), *Repastinatio dialectice et philosophie*, ed. Gianni Zippel (Padua: Antenor, 1982) I:355: "Hunc ego, si enthymema est (nam multis modis 'enthymema' dicitur), potius appellarim 'imperfectum syllogismum,' quam 'rhetoricum' sive 'oratorium syllogismum.' "

word. It hardly matters whether the word is present in Aristotle's text, because his enthymeme will be understood as though the word were there all the same. The story in the Latin West is paralleled by what happens in Arab thinking. In the 9th century, Alfarabi produced a lengthy commentary on Aristotle's *Rhetoric* (a commentary that was rediscovered only in 1951). In keeping with Arabic thinking that considered rhetoric, dialectic, and poetics all as subdivisions of logic, Alfarabi defines Aristotelian rhetoric as "un art syllogistique" and devotes a major part of the commentary to "persuasion par la forme des enthymèmes."[68] The enthymeme itself was a truncated syllogism, with the hidden (*caché*) premise being discovered in the mind (*se trouve dans la conscience*) of the auditor. The persuasive force of the enthymeme lay largely in the fact that the omitted premise suddenly and immediately calls into play shared understandings in the audience.[69] Alfarabi's commentary provided the basis in the 13th century for the *Didascalia* of Hermannus Alemannus, in which Hermannus defines Aristotle's enthymeme in the *Rhetoric* as a subset of the syllogism and refers explicitly to the *Prior Analytics* to justify reducing enthymemes to syllogistic figures.[70] In the 12th century, Averroes composes an extensive commentary on the *Rhetoric*, in which he discusses the enthymeme as though it were incomplete; and in the 15th century the Junctas edition of Averroes clearly translates *Prior Analytics* 2.27 as "imperfectus."[71] Averroes was available in the West from the 12th century, and Averroist thinking in Aristotelian studies was particularly strong in Padua; in 1579 Jacopo Zabarella, the Professor of Logic at Padua, could offer with confidence a specious etymology of the word *enthymeme* as coming from ἐν θυμῷ, that is, "*in the mind*, because the omitted proposition remains in the mind."[72]

---

[68]Alfarabi (Al-Fârâbî, ca. A.D. 873–950), *Commentaire de la rhétorique d'Aristote*, trans. Jacques Langhade, *Al-Fârâbî: Deux ouvrages inédits sur la rhétorique*, ed. Jacques Langhade and Mario Grignaschi (Beirut: Dar El-Machreq, 1971) 30 [248 b].

[69]Alfarabi, *Commentaire de la rhétorique d'Aristote*, 62: "L'enthymème est une affirmation composée de deux prémisses conjointes que l'on utilise en omettant l'une de ces deux prémisses conjointes. On l'appelle enthymème parce que celui qui l'utilise cache certaines de ses prémisses et ne les déclare pas; il l'utilise aussi en fonction de ce qui se trouve dans la conscience de l'auditeur qui est censé connaître les prémisses qu'il a cachées. Et il faut dire que l'enthymème ne devient persuasif pour le sens commun immédiatque parce qu'on y opère la dite omission. Car sans cette omission il ne serait pas persuasif."

[70]Hermannus Alemannus (Herman the German, d. 1272), *Didascalia in Rethoricam Aristotelis ex Glosa Alpharabi*, ed. Grignaschi, in Langhade and Grignaschi, *Al-Fârâbî: Deux ouvrages* 208–209 (sect. 36): "Enthimemata sunt sillogismi, quorum alique propositionum subtrahuntur vel subcitentur propter causas. . . . Et iam patuit in Libro (Analyticorum) similiter qualiter deducuntur enthimemata omnia in sillogismorum figuras."

[71]Averroes (Ibn Rushd, 1126–1198), *In libros rhetoricorum Aristotelis paraphrases. Abramo de Balmes interprete*, 75ᵛ–76ʳ; *Aristotelis priorum resolutoriorum, Ioanne Francisco Burana Veronensi interprete*, 166ʳ; in *Aristotelis opera cum Averrois commentariis*, vols. 1 and 2 (Venice, 1562).

[72]Jacopo Zabarella (Giacomo, Jacobus, 1533–1589), *Tabulae logicae* (1579; Padua, 1594) 169: "Enthymema est syllogismus imperfectus constans ex verisimilibus, vel ex signis. Imperfectus est quia deest ei altera propositio vel maior, vel minor, quae ut nota omittitur, unde etiam dictum est enthymema quasi ἐν θυμῷ, id est in animo, quia propositio, quae omittitur, in animo manet."

This predisposition to view Aristotle's enthymeme as a formula explains why Giulio Pace's thorough discrediting of the word ἀτελής during the Renaissance remained all but irrelevant. So deeply rooted was the predisposition that even Peter Ramus, who made his reputation attacking Aristotle, accepted the doctrine in its entirety: "Tel syllogisme imperfaict est nommé par Aristote, enthymeme au deuziesme du Syllogisme. L'esprit de l'homme autrefois est content de la seule proposition, autrefois de l'assomption, autrefois conçoit plustot la conclusion, qu'elle se puisse dire & exprimer: neantmoins en examinant ce ingement syllogistique, il fault remplir les parties qui sont seullement entendues, & acheuer le syllogisme."[73] A whole new industry in logical thinking developed in the wake of Ramus' work,[74] one that did not need to attend closely to the Renaissance debates about Aristotle's own logic and that thus provided an independent path of survival for the doctrine of truncation, immune to Pace's arguments. But even within the world of Aristotelian studies, life went on as usual, untroubled by Pace's assault. The Jesuits provide but one of many examples. The anonymous or, rather, corporate commentary from the College of Coimbra on Aristotle's logic was reprinted numerous times during the early 17th century.[75] The discussions of the enthymeme rehearse all the traditional positions, including the doctrine of truncation, drawing extensively upon Cicero, Quintilian, Boethius, Agricola, and even Averroes to explain Aristotle.[76] And the Latin translation of the *Organon* upon which this commentary was based was that of John Argyropolous, the one that did not have the suspect word ἀτελής.

PART FOUR

During much of this time, the text of Aristotle's *Rhetoric*, with its several different accounts of the enthymeme, was nowhere to be seen.[77] Such Aristotle as the western world knew was the Aristotle of the *Organon*, and even Aristotle's *Topics*, which is so closely allied with the *Rhetoric*, was kept with and understood in terms of the analytical treatises. With the reintroduction of Aristotle's *Rhetoric*, the intervening centuries of logical discussion were read back into the *Rhetoric*. Giles of Rome (ca. 1290) provided an extensive commentary on Moerbeke's Latin translation of the *Rhetoric* in which he declared that *enthimema est quidam defectivus syllogismus*,

[73]Pierre de la Ramée (Ramus, 1515–1572), *Dialectique* (Paris, 1555) 114–115.

[74]Modern philosophers "find little of value either in Ramus's criticisms of Aristotle or in his own original work"; see William Kneale and Martha Kneale, *The Development of Logic* (1962; Oxford: Clarendon Press, 1984) 302ff.

[75]*Commentarii Collegii Conimbricensis e Societate Iesu in universam dialecticam Aristotelis* (Cologne, 1607; Hildesheim: Georg Olms, 1976); other editions in Coimbra, 1606; Lyon, 1607; Lyon, 1610; Cologne, 1611; Venice, 1616; Lyon, 1622; Cologne, 1630; also Frankfurt[?], 1604.

[76]*Commentarii Collegii Conimbricensis*, 2.266–270; 2.401–406; 2.507–510.

[77]See Lawrence D. Green, "The Reception of Aristotle's *Rhetoric* in the Renaissance," in Fortenbaugh and Mirhady, *Peripatetic Rhetoric After Aristotle* 320–348.

short one premise and reducible to a syllogism.[78] With the rediscovery of the complete text of Quintilian's *Institutio oratoria* in the early 15th century, commentators found what must have seemed like confirmation of what they had already concluded long before: "Some again call [the enthymeme] a rhetorical syllogism, others an incomplete syllogism, because its parts are not so clearly defined or of the same number as those of the regular syllogism, since such precision is not specially required by the orator."[79] The commentators who rely upon Quintilian show little awareness that the conflation of Stoic and Peripatetic notions had begun long before Quintilian, or that his summary of Peripatetic positions might have little to do with Aristotle's own treatises.

Even the distinctions that Alexander of Aphrodisias had drawn with such care in the century after Quintilian were completely obliterated during the Renaissance. Marc-Antoine Muret's influential Latin translation of Alexander's *In topica* (1544) freely uses the Latin phrase *syllogismus imperfectus* where the word ἀτελής never appeared in Alexander's text.[80] Those who relied upon Muret's translation found confirmation for what they were already prepared to believe.[81] As early as 1545 Danielo Barbaro glosses Hermolao Barbaro's translation of the *Rhetoric* by explaining that the enthymeme was an imperfect and incomplete syllogism.[82] Johann Sturm's influential edition of the *Rhetoric* in 1570 glossed the word *syllogism* by saying that it is what orators called an enthymeme and then gives the standard explanation about truncation and probable premises.[83] But Sturm also

---

[78]Giles of Rome, *Expositio super tribus libris rhetoricorum* [ca. 1290] (Venice, 1515) 2ʳa, 4ʳb. Giles refers to his own earlier commentary on the *Prior Analytics* (see footnote 66) in thinking about the *Rhetoric* in terms of the Organon, saying that enthymemes and examples are the tools (*instrumenta*) of rhetoric; *Rhetoricorum*, 8ʳa, 9ʳa–10ʳb.

[79]Quintilian, *Institutio oratoria*, trans. H. E. Butler (London: Heinemann, 1921) 5.10.3: "Hunc alii rhetoricum syllogismum, alii imperfectum syllogismum vocaverunt, quia nec distinctis nec totidem partibus concluderetur; quod sane non utique ab oratore desideratur." See 5.14.23ff.

[80]Marc-Antoine Muret (Muretus, 1526–1585), *Alexander Aphrodisiensis in octo libros topicorum Aristotelis explicatio* [1544?] (Venice, 1554) 2ʳb. On the other hand, the earlier translation by Guilelmus Dorotheus Venetus does not read *imperfectus* into Alexander's text; *Alexandri Aphrodisei summi peripatetici, in octo libros topicorum, vel de locis sedeque argumentorum Aristotelis commentatio lucidissima* [1538?] (Venice, 1541).

[81]So also the anonymous Greek commentary on the *Rhetoric* (*CAG* 21.2) would have confirmed the predispositions of the Renaissance commentators, and it would have been available after its printing in 1539, but I have found no evidence of commentators drawing upon it; see the earlier discussion on this commentary.

[82]Hermolao Barbaro (Hermolaus Barbarus, 1454–1493), Danielo Barbaro (Danielus Barbarus, 1514–1570), *Aristotelis rhetoricorum libri tres, Hermolao Barbaro Patricio Veneto interprete, Danielis Barbari in eosdem libros commentarii* (Basel, 1545) 30. Hermolao's translation reads "Enthymema autem est ratiocinatio et syllogismus quidam," which Danielo glosses as "Enthymema esse quendam syllogismum, imperfectum scilicet et inchoatum." Danielo later rehearses several different uses of the word *enthymeme* by various writers and again concludes that Aristotle intends "Enthymema, id est commentatio, imperfectus syllogismus" (81).

[83]Johann Sturm (Sturmius, 1507–1589) *Aristotelis rhetoricorum libri III* (Strassburg, 1570) 20: "συλλογισμός: Latine Ratiocinatio, apud oratores vocatur enthymema." See especially Sturm's discussion on p. 10.

provides a psychological explanation that owed more to Stoicism than to Aristotle: The speed and the condensed form of the enthymeme could make auditors grant their assent to that which they really do not understand.[84] By the late Renaissance, the doctrine of the truncated Aristotelian enthymeme was secure and was further complicated not only by Renaissance efforts to make Aristotle's *Rhetoric* consonant with topical proceeding in the *Topics* (which also got confused with Ciceronian *Topics* and Boethian topics) but also by efforts to coordinate that treatise with Aristotle's analytical works.

Antonio Riccobono (1606) is no longer translating Aristotle's *Rhetoric* but merely summarizing the views of some of the best thinkers of the preceding century when he explains that "enthymema sit syllogismus imperfectus."[85] Riccobono is nervous about trying to make sense of the enthymeme in this way, and he engages in extended argument with Marc Antonio Maioragio on this subject.[86] The doctrine of truncation, as Riccobono points out, stipulates that enthymemes are for those auditors who cannot grasp a syllogism; but he is unconvinced by this explanation, because it surely must be more difficult for an auditor to follow an incomplete syllogism than a complete syllogism. Riccobono was not the only Renaissance commentator to be troubled by the entire issue. In 1549, the magisterial Pier Vettori repeats the doctrine of rhetorical truncation, but when he comes to the topical discussion of enthymemes in book 2 of the *Rhetoric*, he realizes that the doctrine is insufficient.[87] Like Riccobono later, Vettori is puzzled and finally resorts to the theory of truncation as an explanation of last resort. So also when the *Rhetoric* is finally printed in England in 1619; in the preface Theodore Goulston tries to approach the enthymeme as a fuller concept that organizes Aristotelian rhetoric, but in his local commentary he is reduced to explaining the enthymeme with medieval diagrams for syllogistic completion and reduction.[88]

For Riccobono and other commentators on the *Rhetoric*, completeness and perfection seem to mean the same thing, but they are not—at least, not in Aristotle—and this raises one last problem in this long tradition. Formal completeness refers to the number of parts present; hence the notion of truncation. Perfection, however, is a notion that emerges out of the *Prior Analytics*, when Aristotle

---

[84]Sturm, *Rhetoricorum libri III*, 20: "Enthymemata vero magis perturbant: quia requirunt celerem auscultatorum assensiorem. Saepe etiam condensantur, ut auditor nesciat, quare credat, et tamen cogitur assentiri: quia audit sententias uniuersales et graves, et putantur quasi es thesauro ingenij alicuis magni adferri."

[85]Antonio Riccobono (Riccobonus, 1541–1599), *Paraphrasis in rhetoricam Aristotelis, interiecta rerum difficiliorum explicatione, & collata ipsius Riccoboni multis in locis conversione, cum Maioragii, Sigonii, Victorii, Mureti conversionibus* (Hanau, 1606) 25.

[86]This argument is summarized in Green, "The Reception of Aristotle's *Rhetoric* in the Renaissance" 342–344.

[87]Pier Vettori (Victorius, 1499–1585), *Commentarii in tres libros Aristotelis de arte dicendi* (Florence, 1548) 414: "Enthymema hic appellat, non imperfectum syllogismum, sed ut fere magistri dicendi capere hoc nomen consuerunt, sententiam ex contrariis conclusam. Verba autem quae sequuntur oratoris, id manifesto declarant." Compare 44–45.

[88]Theodore Goulston, *De rhetorica seu arte dicendi libri tres* (London, 1619).

described four, and then two, syllogistic forms that are "perfect." Unfortunately, there is little agreement on what Aristotle means by a "perfect" syllogism. Apparently, an Aristotelian syllogism is perfect when its validity is immediately apprehensible upon first articulation, and any syllogistically valid set of propositions in the other more convoluted Aristotelian modes and figures ultimately can be expressed as an uncomplicated and clearly apprehensible syllogism. That is, any imperfect syllogism can be rendered as a perfect syllogism. Thus it makes sense to propose that either Aristotle or his unknown glossator might have used the word ἀτελής at *Prior Analytics* 2.27. An enthymeme is rarely expressed in the form of a perfect syllogism and does not depend upon such perfection for its immediate apprehension by an audience. But anyone, with time and effort, could reduce an enthymeme to a perfect syllogism. The word ἀτελής is defensible in the context of the *Prior Analytics*, even if it is mistaken. But that context is not the context of the *Rhetoric*.

It remains open to debate whether it is useful at all to think of Aristotelian syllogistic in terms of inferential proceeding; as Ernst Kapp points out, even the name of what we call logic "indicates that logic was originally conceived as a science of what happens, not when we are thinking for ourselves, but when we are talking and trying to convince one another."[89] It is widely recognized that trying to turn Aristotle's syllogism to practical account and, at the same time, to preserve its status as an inferential categorical proceeding leads quickly to absurdity. The discussions on the so-called practical syllogism offer a case in point.[90] When we act in this world, it is simply not the case that we start from premises and work our way toward a conclusion, in the following fashion:

(*major premise*) Any act of mine that results in my knowing the time is desirable;

(*minor premise*) Looking at my watch will result in my knowing the time;

(*conclusion*) Therefore, I look at my watch.[91]

There may be a syllogism inherent in the act of looking at one's watch, but it is silly to think of this instantaneous act as a truncated syllogism.[92]

---

[89]Ernst Kapp, *Greek Foundations of Traditional Logic* (New York: Columbia University Press, 1942) 19. See also Ernest Kapp, "Syllogistik," in Georg Wissowa (orig.), *Paulys Real-Encyclopädie der classischen Altertumswissenschaft*, 2nd ser., 4:1 (Stuttgart: Metzler, 1931) cols. 1046–1067; reprinted in Ernest Kapp, *Ausgewählte Schriften* (Berlin, 1968) 254–277; reprinted in Jonathan Barnes, Malcolm Schofield, Richard Sorabji, eds., *Articles on Aristotle: 1. Science*, trans. Mary Humboldt Dill and Peter Dill (London: Duckworth, 1975) 35–49.

[90]For a review of the literature and problems, see W. K. C. Guthrie, *A History of Greek Philosophy*, 8 vols. (Cambridge: Cambridge University Press, 1981) 6:349–352.

[91]Quoted in Guthrie, *A History of Greek Philosophy* 6:350n.

[92]For efforts at a more nuanced understanding of Aristotle's practical syllogism, see Takatura Ando, "The Practical Syllogism," *Aristotle's Theory of Practical Cognition*, 3rd ed. (1958; The Hague: Martinus Nijhoff, 1971) 214–265; Anthony Kenny, "Practical, Technical and Ethical

So also with Aristotle's enthymeme. The process starts not with premises but with conclusions, and we work backwards; first we seize upon what we want another person to think or do, and then we seek reasons sufficient for that goal. There may be a syllogism inherent in some enthymemes,[93] but this is hardly the entire story. Aristotle's enthymeme has suffered from two thousand years of conflating Stoic and Peripatetic ideas, and this conflation has provided fertile ground for enduring misperceptions.[94] People accept limited evidence that the enthymeme is merely a mechanistic formula, because they are already predisposed to view the enthymeme as part of a deductive inferential machine. And when this machine fails to operate as required, as inevitably it must fail, Aristotle's enthymeme can only appear naively reductive—and even *imperfectus, inchoatus, defectivus, mutilus, curtatus, truncatus.*

Syllogisms," *Aristotle's Theory of the Will* (New Haven: Yale University Press, 1979) 111–124; and Norman O. Dahl, *Practical Reason, Aristotle, and Weakness of the Will* (Minneapolis: University of Minnesota Press, 1984). Kenny and most editors read *Ethica Nicomachea* 1144ᵃ31 as συλλογισμοὶ τῶν πρακτῶν, whereas Guthrie reads συλλογισμοι τῶν πρακτικῶν.

[93] See the comments and materials in Kennedy, *Aristotle. On Rhetoric* 42n, 297–298, 310.

[94] Sten Ebbesen provides an interesting comparison for how ideas conflate and separate over time: "Medieval logicians surpassed the ancients. But they were deeply influenced by the men from Porphyry to Philoponus; both in nominalistic periods and in realistic ones. The ancient scholastics were chimeras with an Aristotelian body barely managing to keep the Platonic head and the Stoic tail from either running in opposite directions or engaging in a deadly fight with each other. The medievals saw the monster from both ends." See Sten Ebbesen, "Philoponus, 'Alexander' and the Origins of Medieval Logic," in Sorabji, *Aristotle Transformed* 459.

Chapter 2

Cicero's Response to the Philosophers in *De oratore*, Book 1

Robert Gaines
University of Maryland

In their recent and authoritative commentary on *De oratore*, Leeman and Pinkster propose that book 1 is a *disputatio in utramque partem* which discloses a skeptical suspension of judgment by Cicero regarding the main positions represented in the book.[1] Thus, within their view, when Crassus' position that the orator must know all important matters and arts is challenged by Antonius, who says the orator has no time and no need to acquire such knowledge, this is Cicero's device for showing that both accounts are probable and neither may be chosen with any certainty.[2]

Despite the obvious attractions of this proposal, I find it unacceptable on several grounds. One has to do with Cicero's comments related to the discussion of Crassus and Antonius at the outset of book 2. Noting that Crassus chose a reputation for looking down on learning whereas Antonius disdained appearance of any study at all, Cicero remarks in his own voice at section 5 as follows: "What was the prudence of these choices, pertains not at all to the present; however, the following is for this composition undertaken and this time to say, that no one has ever been able to shine and excel at eloquence, not just without

---

[1]Anton D. Leeman and Harm Pinkster, *De oratore libri III/Kommentar*, vol. 1 (Heidelberg: Carl Winter Universitätsverlag, 1981) 11–12; compare A. D. Leeman, "The Structure of Cicero's *De oratore* I," *Ciceroniana: Hommages à Kazimierz Kumaniecki*, ed. Alain Michel and Raoul Verdière, *Roma Aeterna*, 9 (Leiden: E. J. Brill, 1975) 148–149.

[2]Leeman and Pinkster, *Kommentar* 11; see also Leeman ("Structure" 149), who understands the *disputatio in utramque partem* as reflecting Cicero's adherence to Academic methods (on the principles of Academic inquiry, consult, e.g., Cicero, *Academica* 1.45–46, 2.124).

instruction in speaking, but even without all wisdom."[3] To my mind, these are not the words of a man carefully preserving the conditions of a skeptical suspension. Rather, they represent a firmly held conviction and one of which Cicero is at great pains to persuade his reader.[4] Not only does Cicero force the constructed nemesis of his view, Antonius, to recant opposition to the knowledge doctrine at the beginning of book 2 (37–40), but he allows his constructed champion, Crassus, to digress repeatedly on behalf of the doctrine through the first half of book 3 (see 3.54–61, 74–81, 82–89, 122–125, 142–143).

Of course, if Cicero did not himself suspend judgment about the positions expressed in *De oratore*, book 1, we are left with three significant problems. The first is the failure of book 1 to conclude Cicero's theoretical conviction with finality. This difficulty is easily resolved, I think, when the position opposed to Cicero's view, that of Antonius, is closely scrutinized. At 1.223, Antonius confronts Crassus' notion of the learned orator with a conception of his own that is laid out with some care: "It is essential for us to have a shrewd man, clever by nature and experience, who can diligently track down with keenness of scent, what his countrymen (and those men he might wish to persuade on something by speaking) think, feel, believe, hope for."[5] What is characteristic about this description is Antonius' insistence that, to be successful, the orator needs only a kind of shrewdness derived from nature and experience. Particularly within its context—namely, opposition to Crassus' view—such a description seems provocative, for it is essentially identical to the description of the orator that Cicero ascribes to Quintus in the prologue to book 1 at section 5: "And you make it a practice on various occasions to disagree with me on this matter in our discussions, because I posit that eloquence is dependent upon the culture of the most learned men, while you think it ought to be dissociated from refinement of training and located in a certain kind of talent and practice."[6] Given the close similarity of the two descriptions, what I propose is that within book 1 Cicero uses Antonius to present a fully developed version of the view to which Quintus

---

[3]"Quorum consilium quale fuerit, nihil sane ad hoc tempus; illud autem est huius institutae scriptionis ac temporis neminem eloquentia non modo sine dicendi doctrina, sed ne sine omni quidem sapientia florere umquam et praestare potuisse." Here and elsewhere, with exceptions noted, citations in Cicero's *De oratore* refer to Kazimierz F. Kumaniecki, ed., *M. Tulli Ciceronis scripta quae manserunt omnia*, Fasc. 3, *De oratore* (Leipzig: BSB B. G. Teubner Verlagsgesellschaft, 1969). Translations are my own.

[4]Cicero announces this position at 1.20.

[5]"acuto homine nobis opus est et natura usuque callido, qui sagaciter pervestiget quid sui cives iique homines, quibus aliquid dicendo persuadere velit, cogitent, sentiant, opinentur, expectent."

[6]"solesque non numquam hac de re a me in disputationibus nostris dissentire quod ego eruditissimorum hominum artibus eloquentiam contineri statuam, tu autem illam ab elegantia doctrinae segregandam putes et in quodam ingenii atque exercitationis genere ponendam." On the comparability of the positions of Quintus and Antonius (in book 1), see George Kennedy, *The Art of Rhetoric in the Roman World: 300 B.C.–A.D. 300* (Princeton: Princeton University Press, 1972) 211; however, compare Leeman, "Structure" 146.

actually adhered. The book thus becomes, inter alia, a theoretical amplification of the *disputationes* that Cicero had previously held with Quintus. Considering the special status of Quintus—brother and dedicatee of *De oratore*—I believe it is no mystery that the dispute in book 1 is not settled decisively in favor of Cicero's position. This much Cicero could postpone to the later books.

A second and related problem is posed by the form of book 1—a *disputatio in utramque partem*. Leeman and Pinkster believe that this form signifies a skeptical commitment on Cicero's part concerning the matter under discussion. However, Cicero's presentation of arguments on both sides of the subject need not signify such a commitment. For Cicero conceived of speech or discussion *in utramque partem* as belonging to orators at least as much as to philosophers.[7] And what better place to display the orator's facility than a dialogic dispute in which the scope of the orator's facility is at stake? Accordingly, it seems quite possible that Cicero's exploitation of *disputatio in utramque partem* is simply an illustration of the main point he is trying to make in the book—that the complete orator knows all important matters and arts.

The third problem is the place of book 1 in the overall scheme of *De oratore*. Within the account of Leeman and Pinkster, the indecisive—and, to them, undecidable—outcome of book 1 serves only to prepare for a return to and expansion of certain of its philosophical themes in books 2 and 3, where Cicero furnishes a self-styled τεχνολογία.[8] However, presuming that Cicero adopts—and intends for us to adopt—what I have called his knowledge doctrine, then we must take book 1 as a kind of theoretical accomplishment alongside which the philosophical *ars oratoris* of books 2 and 3 had to be prosecuted. That Cicero, at least, was mindful of such an accomplishment is indicated by the placement of Antonius' confession of dissemblance in book 2. Coming early in the book, Antonius' announcement of a position that is compatible with, if not identical to, the knowledge doctrine allows the account of Cicero's *ars oratoris* to proceed without danger of contradiction or inconsistency.

The question remaining, then, concerns the sort of theoretical accomplishment realized by Cicero within the first book of *De oratore*. In what follows, I develop an answer to this question in three stages. Within the first, I explore Cicero's general argument related to the knowledge doctrine, focusing on the manner in which he specifically supports and eventually augments that doctrine. In the second stage, I demonstrate that this argument constitutes Cicero's reply to the philosophers, particularly those who would disparage rhetoric.[9] In the concluding

---

[7]*De oratore* 1.158, 263, 3.80; *Orator* 46.

[8]Leeman and Pinkster, *Kommentar* 26; compare Leeman, "Structure" 149. The evidence for Cicero's conception of *De oratore*, books 2 and 3, derives from *Ad Atticum* 4.16.3, where Cicero describes the books as containing a τεχνολογία.

[9]The general view that Cicero's requirement of broad knowledge for the orator responds in some way to philosophical criticism of rhetoric may be found in Jakob Wisse, *Ethos and Pathos from Aristotle to Cicero* (Amsterdam: Adolf M. Hakkert, 1989) 175; and Brian Vickers, *In Defence of*

stage, I argue that this reply is best understood as a self-conscious philosophy of rhetoric.

PART ONE

Much of Cicero's argument on the knowledge doctrine is represented in the earliest formulation of the view. Writing in his own voice at 1.20–21, Cicero declares:

> And certainly in my view, no one will be able to be an orator abounding in every excellence, unless he will have acquired knowledge of all great matters and arts. For, his speech must blossom forth and be copious from a comprehension of things and, unless there is an underlying matter, perceived and understood by the orator, his speech finds a sort of hollow and nearly childish expression. Yet I shall not impose so much of a burden upon orators, especially ours, in such an occupation with the city and its life, that I believe it is permitted to these men to be ignorant of nothing; however the force of "orator" and the very act of professing to speak well seems to undertake and to promise this, that whatever matter has been proposed, everything about the matter is spoken by him ornately and copiously.[10]

Embedded in this passage is the knowledge doctrine, along with two reasons for its acceptance. Cicero's claim is that the *orator perfectus* (or, in this case, orator *cumulatus omni laude*) must acquire knowledge of every *ars et magna res*, the only proviso being that acquisition of these things does not entail their absolute

---

Rhetoric (Oxford: The Clarendon Press, 1988) 164–167. However, the knowledge doctrine is more typically conceived as a means of philosophizing rhetoric than as a foundation for counterattack against the philosophers; see, for instance, Wilhel Kroll, "M. Tullius Cicero (Rhetorische Schriften)," *Paulys Real-Encyclopädie der classischen Altertumswissenschaft*, 7:1 (Stuttgart: J. B. Metzlersche Verlagsbuchhandlung, 1939) 1095–1097; A. D. Leeman, *Orationis Ratio: The Stylistic Theories and Practice of the Roman Orators, Historians, and Philosophers* (Amsterdam: Adolf M. Hakkert, 1963) 1: 116–117, 123–124; Kennedy, *The Art of Rhetoric in the Roman World* 226–227; Alain Michel, "La théorie de la rhétorique chez Cicéron: éloquence et philosophie," *Éloquence et rhetorique chez Cicéron*, ed. Walther Ludwig, Entretiens sur l'Antiquité Classique, 28 (Genève: Fondation Hardt, 1982) 117–118; Harald Merklin, "System und Theorie in Ciceros 'De oratore'," *Würzburger Jahrbücher für die Altertumswissenschaft*, n.F. 13 (1987): 158–160; Guy Achard, "Pourquoi Cicéron a-t-il écrit le *De oratore?*" *Latomus* 46 (1987): 320–321; Peter Steinmetz, "Beobachtungen zu Ciceros philosophischem Standpunkt," *Cicero's Knowledge of the Peripatos*, Rutgers University Studies in Classical Humanities, 4 (New Brunswick: Transaction Publishers, 1989) 6–7; Eckart Schütrumpf, "Cicero *De oratore* I and Greek Philosophical Tradition," *Rheinisches Museum für Philologie* 133 (1990): 315–317.

[10]"ac mea quidem sententia nemo poterit esse omni laude cumulatus orator, nisi erit omnium rerum magnarum atque artium scientiam consecutus. etenim ex rerum cognitione efflorescat et redundet oportet oratio; quae nisi subest res ab oratore percepta et cognita, inanem quandam habet elocutionem et paene puerilem. neque vero ego hoc tantum oneris imponam nostris praesertim oratoribus in hac tanta occupatione urbis ac vitae, nihil ut iis putem licere nescire, quamquam vis oratoris professioque ipsa bene dicendi hoc suscipere ac polliceri videtur, ut omni de re quaecumque sit proposita ornate ab eo copioseque dicatur."

mastery. The reasons Cicero gives for his claim are of two different sorts. The first is related to the oratorical outcomes of knowledge and its lack: Oratory derived from knowledge inevitably blooms forth and manifests copiousness, and oratory not so derived must be inane and puerile. The second reason has to do with the fundamental basis for Cicero's claim. To be an orator simply means being able to speak on any subject copiously and ornately.[11]

Cicero's views on the knowledge doctrine as well as its outcomes and basis are developed throughout book 1. In explication of the basis, for example, Crassus defines the *orator perfectus* at 1.59 as that man "who is able to speak concerning all matters copiously and diversely."[12] This definition is clarified and expanded at 1.64, where Crassus argues as follows: "Wherefore, if anyone wishes to define and sum up the general and particular power of the orator, he will be an orator, in my view, worthy of this name so grand, who, whatever matter should present itself to be set out in words, would speak with sagacity and order and embellishment and good memory, adding a certain impressiveness of delivery."[13] Here Cicero suggests why it is that the very definition of the orator leads to the knowledge doctrine. Because the orator must speak on every subject with understanding, the orator must acquire a knowledge of all matters that is adequate to this purpose.

The outcomes of the orator's knowledge are developed similarly. At book 1.48–50 Crassus requires understanding of the subject for manifestation of *virtus dicendi* and affirms that the style of those who speak well shall either amount to nothing at all or result in derision, if the stylist does not comprehend the *res*. So, too, at 169 he criticizes as unseemly and presumptuous the actions of those who would speak at the bar without thorough training in civil law.[14] In a similar vein, Crassus denies at 53 and 60 that the orator will be able to arouse or allay emotions without a complete grasp of the minds and characters of men. But Cicero's account of outcomes is not concerned exclusively with instrumental matters; it also includes effects attributable to mastery of much that is collateral to the immediate subject and audience. Specifically, at 1.72 Cicero has Crassus opine that "no one should be held of account among the orators, who is not polished in all those arts which are appropriate to a free man, which very arts, if we do not use them in our speaking, still it appears and is obvious, whether we are ignorant or informed of them."[15]

---

[11]Compare Quintilian, *Institutio oratoria* 2.21.5.

[12]"sed oratorem plenum atque perfectum esse eum, qui de omnibus rebus possit copiose varieque dicere."

[13]"quam ob rem si quis universam et propriam oratoris vim definire complectique volt, is orator erit mea sententia hoc tam gravi dignus nomine, qui quaecumque res inciderit quae sit dictione explicanda prudenter et composite et ornate et memoriter dicet cum quadam actionis etiam dignitate."

[14]Compare 1.167, 184.

[15]"sic sentio neminem esse in oratorum numero habendum, qui non sit omnibus iis artibus, quae sunt libero dignae, perpolitus; quibus ipsis si in dicendo non utimur, tamen apparet atque extat, utrum simus earum rudes an didicerimus."

As might be expected, Cicero elaborates the knowledge doctrine itself in coordination with his account of knowledge outcomes. Within book 1 he represents Crassus as requiring that the orator have knowledge of the subject at 48, 60, 159, 167, and 201; knowledge of human nature at 48, 53, 60, and 67; and knowledge of liberal arts at 72. Of these requirements, only the first is given further treatment. Beginning at 65, Crassus lays out several limitations on the demand for knowledge of the subject matter. The orator, Crassus admits, does not need to know everything about every matter; in fact, of the three general subjects of philosophy—nature, discussion, and life and morals—the orator must grasp only the last (68–69). And even here, Crassus says, the orator need not be troubled with details, because there is always a specialist to consult for what is really technical about each subject (66–67). As for matters other than life and morals, the orator can learn enough to speak about them, provided that they are imparted and reported to him (69). Of course, such limitations are clearly foreshadowed by Cicero's proviso to the first statement of the knowledge doctrine. True to his proviso, Cicero does not prohibit initial but, rather, continued ignorance of the orator's subject.[16]

I think that by now the argument offered by Cicero on behalf of his knowledge doctrine is fairly clear. He took as his basis the proposition that the true orator could speak on any subject with knowledge and grace. He then insisted that the outcomes of intellectual respectability, effectiveness, and sophistication were inaccessible apart from knowledge of the subject, psychology, and the liberal arts. In these he found two lines of reasoning on behalf of the doctrine that the ideal orator must know all important matters and arts.[17]

Having arrived at this doctrine, however, Cicero apparently realized it had significance far beyond the question it was initially supposed to answer, namely, what is required of the orator? For within book 1, he seizes upon the doctrine as the ground for a new and startling implication—the *orator perfectus* demonstrates superiority over the practitioners of all the other arts. He arrives at this implication in the following way.

At 1.42–44, Cicero has Scaevola pose the problem that philosophers and other artists display the resources of eloquence, although their arts are not allied with rhetoric. To this Crassus replies that although philosophers and others may speak eloquently on subjects within their own arts, the style that makes them eloquent is a product of the rhetorical faculty (49, 62). His argument for this view involves two interlocking considerations. The first is that eloquence is not essential to the competent practice of arts other than rhetoric. Crassus reasons on behalf of this

---

[16]Brian Vickers' complaint (*In Defence of Rhetoric* 164–165) that Cicero's knowledge doctrine demands a kind of "omni-competence" seems to ignore the very practical minima set down by Cicero in defining the orator's mastery.

[17]Given the structure and development of Cicero's defense of the knowledge doctrine, I cannot accept Kennedy's general dismissal of the position as shallow and poorly argued (see Kennedy, *The Art of Rhetoric in the Roman World* 226–228).

consideration at 50 with a brief reference to the case of philosophy. Some philosophers, he says, present their subjects in a thin and meager fashion, yet they are not discounted as philosophers, despite their lack of eloquence.

The second consideration is that the style that separates eloquent speakers from meager ones belongs exclusively to oratory. Crassus substantiates this position in two steps. At 50 he insists that when knowledge of the subject is assumed, the single mark of the accomplished speaker is a style that is "studied, ornate, and distinguished by a certain artifice and polish." Later, at 54, he adds that the same style—now described as "impressive, ornate, and accommodated to the perceptions and minds of men"—is a peculiar property of the orator (*proprium oratoris*).

The upshot of Crassus' reply to Scaevola is a firm distinction between disciplinary or artistic knowledge of subject matters and the strictly rhetorical ability to express such knowledge eloquently. Cicero's purpose in the exchange seems quite obvious, for when this new distinction is coupled with the knowledge doctrine, it immediately falls out that orators surpass the practitioners in all other arts, because they alone possess both the knowledge and the expressive ability requisite for eloquent speaking.

That Cicero cherished this conclusion is indicated, I think, by its frequent repetition in various forms within book 1. At 51, for instance, Crassus declares that provided the subject matter is grasped and understood by the orator, then "whatever the matter will be from whichever art and concerning whichever genus, the orator, just as if he has mastered the case of a client, will speak better and more ornately than the very inventor and practitioner of the art."[18] This version of the conclusion is amplified at 56 with a particular application to philosophy. Here, noting the philosophical schools deny that topics such as the gods, friendship, and virtue pertain to the orator, Crassus continues as follows (57): "When I shall have allowed that they dispute concerning these matters in their secluded corners, to occupy their leisure, I shall nevertheless ascribe and attribute this to the orator, that the same things, concerning which those men debate in a certain plain and paltry style, this man expands with all charm and gravity."[19]

We meet the conclusion in a slightly different form at 65. Crassus acknowledges that the assumption of polymathy in the orator may be objectionable; accordingly, he develops the idea that the orator may need to learn some subjects before speaking. But even in such cases, Crassus maintains, the orator will surpass his extradisciplinary colleagues. For when he has learned about the relevant arts from those who possess them, he will speak about these "far better than those very men whose arts they are." Crassus immediately elaborates this version of

---

[18]"quicquid erit igitur quacumque ex arte, quocumque de genere, orator id, si tamquam clientis causam didicerit, dicet melius et ornatius quam ipse ille eius rei inventor atque artifex."

[19]"quibus ego ut his de rebus in angulis consumendi oti causa disserant cum concessero, illud tamen oratori tribuam et dabo, ut eadem, de quibus illi tenui quodam et exiguo sermone disputant, hic cum omni iucunditate et gravitate explicet."

the conclusion with reference to three particular arts—tactics (66), civil law (66), and philosophy (67). In each of these cases, Crassus insists that the orator, once informed, will account himself far better than the master from whom he has learned the art.

Thus Cicero records and amplifies this crucial implication of the knowledge doctrine. Having carefully grounded that doctrine in the orator's responsibility and the outcomes of knowledge in rhetorical practice, he discloses in these passages the doctrine's ultimate significance—the orator, who combines knowledge of all arts with eloquent expression, is superior to every other artist.

PART TWO

To this point, we have seen that within *De oratore*, book 1, Cicero offers an argument that explicates and elaborates his personal view on the orator's obligation to know all important matters and arts. We have seen, too, that Cicero is at pains to show the pointed implication of this view for the practitioners of all arts and disciplines. Now, that Cicero meant his argument as a reply—especially and in particular—to one group of practitioners, the philosophers, is indicated by several features of its presentation, originally in book 1 and then summarily in book 3.

Within book 1, perhaps the most obvious indications of Cicero's intentions are literary. For twice, here, he expressly characterizes Crassus' main argument as a response to philosophical views on rhetoric. The first occurs at 45–47. Having just heard Scaevola's complaints against his expansive view of oratory, Crassus likens them to the critique of rhetoric previously furnished by the Greek philosophers (45). These philosophers had banished orators from civic government, excluded orators from knowledge of important matters, and restricted orators to law courts and assemblies (46). "But," Crassus adds, "I could agree neither with those men nor with the inventor and source of these arguments, . . . Plato" (47).[20] Crassus proceeds to address Scaevola's complaints in a larger context of dispute with the philosophers. At the middle of this discussion we find the second characterization of Crassus' argument. Having already presented the knowledge doctrine, its justification in rhetorical outcomes, and its consequences for the surpassing status of orators, Crassus now discloses, "These matters I used to argue with the philosophers themselves back in Athens" (57). The polemical significance of these two characterizations seems unmistakable, because in both instances the argument of Crassus—and thus of Cicero—is placed squarely in opposition to those philosophers who derogate rhetoric.

In addition to such literary indications, there are also theoretical grounds for believing that Cicero had the philosophers in mind as he presented his argument

---

[20]Compare Kennedy, *The Art of Rhetoric in the Roman World* 218.

on the knowledge doctrine. Within book 1, these grounds arise from the meticulous way in which Cicero responds to the philosophers brought forward by Scaevola, Crassus, and Antonius. The main elements of the philosophical position on rhetoric sketched by the discussants—namely, that rhetorical activity is limited to courts and assemblies and that knowledge of important matters does not belong to the orator—are both confronted directly by Cicero's explication of the knowledge doctrine. And within this confrontation, Cicero so contrives his argument that it incorporates a number of the propositions that the philosophers had counted against rhetoric—most notably, the inadequacy of rhetorical instruction and the crucial importance of philosophical knowledge in rhetorical practice. In this fashion, Cicero not only contends with the philosophers but turns many of their own weapons against them.

In book 3, another sort of response may be observed in five thematically interrelated digressions, where Cicero reconsiders the knowledge doctrine and its implications, this time with special reference to the philosophers (54–61, 74–81, 82–89, 122–125, and 142–143, as mentioned earlier).[21] Within the earliest of these, Crassus proposes that in ancient Greece, wisdom and eloquence were originally combined under the general rubric of philosophy (56–57, 60). However, at the prompting of Socrates, persons too plentifully supplied with leisure separated the two and arrogated the term *philosophy* for their own pursuit of wisdom (56–60). This separation, Crassus insists, was a theoretical mistake, because thinking wisely and speaking magnificently are intimately connected (60). As a corrective for this mistake, Crassus reconstitutes the ancient conception of the orator. The true orator, he says, should not be satisfied with ornate expression alone. Instead he "ought to inquire about, attend to, read of, reason out, deal with, and think over all things which exist in the life of men, seeing that the orator is concerned with this and it is the subject matter for him" (54). Here, of course, we meet a version of the knowledge doctrine that grants the orator wisdom in the sense required for his reconstitution. Through recourse to the doctrine, Crassus shows that the orator properly combines in practice what philosophers ineptly separate in theory—acuteness of thought and eloquence of expression. To be sure, Crassus had made a similar point before, but in that place his concern was to establish the knowledge doctrine as a reasonable alternative to the narrow philosophical notion of the orator. In this place, he exploits the doctrine to attack the philosopher's position at its very foundation.

Crassus' attack is continued in two digressions that pursue the main themes introduced at 3.56–61, specifically, the sort of knowledge required for the true orator and the sort of knowledge attained by the otiose philosophers (3.82–89, 122–125). At 3.82–89, Crassus deals with an obvious question: If the orator is to know all important matters and arts, how will he ever have time to achieve such

---

[21]These digressions form only part of the two major excursive discussions that occupy Cicero in book 3, namely those at 54–90 and 122–143.

mastery? Crassus' reply is complex, for he wishes to explain why mastery can come quickly as well as why some arts are studied by men into their old age. The former matter is dispatched with some speed (87): "Those things," Crassus insists, "are easily learned, if you take in just so much as is essential and you have someone who is able to teach accurately and in addition you yourself know how to learn."[22] As regards those who study single arts for their entire lives, Crassus proposes a distinction. "All arts are pursued differently," he says, "by those who apply them to use as opposed to those who pursue the arts themselves for pleasure and seek nothing else in life" (86). In fact, he continues that if one wishes to devote a life to study, every new day poses a question for pursuit with "indolent pleasure" (*cum desidiosa delectatione*, 88). Crassus concludes, therefore, that "there is nothing that anyone should fear in the scope of arts from the fact that aged men pursue them. For either they have resorted to them as old men, or they have remained fixed on their studies into old age, or they are very slow-witted. Indeed, in my view the matter stands thus, that if someone has not been able to learn something quickly, he will never be able to learn it at all" (89).[23]

This much would seem to apply to all specialists in the arts. However, at 3.122–125, Cicero makes it clear that Crassus' argument has particular reference to the philosophers. Here Crassus complains that rightful properties of the orators have been invaded by the philosophers (122):

> Ours, I say, is that entire estate of prudence and learning, in which, as if the estate were lapsed and vacant, men over-rich with leisure have rushed while we were occupied and either they banter, ridiculing the orator, as does Socrates in the *Gorgias*, or they propound something concerning the art of the orator in a few little books and entitle them "rhetorics," as if those things were not the property of rhetors, which are asserted by these same men concerning justice, duty, institution and management of states, the whole theory of living, and finally even the theory of nature.[24]

Having targeted the philosophers in this way,[25] Crassus underscores the futile vanity of their indolent pleasures (123–124):

---

[22]"ista discuntur facile, si et tantum sumas, quantum opus sit, et habeas qui docere fideliter possit, et scias etiam ipse discere. . . ."

[23]"quare nihil est quod quisquam magnitudinem artium ex eo, quod senes dicunt, pertimescat. namque aut senes ad eas accesserunt aut usque ad senectutem in studiis detinentur aut sunt tardissimi. res quidem se mea sententia sic habet, ut, nisi quod quisque cito potuerit, numquam omnino possit perdiscere."

[24]"nostra est, inquam, omnis ista prudentiae doctrinaeque possesio, in quam homines, quasi caducam atque vacuam, abundantes otio nobis occupatis involaverunt atque etiam aut inridentes oratorem, ut ille in Gorgia Socrates, cavillantur, aut aliquid de oratoris arte paucis praecipiunt libellis eosque rhetoricos inscribunt, quasi non illa sint propria rhetorum, quae ab isdem de iustitia, de officio, de civitatibus instituendis et regendis, de omni vivendi, denique etiam de naturae ratione dicuntur."

[25]See Karl Wilhelm Piderit and O. Harnecker, eds., *Cicero, De oratore*, 6th ed. (Leibzig: B. G. Teubner, 1890) 455–456; Augustus S. Wilkins, ed., *M. Tulli Ciceronis De oratore libri tres* (Oxford: The Clarendon Press, 1892) 475.

Seeing that now we cannot get those things from elsewhere, it is necessary that we take them from the very ones by whom we were despoiled, as long as we apply these things to that political science, to which they pertain and to which they are directed, and yet not, as I said earlier, use up all our life in their learning; but rather, when we shall have looked into their basic principles, which unless someone will have learned quickly, he never will learn entirely, we will, whenever necessary, derive from these things only as much as the matter will call for. For, neither is there such a sharp discernment in the natures and intellects of men, that anyone can comprehend matters so great unless they have been taught, nor is there so great an obscurity in things, that a man of sharp intellect does not discern them thoroughly, if only he will have investigated them.[26]

According to this account, the philosophers' pursuit of knowledge is misdirected, because it is not applied to political science, and it is wasteful, because the philosophers' attainments are both time-consuming and useless. Thus, despite their continuous study of technicalities, they can demonstrate no worthwhile superiority over the orators, who quickly acquire (and properly exploit) all that is important in every art. By way of this comparison, then, Cicero repositions the knowledge doctrine of book 1 with a singular consequence—all the specialized and lifelong activities of the philosophers are now reduced to a kind of noisome pettifoggery.

A different and even more pointed comparison of philosophers and orators is presented by Cicero in the remaining two digressions mentioned earlier (3.74–81, 142–143). At 3.74–81 Crassus explains why—despite his limitations as an orator—he need not yield much ground in debate (*in disputatione* [78]) with philosophers. His argument is very telling (79):

Philosophy is not like the rest of the arts. For what does one say in geometry who has not learned geometry? What in music? Either he will have to be silent or be judged not even sane. However, those things which are in philosophy are brought to light by minds shrewd and penetrating at this, educing what is plausible in each matter, and these are polished by trained speech. Hence, this common orator of ours, if he is not learned but yet trained in speaking, with this very ordinary training he will batter even these philosophers and not let himself be condemned and despised by them.[27]

---

[26]"quae quoniam iam aliunde non possumus, sumenda sunt nobis ab iis ipsis, a quibus expilati sumus, dummodo illa ad hanc civilem scientiam, quo pertinent et quam intuentur, transferamus neque, ut ante dixi, omnem teramus in his discendis rebus aetatem; sed, cum fontis viderimus, quos nisi qui celeriter cognorit, numquam cognoscet omnino, tum, quotienscumque opus erit, ex iis tantum, quantum res petet, hauriemus. nam neque tam est acris acies in naturis hominum et ingeniis, ut res tantas quisquam nisi monstratas possit videre, neque tanta tamen in rebus obscuritas, ut eas non penitus acri vir ingenio cernat, si modo aspexerit."

[27]"non est enim philosophia similis artium reliquarum. nam quid faciet in geometria, qui non didicerit? quid in musicis? aut taceat oportebit aut ne sanus quidem iudicetur. haec vero, quae sunt in philosophia, ingeniis eruuntur ad id, quod in quoque veri simile est, eliciendum acutis atque acribus eaque exercitata oratione poliuntur. hinc hic noster vulgaris orator, si minus erit doctus ac tamen in dicendo exercitatus, hac ipsa exercitatione communi istos quidem †nostros† verberabit neque se ab iis contemni ad despici sinet."

Crucial to this argument is Crassus' insistence that the orator may surpass the philosopher in discussion on account of the twofold nature of this philosophical activity—drawing probable conclusions and refinement of these in practiced speech. Of course, this is a special version of the general argument in book 1 that posited the orator's ability to surpass all practitioners of arts in speaking about their subjects. There, Cicero had chided the philosophers alone and among other practitioners. But whether the philosophers were a particular target was left ambiguous. Here he removes all doubt, distinguishing philosophy from the other arts and demanding recognition of the orator's superiority in debate—a time-honored province of philosophical activity.

This special advantage of the orators over the philosophers is generalized at 3.142–143. Here, Cicero has Crassus deliver the ultimate blow to the prestige of the philosophers. Crassus says he is willing to allow anyone to give the name orator to a philosopher "who gives to us an abundance of matter and speech"; likewise, he will permit the name of philosopher to be given to the orator "who possesses wisdom conjoined with eloquence" (3.142). He then considers possession of wisdom or eloquence alone, approving more of the former. But in the final analysis, Crassus concludes as follows (3.143):

> If we ask what one thing is pre-eminent out of all, first place must be given to the learned orator; whom if they grant him also to be a philosopher, the controversy is eliminated. But if they separate them, they will be inferior in this, that all the knowledge of those men is present in the complete orator, however eloquence is not necessarily present in the knowledge of the philosophers; which eloquence, although it is despised by them, nonetheless, must needs be understood to add a certain consummation to the arts of those men.[28]

Within this passage, Cicero quite clearly applies the main implication of his knowledge doctrine to the philosophers and particularly to those who disparage rhetoric. To my mind, the fact that Cicero similarly particularizes his account of the knowledge doctrine throughout book 3 leaves no doubt that he meant his position on the knowledge doctrine as a response to the philosophers.

PART THREE

Consistent with the foregoing, in my final remarks I would like to consider the status of Cicero's reply to the philosophers within the general plan of *De oratore*.

Following Wilkins (*De oratore* 451–452) and Piderit and Harnecker (*De oratore* 435), I have indicated a textual problem with Kumaniecki's *nostros* and omitted the word in my translation; fortunately, despite this difficulty with the text, the general sense of the passage is quite clear.

[28]"si quaerimus quid unum excellat ex omnibus, docto oratori palma danda est; quem si patiuntur eundem esse philosophum, sublata controversia est. sin eos diiungent, hoc erunt inferiores, quod in oratore perfecto inest illorum omnis scientia, in philosophorum autem cognitione non continuo inest eloquentia; quae quamquam contemnatur ab eis, necesse est tamen aliquem cumulum illorum artibus adferre videatur."

As I indicated earlier, we know that Cicero conceived of book 1 as quite distinct from books 2 and 3, which he characterized as a τεχνολογία. We also know that he believed the whole of *De oratore* to contain everything about the theory of speaking "which anyone could have considered possible to be known and grasped by men of the utmost talent, the most serious study, the best training, and the most extensive practice" (2.11).[29] The ultimate question is, then, how was the largely polemical argument of book 1 meant to complement the technical theory supplied in the remainder of the work?

I believe that *De oratore*, book 1, in particular Cicero's defense and elaboration of the knowledge doctrine, is best understood as a self-conscious philosophy of rhetoric. I say this for two main reasons. First and perhaps most obvious, Cicero's argument concerning the knowledge doctrine addresses and, in a way, settles nearly every philosophical problem that had arisen in the historical debate between philosophy and rhetoric. For the argument clearly resolves questions that had initially arisen in the Hellenic Academy and Peripatos concerning the knowledge required of the orator as well as the subject matter, function, scope, and disciplinary relations of rhetoric. Moreover, it likewise responds to two of the chief issues raised by these schools in the Hellenistic period, namely, the limits and practical utility of rhetorical instruction as well as the propriety of rhetorical treatment of all themes, whether limited or unlimited.[30]

My second reason is that even where Cicero's argument omits decisive treatment of an issue that loomed large in Hellenistic times, specifically, the artistic status of rhetoric, his handling of the subject discloses an important philosophical objective. As a theoretical matter, Cicero devotes two significant discussions to the art problem: Crassus speaks to the issue at 1.102–109 and Antonius treats it at 2.30–32. Within both discussions, the artistic status of rhetoric is handled as a kind of adjunct to the real business at hand; in fact, Crassus initially dismisses the art problem as unsuitable for anyone but a "talkative Greekling." Nonetheless, both discussions eventually handle the issue with great precision, arguing—in essential agreement—that speaking is not an art in the sense of exact knowledge, though it may be considered an art in the sense of an analytical or methodical set of principles (1.107–109, 2.32). The ultimate conclusion of the discussions is that although oratory may not be an art in the strictest terms, its study is still profitable for speaking and crucial to the complete orator (1.109, 2.33). What is important about this conclusion, I believe, is that it reflects Cicero's recognition of a new way to think about the theory of speaking.

From the time of Plato onward, the standard conception of rhetoric was disciplinary. Accordingly, philosophies of rhetoric were concerned with such matters

---

[29]"nihil enim mihi quidem videtur in Crassi et Antoni sermone esse praeteritum, quod quisquam summis ingeniis, acerrimis studiis, optima doctrina, maximo usu cognosci ac percipi potuisse arbitraretur. . . ."

[30]My account of the issues involved in the dispute between philosophy and rhetoric follows Hans von Arnim, *Leben und Werke des Dio von Prusa. Mit einer Einleitung: Sophistik, Rhetorik, Philosophie in ihrem Kampf um die Jugendbildung* (Berlin: Weidmannsche Buchhandlung, 1898) 87–114.

as the subject or function of the discipline as well as the level of certainty or success that it afforded. Within this framework, rhetoric was necessarily subordinate to exact arts such as grammar and geometry, because it had no substantial subject of its own and could succeed at its persuasive function only unreliably. Cicero clearly understood this difficulty and sought to offer a corrective by conceiving of rhetoric and the other arts not simply as disciplines, but as disciplinary contributions to the powers of their possessors and practitioners. The result of this conception was a philosophy of rhetoric that took as its focus the orator and, as its function, the description of requirements for oratorical success. As the most revolutionary contribution to this philosophy, Cicero's knowledge doctrine particularized the orator as a principal object of theoretical investigation and at the same time constituted the orator with reference to the kinds and levels of knowledge essential to his rhetorical activity. Cicero, himself, was certainly conscious of the conceptual innovation represented by the knowledge doctrine. For he deliberately and effectively prosecuted its consequences against the long-standing philosophical critique of the rhetorical discipline. He also elected to name his work *De oratore*—as opposed to, say, *De oratoria*—and, subsequently, he maintained the orator as the single focus of his own theoretical program.[31] Accordingly, it is my conclusion that Cicero's knowledge doctrine, by means of which he announced his new philosophy of rhetoric, with recourse to which he responded to the philosophers, and alongside of which he presented his own magisterial *ars oratoris*, must certainly be counted as Cicero's main theoretical accomplishment in *De oratore*, book 1.

ACKNOWLEDGMENTS

The research reported in this chapter was supported in part by an award from the General Research Board of the University of Maryland at College Park; the author gratefully acknowledges this support.

---

[31]On this point, see Alain Michel, *Rhétorique et philosophie chez Cicéron: Essai sur les fondements philosophiques de l'art de persuader* (Paris: Presses Universitaires de France, 1960) 41–42.

Chapter 3

Cicero's Court Speeches: The Spoken Text Versus the Published Text Some Remarks From the Point of View of the Communication Theory of Text

Jerzy Axer
University of Warsaw

As is generally known, the relation between a text as delivered and the same text as it was published has repeatedly puzzled scholars dealing with Cicero's speeches, especially those delivered in court. The question of the character and scope of the changes made by the orator for publication purposes has been raised over and over again, both in synthetically oriented studies and in analyses of individual speeches. This question is implicit even in the works of those scholars who explicitly renounce asking it.

Until quite recently the problem has not seemed to me an attractive one. The work of generations of philologists, who took pains to reconstruct hypothetical amendments and corrections Cicero introduced to his speeches after their delivery and before their publication, has proved to be decidedly unrewarding and of little practical use. Analysts focusing on the problem have tended to aim at isolating from the published texts all that was contained in the original delivered speeches, in order to derive from that material the defense tactics, the course of proceedings, and the ideological motivation of the contestants. Fragments regarded as added or reworded afterward have been construed either as insertions due to (chiefly political) circumstances around the moment of publication or as the author's self-corrections intended to expurgate the form and content of those elements in a speech that had proved to be ineffective in the course of the trial or had been found erroneous after it. What is particularly discouraging in inquiries of this kind (and even more discouraging in their reception by historians and lawyers) is a distinct—unconscious or sometimes conscious—tendency to view Cicero's revisions as a specific adulteration, as a distortion that was to conceal various aspects of the actual oration from the reader of the published version, in other words, a tendency to see the recasting as a morally suspicious practice.

Whenever I have read works like this, they have generally appeared to me to be attempts at solving equations with too many unknown quantities. Such attempts are futile and hardly appealing to a scholar, because they easily trap him in circular argument. I welcomed, then, Wilfried Stroh's discussion[1] in which he brilliantly disposed of the thesis of Jules Humbert, the author of a book that for half a century had served as a main support for that trend of studies.[2] I also found Stroh's view on the relation of the delivered speeches to the published ones quite convincing; even more acceptable to me is Joachim Classen's methodological position formulated with measure and precision in *Recht-Rhetorik-Politik*.[3] Classen considers endeavors to reconstruct the speeches as they were originally delivered to be largely utopian projects. Both Stroh and Classen agree that the principal motive underlying publication of the speeches was a didactic ambition; the very intent behind presenting a model to be followed made stripping content appropriate to court speeches quite unlikely. Thus what is in question is another currently fashionable tendency: the assumption that it was a changed intent that made Cicero thoroughly recast his speeches when preparing them for publication. In that view, a published oration is supposed to be primarily a contribution to political disputes of the time, and is not a court speech. The two authors' final conclusions are fairly similar and are formulated as follows. Stroh writes: "Full identity of a speech as it was delivered with the same speech as it was published may to some extent be a fiction, yet if we wish to make a correct rhetorical interpretation we must, however paradoxical it may sound, consider this fiction as reality."[4] Classen writes: "Even if the published speeches are not a literal reproduction of the delivered ones, any divergences may have only a strictly limited extent."[5]

Thus, I thought that reformulating the correspondence between the delivered and the published speeches would be methodologically most promising,[6] because I felt that the unrewarding discussions concerning differences between the two versions could be treated as having come to a close, at least from the point of view of a student whose main interest was the analysis of individual orations.

And yet it was precisely such practical interpretive difficulties I confronted while working on the "Pro Milone" speech that made me change my mind. The speech is notorious for the striking contrast between the unfavorable impression

---

[1]Wilfried Stroh, *Taxis und Taktik. Die advokatische Dispositionskunst in Ciceros Gerichtsreden* (Stuttgart: B. G. Teubner, 1975) /2 *Exkurs: Zur These von Jules Humbert und dem Problem der schriftlichen Redaktion von Ciceros Gerichtsreden*/.

[2]Jules Humbert, *Les plaidoyers écrits et les plaidoiries réelles de Cicéron* (Paris, 1925).

[3]Joachim Classen, *Recht-Rhetorik-Politik. Untersuchungen zu Ciceros rhetorischer Strategie* (Darmstadt: Wissenschaftliche Buchgesellschaft, 1985) 1–13.

[4]Stroh, *Taxis und Taktik* 54.

[5]Classen, *Recht-Rhetorik-Politik* 8.

[6]Compare Stroh, *Taxis und Taktik* 53–54.

Cicero's oration made on the Forum in April 52 B.C. and the stunning success of its published version. No wonder, then, that philologists have traditionally devoted much time to speculations on two possible versions of the speech. I had, of course, fully intended to break with the tradition; some time later, however, there arose questions that made the problem return through the back door, so to speak. For it occurred to me that in the "Pro Milone" speech Cicero had sought— within the frame of the defense tactics—to arouse the audience's emotions by appealing to their experience as spectators and fans of gladiatorial fights. Gradually, I came to believe that the case in question was an instance of a broader phenomenon, which I called the modification of the communication context in Cicero's court speeches. What I mean is that the orator could seek to suggest to his listeners a reception convention that differed from the one associated with being present at the court trial. In the "Pro Milone" speech such a frame of reference was provided by gladiators' contests; in "Pro Q. Roscio Comoedo" it was provided by the theatre.[7]

As I was elaborating the idea it became clear to me that I could not escape the question of the relation between the delivered speeches and the published ones. And the reason was not that in the case of "Pro Milone" the two versions seem to have differed considerably, but that in considering manipulations involving the communication context one cannot avoid reconstructing the communication act itself. Once I realized that, many of the difficulties were solved. A similar approach might be useful in various kinds of studies on the texts of court speeches.

I do not propose here to upset the methodological position represented by Stroh and Classen, or to defend the view that Cicero's orations underwent thoroughgoing changes before their publication. I do point out, however, that there are shifts that are bound to occur when a speech that was originally delivered orally is published and that these shifts are inevitable even when the author did not change a single letter in his text. They are totally beyond his volition (which does not mean, however, that he is unaware of them); and in certain types of studies, they should be considered deeper and more radical than any reformulation or recasting of the text.

Recall, of course, that in the case of court speeches the communication situation of a text delivered orally is essentially different from that of a published one. This difference seems quite obvious; yet it has not always been given due attention. And I do not mean that the difference consists in a text's being readdressed, as it were, changed from a court speech into a political pamphlet, as some would have it. As I have already mentioned, I accept the thesis that the main function of Cicero's published texts was a didactic one, that they were to serve as a model to be imitated. Neither do I wish to repeat what has by now been generally noted—the fact that while reading the speeches we should bear

---

[7]See Jerzy Axer, "Tribunal-Stage-Arena: Modelling of the Communication Situation in M. Tullius Cicero's Judicial Speeches," *Rhetorica* 7 (1989): 299–311.

in mind their actually paratheatrical performance, the effect of the spoken word and gesture on the audience, and the difference between listening and reading. My point is that the principal transformation consists in something else: The subject of the transformation is, in fact, the whole act of communication.

First of all, there is a shift in the status of the author, as well as in the status of the audience; the very character of the dialogue they are engaged in also changes considerably. From the point of view of the essence of that communication drama that took place in the past, each version of Cicero's speeches should be taken as a distinct kind of discourse.

Let us, then, take a look at the main differences between them. I do not claim that my observations are new; anyone could make such a comparison for analytic purposes. And yet, to students of Cicero's speeches, many of the differences still seem irrelevant.

First, it is undeniable that the text of a published speech, as compared with that of the delivered one, is to an incomparably greater extent a literary text. And this is not because the listener has changed into the reader. This shift was perhaps less substantial than it seems to the present-day reader—after all, at that time reading was an act performed vocally rather than mentally. A published text becomes a literary text insofar as it—more clearly than its spoken counterpart—provides the reader with conventions according to which it was composed. What is more, it was precisely those conventions on which the reader was supposed to focus when approaching the text in order to learn the rules of its composition and to master the techniques that would enable him to imitate it.

Second, a published text is close to a literary one in its specific fabulation; there emerges in it a category akin to, if not identical with, the category of *presented world* in literary fiction. A published speech describes (or suggests) the entire spectacle of the trial; the orator himself, as well as his audience, are a part of that presented world. This use of reality is not unlike that in modern "literature of fact."

Third, the status of the author alters as well. In a speech he is delivering, he is engaged in a judicial contest with the prosecutor, but those primarily addressed—by way of *allocutio obliqua*—are the jury, as it is on them that the result depends. From the point of view of the jury and the court public he is representing one of the parties, but at the same time he is acting a part he has written for himself. In the published speech, the orator's situation becomes quite complicated. The author of the text addresses, first and foremost, the reader, whom he treats as a disciple (and partly, in the sphere of political meanings of the speech, as a representative of the public opinion whose support he wants to gain). All other addressees belong to the past, to the presented world that the reader is to reconstruct imaginatively.

Fourth, the shift also involves the addressee. The reader's situation, as compared to that of the jury and the court public listening to a speech, is a complex one. First of all, he finds himself in the position of an apprentice, for he seeks to acquire skills that would qualify him to take the author's position. On the other hand, participating imaginatively in a trial that took place in the past he must to some extent cast himself in the role of the court public and expect that the orator intends to win him over. The situation of the reader least resembles that of the chief addressee of the delivered speech—the jury. The reader does not pass the verdict but knows it; it was already pronounced.

A fifth significant factor is the fact that the information available to the listener differs considerably from the information available to the reader. The listener had to compare what he heard with what the prosecutor and the witnesses said. For him, the oration was only one of the voices in the dispute, whereas for the reader, the author's voice is the only one, and the counterarguments of the opposing party reach him only in the form Cicero gave them. In addition, it is worth noting that the reader has no access to all the information provided for a participant in the trial by the referential aspects of the text, its immediate references to the extratextual reality. While preparing a speech for publication the author must take into account the reader's situation. To make the text coherent he has to perhaps add some information that will serve to construct a kind of fake extratextual reality and help the reader to visualize certain elements of the court spectacle.

Sixth, the defense strategy necessarily takes on a different character as well, even if the orator wants the published version to reproduce faithfully the strategy he actually pursued. In the speech as delivered, the main goal was to convince the main addressee of the speech, the jury, and to win the case. In the published speech, the adopted strategy had a different purpose. Although recently, in philological studies, it has been emphasized that in the published version, too, everything must be subordinated to the same objective, which is the successful defense, this is true only in a sense, because the chief objective in the published speech is for the strategy to be followed with appreciation by the reader. Thus, the difference is somewhat akin to that between a war and maneuvers.

I will not try the reader's forbearance with any further enumeration of the differences between the two communication situations. After all, my aim in this chapter is not to test the prescriptions of a popular handbook on communication theory applied to Cicero's court speeches. The preceding observations suffice, I think, to make it clear why the difference I have discussed between the delivered and the published versions is significant in certain types of studies. What kinds of studies do I mean? Within the already overextended limits of this chapter, I can give only a few examples.

The first kind includes those inquiries in which the main focus is on the manipulation discussed earlier of a speech's reception by the audience, which I called modification of the communication context. It is quite evident that taken in these terms, a speech must be considered on two levels: in its original communication context and in the new one. An additional question is whether in the published text the author tries to disclose to the reader his secret weapon, so as to make it serve the didactic purpose, or whether we find in the text vestiges of a technique that was fully meaningful only in its original communication context and that the author made no attempts to render readable.

The second kind covers various types of historical readings of the court speeches. These range from reading oriented toward the reconstruction of the facts, in which it is vital to separate carefully (or at least to try to separate) the facts belonging to the presented world of the published speech from the circumstances during the trial and to see the former as only indirectly testifying to the latter, even if the orator did not intend to deceive anyone, to that type of historical reading that is characteristic of the sociology of culture. We know now that every discourse carries as much information about its addressee as it carries about its author. One can, therefore, seek in Cicero's court speeches a reflection of the community originally addressed by the orator. In this view, the delivered and the published speeches serve as material into which two probes of Roman society in the 1st century B.C. can be made. This may compensate for the obvious impossibility of actually conducting such an experiment. But if one confuses the two samples, one may be sure of arriving at results that cannot be valid.[8]

As a third type of example, all kinds of studies requiring a reconstruction of the reception of a speech by the audience must not overlook the fact that the author of a published speech is felt to be a somewhat different person from the author of the spoken speech and that his authority derives from different sources. I will not dwell on the point at any length; generally, Cicero as the author of published speeches, as compared to Cicero the attorney, decidedly also took on his other social roles—those of a statesman, a philosopher, an oratory theoretician. Sometimes this occurred even against his own will—hence his outrage at "fools" (as he used to call them) who falsely construed his views in the published speeches. Yet this is to be treated as a natural consequence of the changed communication situation.

Finally, not to make the list of examples unduly long, I would like to point out that the careful distinction between the two communication situations is likely to be useful for those dealing with textual criticism from the philological point of view, as it should help them escape many needless conjectures.

To conclude, attempts at reconstructing the verbal shape of Cicero's original speeches are a futile and utopian trend of inquiry, irrespective of the character and scope of the changes and amendments introduced by the orator before publication. One can, however, be sure that another explanation for the differences between the spoken speech and the published speech should be considered besides political interpolations and artistic improvements—namely, the rewording, additions, and omissions that were necessary to make the text intelligible in the new

---

[8]Compare Jerzy Axer, "Cicerone e la società alla luce delle orazioni giudiziarie," *Ciceroniana* 7 (1990): 175–182; and Jerzy Axer, "Remarks on the 'Historical Reading' of Cicero's Legal Speeches," *Index* 17 (1989): 205–215.

communication situation. We must constantly bear in mind the distinct patterns of the two communication situations and take into account when reading an existing text both its function in the author–reader relation and its applicability in the court spectacle. It is only such a reading—by no means very popular among philologists, and even less so among historians and lawyers—that may lead to the right conclusions.

The act of delivering a speech was part of an event that was distinctly a kind of spectacle; it worked as an element of the contest between two parties with contradictory interests. The published text of the speech belongs to the world of books, and within this world it competes with other written texts. Speaking to someone has largely changed into speaking for someone. The discourse has changed its addressees, its information channels, and the relations between the author and his audience. The whole communication drama has drastically changed its character; a single, unique event with its pragmatic context has changed into a text that can be reproduced an infinite number of times, though each time for a different audience with a different context. It is this fact, perhaps, that turns a historical reading, that cherished ideal of scholars, from a task that has always been hardly possible into one that is nearly impossible.

ACKNOWLEDGMENTS

An earlier version of this chapter was delivered at the ISHR Congress in Göttingen, July 1989. The chapter was translated by Maria Bozenna Fedewicz.

Chapter 4

Attitudes Toward Authority in the Teaching of Rhetoric Before 1050

George A. Kennedy
University of North Carolina

Writing about the "Survival of the Classical Traditions" in *Rhetoric in the Middle Ages* (89–90), J. J. Murphy said, "It would be unrealistic to assume that the classical works received unqualified acceptance, or even unqualified respect, in comparison to treatises produced during the Middle Ages. Rather, it might be more accurate to say that the ancient *artes* are to be seen competing for the attention of the medieval writer and speaker—competing, that is, against the lure of the 'modern' and specialized works which sprang up in various fields after about 1050—but competing with the advantage of *antiquitas*." As a footnote to Professor Murphy's observation I briefly explore in this chapter the attitudes toward their predecessors shown by teachers and writers in the western tradition of rhetoric before 1050.

There is a marked resistance, sometimes expressed, sometimes implied, to the authority of predecessors among rhetoricians in almost all periods. This can result, as with Isocrates and Petrus Ramus, from a personal, professional assertiveness in competition with their peers; an individual teacher claims authority for himself in understanding the subject better than others. It seems worth asking whether such a view reflects an assumption that there are natural principles of rhetoric, common to all societies, which a particular teacher has understood better than his predecessors; or an assumption that rhetoric changes with historical, social, political, and religious conditions, in which case a particular teacher is claiming a better understanding of what is effective in these new conditions. The rejection or partial revision of the authority of earlier teachers on the subject of the *precepts* of rhetoric is, however, to be contrasted with a wider approval of the *practice* of the ancients, including Cicero and Demosthenes as authoritative models, which in its turn may reflect the belief that these men were in some sense unique geniuses who grasped better than others the basic principles of rhetoric, or that they lived in a time when eloquence had opportunities for greater development.

The absence of appeal to earlier theoretical authority and the failure of any one teacher to achieve permanent authoritative status characterize the teaching of rhetoric from the earliest times in Greece, but authorities on other subjects were canonized from an early time. The Homeric and Hesiodic poems were authoritative epics by the 6th century B.C., and the rhapsode in Plato's *Ion* regards them as authoritative sources of knowledge on many subjects. Early Greek lyric poets were already educational classics by the 5th century B.C. In the *Poetics*, Aristotle seems to canonize Sophocles' *Oedipus Tyrannus* as embodying the theory of tragedy. The parameters of the study of history were established by Herodotus and Thucydides. In the 5th century Hippocrates acquired an authoritative reputation in medicine. Even in philosophy, though many innovations were to come, some of the fundamental questions had already been asked by the 5th century, and both Plato and Aristotle appeal to earlier authorities that need to be taken into account even when they disagree with them. One of the bases of Aristotelian dialectic is the opinion of the wise, or of most of them, or of the wisest of them (cf. *Topics* 1.2). Epicurus took on an authority among his followers that left rather little room for the further development of Epicureanism. Euclid, in geometry, Ptolemy, in astronomy, and Galen, in medicine wrote fundamental works that were regarded as permanently authoritative for centuries. Donatus later acquired almost the same status on grammar, despite the view that grammar was more a matter of *usus* than of nature. Boethius became a recognized authority on dialectic and music.

In the teaching of rhetoric there is really nothing like this, although, beginning in the Hellenistic period, imitation of approved models of style and genre became a convention of rhetorical education. To judge from the brief references of Plato and Aristotle, the writers of early handbooks tended to assert their own originality, for example, in multiplying the number of parts of an oration, and both Plato's Socrates and Aristotle claimed originality for their views of rhetoric. Aristotle did not even have authoritative examples of rhetorical usage to cite. If the speeches of Pericles or other great figures of the 5th century had been written down and published, they could perhaps have functioned as models for his analysis, as did the Greek tragedies in poetics; but all he seems to have had is a memory of some phrases, transmitted by an oral tradition or by quotation in other writers. Aristotle, of course, frequently quoted bits from orators of his own time as examples of rhetorical technique. Among his favorite sources were the Athenian general Iphicrates, whom he probably heard in person in Athens in the period from 367 to 347 B.C. and whose speeches, so far as we know, were not published or much quoted by others; he also repeatedly quoted his friend Theodectes and his rival

Isocrates. But Aristotle's quotations of oratory were illustrations, sometimes illustrations of faults rather than appeals to authority. His attitude toward earlier technical writing about rhetoric was consistently denigrating, and though he drew ideas from Plato's *Gorgias* and *Phaedrus*, he never presented Platonic dialogues as authoritative treatments. It seems to have been Aristotle's view that there was a single art of rhetoric whose universal principles, most evident in public address, could be formulated through observation and reason. Clearly, these principles were best seen in a democratic state like Athens, but they could also be applied under other kinds of constitutions (cf., e.g., *Rhetoric* 1.8) and to forms of discourse other than public address. Nor did Isocrates regard any predecessor as an authority on rhetoric. One purpose of his *Encomium of Helen*, for example, was to show that Gorgias had not treated the subject properly. Isocrates' equation of rhetoric with philosophy seemed to suggest that he regarded its precepts as having universal validity.

Neither Aristotle nor Isocrates became the established authority on rhetoric for succeeding teachers. Aristotle's student Theophrastus began a process of recasting Aristotelian theory. According to Quintilian (3.8.62), Theophrastus often disagreed with Aristotle. The *Rhetoric* of Aristotle was apparently not available to most Hellenistic teachers, though there is evidence of interest in the work on the part of Cicero, Dionysius of Halicarnassus, and others after its publication in the 1st century B.C. Only certain Aristotelian concepts—for example, the three species of rhetoric and the doctrine of topics—were commonly labeled Aristotelian. Although Isocrates' style was admired and his speeches were to some extent taken as models by later sophists, there was doubt about the authenticity of the small handbook attributed to him (cf. Quintilian 2.15.4), and there is no clear body of rhetorical theory that can be confidently labeled Isocratean. By the 1st century B.C. the speeches of Demosthenes emerged as authoritative examples of eloquence. A theory can be deduced from these orations, but what that theory is differs in the treatments of Cicero, Dionysius, Hermogenes, and others.

The most influential Hellenistic teacher of rhetoric was Hermagoras, the father of stasis theory, but rather than teaching Hermagoras' system, later teachers of rhetoric constantly exercised their originality in revising it, as is clear from Quintilian's discussion in *Institutio* 3.6. The Hermagorean system is best known to us from *Rhetorica ad Herennium* and *De inventione*, but the name of Hermagoras never appears in the text of the *Ad Herennium* (thus taking no authority from Hermagoras himself) and appears only once in *De inventione* in 1.8, where Cicero criticizes Hermagoras for not understanding the subject of special and general questions. In fact, both the youthful Cicero and the *Auctor ad Herennium* asserted their own originality. Because there is every reason to believe these works were not very original, this authorial pose can be viewed as a convention among teachers of rhetoric. In *De oratore* Crassus and Antonius were treated as authorities on rhetoric, but clearly this was largely a reflection back onto the speakers in the dialogue of Cicero's own views. Antonius' rhetorical handbook is mentioned but not given authoritative status. It was the success of Crassus and Antonius as orators that really impressed Cicero. Cicero's writings on rhetoric do not seem to have been immediately taken up as authoritative statements. This was the time of the emergence of the rival schools of the Apollodoreans and Theodoreans, neither of whom had any visible debt to Cicero. Cicero's death was in fact followed by a century of reaction against his style, and what we know or can guess about the teachers of declamation does not suggest any agreement on Ciceronian authority.

It is only with Quintilian that Cicero emerged as the great figure in the history of rhetoric. As a political orator and literary stylist, Cicero was clearly supreme in Quintilian's view, but as a theoretician about rhetoric he was only moderately preferred to others. Quintilian did not claim for himself great originality; instead (1.1.2), in response to complaints of his friends that previous writings about rhetoric were contradictory, he collected and weighed the views of a large number of earlier teachers of rhetoric into his own synthesis. In several passages he commented on changes in the circumstances of public address that led to the conclusion that there were ways in which it was now appropriate to go beyond Cicero. The same conclusion might be derived from Tacitus' *Dialogus*. Longinus in *On the Sublime* began by questioning the authority of Caecilius of Calacte, one of the best known writers on rhetoric of the early empire. He implied the originality of his own work, did not identify any earlier Greek teacher as holding preeminent rank, and commented on the changing circumstances of oratory.

In the Greek East, the works on rhetoric by or attributed to Hermogenes did indeed acquire authoritative status. It is, however, in contrast to this canonization that the situation in the Latin West may be viewed. For all the authoritarian stance of Western medieval society, it was much less culturally unified than the Byzantine Empire. The major works of Roman rhetorical theory, Cicero's *De oratore, Brutus*, and *Orator*, and Quintilian's *Institutes*, were first neglected and then to a considerable extent lost. *De inventione* and *Ad Herennium* were the established authorities, but it is noteworthy that the name of Cicero was rarely mentioned explicitly even when the views stated by medieval authors were derived from these works (both of which were regarded as by Cicero). The authority of doctrine was rarely established by asserting its Ciceronian origin. The chief exception was Victorinus, whose work was of course a commentary on *De inventione* and thus clearly took Cicero as an authority. The opening pages of Victorinus' commentary are interesting in that they make explicit the dialectical principles implicit in Cicero's account of the nature and origins of rhetoric. Rhetoric emerges as something inherent in *natura* and *ratio*, and though in application an art rather than a science, its precepts take on universal validity. It is perhaps this widely held assumption, rather than authoritarianism per se, that accounts for the general failure of rhetoricians of late antiquity to develop a theory of rhetoric directly applicable to the conditions of their own time.

Turning to other *rhetores Latini minores*, we find that Fortunatianus cited examples from Cicero from time to time, but, I believe, he only once (1.22) cited Cicero by name as an authority on a matter of theory. The *Rhetorica* attributed to Augustine prefers Hermagoras as an authority. Sulpitius Victor, like Fortunatianus, cited examples from Cicero but, so far as I can see, only once (1.4) cited him as an authority on theory, and then to disagree with him, preferring unnamed "Greek" sources. In Julius Severianus, only Ciceronian practice is specifically cited; and much the same is true in the work of Julius Victor. Martianus Capella cited Hermagoras (5.11), Cicero (5.31), and Theodorus of Byzantium (5.46) once each on theoretical points. Cassiodorus (*Inst.* 2.2.10) included Victorinus, Quintilian, and Fortunatianus with Cicero as his authorities on an apparently equal basis.

By the time of Cassiodorus the function of the study of rhetoric had significantly changed from that of the classical period. Augustine had of course initiated this in the fourth book of *De doctrina Christiana*. For Cassiodorus, Isidore, and Bede, rhetorical theory, especially the doctrine of tropes and figures, was primarily useful in the study of scripture. Isidore's compendium (2.1) names Gorgias, Aristotle, and Hermagoras, *translata a Tullio videlicet et Quintiliano*, as its sources in an opening statement and subsequently adds Victorinus. This again implies that there was a single system of universal rhetoric variously apprehended by different writers and perhaps by late classical times fully comprehended. The famous 10th chapter of Isidore's compendium on rhetoric with its discussion of the law was perhaps intended to adapt rhetoric to some contemporary uses. It seems clear that by this time in the Middle Ages rhetoric was regarded as a body of knowledge discovered by classical writers; but they were in fact only names to Isidore, and the actual doctrine he set out came from intermediate sources. He did not give clear priority to any one of these. Bede's work on rhetoric never mentions Cicero or any other writer on rhetoric. In the introduction Bede attributed discovery of tropes and figures to "the Greeks," and he pointedly rejected all authorities except the Scriptures: Their authority is both divine and ancient.

The situation with Alcuin is somewhat complex. His account of rhetorical theory relies heavily on Cicero's *De inventione*, but without naming Cicero until section 39, when, in response to a question about memory as a part of rhetoric, Alcuin mentions Cicero and quotes his opinion about the importance of memory from *De oratore*. Alcuin claims that, in apparent contrast to invention, arrangement, and style, there are no rules for memory except practical exercise, though some rules could have been found in *Rhetoric for Herennius* and are alluded to in Cicero's works. Similarly, in sections 40 and 41 Alcuin again quotes *De oratore* on the subject of delivery. Because Alcuin does not claim originality for himself, the result is that a reader who did not know Cicero's *De inventione* could assume that the rhetorical theory set out in the *Dialogue with Charlemagne* represents a body of knowledge traditionally held by those learned on the subject of universal validity. Whatever its wider objectives for Carolingian society, the ostensible objective of Alcuin's dialogue is to provide Charlemagne himself with a conceptualized knowledge of a universal rhetoric. Differences between the rhetorical situations of the classical past and the Carolingian present are not noted. It is true that Alcuin speaks at the very end of his work "de volubili civilium quaestionum ingenio," which W. S. Howell translated (p. 155) as "the changing modes of civil questions," but I wonder if that is not a misunderstanding. Because the volatility of public debate is a commonplace, reaching back to the Greek democracies as described by Thucydides and Plato and the Roman republic as known from Cicero, *volubili* could be taken as a transferred epithet, and Alcuin may have meant the innate character of voluble civic disputes. The two quotations from *De oratore* represent two special cases where a rather little known work by a famous person is cited on subjects not treated within the common tradition. Alcuin draws on Julius Victor for material not found in *De inventione*, again without acknowledgment. This reflects, I believe, his view that the theory he is setting out is the property of no one authority. Much the same system could be found in a variety of works. There is a body of definitive knowledge about rhetoric, unchanging over time. If that is the case, rhetoric is like grammar, dialectic, arithmetic, and the other arts in having universal application and thus truth value in its propositions. It is not something inductively arrived at from contemporary practice. The opening of Alcuin's dialogue indicates that he has already expounded the rules of arithmetic and astronomy to Charlemagne and had begun discussion of dialectic and rhetoric earlier, and the conclusion of the dialogue sets out some of the basic principles of ethics. Alcuin's dialogue is thus inserted into the encyclopedic context of the liberal arts.

What was the prevailing view on the origin of rhetoric in late antiquity and the Middle Ages? The answer seems to be that it was the view set out in the preface to *De inventione* (1.2–3), which Alcuin copied (section 2), as did many other writers on rhetoric: "Nam fuit, ut fertur, quoddam tempus, cum in agris homines passim bestiarum more vagabantur. . . ." After some period of primitive life, there suddenly appeared a man, great and wise, who discovered what latent genius was in the human soul and discovered how, by force of reason, to organize men into civilized life and useful activities. Wise though he was, he could not have accomplished this if he had not also been eloquent. A rather different view, in specific reaction to the claims of *De inventione*, could be found in the second chapter of the third book of Quintilian's *Institutio*, where understanding of rhetoric was attributed to observation, over a long period of time, of what is effective in public address and not to a single inspired individual of the past. Cicero's youthful description was perhaps preferred, even in late antiquity when Quintilian's work was still known, because it seemed to imply a sudden revelation of a deep natural truth, which may have been congenial to Christian readers. It is curious, however, that Christian writers, including Alcuin and, later, Thierry of Chartres in his commentary on *De inventione*, made no attempt to reconcile the Ciceronian account of the origins of rhetoric with the Biblical account of the origins and fall of man and the Jewish lawgivers. This does appear later in writings of, for example, Fénelon and Vico.

I must leave to others the examination of attitudes toward authority in the complex developments of ensuing centuries. In the quotation with which I began, Professor Murphy takes the year 1050 as marking a change in which modern authorities began to compete more aggressively with ancient authorities in rhetoric, or, as I would prefer to say, with universal rhetoric as thought to have been perceived by classical rhetoricians. On the one hand, the multiplication of commentaries on *De inventione* and *Ad Herennium* in this later period shows teachers clinging to older views, whereas the *Rhetorica novissima* of Boncampagno of Signa (1235) represents the opposite extreme: a specific effort to replace Cicero with a new work more appropriate to the conditions of the time, which saw the development of the dictamen. In the Renaissance the rediscovery of complete texts of rhetorical works of Cicero and Quintilian produced, for a time, extreme authoritarianism in some circles, followed by a variety of new rhetorics like that of George of Trepizond or, later, Petrus Ramus and a reaction against Ciceronianism in style. In the 20th century, Aristotle has enjoyed new prestige as a rhetorical authority at the same time that "new" rhetorics, some overtly anti-Aristotelian, continue to emerge. Professor Murphy's research and teaching has consistently shown a happy synthesis of respect for the grand tradition of rhetoric, attention to its changing forms and contexts, and an openness to theoretical approaches. We are also greatly indebted to his organizational abilities in the resurgence of rhetorical studies and to the personal encouragement he has graciously given to other scholars.

Chapter 5

Teaching the Tropes in the Middle Ages: The Theory of Metaphoric Transference in Commentaries on the *Poetria nova*

Marjorie Curry Woods
The University of Texas at Austin

In a plenary lecture at the 1983 Fourth Biennial Conference of the International Society for the History of Rhetoric, Brian Vickers argued that we should stop studying medieval rhetoric: C. S. Baldwin had been right in his condemnation of this confused and confusing field 50 years earlier.[1] Time spent on medieval rhetoric and poetic could, according to Vickers, be spent more profitably on the history of rhetoric during other periods.

There are many who agree with Vickers and Baldwin, although few are so bold as to say so. Those of us in the academy who, following James J. Murphy's example, began to work on medieval rhetoric because it was there must provide

---

[1]Vickers' lecture was entitled "The Fragmentation of the Rhetorical Tradition." A revised version has appeared as a chapter, "Medieval Fragmentation" (214–253), in his book, *In Defence of Rhetoric* (Oxford: Clarendon Press, 1928). In the book, Vickers relies less overtly on Baldwin, but his discussion of medieval rhetoric hardly lives up to the promise in his preface "to remove the misapprehensions and prejudices that still affect our appreciation of rhetoric" (vii). Indeed, those scholars trying to accomplish this goal for medieval rhetoric are dismissed by Vickers as "overly respectful towards the authors and topics they study, as if any criticism of them might reflect badly on themselves" (233).

I have taken up the issue of fragmentation in Marjorie Curry Woods, "The Teaching of Writing in Medieval Europe," *A Short History of Writing Instruction From Ancient Greece to Twentieth-Century America*, ed. James J. Murphy (Davis, CA: Hermagoras Press, 1990) 80; and I will do so in greater detail in the future. What I wish to emphasize here is the devastating effectiveness and longevity of Baldwin's assertions so many academic generations ago; see Charles Sears Baldwin, *Medieval Rhetoric and Poetic [to 1400] Interpreted from Representative Works* (New York: Macmillan, 1928).

a more compelling motivation for others to take seriously what we are studying. This chapter is an attempt to reevaluate one aspect of medieval rhetoric in terms of how it was approached in the medieval schoolroom and of how this approach relates to issues now under discussion by modern theorists and teachers.

The medieval rhetorical text for which Baldwin reserved some of his choicest comments was the *Poetria nova*, which was the teaching text par excellence for rhetoric and poetry during the High Middle Ages. The *Poetria nova* is a 2,000-line poem about the composition of verse according to rhetorical principles; it was written in about 1215 by Galfridus Anglicus, also known as Galfridus de Vino Salvo and usually referred to in English as Geoffrey of Vinsauf. This text has survived in almost 200 manuscripts copied all over Europe for three centuries.[2]

The most important aspect of the *Poetria nova* is that it exemplifies the identification of rhetoric and poetic that many modern critics have found so distressing. As Baldwin noted about the *Poetria nova*, "[a] rhetoricated poetic . . . is always a perversion" (295).

Further, the *Poetria nova* was a combination of theory and practice, and this mixture often has not been appreciated by our predecessors. Because Geoffrey of Vinsauf both taught and demonstrated his methods of poetic composition, the value of what he taught had to be determined by what he wrote; and for Baldwin and others who shared Baldwin's assumptions, what Geoffrey wrote was bad. To quote Baldwin again, "[t]o suppose that [the *Poetria nova*] was cherished for its literary achievement is to impute to several centuries a larger and more general appetite for bombast than other evidence warrants" (187).

Finally, that the *Poetria nova* was written for an audience of boys—although it was not their first composition text, as Douglas Kelly has shown[3]—makes it a problematic text for us. One of the legacies of Romanticism that accompanied the idealization of childhood was the exclusion of what were considered to be the proper accomplishments of adulthood, including the composition and study of verse.[4] The term *school texts* became synonymous with bad poetry, and popular medieval pedagogical texts were criticized by 19th- and 20th-century critics for

---

[2]The standard edition of the *Poetria nova* is by Edmond Faral, *Les arts poétiques du xiie et du xiiie siècle; Recherches et documents sur la technique littéraire du moyen âge* (1924; Paris: Champion, 1962). It has been translated into English three times: by Margaret F. Nims, *Poetria nova of Geoffrey of Vinsauf* (Toronto: Pontifical Institute of Mediaeval Studies, 1967); by Jane Baltzell Kopp, in *Three Medieval Rhetorical Arts*, ed. James J. Murphy (Berkeley: University of California Press, 1971); and by Ernest Gallo, *The Poetria Nova and Its Sources in Early Rhetorical Doctrine* (The Hague: Mouton, 1971). A descriptive list of the manuscripts of the *Poetria nova* and the commentaries on it is in preparation by John Conley, Margaret F. Nims, and myself.

[3]Douglas Kelly, "The Scope of the Treatment of Composition in the Twelfth- and Thirteenth-Century Arts of Poetry," *Speculum* 41 (1966): 261–278.

[4]For a discussion of post-Romantic antipedagogy in the academy, see Marjorie Curry Woods, "Among Men—Not Boys: Histories of Rhetoric and the Exclusion of Pedagogy," *Rhetoric Society Quarterly* [special issue: *Feminist Rereadings in the History of Rhetoric*, ed. Susan C. Jarratt] 22 (1992): 18–26.

the very aspects that rendered them successful. My final quotation from Baldwin is his "charitable" description of the *Poetria nova* as "a museum for boys" (187).

Yet these three aspects of the *Poetria nova*—its basis in rhetorical principles, its combination of precept and example, and its exploitation of the structures successful in preadult discourse—were all highly valued and emphasized by the medieval teachers who used the *Poetria nova* in their classrooms. Furthermore, these are the very aspects that we are now beginning to appreciate ourselves. For example, the study of rhetoric is one of the most vital areas of modern composition studies and literary theory. Rhetoric is now becoming for many teachers, critics, and theorists, as it was for the medieval teachers who used the *Poetria nova* in their classrooms, the generic mode of shaping and interpreting discourse, whether in verse or in prose. Because the rhetorical nature of Geoffrey's poetic has received the most revisionist treatment of these three aspects of his work,[5] I concentrate here on the second and third objections to Geoffrey's work outlined earlier.

These latter issues, Geoffrey's exemplification of his theory of composition and the pedagogical nature of that theory, have been particularly problematic with regard to Geoffrey's tropes and his treatment of tropology. But these aspects of his work, perhaps because of Margaret F. Nims' seminal article on medieval *translatio*,[6] are now receiving special attention.

Geoffrey's exemplification of his teaching about metaphor was recently praised by Alexandre Leupin, who devotes attention to Geoffrey's own metaphors, an aspect of the *Poetria nova* on which medieval schoolteachers also focused.[7] Leupin notes that Geoffrey's use of metaphors is not limited to his discussion of tropes but is found all through his 2,000-line text and that they cluster around several important images of poetic creation and textual rhetoric (129–130), exactly those subjects that Geoffrey is teaching in his text. Further, as Leupin argues,

> Geoffroi actually exemplifies the utopic dissolution or fusion of theorist and writer promoted by Barthes more than seven centuries after the *Poetria nova*. . . . [M]edieval discourse—whether poetic, romantic, epic, or didactic—bears in itself all of the premises and conclusions necessary to its own theory. (124)

As the Early Commentator whose work I edited and translated puts it, "the text and the teaching reinforce each other in everything" (690).[8] For this Early Com-

---

[5]See, for example, the essays by Kelly, Leupin, Nims, and Woods cited in the footnotes to this chapter.

[6]Margaret F. Nims, "*Translatio*: 'Difficult Statement' in Medieval Poetic Theory," *University of Toronto Quarterly* 43 (1973–1974): 215–230.

[7]Alexandre Leupin, "Absolute Reflexivity: Geoffroi de Vinsauf," *Medieval Texts & Contemporary Readers*, ed. Laurie A. Finke and Martin B. Shichtman (Ithaca: Cornell University Press, 1987) 120–141.

[8]"Et hic agit ut in omnibus res et doctrina sibi conueniant." Marjorie Curry Woods, ed. and trans., *An Early Commentary on the 'Poetria nova' of Geoffrey of Vinsauf*, Garland Medieval Texts, vol. 12 (New York: Garland, 1985). I refer to this commentator (presumably male) in the singular although the commentary actually exists in two versions, one intended for older and one for younger students;

mentator, who, like Leupin, cites the great authorities of his age, such reinforcing is the most important aspect of the work. The Early Commentator's own most extended rhetorical example appears in his introduction, or *accessus*, where he praises Geoffrey in a series of parallel statements. He begins this section by pointing out that the author of the text is both a rhetorician and an orator in that he speaks about rhetoric rhetorically (*accessus* 44–46). The Early Commentator then continues:

> [I]t is one thing to write about verse, another to write in verse. Virgil wrote in verse, but not about verse; Donatus wrote about verse, but not in verse. This author does both. Similarly, it is one thing to speak about an art (*de arte*), another to speak artfully (*ex arte*). To speak about an art is to give the precepts of the art. To speak artfully is to imitate the precepts, which is more difficult, just as it is more difficult to write verse than to give the precepts of verse. This author does both: he says about his art what he demonstrates from it; he writes verse while giving the precepts of verse. And thus he does what he teaches, which is the custom of a good teacher. . . . (*accessus* 47–54)[9]

Here we see the emphasis that the Early Commentator places on Geoffrey's double roles: Geoffrey is rhetorician/orator, poet/theorist, teacher/practitioner. This inclusiveness and nonhierarchical enumeration of roles was an important aspect of the appreciation of Geoffrey in the medieval schools.

Medieval institutions of higher learning also found room for the *Poetria nova* in their hierarchical structure of areas of learning, but more as a repository of rhetorical doctrine, less as an exemplary text. Inclusiveness of appreciation of the *Poetria nova* during the Middle Ages was an aspect of primary (in both of its senses) teaching, and as such it is alien to both our own inherited adult hierarchization of disciplines and our own limitation of the serious study of poetry and poetics to adult discourse. But during the Middle Ages the adult discourse of choice concerned not poetry and theories of poetry but, rather, philosophy and theology and theories of philosophy and theology. And because adult discourse privileges division and restrictiveness rather than inclusiveness and association, the commentaries developed for institutions of higher learning concentrate on the art of rhetoric, that is, on

see Woods, *An Early Commentary* xxix–xxx; and Marjorie Curry Woods, "Classical Examples and References in Medieval Lectures on Poetic Composition," *Allegorica* 10 (1989): 3–12. The aspects outlined here fall within the parameters of the texts intended for students at schools rather than of those used at institutions of higher learning as outlined in "A Medieval Rhetoric" (see footnote 10).

9

[A]liud est agere de uersibus et aliud uersifice. Virgilius agit uersifice et non de uersibus, Donatus autem de uersibus et non uersifice. Iste auctor utrumque facit. Item aliud est de arte loqui, aliud ex arte. Loqui de arte est dare precepta artis. Loqui ex arte est artis imitari precepta quod est difficilius, sicut uersificari difficilius quam dare precepta de uersibus. Iste auctor utrumque facit; loquitur de arte ita quod ex arte, versificatur dans precepta de uersibus. Et ita ipse agit quod docet, quod est boni doctoris de consuetudine. . . .

rhetorical doctrine—its constituent parts and the divisions and subdivisions of those parts. The school commentaries, on the other hand, emphasize the *Poetria nova* as a text in itself: how the parts are interrelated and how they connect, how one part brings to mind another and how one aspect reinforces another. These school commentaries proceed by transition and association rather than by distinction and division.[10]

Such emphases in the school commentaries are particularly apparent in what is said about Geoffrey's own treatment of tropes. Geoffrey's discussion begins with the general concept of *transsumptio*, transsumption, or what we might call metaphoric transference.[11] This generic term for the tropological function has received very full treatment in a recent article by William Purcell;[12] thus I concentrate here on Geoffrey's emphasis on the basis of *transsumptio* in the perception of similitude, or resemblance.

As the Early Commentator put it,

> [The author] says that those making Transsumptions ought to utilize similitude, and that the transference (*translatio*) ought to be made from one thing to another that seems transferable because of a certain similitude. And if a Transsumption is made where there is no similitude (*transsumptio sine similitudine*), it does not adorn the expression but rather muddles it. (739, 1–2)[13]

In fact, the concept of composition *per similitudinem* is one of the most important aspects of the *Poetria nova* according to the Early Commentator, who uses the phrase often, not only in the section of the *Poetria nova* devoted to tropology but throughout his discussion of the work when he points out the author's own metaphors, such as the comparisons of the poet to an architect, a painter, a traveler—metaphors that Leupin also comments on.

Other medieval commentators on the *Poetria nova* emphasize the nonverbal nature of the perception of similitude in creating tropes. For example, an anonymous, late 13th- or early 14th-century commentary states that there are two kinds of *transsumptio* or metaphoric transference. One of these, *transsumptio gravis*, or the weighty kind, pertains to invention; the other, *transsumptio levis*, or the

---

[10]See Marjorie Curry Woods, "A Medieval Rhetoric Goes to School—and to the University: The Commentaries on the *Poetria nova*," *Rhetorica* 9 (1991): 55–65. I use the term *university* in this article in a nontechnical sense, to distinguish the commentaries developed for use in institutions of higher learning from those developed for the schools.

[11]Following Nims' translation of the *Poetria nova*, I translated this term as "transposition" in my edition of a commentary on the text, but I am convinced by Purcell's essay (see footnote 12) that the English cognate is more appropriate and so use it here.

[12]William M. Purcell, "*Transsumptio*: A Rhetorical Doctrine of the Thirteenth Century," *Rhetorica* 4 (1987): 369–409. See also discussion in Leupin, "Absolute Reflexivity," especially 127–129.

[13]The translation is revised somewhat from the published version. "Dicit quod transumentes debeant uti similitudine et quod translatio debeat fieri ab una re ad aliam que uideatur propter aliquam similitudinem recte posse transferri."

light kind, corresponds to disposition or arrangement.[14] A variation on the concepts of *transsumptio gravis* and *transsumptio levis* was taught by the Dominican Reiner von Cappel in his late 14th-century commentary on the *Poetria nova*, probably intended for younger students.[15]

These kinds of transsumption, which refer to the perception of tropological similitude at the levels of invention and disposition, are distinct from the verbal phase of rhetorical composition, and Geoffrey of Vinsauf's emphasis on nonverbal similitude is one of the most important aspects of his tropology, according to modern theoreticians of language as well. For example, Paul Ricoeur notes that "as [Geoffrey of] Vinsauf and later [Hedwig] Konrad both saw, substitution at the level of expression is only the final phase, itself grounded in the equivalence that is the essential phase."[16] In his own work on metaphor and metonymy, Albert Henry has also examined several aspects of Geoffrey's tropology, focusing on Geoffrey's expression of similitude as a function of the normative.[17]

Similitude at the nonverbal levels of invention and arrangement complements the pedagogical use of etymology at the verbal level, the level most emphasized by medieval schoolteachers.[18] Because of their emphasis on interpretation and composition at the verbal level and their exploitation of the pedagogical usefulness of etymology, the writers of medieval school commentaries realize why

---

[14]"Docet hanc transumptionem gravem et levem. gravem est quo ad inventionem, levem est quo ad dispositionem pertinet" (Barcelona, Archivio de la Corona de Aragon, MS Ripoll 103, fol. 18v, glossing line 830).

[15]"EGREGIE Hic commendat istum transumpcionis modum, ostendens quod grauis est ad inueniendum, leuis ad vtendum" (Wolfenbüttel, Herzog August Bibliothek Cod. Guelf. 286 Gud. lat., fol. 14v, glossing line 830). For information about Reiner von Cappel, see Loris Sturlese, "Der Soester Lektor Reiner von Cappel O.P. und zwei Wolfenbütteler Fragmente aus Kapitelsakten der Dominikanerprovinz Saxonia (1358, ca. 1370)," *Wolfenbütteler Beiträge* 6 (1983): 186–201. A more detailed discussion of both of these commentaries is found in "Some Techniques of Teaching Rhetorical Poetics in the Schools of Medieval Europe," *Learning from the Rhetorics of History: Essays in Honor of Winifred Bryan Horner*, ed. Theresa Enos (Carbondale: Southern Illinois University Press, 1993) 91–113.

[16]Paul Ricoeur, *The Rule of Metaphor*, trans. Robert Czerny (Toronto: University of Toronto Press, 1977) 204–205. "[L]a substitution au niveau de l'expression, comme l'avait vu Vinsauf et après lui Konrad, est seulement l'acte terminal, fondé lui-même sur l'équivalence, qui est l'acte essentiel"; Paul Ricoeur, *La métaphore vive* (Paris: Seuil, 1975) 260. Although drawing on Geoffrey's discussion of the generic trope *transsumptio*, Ricoeur is actually speaking here of metonymy (which I discuss further at a later point).

[17]

Il en résulte que la métaphore nommerait un objet par le 'représentant le plus typique d'un de ses attributs': on dit *queue* pour *file*, parce que la queue serait le symbole le plus parfait de l'attribut 'retenu'. C'était déjà le point de vue de Geoffroi Vinsauf, mais, selon l'esprit de l'ancienne rhétorique, il l'avait exprimé sous une forme normative: quand vous désirez caractériser métaphoriquement un objet, recourez au représentant le plus typique de l'attribut visé, la *neige* ou le *lait*, par exemple, si vous songez à la blancheur. (Albert Henry, *Métonymie et métaphore* [Paris: Editions Klincksieck, 1971] 54)

See also the references to Geoffrey on pages 71 and 79.

[18]Compare Woods, "Teaching of Writing" 87.

Geoffrey of Vinsauf rearranges the order of tropes in the *Poetria nova* from the order in his source, the *Rhetorica ad Herennium*. While his new order, based on etymological resonance, has eluded even the most sympathetic of Geoffrey's modern readers, the medieval school commentators know that Geoffrey knows what he is doing. They perceive the etymological transitions from trope to trope that provide Geoffrey's important pedagogical substructure.

The first problem for modern readers is the transition from *transsumptio*, the generic trope of transsumption, to *translatio*, or metaphor, the first specific trope or kind of *transsumptio* (see Appendix, page 82 of this volume). The exact location of the transition is so difficult to pinpoint because: (a) all of the examples that Geoffrey gives of *transsumptio* are of *translatio*; (b) the root meanings of both terms are almost identical: *transsumptio* means 'taking across', whereas *translatio* means 'carrying across'; and (c) Geoffrey (deliberately, I would argue) uses both verbs on which the nouns are based, *transsumo* and *transfero*, to describe what happens in each.

Yet, despite the potential confusion, the medieval commentators that I have read so far are in complete agreement about where the transition takes place: at lines 893–894 of the *Poetria nova*, the point at which the general theory of *transsumptio* becomes a discussion of specific kinds found in particular parts of speech. The imprecision and overlap, however, is recognized by the medieval commentators as an indication that the most important aspect of the relationship between *transsumptio* and *translatio* is their resemblance to each other rather than the differences (or transition) between them. The distinction between *transsumptio* and *translatio*, according to these commentators, is one of degree, not essence.

The commentators note that under *translatio*, Geoffrey discusses the metaphoric transference of a verb in relation to subject, complement, or both.[19] Then, according to the commentators, after the metaphoric use of the verb Geoffrey discusses adjectives that are metaphoric in relation to their nouns or their complements. Third, he discusses metaphoric nouns. As the Early Commentator explains it, metaphoric transference of the first kind of noun brings us to the second trope, that is, to *nominatio* ('designation' or 'onomatopoeia'), literally 'nouning', because *nomen*, 'noun', is the root of *nominatio*. *Nominatio* is the metaphoric transference of common nouns. Metaphoric transference of the second kind of nouns, that is, of proper nouns, is the next trope, called *pronominatio* ('name substitution' or 'antonomasia'), also based on the root *nomen*, 'noun' (see Appendix).

This etymological overlap renders absurd the issues of logical distinctions, parts, and subcategories so beloved of scholastic commentaries. For example,

---

[19]For a modern discussion of this concept of the "métaphore verbale bi-vectorielle," see Albert Henry, "Métaphore verbale et métaphore adjective," *Recherches de Linguistique: Hommages à Maurice Leroy* (Brussels: l'Université de Bruxelles, 1980) 89–99, especially 89.

Item 3.a in the Appendix (*discretum nomen*, 'common noun') is under III. B. *nominatio*, whereas 3.b (*nomen proprium*, 'proper name') is under III. C. *pronominatio*. That is, the subdivisions run through and are in some ways, therefore, independent of the larger categories that should contain them. As modern teachers, we may find such a slippage of subsets disturbing to our sense of analytical decorum, but modern students, like their medieval predecessors, have no trouble following the important distinction between more general and more specific categories, rather than the positioning of the more specific categories entirely within an individual general one.

The interweaving in the *Poetria nova* of specific with general categories, rather than strict hierarchical subdividing of specific within general categories, at least according to the Early Commentator, stands in sharp contrast to the treatment given by the author of another medieval art of poetry, Gervais of Melkley. Gervais' treatment, as summarized in outline form by Purcell, contains general groupings and subcategories; but subcategories do not transgress the boundaries of the larger groupings, as is the case with Geoffrey of Vinsauf.[20] Unlike Geoffrey, Gervais often keeps the Greek terms, although he explains them. As Purcell describes Gervais's treatment:

> [H]e organized the figures under general headings that described their functions in clear, descriptive Latin. He further subdivided the various phenomena under other equally descriptive Latin expressions.... Gervasius . . . arranged [the various phenomena] in a scheme designed to show a systematic progression of thought. His account thus imparted an order and concision not found in the traditional accounts and placed an emphasis on figurative function rather than names. (79)

In contrast to Gervais, Geoffrey of Vinsauf emphasizes names and overlapping functions rather than distinctions among functions. Purcell argues that Gervais's approach is particularly useful for the small boys whom Gervais describes as his audience. But with regard to his careful subdivisions and systematic progression, Gervais's approach is, in fact, closer to that used in more advanced commentaries on the *Poetria nova* than to those intended for younger students. In this (as in several other respects[21]), Gervais's pedagogical methods are more attractive to modern teachers than they seem to have been to medieval ones—his text has survived in only three manuscripts. Medieval teachers focused first on putting things together, on overlap and resemblance in both function and name; the focus on distinction and difference came later in a student's career.

But like Gervais, Geoffrey does organize the figures under general headings, a pedagogical technique that emphasizes resemblance. As you can see from

---

[20]William M. Purcell, "*Identitas, Similitudo*, and *Contrarietas* in Gervasius of Melkley's *Ars Poetica*: A *Stasis* of Style," *Rhetorica* 9 (1991): 67–91, especially Fig. 2 on p. 84.

[21]See Marjorie Curry Woods, "*Poetria nova, Rhetorica nova*; The Newness of 13th-Century Rhetorical Poetics," to appear.

Section III of the Appendix, the first four kinds of *transsumptio*, including those just discussed as well as *permutatio*, or allegory, are treated as a group by Geoffrey and the Early Commentator, and the others are also grouped together, in Section V. One of this second group, *denominatio*, is singled out for special praise because of the slippage of meaning based on its overlapping etymological resonance.

The Early Commentator notes that this trope, *denominatio*, literally 'a naming about', is put first in this group and that it means both metonymy and word derivation. The two meanings of *denominatio* are connected by the Early Commentator in his very long discussion of this trope: 21 sentences, of which only the last is quoted here.

> And thus it seems that the term SICKNESS (*LANGUOR*) is a derived noun (*denominatiuum nomen*), since it is derived from a verbal root ["to be sick" (*langueo*)] in this way, and it seems that SICKNESS is also an example of Metonymy (*denominatio*), since the concept is related to the conception noted in the term SICK (*LANGUENS*). (971, 6)[22]

Thus, whereas the basis of metaphoric transference is similitude, the basis of metonymic resonance is etymology.

Although the metonymic and metaphoric aspects of this tropology would seem to be in polar opposition from a Jakobsonian point of view, the overlap and slippage between them are as clear to medieval commentators as they are to Paul Ricoeur, who notes: "Metaphor is the trope of resemblance *par excellence*. This pact with resemblance . . . is intimately connected to the primacy of naming or denomination and to the other traits that follow from this primacy" (173).[23] Yet, although acknowledging this etymological aspect of *denominatio*, Ricoeur is uncomfortable with it and argues against any definition in which "metonymy is a figure only if the focalization results in a name change" (204).[24] Ricoeur's discomfort here is not echoed by the medieval school commentators.

For modern teachers and critics to rejoice as the medieval school commentators do in such etymological overlap, slippage, and associativeness, we need to focus first on the verbal level of rhetorical pedagogy, that is, on elocution or style before invention and arrangement, which means being as aware as medieval schoolteachers were of the Latin terms for the tropes and the overlapping and slippage of function that these Latin terms and their English cognates indicate. At one point I considered introducing this chapter by stating that the most im-

---

[22]"Et ita uidetur quod iste terminus LANGUOR sit denominatiuum nomen, quia a uoce primitiui uerbi, sui sic denominatur; et quod etiam sit denominatio quia res est propinqua huic rei que notatur in hoc termino LANGUENS."

[23]"La métaphore est, par excellence, le trope par ressemblance. Ce pacte avec la ressemblance . . . est solidaire du primat de la dénomination et des autres traits qui procédent de ce primat" (221).

[24]"[L]a métonymie n'est une figure que si la focalisation aboutit à un changement de nom" (260).

portant fact about the teaching of the tropes in the medieval schools was that the names of the tropes were in Latin, the language used to teach them. Consequently, I have tried to emphasize here (and when I teach them) the Latin names and their English cognates rather than our customary Greek terms. This kind of etymological resonance at the verbal level, like tropological similitude at the nonverbal levels with which it is so intimately related, puts words together, rather than, as we usually associate with the function of etymology, pulling them apart. And putting together is what metaphor is all about.

APPENDIX
TROPES IN THE *POETRIA NOVA*

Transsumptio 'taking across' (737): Transumption, Transposition, Metaphoric Transference

I.   Unconditional *transsumptio*: based on similitude (739)
II. General *transsumptio*: figurative (844) or literal and figurative (886)
III. Specialized application of *transsumptio* through verb, adjective, noun (last two reversed in *EC*): (893)
   A. *Translatio* 'carrying across' (894): Metaphor
      1. Verbs metaphoric in relation to subject, complement, or both
      2. Adjectives metaphoric in relation to noun, ablative complement, or both
   B. *Nominatio* 'designation' 'naming' (919): Onomatopoeia
      3. Metaphoric noun (*nomen*)
         a. Common noun (*discretum nomen*)
   C. *Pronominatio* 'name substitution' (923): Antonomasia
         b. Proper name (*nomen proprium*)
   D. *Permutatio* 'complete change' (926): Allegory
IV. Verbal roots of *translatio, permutatio, pronominatio, nominatio* (952)
V.   Remaining colors of *transsumptio*:
   E. *Denominatio* 'word derivation' (966): Metonymy (abstract for concrete vs. matter for form)
   F. *Superlatio* 'exaggeration' 'carrying above' (1013): Hyperbole
   G. *Intellectio* 'perceiving' (1022): Synecdoche
   H. *Abusio* 'imprecision' (1061): Catachresis
   I. *Transgressio* 'transposition' (957 in *EC*, 1051 in *PN*): Hyperbaton
   J. [*Circuitio* 'going around': Periphrasis]

Note. Summarized from Woods, *An Early Commentary*. Line numbers refer to Faral's edition. Some translations modified.

Chapter 6

Between Grammar and Rhetoric: Composition Teaching at Oxford and Bologna in the Late Middle Ages

Martin Camargo
University of Missouri

When historians of rhetoric speak of the decline, decadence, and disintegration of rhetoric during the Middle Ages they proceed from certain assumptions about what a healthy, pure, and whole rhetoric is (or was). For modern scholars, that authentic, premedieval rhetoric was, in George Kennedy's words, " 'primarily' an art of persuasion; it was primarily used in civic life; [and] it was primarily oral."[1] It was also bound up with certain institutions, such as the Roman law courts and the Roman schools, and with the ideal of what it meant to be a Roman citizen. When the institutions and ideals that sustained this rhetoric were lost, so the official story goes, rhetoric lost its identity. And that identity was not recovered until the Renaissance, when rhetoric was reintegrated into something resembling its original institutional context. Between the fall of Rome and the rise of humanism, rhetoric did not so much cease to exist as retreat from the center to the margins; or, to use a different metaphor, rhetoric fragmented and then fused with several related disciplines more central to medieval life. Insofar as rhetoric was concerned with methods of discovery and proof, it was swallowed up by dialectic; insofar as it was concerned with verbal ornament, it was swallowed up by grammar and poetry; insofar as it was the culmination of the ideal citizen's training, it was swallowed up by moral theology and homiletics. As a distinct and practical art rhetoric either ceased to exist or endured in one of those

---

[1]George A. Kennedy, *Classical Rhetoric and Its Christian and Secular Tradition from Ancient to Modern Times* (Chapel Hill: University of North Carolina Press, 1980) 4.

secondary written forms that Kennedy collectively labeled *letteraturizzazione*.[2] Whether reduced to a catalogue of figures (the *colores rhetorici*) or to the mechanical formulas of the *ars dictaminis*, medieval rhetoric was a poor and diminished thing by comparison with its classical forebear. Even the art of preaching, though arguably a form of primary rhetoric in its concern with oral persuasion in the service of moral virtue, turns out to be just as guilty of the sterile formalism and the divorce of theory from practice, part from whole, and form from function that vitiated its secondary sister arts. During the long medieval interregnum the full and authentic rhetoric lay dormant, preserved in a few precious copies of the *De oratore* and the full text of Quintilian buried in monastic libraries. Or it lived at best a shadow existence in technical treatises such as the *De inventione* and the *Rhetorica ad Herennium*, which generations of scribes and teachers copied and even glossed without fully understanding their contents or applying them to the practical affairs of medieval life.[3]

Recently, historians of medieval rhetoric have begun to challenge this traditional view from a variety of angles. The Middle Ages were not so monolithic as nonmedievalists like to assume, and the fortunes of "primary rhetoric" were not identical for every time and place. In northern Italy, for example, at least by the late 11th century, rhetoric was already well on its way toward recovering many important elements of its classical identity, and elsewhere there were periods of revival as well. Margareta Fredborg and John Ward demonstrated that the medieval commentators understood the classical treatises far better than has been recognized, even if it is still not always clear how students would have applied what they learned from those teachers.[4] Others, notably Marjorie Curry Woods, attacked the established view at its source, arguing that the concept of primary rhetoric is too restrictive, even for the period that the term was coined to describe. Chronologically, socially, and pedagogically, written literary rhetoric is every bit as primary as oral persuasive rhetoric.[5]

Although the evidence adduced by such scholars discloses a much greater continuity between classical and medieval rhetoric, and between medieval and Renaissance rhetoric, than the established view allows, none of that evidence

---

[2]Kennedy, *Classical Rhetoric*, especially 108–119.

[3]A recent version of this argument appeared in Brian Vickers, *In Defence of Rhetoric* (Oxford: Clarendon Press, 1988) 214–253.

[4]See, for example, Karin M. Fredborg, ed., Thierry of Chartres. *The Latin Rhetorical Commentaries* (Toronto: Pontifical Institute of Mediaeval Studies, 1988); and John O. Ward, "From Antiquity to the Renaissance: Glosses and Commentaries on Cicero's *Rhetorica*," *Medieval Eloquence: Studies in the Theory and Practice of Medieval Rhetoric*, ed. James J. Murphy (Berkeley: University of California Press, 1978) 25–67. Ward's more detailed and up-to-date volume on the study of the classical rhetorics during the Middle Ages is forthcoming in the series Typologie des sources du moyen âge occidental.

[5]See especially Marjorie Curry Woods, "The Teaching of Writing in Medieval Europe," *A Short History of Writing Instruction From Ancient Greece to Twentieth-Century America*, ed. James J. Murphy (Davis, CA: Hermagoras Press, 1990) 77–94.

challenges the traditional assertion of a sharp contrast between the institutions that generated and sustained classical rhetoric and those that performed the same function for medieval rhetoric. And that institutional contrast was probably responsible for the established view in the first place. In other words, we are still left with the fact that the Middle Ages did not produce a distinct, relatively autonomous *ars rhetorica* to stand on equal terms beside the *ars grammatica* and the *ars dialectica* in the curriculum of the schools. In fact, the more extensive and the more sophisticated medieval theory and practice of rhetoric are shown to be, the more acute rhetoric's marginality *qua* Rhetoric becomes.[6] Given the absence of Roman political and social institutions, it is unreasonable to expect that any degree of familiarity with the classical model would have sufficed to revive the ancient *ars rhetorica* in medieval society. But those factors do not explain why a new, distinctively medieval synthesis never emerged.

The period from the late 11th through the early 13th centuries did witness the emergence of three distinctly medieval arts, each with clear ties to classical rhetoric, and each defined by its own variety of textbook: the so-called letter writer's art or *ars dictaminis*; the versifier's art or *ars versificandi*; and the preacher's art or *ars praedicandi*.[7] There is even evidence to suggest that the earliest of these, the *ars dictaminis*, may have served as a stimulus for the second.[8] Before the mid-12th century, the northern Italian treatises on *dictamen* had reached central France,[9] where they were rapidly assimilated by grammar masters at centers such as Tours and Orléans. The earliest original French *artes dictandi* were composed there during the second quarter of the 12th century, not long before the earliest full-fledged treatise on the *ars versificandi*, Matthew of Vendôme's *Ars versificatoria*, was composed in the same region.[10] Yet despite

---

[6] This anomaly is the focus of Richard McKeon's seminal essay "Rhetoric in the Middle Ages," *Speculum* 17 (1942): 1–32.

[7] The standard source on the medieval rhetorical arts is James J. Murphy, *Rhetoric in the Middle Ages: A History of Rhetorical Theory from St. Augustine to the Renaissance* (Berkeley: University of California Press, 1974) 135–355. For some of the many important new studies that have appeared since the publication of Murphy's pioneering survey, see also James J. Murphy, *Medieval Rhetoric: A Select Bibliography*, 2nd ed. (Toronto: University of Toronto Press, 1989) 76–156. Separate monographs on each of the three arts have appeared in the series Typologie des sources du moyen âge occidental: fascicle 59: Douglas Kelly, *The Arts of Poetry and Prose* (Turnhout: Brepols, 1991); fascicle 60: Martin Camargo, *Ars Dictaminis, Ars Dictandi* (Turnhout: Brepols, 1991); fascicle 61: Marianne G. Briscoe, *Artes Praedicandi*, and Barbara H. Jaye, *Artes Orandi* (Turnhout: Brepols, 1992).

[8] Martin Camargo, "Toward a Comprehensive Art of Written Discourse: Geoffrey of Vinsauf and the *Ars Dictaminis*," *Rhetorica* 6 (1988): 167–194, especially 173–174.

[9] Monika Klaes, "Die 'Summa' des Magister Bernardus: Zu Überlieferung und Textgeschichte einer zentralen Ars dictandi des 12. Jahrhunderts," *Frühmittelalterliche Studien* 24 (1990): 234 n. 154a.

[10] The earliest such treatise was the *Aurea gemma Gallica*, composed in about 1153 to 1155, probably at Meaux (though an earlier version may have been composed at Tours). See Franz Josef Worstbrock, Monika Klaes, and Jutta Lütten, *Repertorium der Artes dictandi des Mittelalters, Teil I: Von den Anfängen bis um 1200*, Münstersche Mittelalter-Schriften 66 (Munich: Fink, 1992)

a common concern with composition and common roots in traditional instruction in grammar and rhetoric, the *ars dictaminis*, the *ars versificandi*, and the later *ars praedicandi* never fused into a unified art of medieval rhetoric, even though all three continued to be taught throughout Europe for several centuries.

The autonomy of the three medieval rhetorical arts is easiest to understand in the case of the latest born, the art of preaching. On the one hand, it was more primary (in Kennedy's use of the term) than the other two, being not only explicitly concerned with persuasion but also bound up with oral delivery in a public context.[11] Moreover, its central concern with communicating the truth in a clear, unadorned fashion aligned it more with the study of dialectic and moral theology than with the compositional component of the arts course.[12] By contrast, in France and England, and in Italy at least up to the late 13th or early 14th century, the same grammar masters who taught the *ars versificandi* would also have taught the *ars dictaminis*. There were even some early attempts at fusing the two, by Geoffrey of Vinsauf and by several writers influenced by him. Why then did these two arts grow apart rather than together with the passage of time?

Here, too, it is tempting to cite the traditional divisions of the curriculum. The roots of the *ars versificandi* were fixed as strongly in grammar, which traditionally included the *enarratio poetarum* or explanation of the poets, as in rhetoric. For this reason, James J. Murphy distinguished the arts of poetry from the other medieval rhetorical treatises, preferring to call them "preceptive grammars."[13] If it were possible to argue that the *ars dictaminis*, by contrast, resembled the *ars praedicandi* in being more exclusively an outgrowth of classical rhetoric, it might be easier to maintain that the *ars dictaminis* represented a body of material that, although closely related to preceptive grammar, was neither assimilable into it nor capable of fully assimilating it. In reality, the *ars dictaminis* and the *ars versificandi* originated in the same 12th-century revolution in language arts pedagogy, and the boundaries between the two arts were frequently renegotiated in the medieval schools from the 13th through the 15th centuries.[14]

119–122. Exactly contemporary with Matthew of Vendôme's pioneering treatise was an anonymous *ars dictandi* from Tours (*inc.*: "Floribus rethoricis verba non facile depinguntur"), which survives in seven copies, the earliest dated 1171 and the latest, 1445. See Worstbrock, Klaes, and Lütten, *Repertorium* 164–167. For a critical edition based on six manuscripts, see Martin Camargo, "A Twelfth-Century Treatise on *Dictamen* and Metaphor," *Traditio* 47 (1992): 161–213.

[11]The written/oral contrast should not be exaggerated. Giles Constable, for one, has noted how frequently the letters and other documents produced by the *dictatores* and their students were intended to be read aloud in a public setting, in Giles Constable, *Letters and Letter-Collections*, Typologie des sources du moyen âge occidental 17 (Turnhout: Brepols, 1976) 13–14, 53–55.

[12]See Harry Caplan's essays on the arts of preaching, collected and reprinted in Anne King and Helen North, eds., *Of Eloquence: Studies in Ancient and Mediaeval Rhetoric* (Ithaca: Cornell University Press, 1970), especially 42–45, 114–120.

[13]Murphy, *Rhetoric in the Middle Ages* 135–193.

[14]William D. Patt points to grammar study as an important and frequently neglected source for the *ars dictaminis*: William D. Patt, "The Early 'Ars Dictaminis' as Response to a Changing Society,"

Nor was the specialization of either art ever quite so narrow as is commonly supposed. The preceptive grammars are often regarded as treatises on verse composition, perhaps because they owed as much to Horace's *Ars poetica* as did the *artes dictandi* to the Ciceronian rhetorics. The difference between the preceptive grammars and the *artes dictandi* is then represented as the difference between an art of poetry and an art of prose. In reality, as Douglas Kelly has been reminding us, the preceptive grammars, including even Geoffrey of Vinsauf's versified *Poetria nova*, were clearly intended to serve as general composition textbooks, suitable for teaching composition in verse or prose.[15] Conversely, although the very term *dictamen*, derived from the verb *dictare* 'to compose', suggests composition in general, it acquired a narrower sense in practice if not in theory. Most *artes dictandi* began by distinguishing among prose, metrical, and rhythmical *dictamen*, only to exclude the latter two from consideration. Nonetheless, though few *artes dictandi* treated verse composition, all but the most schematic ones devoted substantial space to general composition topics such as figurative language, the structure of complex sentences, and the vices and virtues of style.

Such affinities notwithstanding, it must be admitted that the efforts by certain preceptive grammarians to incorporate into their own textbooks the varieties of prose and the teaching methods that characterized the *ars dictaminis* never achieved more than a limited and temporary success. Why did several prose genres seem to resist amalgamation into the general composition program that the preceptive grammars served? The resistance seems to have been due to a combination of factors, including the nature of the prose genres, the context of their use, the methods used by the *dictatores*, and certain conflicts of emphases in the precepts of the two arts.

Probably the single most important factor has already been mentioned: The preceptive grammars were general composition textbooks, whereas the treatises on *dictamen* concentrated on a particular set of genres, broadly defined as epistolary, which included not only public and private letters but also privileges, deeds, testaments, and other legal instruments.[16] Accordingly, in their treatises

---

Viator 9 (1978): 149–151. Paul F. Gehl also issues some useful cautions regarding the tendency to see the 12th-century *ars dictaminis* as an abrupt departure from the traditional curriculum of the monastic schools (in which grammar and rhetoric were difficult to separate): Paul F. Gehl, "From Monastic Rhetoric to *Ars Dictaminis*: Traditionalism and Innovation in the Schools of Twelfth-Century Italy," *The American Benedictine Review* 34 (1983): 33–47.

[15]See especially Kelly, *Arts of Poetry and Prose*. Marjorie Curry Woods makes the same point in her studies of the commentaries on Geoffrey of Vinsauf's *Poetria nova*. See, for example, Marjorie Curry Woods, "A Medieval Rhetoric Goes to School—and to the University: The Commentaries on the *Poetria nova*," *Rhetorica* 9 (1991): 60 n. 15.

[16]Charles Vulliez traces the expansion of the *ars dictaminis'* scope from the epistle proper to include a broader range of official documents, a development that occurred first in France during the second half of the 12th century: Charles Vulliez, "L'apprentissage de la rédaction des documents diplomatiques à travers l'*ars dictaminis* français (et spécialement ligérien) du XIIe siècle," *Cancelleria e cultura nel medio evo* (Vatican City: Archivio Segreto Vaticano, 1990) 77–95.

the *dictatores* placed much more emphasis on the structure of the whole document, on the function and order of its constituent parts, than did the preceptive grammarians, who tended to focus more exclusively on small details of composition (Franz Quadlbauer's "Tendenz zur kleinen Einheit"[17]) Although an *ars dictandi* might devote considerable space to the same stylistic matters that made up the bulk of an *ars versificandi* (along with certain stylistic features, such as cursus, that were more specific to epistolary prose), the focus was generally on the parts of a letter and their contribution to the rhetorical goals of the letter writer. The model salutations, *exordia*, and entire letters that filled the longer treatises were not easily transferred to other uses, and as this component came to predominate, the gap between the *artes dictandi* and the *artes versificandi* widened.

The pedagogical procedures were correspondingly different, though here it is more difficult to generalize safely. The preceptive grammarians seem to have made greater use of exercises in which students reworked an existing text, whereas the *dictatores* more typically presented their students with a practical problem that they were to solve by composing an appropriate document.[18] This is not to say that the *dictatores* made less use of model texts than did the preceptive grammarians, for more often than not the solution amounted to choosing correctly from a finite set of alternatives, whether a collection of ready-made letters, an array of formulas, or even the branching tables popularized by Lawrence of Aquilegia.[19] Given their concern for a clearly articulated structure, the *dictatores* not surprisingly made brevity the chief virtue of style. By contrast, the preceptive grammarians' concern with stylistic plenitude (*copia*) caused them to emphasize amplification over abbreviation. Finally, the two arts envisioned a different sort of typical student. Preceptive grammar was part of one's basic education and led directly to no particular career, whereas the *ars dictaminis* provided vocational training for a career in administration or the law. The difference is roughly comparable to that between a present-day freshman composition course and a business and technical writing course. Students of preceptive grammar would normally be younger than students of the *ars dictaminis*, a contrast that indeed characterized the northern universities such as Oxford, where the arts faculties were more prominent and the students younger, as opposed to the southern universities such as Bologna, where the arts faculties were relatively small adjuncts to the dominant law faculties and where the students were older.[20]

---

[17]Franz Quadlbauer, *Die antike Theorie der genera dicendi im lateinischen Mittelalter* (Vienna: Böhlaus 1962) 71–73.

[18]An excellent recent study of the composition practices in the classrooms of the preceptive grammarians is Robert Glendinning, "Pyramus and Thisbe in the Medieval Classroom," *Speculum* 61 (1986): 51–78.

[19]See Murphy, *Rhetoric in the Middle Ages* 259–263.

[20]A. B. Cobban, *The Medieval Universities: Their Development and Organization* (London: Methuen 1975) 190.

These and other differences worked against the emergence of a truly comprehensive medieval *ars rhetorica*, capable of generating its own distinctive treatise and of claiming a position in the medieval arts curriculum equal to that of grammar or dialectic. Had such a rhetoric emerged, the component of it that concerned the teaching of composition probably would have been a synthesis of what developed into preceptive grammar and what developed into the *ars dictaminis*. Although a single, definitive synthesis of this sort never took hold, the nature and degree of separation between preceptive grammar and the *ars dictaminis* was not the same at all times and in all places. Any attempt to describe all the local permutations of the relationship between grammatical and rhetorical approaches to composition during the Middle Ages must wait until a great deal more work with primary sources has been done. But some idea of the range of variation may be obtained from a brief and necessarily incomplete sketch of developments during the 13th and 14th centuries at Oxford and Bologna, two prominent centers for the study of the verbal arts that represent the opposite poles of the relationship between grammar and rhetoric as it applies to instruction in composition.

There are certain broad and obvious similarities between Oxford and Bologna during the period in question. Each was the site of a *studium generale* that belonged to the first generation of European universities. Both universities were centers for the study of law, though Bologna's preeminence in this area far outweighed Oxford's. Each city was also home to thriving grammar schools, which were tied to the universities in ways that are still imperfectly understood. And most important for present purposes, in each city there developed two groups of composition teachers: One group was associated with the grammar schools and the arts curriculum of the universities, the other with a more narrowly focused, more strictly pragmatic course of vocational training.[21]

Within this broad framework of similarity, however, there were striking differences in the position occupied by the teaching and the teachers of the verbal arts in the two cities. Within a generation of Alberic of Montecassino's pioneering treatises,[22] Bologna became the center for the study of the *ars dictaminis*, not only for Italy but eventually for all of Europe. By the early 13th century the *ars dictaminis* had been taught there for a century, and many of the most influential textbooks had been written by Bolognese masters. The doctrines of the *dictatores* not only were an important component of the university's arts curriculum but seem also to have been taught in the secondary grammar schools already in the 13th century.[23]

---

[21]The two writing courses at Oxford are discussed in greater detail in the Introduction to Martin Camargo, *Medieval Rhetorics of Prose Composition: Five English Artes Dictandi and Their Tradition* (Binghamton: Medieval and Renaissance Texts and Studies, 1994) 23–32.

[22]See especially Franz Josef Worstbrock, "Die Anfänge der mittelalterlichen Ars dictandi," *Frühmittelalterliche Studien* 23 (1989): 1–42.

[23]Ronald G. Witt, *Hercules at the Crossroads: The Life, Works, and Thought of Coluccio Salutati* (Durham, NC: Duke University Press, 1983), 6–19.

At Oxford, by contrast, the barest traces of instruction in the *ars dictaminis* began to appear only during the first half of the 13th century, and the evidence suggests that such instruction did not become widespread until the second half of the 14th century. Prior to that time, what instruction there was was based almost exclusively on imported textbooks, in particular those of the 12th- and 13th-century Bolognese *dictatores*. Although Oxford was the chief center for the *ars dictaminis* in England, such study was decidedly local in impact and predominantly derivative. Nor is there any evidence that the *ars dictaminis* was ever taught in the Oxford grammar schools.

Several developments at Bologna during the second half of the 13th century further sharpened the contrast with Oxford. Increasing emphasis was placed on oral eloquence, and treatises on the *ars arengandi* or art of speechmaking began to appear. The reform of the system for educating notaries, ongoing since the early 13th century, was completed with the publication of Rolandino Passageri's definitive textbooks.[24] And near the end of the century a renewed interest in studying the classical rhetorics, especially the *Rhetorica ad Herennium*, began to manifest itself in the first of a wave of new commentaries.[25] By the early 14th century, therefore, the *ars dictaminis* was part of a broader range of formal rhetoric pedagogy that included training in speechmaking and lectures and commentaries on the Ciceronian rhetorics, as well as a separate 2-year course on the notary's art.[26]

These developments culminated in the creation of a chair of rhetoric at the university, to which Giovanni di Bonandrea was appointed in 1292. Although Giovanni's duties were initially to lecture on the *Rhetorica ad Herennium* to students at the university, beginning in 1304 he also offered instruction in the *ars dictaminis* and the *ars oratoria* to members of the notarial guild. Thus the teaching of the *ars dictaminis*, which had formerly been conducted by grammar masters, became explicitly the province of the rhetoric professor.[27] As James R. Banker has shown, this double course in rhetoric, which Giovanni continued to teach until his death in 1321, became the pattern at Bologna for at least the remainder of the 14th century. The *Rhetorica ad Herennium* and Giovanni di Bonandrea's own *Brevis introductio ad dictamen* served as the required textbooks for a succession of rhetoric professors that began with Giovanni's student Bartolini di Benincasa da Canulo (who wrote a commentary on the *Rhetorica ad Herennium*) and included Pietro da Forli, Dino della Valle da Reggio, Pietro da Moglio, and Bartolomeo del Regno. The boundary between rhetorical and gram-

---

[24]Witt, *Hercules at the Crossroads* 20–23.

[25]Ward, "From Antiquity to the Renaissance" 36–39.

[26]See especially James R. Banker, "The *Ars dictaminis* and Rhetorical Textbooks at the Bolognese University in the Fourteenth Century," *Medievalia et Humanistica* n.s. 5 (1974): 153–168; Sandra Karaus Wertis, "The Commentary of Bartolinus de Benincasa de Canulo on the *Rhetorica ad Herennium*," *Viator* 10 (1979): 283–310; and Witt, *Hercules at the Crossroads* 6–23.

[27]Banker, "Rhetorical Textbooks" 154–157.

matical instruction was far from absolute: The professors of rhetoric also taught the rhetorical analysis of classical and contemporary poetry,[28] and the grammar masters doubtless continued to teach *dictamen* in some form. But an unusually explicit rhetorical orientation characterized the more advanced courses in composition at Bologna.

Of the many factors that worked against a repetition of these developments at Oxford, I would single out as especially significant the separation between the study of civil and that of common law, which was formalized by royal edict in 1234. Although civil and canon law were studied at Oxford, those who wished to study the common law used in the courts received practical training at the Inns of Court in London. And when a professional bar eventually formed late in the 13th century, its rules for entry favored those court-trained apprentices over university-trained civilians.[29] The relative absence of the forensic component from the legal curriculum at Oxford removed what might have proved an important stimulus to the growth of a rhetorical culture comparable to Bologna's. There is little evidence of formal study of oral eloquence or the classical rhetorics at Oxford during the 14th and even the first half of the 15th centuries.[30] And though a course of study that included notarial training was offered by teachers such as Thomas Sampson and William Kingsmill, that course did not achieve the same degree of organization as did the notarial curriculum at Bologna, nor did the notarial profession or its teachers achieve anything like the prestige of their Bolognese counterparts.

Thus, despite the fact that at Bologna, no less than at Oxford, the same teacher often taught both rhetoric and grammar, at Bologna the grammatical component of such instruction was subsumed by or was subservient to the rhetorical component, whereas at Oxford grammar subsumed rhetoric even more effectively. This can be seen clearly in the *artes dictandi* written by the Oxford grammar masters, which tended to give disproportionate emphasis to catalogues of figures and to techniques of amplification and which often employed the language of versification to discuss prose rhythm (*cursus*). Three Oxford manuscripts even preserve the short *ars dictandi* of Jupiter Monoculus/Francigena, written in leonine hexameters, with accompanying prose commentary.[31] Moreover, these tech-

---

[28]Banker, "Rhetorical Textbooks" 168 n. 54. See also footnote 37.

[29]J. L. Barton, "The Study of Civil Law Before 1380," *The Early Oxford Schools. The History of the University of Oxford*, vol. 1, ed. J. I. Catto (Oxford: Clarendon Press, 1984) 521–522.

[30]James J. Murphy emphasizes the absence of rhetoric from the university curriculum, in James J. Murphy, "Rhetoric in Fourteenth-Century Oxford," *Medium Aevum* 34 (1965): 1–20.

[31]Inc.: "Si dictare velis et iungere scema loquelis." All three Oxford copies date from the 15th century: Bodleian Library, MS Auct. F.3.9, 428a–435a; Bodleian Library, MS Digby 64, fols. 99v–105r; and British Library, MS Add. 62132A, fols. 199r–204r. At least 23 additional copies are known to exist. Like the slightly later versified *ars dictandi* by Otto of Lüneburg, *Compendium poetrie nove*, the treatise by Jupiter Monoculus was especially popular in southern Germany and Austria during the first half of the 15th century. See especially Franz Josef Worstbrock, "Iupiter (Monoculus, Francigena)," *Die deutsche Literatur des Mittelalters: Verfasserlexikon*, 2nd ed., vol.

nical treatises were taught not in association with the Ciceronian rhetorics and the art of speechmaking but with the preceptive grammars, and the models for imitation that accompanied them in the manuscripts were not the large collections of letters and documents employed at Bologna but stylistic tours de force such as Alain of Lille's *Complaint of Nature*, Jean of Limoges' *Dream of Pharaoh*, and Richard of Bury's *Philobiblon*.[32]

Although no English teacher produced an *ars dictandi* used outside England, with the exception of the *Summa de arte dictandi* uncertainly ascribed to Geoffrey of Vinsauf,[33] three of the four earliest preceptive grammarians whose written works are preserved were Englishmen. And although John of Garland taught mainly in France, both Gervase of Melkley and Geoffrey of Vinsauf spent at least part of their careers teaching in England. More important, their treatises were quickly adopted and widely used in the English schools, of which Oxford was the most important. Indeed, the long and as yet unprinted version of Geoffrey's *Documentum de modo et arte dictandi et versificandi*, the most careful attempt at synthesizing preceptive grammar and *dictamen*, is preserved only in manuscripts of English provenance.[34]

The dominance of these general composition textbooks at Oxford contrasts with composition pedagogy at Bologna. There is no question that when the preceptive grammars reached Bologna from France and England, their influence was felt immediately in the *artes dictandi*. The treatises of Guido Faba and Bene of Florence incorporated considerable material dealing with style and the figures taken directly from the preceptive grammars, particularly the *Poetria nova* of Geoffrey of Vinsauf, who may have taught briefly at Bologna in the late 1190s. As Ronald Witt has shown, this "grammatization" of *dictamen* was in turn criticized, most directly by Boncompagno da Signa, who set out to purge *dictamen*

4, ed. Kurt Ruh, Gundolf Keil, Werner Schröder, Burghart Wachinger, Franz Josef Worstbrock (Berlin: Walter de Gruyter, 1983) cols. 429–430; and Franz Josef Worstbrock, "Otto von Lüneburg," *Die deutsche Literatur des Mittelalters: Verfasserlexikon*, 2nd ed., vol. 7, ed. Kurt Ruh, Gundolf Keil, Werner Schröder, Burghart Wachinger, Franz Josef Worstbrock (Berlin: Walter de Gruyter, 1989) cols. 225–228. Monika Klaes records an earlier *ars dictandi* (before 1226) consisting of 337 hexameters, preserved in Innsbruck, Universitätsbibliothek Cod. 322, fols. 126r–131r. " 'Summa' des Magister Bernardus" 199 n. 5.

[32]On the codicological evidence for the use of these works as models of Latin prose style, see Martin Camargo, "Beyond the *Libri Catoniani*: Models of Latin Prose Style at Oxford University ca. 1400," *Mediaeval Studies* 56 (in press).

[33]The treatise is edited by Vincenzo Licitra, "La *Summa de arte dictandi* di Maestro Goffredo," *Studi medievali*, ser. 3, 7 (1966): 865–913. See also Worstbrock, Klaes, and Lütten, *Repertorium* 65–68.

[34]On this work, see Margaret F. Nims, "Translatio: 'Difficult Statement' in Medieval Poetic Theory," *University of Toronto Quarterly* 43 (1974): 215–230; Traugott Lawler, ed., *The Parisiana Poetria of John of Garland*, Yale Studies in English, 182 (New Haven: Yale University Press, 1974) 327–332; and Martin Camargo, "Toward a Comprehensive Art of Written Discourse: Geoffrey of Vinsauf and the *Ars Dictaminis*," *Rhetorica* 6 (1988): 167–194. Margaret F. Nims is completing a critical edition and translation, for which Martin Camargo will provide an introduction.

of its "literary" excrescences and to restore its pragmatic, rhetorical emphasis.[35] Though most later *artes dictandi* continued to discuss topics borrowed from the preceptive grammars, the proportion of such material decreased, and in general the division between grammatical and rhetorical instruction sharpened at Bologna.[36] As late as 1405–1406, Bartolino Valvassari da Lodi, doctor of grammar and rhetoric at the *Studio* of Bologna, named "Gualfredum Anglicum" as a major source for his *Rhetoricale compendium*. However, his use of the *Poetria nova* was selective and supplementary by comparison with that of his main source, the *Rhetorica ad Herennium*. And the treatise itself, an *ars arengandi* in three books followed by an *ars epistolandi* in one book, clearly embodied the rhetorical orientation of the Bolognese curriculum.[37]

At Oxford, the authoritative source was less the *Rhetorica ad Herennium* than the treatises of Geoffrey of Vinsauf. Composition textbooks such as Giovanni di Bonandrea's *Brevis introductio ad dictamen* and Bartolino da Lodi's *Rhetoricale compendium*, with their clear and extensive dependence on the Ciceronian rhetorics, stand in sharp contrast to the most popular English *ars dictandi*, the *Formula moderni et usitati dictaminis* (ca. 1390) composed at Oxford by Bartolino's contemporary Thomas Merke.[38] Merke's chief sources were Geoffrey of Vinsauf's *Poetria nova* and *Documentum* (short version), which he paraphrased in much the same way as Bartolino did the *Rhetorica ad Herennium*. When he treated the parts of a letter, the *cursus*, or any topic exclusively connected to letter writing, Merke turned to the 13th-century Italian *dictatores* Guido Faba and Thomas of Capua. The curriculum in which such a textbook could find a place was clearly oriented toward grammar.

The observations that I have made here, and particularly those regarding the contrast between Oxford and Bologna, will have to be refined in the course of further investigation of primary materials. My point is to suggest that in evaluating what can broadly be called the teaching of composition in the Middle Ages, we need to look more closely at what was happening at a variety of specific schools, and we need to pay more attention to the whole institutional context rather than

---

[35]Ronald G. Witt, "Boncompagno and the Defense of Rhetoric," *The Journal of Medieval and Renaissance Studies* 16 (1986): 1–31.

[36]Paul Oskar Kristeller, "Humanism and Scholasticism in the Italian Renaissance," *Byzantion* 17 (1944–1945): 364.

[37]On Bartolino, see Giovanni Cremaschi, "Bartolino da Lodi, Professore di Grammatica e di Retorica nello studio di Bologna agli inizi del Quattrocento," *Aevum* 26 (1952): 309–348. Cremaschi discusses the *Rhetoricale compendium* (322–335) and prints excerpts from it (342–348). Bartolino, who referred to himself as "grammatice ac rhetorice doctor" (Cremaschi, "Bartolino da Lodi" 346), also apparently taught verse composition and the rhetorical analysis of Latin poetry, elements of his instruction that were embodied in his other surviving work, the *Oratio composita una cum metris pro principio facto super Ovidio Metamorphoseos* (see Cremaschi, "Bartolino da Lodi" 312–321, 336–341).

[38]On Merke and the *Formula*, see James J. Murphy, "A Fifteenth-Century Treatise on Prose Style," *The Newberry Library Bulletin* 6 (1966): 205–210; and Camargo, *Medieval Rhetorics of Prose Composition* 105–147 (critical edition: 122–147).

artificially isolating its components for the purpose of matching them with their classical antecedents. There are real and important differences between an advanced composition course conceived as an *ars rhetorica* at Bologna and one conceived as an *ars grammatica* at Oxford, and those differences could be counted as further evidence for the medieval fragmentation of classical rhetoric. But I would prefer to regard both courses as new syntheses, each appropriate for its particular time and place.

Part II

RENAISSANCE TEXTBOOKS AND RHETORICAL EDUCATION

The Lectures of Guarino da Verona on the *Rhetorica ad Herennium*: A Preliminary Discussion

John Ward
University of Sydney

Guarino da Verona and Jerry Murphy have much in common. Both have been inspired teachers of rhetoric for many generations of students and both have gone down or will go down in history as great facilitators and promoters of their disciplines. Both have combined a deep concern for the classical sources of rhetorical theory with more modern didactic and practical preoccupations. In one major respect, however, they differ. Surprisingly, perhaps, in view of the publishing record of contemporaries such as Leonardo Bruni or Poggio Bracciolini,[1] Guarino da Verona published little: "Ancorché dottissimi" Eugenio Garin wrote of the great humanist teachers of the early 15th century,[2] "non scrissero libri originali; prepararono solo qualche sussidio al loro insegnamento: Vittorino un trattatelo d'ortografia, Guarino delle regole grammaticali, edizioni di testi, versioni, orazioni. Consegnarono, come Socrate, la loro parola non alle pagine mute, ma alle anime vive."[3]

---

[1] See G. Griffiths, J. Hankins, and D. Thompson, trans., intr. *The Humanism of Leonardo Bruni: Selected Texts* (Binghamton, NY, 1987); J. W. Oppel, "Peace vs. Liberty in the Quattrocento: Poggio, Guarino, and the Scipio-Caesar controversy," *The Journal of Medieval and Renaissance Studies* 4 (1974): 221–265; and P. W. Gordon, *Two Renaissance Book Hunters: The Letters of Poggio Bracciolini to Nicolaus de Niccolis* (NY, 1974).

[2] Eugenio Garin, *L'Educazione in Europa 1400–1600* (1957; Bari, 1976) 129–130.

[3] J. Burckhardt, *The Civilization of the Renaissance in Italy*, trans. S. G. G. Middlemore (NY, 1960) 169. Burckhardt seems astray in his assertion that despite his teaching preoccupations, Guarino "still found time to do translations from the Greek and to write voluminous original works." Guarino's publications include some 900 **letters** (Poggio left behind some 600), never collected as such by him and written across a 55-year period (1405–1460). See R. Sabbadini, *Epistolario di Guarino Veronese*, vols. 1–2 *testo*, 3 *commento* (Miscellanea di Storia Veneta ser. 3, vols. 8, 11, 14, 1915,

1916, 1919), henceforth *Epist.*; E. Garin, ed., *Prosatori Latini del Quattrocento* (Milan/Naples, 1952) 313–377, containing Guarino's long letter to Poggio in defense of Caesar, separately published in 1977 (Turin: Einaudi), with the same pagination, and henceforth *Pros.*; M. Sancipriano, ed., *Guariniana* (Turin, 1964) vol. 2, *Scuola* 83ff. This publication contains reprints of two major works of Remigio Sabbadini: *Vita di Guarino Veronese* (Genoa, 1891), and *La Scuola e gli studi di Guarino Veronese* (Catania, 1896), henceforth cited as Sabbadini, *Vita* or Sabbadini, *Scuola*. The name of Remigio Sabbadini (1850–1934) is inseparable from that of Guarino. Born near Vicenza, Sabbadini taught Latin literature at the University of Catania (1886–1900) and in the Accademia Scientifico-letteraria, later Università di Milano (1900–1926). A pioneer of precise inquiry into the classical philology of the humanists, Sabbadini's edition of Guarino's letters and his life of the scholar are still the fundamental ports of call for all interested in the subject (cf. *Enciclopedia Italiana*, 1949 ed., vol. 30, 375). Some of Guarino's letters are mini-treatises, for example, that on historiography of A.D. 1446 (*ep.* 796, *Epist.* vol. 2, 458ff, and cf. Sabbadini, *Il Metodo* 43ff) or *ep.* 823, *Epist.* vol. 2, 519ff, a long defense of the classics "fratri Iohanni Pratensi." Guarino's **orationes** and **prolusiones** (the latter divided into *familiari, solenni,* and *solennissimi*) were also much copied: M. King, *Venetian Humanism in an Age of Patrician Dominance* (Princeton, 1986) 10. See: R. Sabbadini, *Classici e Umanisti da Codici Ambrosiani* (Florence, 1933) 104–113 (*oratio in laudibus Guarini* from MS Milan Ambros. O 66 sup. f.21r); R. Sabbadini, "Una prolusione di Guarino Veronese sulle arti liberali," *La Biblioteca delle Scuole Italiane* 7 (1897): 33–37; Sabbadini, *Scuola* 62ff, 170ff, 182ff; R. Sabbadini, *Il Metodo degli Umanisti* (Florence, 1920) chap. 4, 35ff; K. Müllner, "Acht inauguralreden des Veronesers Guarino und seines Sohnes Battista: ein Beitrag zur Geschichte der Pädagogik des Humanismus," *Wiener Studien* 18 (1896): 283–306; see footnote 115. Guarino also wrote some verse, short **treatises** on Latin grammar and lexicography, and collections of philological notes. Sabbadini (*La Scuola* 73, 228–230, *Il Metodo* 61) mentions a "trattatello in versi memoriali" on composition, MS Vat. BAV Urbin.lat.1180. The topic of euphonious prose is also touched upon in Guarino's short *Regule de ornatissimo et rhetorico dictamine Latino*: Parisius impresse/facte Ferrarie (n.d.) containing the *sinonima Guarini Veronensis* (oriented toward epistolography) and possibly by Guarino or by his disciple (cf. the verses at the end in the Paris B.N. Rés X.1416, 1417 and Rés X 156 copies). This is not the well-known short grammatical treatise of Guarino (*Grammaticales regulae*, on which see W. Keith Percival, "The Grammatical Tradition and the Rise of the Vernaculars," *Current Trends in Linguistics*, ed. T. A. Sebeok, vol. 13 [The Hague: Mouton, 1975] 238–239; and "Textual Problems in the Latin Grammar of Guarino Veronese," *Res Publica Litterarum: Studies in the Classical Tradition* 1 [1978]: 241–254) or his *De dipthongis*, a list of correct dipthongs in various positions within a word. Guarino's **lectures**, usually reported by way of student *reportationes*, seem to have covered such texts as the *Facta et dicta memorabilia* of Valerius Maximus (with a preface, E. Fryde, *Humanism and Renaissance Historiography* [London, 1983] 60, reprinting earlier articles for the most part); Cicero's *Pro Roscio Amerino, Paradoxa, Epistles, De officiis, De senectute, De amicitia*; Terence's *Heautontimorumenos* (J. Monfasani, *Renaissance Quarterly* 41 [1988]: 36); and the poetry of Juvenal (Sabbadini, *Scuola* 96 could not find actual MS evidence of this but cf. *CTC* [for this abbreviation see the foot of the present note] I, 205–208), Martial (? See *CTC* 4, 295), Persius. On these see Sabbadini, *Scuola* 90ff. Guarino's **translations** included some from Plutarch's biographies (of. Caesar [Fryde, *Humanism* 70, being revised A.D. 1435], Alexander, Marcellus, Phocion, Dion, Eumenes, Pelopidas, Philopoemen, Flaminius, Coriolanus, and Themistocles [apparently the work of his Venetian days, cf. *ep.* 95, *Epist.*, vol. I, 176, A.D. 1418, I, 407, no. 681 II, 272, no. 706 II, 310 A.D. 1437]), from the orations of Isocrates, from St. Basil of Caesarea, Lucian's *Calumnia*, (ps-) Plutarch's *Liber de educatione* with preface (Birnbaum, [see footnote 19] 35), and "a work of his old age" (Fryde, *Humanism* 72), Strabo's *Geographica*, with some marginalia, here and there extensive (Fryde, *Humanism* 81). He also edited and translated into Latin "the little manual of Greek accidence which Chrysoloras dictated to his pupils in lecture and for many years this remained the only introduction to Greek available to western students," W. H. Woodward, *Vittorino da Feltre and Other Humanist Educators: Essays and Versions: An Introduction to the History of Classical Education* (Cambridge, 1897). His **original compositions** included a life of Plato (J.

Jerry Murphy, on the other hand, has produced a prolific series of guides, aids, manuals, translations, and monographs to match his vigorous role as teacher and facilitator. Although the present chapter is devoted to some of the problems raised by a consideration of the teaching career of one of the great masters of the 15th

Hankins, "A Manuscript of Plato's *Republic* in the Translation of Chrysoloras and Uberto Decembrio with Annotations of Guarino Veronese [Reg.lat.1131]," 149ff of J. Hankins, J. Monfasani, F. Purnell Jr., eds., *Supplementum Festivum: Studies in Honor of Paul Oskar Kristeller* [Binghamton, 1987]; *Fryde, Humanism* 62ff, ca. A.D. 1430) and lives of Homer and Aristotle. His **textual work** concentrated upon both Plinys' *Natural Histories* and *Epistles*; Aulus Gellius' *Attic Nights* (A.D. 1432–1433); Caesar's *Commentaries*; works of Cicero, Plautus, Servius, and Cornelius Celsus. It is highly likely that unidentified works of Guarino still lie in the MSS. In MSS Bd Petrarch P.P49P8, for example, of the Cornell University collection, we find a rhetorical treatise with the incipit *tametsi dicendi venustas duas in partes presertim distributa sit* attributed to Guarino, and MS Paris B.N. nouv.acq.lat. 166 contains a text described in L. Delisle's "Inventaire des MSS latins de la B.N. insérés au fonds des nouvelles acquisitions, du Ier août 1871 au Ier mars 1874," *Bibliothéque de l'École des Chartes* 35 (1874): 78 as "Rhétorique de Guérin de Vérone avec gloses. . . ." This latter text has across the top margin of its first page, in the hand of the glossator, who has added extensive marginalia to the text, "Guarini Veronensis latinitatis componende feliciter incipit" and begins, "Quamdiu profecto elegans ornata que latinitatis permaximum hominibus decus prestare assuevit cuius sane ab institutis nostre tempestatis homines sepe numero de more solent quocirca. . . ." The text, which begins the MS and ends on f.92v, is entitled in the colophon *rhetorica* and contains letters of Iohannes Serra (and also of Guarino himself, e.g., f.15v *ut in serie Guarini licterarum scribis*), sections on the *modi* of amplification and *abbreviatio*, on concluding a speech, on punctuation and *de viciis dictaminis*. A large section on the *colores* is found in the second part of the book, fols. 47v and following. It is highly unlikely that Guarino ever taught routine business *dictamen* sufficiently extensively to compose a textbook on it (yet cf. P. F. Grendler, *Schooling in Renaissance Italy: Literacy and Learning 1300–1600* [Johns Hopkins University Press, 1991] 206 [Cicero's *Epistles* were more popular than his *Rhetorics*, a fact borne out by the pattern of early printed editions], 227ff, 231, and note Janus Pannonius' language in his *Panegyric* to Guarino [*Iani Pannonii Quinquecclesiensis episcopi Sylva Panegyrica ad Guarinum Veronensem, praeceptorem suum et eiusdem epigrammata* (Basle, Frobenius 1518) 19] "Principio recte das fundamenta loquendi/ Recte scribendi compendia tradere calles:/ Ne lingua accentu: calamo ne dextera peccet./ Mox argumento formatur epistola ficto:/ Proxima volvendis annalibus ocia dantur:/ Declamare dehinc: et carmina fingere monstras:/ Dum matura suam facundia crescat in arcem"). Probably a later user extrapolated from the inclusion of letters by Guarino in some dictaminal text not composed by Guarino, of which the present MS is a copy. Professor Emil Polak was unable to identify the text (by letter). On Guarino in general, see: Carlo de Rosmini, *Vita di Guarino Veronese e de' suoi discepoli*, 3 vols. (Brescia, 1805); P. O. Kristeller, V. Brown, and F. Cranz, eds., *Catalogus Translationum et Commentariorum Medii Aevi* (henceforth *CTC*) I, 205–208; II, 229–230; III, 255; IV, 295; V, 358–359; Woodward, *Vittorino da Feltre* (159–178 contain the treatise by Guarino's son Battista *De ordine docendi et studendi*, which is recognized to contain much evidence for the father's teaching methods); G. Billanovich, "L'insegnamento della Grammatica e della Retorica nelle Università italiane tra Petrarca e Guarino," 356–380 of J. Ijsewijn and J. Paquet, eds., *The Universities in the late Middle Ages* (Louvain, 1978—not especially revealing on either rhetoric or Guarino); A. Rabil, ed., *Renaissance Humanism: Foundations, Forms and Legacy*, vol. 3 (Philadelphia, 1988) 15ff and compare index; Voigt, *Il Risorgimento dell' Antichità Classica ovvero il primo secolo dell'Umanismo*, 2 vols., trans. D. Valbusa (Florence, 1888–1890), with *giunte e correzioni* of 1897) I, 437, 547ff; Grendler, *Schooling* 126–129. For Guarino's teaching and intellectual interests down to and including his Verona period, see Rino Avesani, *Verona nel Quattrocento: la civiltà delle lettere*, (Verona, 1984) chap. 2.

century, its resonance with the commemorative purpose of the present volume should not be forgotten.

Guarino da Verona (1374–1460) was the last to die, the longest lived, and in some ways the most memorable of the first generation of post-Petrarchan Italian humanists, for whom Latin was a kind of new mother tongue, and Greek a newly acquired and exciting challenge.[4] Current interest in Guarino, however, has been enriched by a recent assault on the novelty and originality of his rhetorical teaching by Anthony Grafton and Lisa Jardine.[5] Since the time at least of Hanna Gray's 1960 article "Renaissance Humanism: The Pursuit of Eloquence,"[6] it has been customary to set up some sort of a contrast between medieval and Renaissance cultures. It has been customary to view the former as didactic, adapted to the world of the school rather than to that of the market place, to the world of logical and theological truth[7] rather than to the negotiability of the forum, a culture without a sense of the distance that separated medieval from antique ways, a culture divorced from the burgeoning lay world around it. Renaissance culture, on the other hand, is traditionally seen as a culture of the world outside the school, a culture of the court, of the chancery, of political life, a culture with an acute sense of the divide between contemporary and classical times, a lay culture, in fact, perhaps the first such lay culture since Roman times. The place of classical humanism within this Renaissance culture, according to the conventional paradigm, is well put by the chapter on "Guarino Veronese e

---

[4]The others are: Antonio Loschi (1368–1441), Gasparino Barzizza (1370–1430), Poggio Bracciolini (1380–1446), and Vittorino da Feltre (1373 or 1378–1446/1447).

[5]Anthony Grafton and Lisa Jardine, *From Humanism to the Humanities: Education and the Liberal Arts in Fifteenth- and Sixteenth-Century Europe* (Cambridge, MA, 1986) xii–xiv and chap. 1 ("The School of Guarino: Ideals and Practice"). Chapter 1 first appeared in the journal *Past and Present* 96 (1982): 51–80. There the authors asked, in regard to the core of Guarino's teaching curriculum in rhetoric, "whether the accumulation of fragments which the student made his own could ever take shape as the whole from which they originated" (72). This dubbing of *Renaissance* rhetoric (rather than *medieval* rhetoric) as fragmentary is in itself a polemical assertion (cf. B. Vickers, *In Defence of Rhetoric* [Oxford, 1988] chaps. 4 and 5). In *Schooling* Grendler shares Vickers' view of medieval rhetoric (205, 221, etc.).

[6]See P. O. Kristeller and P. P. Wiener, eds., *Renaissance Essays from the Journal of the History of Ideas* (NY, 1968) 199–216. The same year saw, curiously, the publication of several papers that similarly stressed the connections between Renaissance humanism and eloquence: Q. Breen, *Christianity and Humanism: Studies in the History of Ideas* (Grand Rapids, 1968). Breen's studies go back, in fact, to the years 1947–1957. Eugenio Garin's *Der italienische Humanismus* (1947), translated by P. Munz as *Italian Humanism: Philosophy and Civic Life in the Renaissance* (NY, 1965) had also stressed humanist emphasis on "human and social communication and conversation . . . language as the exemplary manifestation of mankind . . . conversation . . . dialogue" (cf. 158–159). Since Gray's article, numerous studies have stressed the centrality of eloquence and rhetoric in and for Renaissance culture. Compare J. J. Murphy, ed., *Renaissance Eloquence: Studies in the Theory and Practice of Renaissance Rhetoric* (University of California Press, 1983) 126; J. Tinkler, "Erasmus' Conversation with Luther" *Archiv für Reformationsgeschichte* 82 (1991): 59; and B. Vickers, *In Defence.* For a conventional view of the beginning of Renaissance rhetoric, see Grendler, *Schooling* 207.

[7]Hence the need for such books as R. Morse, *Truth and Convention in the Middle Ages: Rhetoric, Representation and Reality* (Cambridge, 1991).

la cultura a Ferrara" by Eugenio Garin in his *Ritratti di Umanisti.*[8] Guarino's teaching lay at the basis of the programme of studies destined to become widely diffused throughout Europe; he contributed in a decisive manner toward the definition of 15th-century Italian *paideia*: not a professional, technical *paideia* such as characterized the medieval university, not a *paideia* concerned with elementary notions necessary for everyone, but a *paideia* educative of the whole man, capable of developing in the child a free rather than a conditional moral personality, open to all the possibilities of specialization but first of all wholly human, linked socially to every man and endowed with means suited to the acquisition of every instrument, yet in full possession of himself and aware of the dangers involved in becoming but an instrument. In the new conditions of the 15th century in Italy, lordship, unstable in both its origins and pretensions, lacking nobility of blood, drew on the new nobility of works and substance: Humanist, lettered culture identified itself with the chancellors and secretaries of the republics of the day: "è molto vicino al potere, collabora, consiglia, educa." Lettered activity was not merely propaganda; the muses in a sense governed insofar as they influenced, advised, and contributed toward the creation of a climate in which an unlettered prince was indeed a crowned ass. Letters elaborated doctrines, forms of living together, relations between states and within the state; they elaborated rules for the conduct of life according to reason, whether the art of war, politics, science, architecture, agriculture, or similar sciences and disciplines. The humanists were not "oziosi sognatori: erano vomini di stato." Guarino founded a tradition, a method that would influence fields far beyond letters and would develop "una filosofia non servile" that would question the very principles of authority and expose the multifaceted nature of humanity and its institutions.[9] Such was the orthodoxy before the attack of Jardine and Grafton.

For Jardine and Grafton, humanist culture was a culture of conformity and conformism, of service, of obedience, an ideal[10] that flourished within the privileged, male world of patricians and princes, an ideal deprived of the substance of reality. For the humanists, classical texts had become part of an elaborate symbolic ritual of obeisance and deference toward a vanished cultural world. The scholastic culture of the Middle Ages, on the other hand, was vigorous, independent, tied umbilically to the sinewy practical world of debate in all walks of intelligent life, geared to the marketplace, profoundly and productively linked to the lay world outside the universities. The commentary on the *Rhetorica ad Herennium* of the school of Guarino, for Jardine and Grafton, epitomized all that was otiose, antiquarian, and divorced from reality about high Renaissance culture. The rhetorical curriculum, indicated by the surviving *reportationes* from the school of Guarino, was long, tedious, and without value for contemporaries, except in the narrow sense of acquiring, laboriously, a command of classical Latin idiom.

---

[8]Eugenio Garin, *Ritratti di Umanisti* (Florence, 1967) 69ff.
[9]Garin, *Ritratti* 74–75, 84–85, 94–95.
[10]Grendler was not worried by the term: "Education always involves utopian dreaming..." (*Schooling* 234).

Such a view of Renaissance humanism in general and of Guarino, in particular, is not, indeed, unprecedented;[11] but it is freshly and forcefully stated, even if based on only a partial and initial acquaintance with Guarino's "long and tedious" lectures on the *Ad Herennium*.[12] It is also a view of Guarino that his contemporaries, for the most part, do not seem to have shared. Ludovico Carbone, for example,[13] in his funeral oration for Guarino, urged the muses to come running, clothes torn, cheeks lacerated, hair awry: "Iacet ecce Guarinus, alumnus vester, periit litterarum specimen . . . manibus date lilia plenis, pueri innuptaeque puellae: doctrinae probitatisque parentem perdidistis."[14] Poggio, too, said in a letter to Guarino[15] that he had heard someone say that of four "latine lingue principes . . . in Italia," the first was Leonardo Bruni and the second, Guarino da Verona. Pope Pius II, in his commentaries, described Guarino as "the teacher of almost all who have attained distinction in the humanities of our day"[16] and, in connection with Guarino's death, asserted that no *letterato* "of our time left behind him a greater reputation (*fama*) than he."[17] Beatus Rhenanus called Guarino "ille Veronensis latinae linguae restitutor."[18] Guarino's most celebrated pupil, the Hungarian Janus Pannonius (1434–1472), who attended Guarino's school in Ferrara at the age of 13 (1447) and became the most celebrated epigrammatist and poet of his age, expressed the same idea in one of his epigrams.[19] Another[20] compared Guarino to Phoebus, Faunus, Hammon, and Serapis, whereas yet another[21] claimed

---

[11]Compare, for example Voigt's view of the matter (*Risorgimento* vol. 2, 425): Although he deplored the fact that at the time Guarino's letters had not been collected and edited—"le lettere del Guarino che pure va annoverato fra i più illustri benefattori dell' umanità"—he yet declared Guarino to be "come scrittore" a man "di secondo ordine." Though of congenial and tranquil temperament— unlike most of his humanist peers—his innumerable discourses and orations "hanno un' impronta di compassata pedanteria," being "prolissi e tagliati tutti sullo stesso stampo," as, indeed, are his letters (Voigt, *Risorgimento* vol. 1, 549–550).

[12]Jardine and Grafton's examination of Guarino's *Ad Herennium* commentary and its sources does not seem to have been extensive. My own as yet unfinished analysis suggests that their statement that Guarino "sedulously pillaged" the commentary by the 12th-century (?) Alanus for his own lectures is wide of the mark. I return to this subject.

[13]Carbone (1435–1482) was a pupil of Guarino's.

[14]Garin, *Pros.* 382.

[15]*Ep.* 622, Sabbadini, *Epist.* vol. 2, 169, A.D. 1433.

[16]M. Baxandall, "Guarino, Pisanello and Manuel Chrysoloras," *Journal of the Warburg and Courtauld Institutes* 28 (1965): 199, n. 44.

[17]Rosmini, *Vita* vol. 2, 124.

[18]*Iani Pannonii Quinquecclesiensis episcopi Sylva Panegyrica ad Guarinum Veronensem, praeceptorem suum et eiusdem epigrammata* (Basel, 1518, pref.).

[19]No. 13, p. 60, and cf. no. 89, p. 114, of A. Barrett, ed. and trans., *Ianus Pannonius Epigrammata* (Gyomaendröd, 1985). I owe my knowledge of Pannonius to discussions with Dr. Imry Téglásy (Budapest), whose friendship while I was in Wolfenbüttel during April and May of 1991 is a pleasure to recall here. See also Marianne D. Birnbaum, *Janus Pannonius: Poet and Politician* (Zagreb, 1981), especially (on the epigrams) 42ff. I hope to make a fuller study shortly of the evidence for Guarino's teaching provided by Ianus' panegyric.

[20]Barrett, *Pannonius* no. 15.

[21]Barrett, *Pannonius* no. 37, p. 76.

Guarino equaled *Nestor Homericus* "linguae dulciloquo nectare."[22] Pannonius called Guarino the glory and *honos* of the Muses Calliope, Clio, and Polyhymnia and claimed he taught the art of poetry to Janus, even though he seems to have disapproved of some of the Hungarian's (frequently erotic) themes.[23] Pannonius praised above all, it seems, Guarino's (oral?) eloquence: In his epitaph for his master[24] he praised Guarino as one who "linguam diffudit in orbem. . . . Latiam; Latio reddidit Inachiam" (= 'the Greek tongue').[25]

The fulsome praises of Guarino's own pupils and adherents, not least Angelo Decembrio, whose *Politia Literaria* encapsulated Guarino and his admirers in their most intimate philological discussions,[26] are one thing, but the Ferrarese master was not without his opponents among the adherents of the younger generation of rhetors. To such teachers and scholars as the ambitious George of Trebizond, for example, Guarino seemed a somewhat outmoded figure.[27] Modern writers, nevertheless, seem on the whole persuaded of Guarino's merits: "La fama del Guarino come maestro ed educatore è ammessa universalmente e senza restrizione alcuna."[28] Guarino is labeled "the greatest teacher in a century of great teachers,"[29] "vomo di grande cultura e di molti legami,"[30] "primo fra i letterati Italiani del secolo xv,"[31] "il grande maestro del secolo,"[32] one "of the three

---

[22]Compare also Barrett, *Pannonius* no. 188, p. 160 and no. 185, p. 159, where Pannonius claims he would prefer Guarino's eloquence to all the beverages offered by the Gods. Pannonius' epigrams sometimes have a biting edge, such as, for example no. 9, p. 57, and no. 258, p. 190, which refer to Guarino's concern for fees, and no. 96, p. 118, which claims that Guarino *mollissime patrum* turned an absent-minded professor's blind eye to his sons' fornication with his maids and to the possibility of his students' flirtations with his daughters!

[23]Barrett, *Pannonius* no. 161 and no. 162, p. 148.

[24]Barrett, *Pannonius* no. 266, p. 192.

[25]For Janus' long hexametric Panegyric to Guarino, see footnote 18.

[26]Printed Basle, 1540 and 1562, but one should still, apparently, use the presentation (to Pius II) copy—MS Vat.lat.1794. See Werner L. Gundersheimer, *Ferrara: The Style of a Renaissance Despotism* (Princeton, 1973) 104ff; P. Viti, *Dizionario degli Biografici Italiani* vol. 33 (Rome, 1987) 483–488, where it is stated that the *Politia* provides a "fondamentale rappresentazione" of Guarino himself. See Sabbadini in *Enciclopedia Italiana* 12 (1949) 457; Paola Scarcia Piacentini, "Angelo Decembrio e la sua scrittura," *Scrittura e Civiltà* 4 (1980): 247–277. Christopher Celenza of Duke University's History Department has completed a master's dissertation at Albany on book I part 10 of the *Politia* (with commentary, translation, and, in part, critical edition). I owe this information to correspondence kindly initiated by Professor John Monfasani (Albany, NY).

[27]J. Monfasani, *George of Trebizond: A Biography and a Study of His Rhetoric and Logic* (Leiden, 1976) 11–12, 22, 29–32; *Collectanea Trapezuntiana: Texts, Documents and Bibliographies of George of Trebizond* (Binghamton, 1894) 364–411; and "In Praise of Ognibene and Blame of Guarino: Andronicus Contoblacas's Invective Against Niccolò Botano and the Citizens of Brescia," *Bibliothèque d'Humanisme et Renaissance* 52 (1990): 311ff.; Rabil, *Renaissance Humanism*, vol. 3, 189ff; Sabbadini, *Epist.* no. 707, vol. 2, 311–312; Sabbadini, *Vita* 67.

[28]Voigt, *Risorgimento* vol. 1, 550.

[29]Jardine and Grafton, *From Humanism* 1.

[30]Garin, *L'Educazione* 131.

[31]Rosmini, *Vita* vol. 1, i.

[32]Voigt, *Risorgimento* vol. 1, 550.

greatest educators of the humanist movement,"[33] "un grande educatore,"[34] "uno dei più insigni umanisti e docenti italiani della prima metà del secolo XV,"[35] "primo ristoratore fra gl' Italiani delle greche lettere dopo i barbari tempi, il qual vivrà sempre immortale e per l'opere sue, e per quelle de' suoi illustri discepoli."[36] Giulio Bertoni, in his *Guarino da Verona fra letterati e cortigiani a Ferrara 1429–1460*,[37] was very specific:

> "Guarino ('celebre umanista Veronese') sta però a centro di tutta quest" accolta di vomini studiosi e colti e la sua luminosa figura si riflette, poco o molto, su tutti o quasi tutti i personaggi che nelle pagine sequenti mi sono proposto di risvegliare talora da un lungo sonno, talora da un oblio completo. É giusto che da queste fioche ombre Guarino sia circondato e onorato! Amici, discepoli, conoscenti subirono invero—tutti o quasi tutti—in maggiore o minor grado, l'efficacia della sua personalità. Ond' egli può esser detto se non l'instauratore, l'animatore della coltura ferrarese, il propagatore più autorevole e fermente dell' umanesimo nella città degli Estensi, il fecondatore del terreno da cui germinarono Tito Vespasiano Strozzi, Matteo Maria Boiardo, Ercole Strozzi e Ludovico Ariosto.…[38]

Guarino has been especially associated with one of the two "most famous examples of schools that attempted [a] union of philosophy and rhetoric in the education of the Italian elite,"[39] and his teaching methods have become celebrated examples of humanist method, from his own day[40] to the present.[41] Even the close philological attention to Guarino's work that derives from the ever more refined tools and techniques of very recent historians of Renaissance humanism has preserved a creditable enough picture of the Veronese master. Fryde, modifying the extremes of praise noticed in the preceding, nevertheless judged Guarino "a very representative figure among a small elite of early humanists [who] had a deservedly high reputation as an efficient teacher of Latin and Greek, and as the author of useful aids to the study of classical languages and literature . . . a fairly typical humanist, though of exceptional technical competence."[42]

---

[33]See King, *Venetian Humanism* 18ff.

[34]C. Vasoli, ed., *Umanesimo e Rinascimento* (Palermo, 1969) 26.

[35]Sancipriano, *Guariniana* v.

[36]Rosmini, *Vita* vol. 2, 127, and on the disciples, Rosmini, *Vita* vol. 3.

[37]Giulio Bertoni, *Guarino da Verona fra letterati e cortigiani a Ferrara 1429–1460* (Geneva, 1921).

[38]Bertoni, *Guarino* v.

[39]Kohl in Rabil, *Renaissance Humanism* vol. 3, 15.

[40]R. R. Bolgar, *The Classical Heritage and Its Beneficiaries* (Cambridge, 1954) 431 (n. to 270); W. H. Woodward, *Studies in Education during the Age of the Renaissance* (Cambridge, 1906) 26–47 (especially 45–46).

[41]Bolgar, *Classical Heritage* 87–88, 269–270; Sabbadini, *Il Metodo*.

[42]Fryde, *Humanism* 55–57. Fryde points to "the old-fashioned background of his (Guarino's) scholarship" (70) and notes his "not . . . very profound knowledge of late Roman Republican history" (71). Hankins, "Plato's *Republic*" 173ff has similar reservations in regard to Guarino's understanding of Platonic philosophy. Compare also footnote 160 and Gundersheimer, *Ferrara* 105: Angelo Decembrio's portrait of Guarino, "whose particular forte is the elaboration of pedantic philological arguments."

Encouraged, then, by recent interest in Guarino's achievements, and by the apparent clash between 15th-century and 19th-/(earlier) 20th-century estimates of his worth, on the one hand, and, on the other, Jardine and Grafton's revelations in regard to the apparently conventional nature of his rhetorical teaching, a colleague[43] and I have undertaken an annotated edition of Guarino's lectures on the *Rhetorica ad Herennium*, with the particular goal of establishing the relationship between Guarino's rhetorical teaching and that of his contemporaries, predecessors, and successors.[44] The task is no mean one, given that Guarino left behind him no complete authorial version of his lectures: One can approach only with trepidation the task of giving to the learned world something that the author specifically withheld. Whatever text we decide upon, from the many versions that are available to us, we must continually remind ourselves that it is not what Guarino actually said in the course of any particular lecture series on the *Ad Herennium*. It is simply what some contemporaries chose to recall of what he said on the occasions that they heard him. We can but glimpse the master behind the façade of scribal ignorance and student inattention or inexperience that each particular manuscript or incunabulum recorded. That the attempt is a worthwhile one, however, we would defend from a number of points of view.

In the first place, the commentary of Guarino stands at the end of a great and continuous tradition of study of Latin eloquence, a tradition based on the survival of two fundamental almanacs of classical Roman eloquence, the *De inventione* of Cicero and the approximately contemporary but anonymous[45] *Rhetorica ad Herennium*. A census of surviving manuscripts of these two works and of commentaries on them, and of certain related works on which I have been engaged for many years, includes more than one thousand manuscripts. Guarino's lectures were the last great products, in this connection, of manuscript culture and, significantly, at the same time the first product of the new world of printing. Stripped of signs of authorship, his commentary initiated another major series of like works, from the era of printing, which has reached a kind of culmination with

---

[43]That colleague is Dr. Caterina Griffante, Librarian of the Instituto Veneto di Scienze, Lettere ed Arti, Venice, who very kindly helped me with the seminar mentioned in the acknowledgments. We are both grateful to the Gladys Krieble Delmas Foundation for a research award, and to the University of Sydney (Australia) for microfilm funds and a funded sabbatical period that enabled us to initiate the project over a period of two months in Venice in 1991. That only certain medieval corners of the Marciana Library were, in fact, open during this period, at times without either light, electric current, or (in February and March) heat, that the Correr Museum Library was on partial strike for much of the period, and that the amiable Querini-Stampalia library was under threat of total closure during the whole period did not prevent a very useful beginning to our labors.

[44]Compare the comparable labors, in regard to *dictamen*, being carried out by Giancarlo Alessio and others: Giancarlo Alessio, "Il *De componendis epistolis* di Niccolò Perotti e l'epistolografia umanistica," *Respublica Litterarum: Studies in the Classical Tradition* 11 (1988): 9–18; and Grendler, *Schooling* 233ff. The picture of medieval rhetoric in Grendler 205, 221 is stereotyped and inadequate.

[45]Professor Calboli is currently less persuaded of the Cornifician authorship of the *Ad Herennium* than he has been in the past. I propose to deal extensively with the history of the *Ad Herennium* in conjunction with forthcoming articles for the *CTC* series on the two "Ciceronian" juvenilia.

the commentaries of Professors Caplan and Calboli.[46] We thus have an unrivaled opportunity of viewing the changing cultural concerns of schoolmen across the centuries that lie between Victorinus and the mature age of Renaissance humanism. Few texts, apart from the Bible, certain works of Vergil and Aristotle, and, perhaps, such texts as Boethius *De consolatione philosophiae* offer such a vantage point. Few texts touch upon so wide a cultural ambit and are so relevant to modern concerns (communications, marketing). Guarino's teaching offers us an unrivaled opportunity to test generations of generalizations about the relationship between medieval and Renaissance cultural and didactic forms.

Second, Guarino himself lived in a tension-filled and vital transitional period. His lifetime was studded with plague, internecine warfare, and revolution and witnessed the passage from the world of the medieval university to that of modern lay culture. His immediate environment was a critical one, as the Venetian republic sought to ward off its opponents, maintain its liberty, and extend its dominion over the hinterland as far as the commune of Verona.[47] In his final formation Guarino was himself very much the servant and product of the new courtly humanism[48] that was becoming so marked a feature of the Italian political scene in the period that preceded the great clash between the national giants, 40 years after his death. Though he seems to have inherited through his wife's dowry some property at Valle Policella[49] (from time to time ravaged by raiders), for most of his life he was, in fact, dependent for his existence on that class of glamorous potentates whose brilliant careers marked the passage from the world of the medieval empire to that of the early modern nation-state: the Renaissance prince.[50] It is very tempting to ask what links existed in this troublous world between humanist studies, rhetorical teaching, and life in general for a man such as Guarino. Is Guarino to be compared with Lupus of Ferrières, from the Caro-

---

[46]Harry Caplan, ed. and trans., *[Cicero] Ad C. Herennium de ratione dicendi (Rhetorica ad Herennium)* (London, 1964); G. Calboli, intr., test. crit., comm., *Cornifici Rhetorica ad Herennium* (Bologna, 1969). See Murphy, *Renaissance Eloquence* 129ff, 142ff.

[47]For a rather old-fashioned but, in its way, gripping presentation of these events, see J. J. Norwich, *A History of Venice* (Penguin Books, 1983) chaps. 20–23.

[48]See John Larner, "Europe of the Courts," *Journal of Modern History* 55 (1983): 669–681. Guarino's own political predispositions have been usefully canvassed, as far at least as they relate to the celebrated Scipio-Caesar controversy that he waged with Poggio the Florentine, by Oppel, "Peace vs. Liberty," especially 244ff. Although earlier in his life Guarino seems to have been variously prepared to oppose Venetian rule in Verona and to profess exaggerated loyalty to the Venetian government (Sabbadini, *Epist.* vol. I, 32; vol. 3, 23; Stocchi [see footnote 65] 117), his position at Ferrara from 1429 onward meant a formal adherence to the supremacy of autocratic, if enlightened, princedoms. King, *Venetian Humanism* 51ff. comments effectively on the need for patronage in order to secure adequate survival, on the part of these early teachers, hence their professed loyalty to their lords and masters. See also Fryde, *Humanism* 26, 31; Baron, *Crisis* (see footnote 130); Hankins, "Plato's *Republic*" 153; and the comments of Diana Robin, *Filelfo in Milan: Writings 1451–1477* (Princeton, 1991) 3.

[49]Valpolicella: Grendler, *Schooling* 127.

[50]For the Renaissance prince in question see Gundersheimer, *Ferrara* (cf. footnote 26) especially 94ff.

lingian period, who certainly copied crucial classical rhetorical works[51] but seems to have written little of importance in an original way, other than letters? How far was Guarino's didactic-rhetorical humanism typical of the Veneto in contrast to the pattern of Florentine humanism—with which Guarino was intimately concerned—as exemplified by Bruni and Poggio? Why did his lectures on the mature rhetorical works of Cicero not survive,[52] and why did neither Poggio nor Bruni seem ever to have had to lecture on the Ciceronian rhetorical juvenilia? What contributions was Guarino able to make to the medieval handling of the juvenilia?

Third, it can be maintained that a routine didactic work such as the lectures on a text like the *Ad Herennium* reflects unconscious modes of thought in an age better than a unique or a highly original work. Consider, for example, the light the following extracts throw on contemporary male intellectuals' understanding of domestic and male/female relations:

Non nulli etiam dixerunt non esse artem (i.e. rhetoricam) hac de causa quia versaretur in omnibus hominibus barbaris et femellis quod in se artem habere viderentur ut conciliare in primis et blandiendo alicere eorum animos a quibus aliquid impetrandum foret . . . sed dicendum tamen esse artem quia ut dixit Cicero nec ars primum nec natura . . . invenit extremum. Nam licet femelle in se artem habere videantur tamen persepe cogitantes se persuadere in dissuasionem incidunt quod non facerent si artis precepta tenuissent.[53]

Philosophia. . . . distinguitur in tres partes—(primam) monosticam . . . secunda vocatur oeconomica quo pacto quis recte pulcherrimeque ancillas, servos, liberos, uxorem regit moderarique possit.[54]

Alii vero intelligant *negociis familiaribus*[55] id est proprie familie, sed dicit magister[56] quod hoc est puerile: non enim credendum est quod tantus homo[57] haberet suam familiam gubernare, quia ipse habebat vel habere poterat famulos infinitos eam gubernantes.

---

[51]*De inventione, Ad Herennium, De oratore*, for example. See C. H. Beeson, *Lupus of Ferrières as Scribe and Text Critic* (Cambridge, MA, 1930); and G. W. Regenos, trans., *The Letters of Lupus of Ferrières* (The Hague, 1966) (*ep.* 1, etc.).

[52]Compare Sabbadini's remark that the *De inventione* and the *Ad Herennium* "interessano molto il medio evo, ma interessano meno noi . . . le opere veramente fondamentali sono le altre tre—il *De oratore*, l'*Orator* e il *Brutus*" ("I codici delle opere rettoriche di Cicerone," *Rivista di filologia e d'istruzione classica* 16 (1887–1888) [97–120]: 98.

[53]Guarino, *Ad Herennium* lectures, Version III MS Fr fols. 7v–8r. (See later discussion.)

[54]Version II(a) MS P f.3r; compare the Version III gloss on *Ad Herennium* 1.7.11 *non apparata*: "nam nimis apparata sic displicet auditoribus, sic mulieres fucate et nimis apparate" MS Fr f.21v. Note also Guarino's equation of the trivial with "women's talk" (Oppel, "Peace vs. Liberty" 253).

[55]*Ad Herennium* 1.1.1. The quotation is from the early 14th-century Italian (Bolognese) glossator Bartolinus (cf. S. K. Wertis, "The Commentary of Bartolinus de Benincasa de Canulo on the *Rhetorica ad Herennium*," *Viator* 10 [1979]: 283–310). The text has been taken from MS Correr VI.669 (854) (on which see Wertis, "Commentary" 300).

[56]Bartolinus: the MS no doubt represents a *reportatio*.

[57]Cicero.

Such incidental remarks, so revealing of ingrained and inherited attitudes, seem to have, for us today, more resonance than they might otherwise have, because they are found in student *reportationes* of commonly repeated lectures on a relatively common textbook. Examples could be multiplied.

Finally, despite some remarks and quotations in the works of Sabbadini,[58] Wisén,[59] Quadlbauer,[60] Baxandall,[61] Jardine and Grafton,[62] the *reportationes* of Guarino's *Ad Herennium* lectures seem to have been little read by modern scholars. Can we be sure they contain so little of interest to our modern communications-oriented society?

GUARINO, TEACHER AND LECTURER

Guarino was born of undistinguished parents[63] at Verona in 1374[64] and completed notarial and grammatical studies at Verona, Padua, and Venice. In the latter town, in 1403, he met Manuel Chrysoloras, whom he accompanied back to Constantinople (1403–1408) to learn Greek. Between 1408 and 1414 he visited Bologna, the papal court, Verona, and Florence, where he taught Greek. Between 1414 and 1419 he enjoyed patrician patronage in Venice, in the house of Francesco Barbaro, where he conducted a private school for patrician sons. The reasons he did not remain in Venice, which undoubtedly possessed the most vibrant economy of the city-states that offered him employment, probably had as much to do with the nature of Venetian humanism as with the emergence of a new intellectual type in the period "non troppo legato alle istituzioni accademiche e dedito alla libera ricerca e allo spregiudicato dibattito culturale, secondo la vocazione e il costume che troviamo stabiliti già con il Petrarca."[65] The former excluded the exponents of professional humanism from the highest level of state administration and was slow to offer them

[58]Sabbadini, *Scuola* 62, 93–95, *Il Metodo* 43ff, *Storia e Critica di Testi Latini* ed. E. and M. Billanovich, 2nd ed. (Padua, 1971) 22.

[59]M. Wisén, *De scholiis rhetorices ad Herennium, codice Holmiensi traditis* (Stockholm, 1905). Compare the discussion in J. O. Ward, *"Artificiosa Eloquentia* in the Middle Ages" (Diss. Toronto, 1972) II no. 71, 511ff.

[60]F. Quadlbauer, *Die Antike Theorie der genera dicendi in Lateinischen Mittelalter* (Österr. Akad. der Wiss. Philos.-Hist. Klasse, Sitzungsberichte 241 Bd 2 Abh., Vienna, 1962) 208–218.

[61]Baxandall, "Guarino, Pisanello and Manuel Chrysoloras" 183–204; M. Baxandall, *Giotto and the Orators: Humanist Observers of Painting in Italy and the Discovery of Pictorial Composition 1350–1450* (Oxford, 1971) index s.v. "Guarino," but, on the Florence (Riccardiana) and Venice MSS of Guarino's *Ad Herennium* commentary, see n. 66 p. 41 (where the shelf mark of the Venice MS is incorrectly given).

[62]See footnote 5.

[63]Though see Rosmini, *Vita*, vol. 1, 1 "of noble family."

[64]Rosmini, *Vita*, vol. 1, 1 "1370."

[65]M. P. Stocchi, "Scuola e cultura umanistica fra due secoli," *Storia della Cultura Veneta dal primo quattrocento al concilio di Trento* I, ed. G. Arnaldi and M. P. Stocchi (Vicenza, 1980) 98. See too the remarks of King in Rabil, ed., *Renaissance Humanism* vol. 1, 209ff.

adequately remunerated state employment,[66] whereas the latter tended to divorce the humanist from the routine world of the schoolmaster:

> The Conversini, the Barzizzas, the Guarinos derive their prestige not from their status as *ludi magistri*, or from their status as private tutors; on the contrary, they derive it from the particular scientific physiognomy that they had acquired exploring fields and undertaking activities to which the didactic profession hardly obliged them, for example, the study of Greek, the renewal of the canon of *auctores*, the philological care of texts, all directions of research arising from the stabilized status of an intellectual freely dedicated to letters rather than to the tradition of the school.[67]

Guarino would thus have looked forward to more congenial forms of humanist employment than the private tutoring of patrician sons that his Venetian situation offered him:[68] "Una condotta a Verona, a Vicenza, a Treviso dava una sicurezza e un' indipendenza evidentemente preferibile per chi non trovasse del tutto rispondente alle sue mire o al suo carattere lo stato di precettore in casa di un patrizio Veneziano o le piccole funzioni burocratiche."[69]

There is, indeed, much evidence that late in his Venetian stay Guarino—though sensible of an obligation to his Venetian students[70]—was anxious to secure preferable employment from, among other places, perhaps, the Roman curia.[71] A peculiarly candid letter,[72] written during his Venetian sojourn, canvassed the possibility of taking a wife—a course many were apparently urging upon him. Sheltering in Padua from the plague toward the end of 1416, he wrote: "Uxores abhorreo nisi quas alii pascunt, ego vero utar." He claimed he was already married, but to *inopia*, which dogged him while he dreamed of learned girls, foreplay, carnal struggle, the sleep of exhaustion. This apparently unsettled period found a welcome conclusion with the offer of a superior contract from the commune of Verona in May 1420, "to lecture on rhetoric, letters and Cicero's speeches, and to teach other *facultates* which pertain to eloquence and whatever else was found pleasing and useful to hearers, and to embrace appropriate doctrine for all willing adolescents and elders of the city and district of Verona."[73] This contract

[66]Stocchi, "Scuola" 102.

[67]Stocchi, "Scuola" 99–100.

[68]Stocchi, "Scuola" 106–110.

[69]Stocchi, "Scuola" 109. There are some apt remarks on the social situation of humanists and teachers in Guarino's day in Griffiths et al., *The Humanism of Leonardo Bruni* 7ff.

[70]Sabbadini, *Epist.* vol. 3, 75–76: "Nam si a patriciis quibusdam adolescentibus impetrare potuerit ut eam stipulationem sibi remittant que ex fide cum eis de bonarum artium doctrina deque litteris grecis tradendis adhuc tenetur...."

[71]Sabbadini, *Epist.* vol. 1, 165–166, 174.

[72]Sabbadini, *Epist.* vol. 1, 125ff.

[73]Stocchi, "Scuola" 113; Sabbadini, *Vita* 21: "Rhetoricam legere, epistolas et orationes Tullianas et alias facultates que ad elloquentiam pertineant docere et alia que fuerint auditoribus placita et utilia omnibus adolescentibus et maioribus civitatis et districtus Verone istiumodi doctrinam capere volentibus."

seems to have freed Guarino from the need to provide elementary and grammatical levels of instruction (the latter including both grammatical theory and the reading of the poets and historians) and enabled him to concentrate on the highest level of humanist instruction of the day, parallel to or even more elevated than that provided by Barzizza at Padua, appropriate, indeed, to the level characteristic of contemporary universities.[74] Toward the end of the 1420s Guarino found himself away from Verona, fleeing the plague, and by a series of accidents he ended up a private tutor at Ferrara and, from 1431 onward, to no less a person than Leonello d'Este (son and designated successor of Marchese Niccolò III of Ferrara), who was at that time 24 years of age. Guarino acted as public orator and diplomat, gave private lessons in Greek, and later was appointed to the august position of "lettore ufficiale" in the refounded *studio* of Ferrara.[75] With some hitches, Guarino remained in this position until his death in 1460, and his youngest son Battista, professor of rhetoric at Bologna (1455–1457), succeeded him at Ferrara.

The priority Guarino gave to rhetoric is indicated in the solemn *prolusio* of October 18, 1447 for the inauguration of the second *quinquiennium* of the *studio* of Ferrara.[76] Seven subjects are covered and the number of lines devoted to them in the *prolusio* is indicated in parentheses: grammar (15), dialectic (11), rhetoric (42), philosophy (19), medicine (38), and jurisprudence (civil [37] and canon [18]). Citing Quintilian[77] and Cicero *De oratore*,[78] Guarino lauds his topic in phrases reminiscent of John of Salisbury:[79]

Rhetoric is third in our teaching (*apparatii*), magnificent, sumptuous and distinguished by its varied abundance of colours and ornaments. Who can adequately explain the dignity and elegance of apt, commodious and abundant systematic discourse? For, since immortal God formed man, a sharer in reason and divinity, and, as it were, a kind of God on earth, to know about everything on earth, in the sea, in and above the sky, what profit could have been derived from cognition of so many important things and otherwise, as it were, dead to each other (*alioquin intermortua*), unless man could have uttered (*proferret*) those things understood, the movements and counsels of minds communicated, and diffused them into the ears of others as things to be shared? . . . For the other arts and disciplines profess

---

[74]So Stocchi, "Scuola" 113, who comments that Guarino's inaugural address at Verona had the character of a University *prolusio*; and Garin, *L'Educazione* 134; A. J. Dunston, *Four Centres of Classical Learning in Renaissance Italy* (Sydney, 1972) 11; Grendler, *Schooling* part 2. For Janus Pannonius' version of Guarino's curriculum, see footnote 18.

[75]On the position of which see P. Burke, *Culture and Society in Renaissance Italy 1420–1540* (NY, 1972) 47; and Gundersheimer, *Ferrara* 100ff. See Griffiths et al., *The Humanism of Leonardo Bruni* 8: "So great was the honor in which the famous teacher Guarino Guarini of Verona was held . . . that he was given the task of delivering the inaugural lecture of the newly-founded University of Ferrara. It is hard to imagine that a fourteenth-century schoolteacher could have done that."

[76]Sabbadini, "Una prolusione."

[77]*Institutes of Oratory* 1.4.2,4,5; 12.1.2.

[78]1.20–21,30,33.

[79]*Metalogikon* 1.1,7.24, trans. D. D. McGarry (Kalamazoo, 1962) 9–11, 26–27, 67.

their own sure, definite and uniquely proposed subject-matter within their own boundaries, but rhetoric does not permit them to remain mute and tongueless; through its office it allows them to speak smoothly, threateningly, severely, urbanely, grandly, softly, gently, bitterly, copiously, and "to pour out the understandings of the mind through the interpreting tongue."[80]

Much the same picture can be deduced from the *Panegyric* of Janus Pannonius:

Non medicina tibi; scitu pulcherrima quanquam
Actu foeda tamen; Logicae aut placuere protervae
Iurgia: inexplicitos frustra nectentia gryphos:
Nec verbosarum discors concordia legum.
Rhetoras: et vateis, studio complecteris omni.
Quos si quis novit: nil ignorare probatur.[81]

Guarino was thus, at heart, a rhetor. The picture we form of him, therefore, is an appropriate one. It is a picture not of edgy[82] brilliance, but of a man forever in society, whether that of fellow scholars and patrician sympathizers; or that of his students, to whom he was, according to Rosmini,[83] father, friend, and teacher; or, in the city, that of his domestics, his numerous children,[84] the laborers constantly expanding the size of his house;[85] or, in the country, where alone he was happy (we are told[86]), with flocks of live-in friends and family members who thronged his walks like starlings or locusts.[87] Guarino worked outward from his teaching, and midst the social turbulence that accompanied his lifestyle, he managed to devote countless hours to the close work of editing, translating, and annotating classical texts, seasoned by *sermo* and the labor of composing often long letters to his friends and acquaintances. His rhetorical lectures seem to have been off-the-cuff efforts based on his ever accumulating close textual work and his growing ability to speak eloquently in Latin; if repeated frequently, however, they seem to have fallen into a routine in the course of which he selected from a stock of suitable illustrations and remarks that recurred from version to version in different combinations. Despite the confused and dangerous times in which he lived, Guarino survived to be 86 years old: "I have described him in 1460 [wrote Rosmini] as a very old father because, in spite of the immense and never

---

[80]Horace, *Ars poetica* 111.

[81]*Iani Pannonii Quinq. . . . Panegyrica* 8.

[82]In his early days, however, Guarino seems to have shared the common humanist penchant for polemic: See Hankins, "Plato's *Republic*" 150–151, and, for his polemic with Trebizond, footnote 27.

[83]Rosmini, *Vita* vol. 1, 87–88.

[84]By 1441 Guarino had 13 children (14 according to Avesani, *Verona* 36), evenly divided between the sexes and all living; he married in 1418 at the age of 44.

[85]Sabbadini, *Epist.* vol. 1, 575, 592; vol. 3, 434.

[86]Rosmini, *Vita* vol. 2, 15; Sabbadini, *Scuola* 155; and see Sabbadini, *Epist.* vol. 1, 574.

[87]Sabbadini, *Epist.* vol. 1, 592.

interrupted labour he devoted to research, teaching, the composition of such notable works, his private and public affairs, the regimen of his numerous family, he arrived happily at the extremest of old age, enjoying robust health almost without a single interruption"—a remarkable achievement and one that seems to fly in the face of the possibilities of the age. "Spicca in Guarino [wrote Sabbadini] un' indole nobilmente umana, con le sue debolezze, ma anche con una gran forza morale; un carattere dignitosamente equilibrato, coi suoi scatti, ma anche con una sicura padronanza di sè. E quella forza morale e quella padronanza di sè egli ripete e deriva dalle lettere del cui ufficio, che in lui diventa missione, ha un elevato e squisito concetto. Il letterato deve essere un vuomo superiore, esempio di virtù agli altri. . . ."[88]

THE COMMENTARY ON THE RHETORICA
AD HERENNIUM

Nineteen manuscripts[89] have come down to us with one or another version of Guarino's lectures on the *Ad Herennium*, together with seven incunable editions between 1481 and 1493.[90] Sabbadini (on the basis of three manuscripts and the incunabulum) seems to have thought in terms of but two main versions ("redazioni") of the lectures. The first he termed the Ambrosiana version, after MS A, completed (as we learn from its rubric) in 1445 by a scholar of Guarino's and then approved by the master. This version, he claimed, was also extant in MS Fr, written in the year 1481, although there are minor differences of text. The second version he termed the Marciana version, after MS *M, "nel fondo" like the Ambrosiana recension, "but it draws away in many places and in general is more extended (*estesa*) and complete."[91] This led Sabbadini to suppose that the Marciana version either derived from another course of lectures by Guarino or else was compiled by a more intelligent pupil from the same course of lectures that led another student to compile the Ambrosiana version. Guarino is rarely cited in the Marciana version, and of the two citations Sabbadini noted, the first was suppressed and the second

---

[88]Rosmini thought Guarino was, in fact, 90 years of age at death: Rosmini, *Vita*, vol. I, 33 n. 1. The quotation, from Sabbadini, is found in *Scuola* 162.

[89]With appropriate *sigla* (* = incomplete text), these are: A—Milan Ambrosiana A.36 inf; B—Basel Öffentliche Bibl. der Universität F.V.32; *D—Donaueschingen FFHofbibl. 12; Fc—Firenze Bibl.Naz.Centr. II.1.67; Fr—Firenze Riccardiana 681; G—Ghent Rijksunivbibl. 10; *L—Oxford Lincoln College (Bodleian Lib.) 84; *M—Venice Marciana XIII, 84 (3997); Ma—Clm (München, Staatsbibl.) 378; *Mb—Clm 28,137; O—Oxford Bodl. Lib. Canon.Misc 165; P—Perugia Bibl. Com. Aug. 730 (I.124); *Pa—Palermo Bibl.Com. 2 Qq D140; S—Shlägl Stiftsbibl. 124; Sg—St. Gall Stiftsbibl. 851; St—Stockholm Kungl.Bibl. Va 10; *V—Vatican lat. 5129; Va—Vatican lat. 5338; *Vb—Vatican lat. 11,441.

[90]The dates of these (with the printers in parentheses) are as follows: 1481 (B. de Tortis), 1483 (17 July, Forlivio/Britannicus; 31 Oct., B. de Tortis), 1485 (Zarotus), 1487 (Saracenus), 1489 (Scinzeler), 1493 (Presbyter/de Quarengiis).

[91]Compare Sabbadini, *Scuola* 93–97 and also 36, 59–65.

changed into a generalized *preceptor meus* in the Venetian incunabulum edition of 1481, 1483, and 1487, in all of which the text of the *Ad Herennium* was framed by the commentary of Guarino, reproduced textually from the Marciana redaction, but from a more correct MS of that redaction than the Venetian MS. My own initial survey of the MSS suggests that there are in fact more than two versions of the lectures, and these may be set out thus:

> *Version I(a)* is the text of the incunabulum, presented reasonably uniformly in the extant editions.[92] MS G (*a*.1486–1487) seems to have been taken from the incunabulum.

A text very similar to but fuller than that of the incunabulum is presented in three MSS or groups of MSS:

> *Version I(b)*: MSS B, O, *Mb, Ma, Sg, *Pa
>
> *Version I(c)*: MS V
>
> *Version I(d)*: MS *M

These versions, and the MSS within them, differ in terms of lacunae and readings and seem to be independent of each other.

> *Version II(a)* is represented by a curious MS, P (*a*.1466), with a new preface and a text similar to that of the incunabulum but much fuller than the MSS that are closest to that text (Versions I[b]–[d]), and different from them in places, with material similar to that found in Versions III and IV.
>
> *Version II(b)*: MS *Vb is a compilation drawn from a version of the incunabulum text of Guarino's commentary, and from medieval *Ad Herennium* commentaries.
>
> *Version II(c)*, the compilation by Jean Poulain recorded in MS St,[93] is another compendium from, apparently, the incunabulum version of Guarino's commentary, and from medieval *Ad Herennium* commentaries.
>
> *Version III* differs considerably from Versions I and II, even to the extent of contradicting them, and is somewhat clumsier than IV, with a new preface contradicting the prefaces of Versions I and IV (in that it does deal with the life of Cicero, which is one of the matters deliberately passed over in the other versions). MSS: A, S, Fr, *D, Va (*a*.1445, 1456, 1481).

---

[92] The Marciana copy (Marc. Inc. 437), however, is a faulty printing. Between gatherings *eVIv* and *fIr'*, the end of *Ad Herennium* book 2 and the beginning of book 3 are missing. In the following listing of MSS for each version I have added some sample dates for particular MSS to give an idea of the moments at which the particular *reportationes* were compiled. The editor of the incunabulum version is not known; presumably he was a *poligrafo* like the later Orazio Toscanella (1520–1579, Grendler, *Schooling* 222ff).

[93] See footnote 59.

Version IV: MSS Fc, *L (a. 1473). In some ways this is the best version of
the commentary, fuller and more intelligent, especially in regard to Greek
words. It is very different from the others (yet clearly a version of the Guarino
commentary), straightforward, but occasionally weaker than the others. This
version may, in fact, be ascribed to Guarino's son Battista,[94] though the extent
of his reliance upon his father's gloss is at present undetermined. The passage
that alerts us to the origin of the gloss is sufficiently interesting to be cited
in full, as it has been used (erroneously) to argue that Guarino suspected the
authorship of the *Ad Herennium*:[95]

(*Ad Herennium* 2.30.47[96]) dixit in numero plurali habito respectu ad partes et
divisionem, quia dividitur in tres partes sicut patet in ipso textu *que apud grecos
epilogi nominantur*, ab ἐπιλέγω que est 'colligo', et bene ac grate facit inserere
memoriam vocabuli Greci quoniam usque ad tempora Ciceronis non erant vocabula
rethorice Latina, sed ipse invenit, et hoc pacto linguam nostram collocupletavit.

Nam constant: ipsa est divisio et unamquamque partem inferius successive diffiniet;
vocatur etiam peroracio apud Latinos. In *quattuor locis*: nunc premonet studiosum
huius artis hanc conclusionem fieri posse in *quattuor locis*: post exordium, post
narrationem, post argumentationem, et in ipsa conclusione. Multi vero et doctissimi
viri, inter quos et prestans ille Ant(onius) Luscus et eloquentissimus vir Guarinus
Veronensis dixerunt hunc textum non esse Ciceronis, sed potius fuisse adiunctum
ab aliquibus volentibus hanc rem subtilius sed non utilius perscrutari, nam minime
quidem[97] videtur convenire quod debeamus uti conclusione in exordio, nam
exordium principium est orationis, conclusio vero est terminus. Itaque non bene
conveniunt. Preterea dicit in *quattuor locis* posse fieri quorum unus est in
conclusione, sed quod dissonantius audiri potest quam conclusionem in conclusione
fieri posse? Tamen posteaquam in omnibus textibus hec pars comperitur. Ea hoc
modo salvari potest per sententiam amantissimi genitoris mei Guarini Veronensis
qui intelligatur conclusionem fieri posse in hiis locis, i.e. sentenciam conclusionis.
Nam cum tres sint effectus in oratore, movere, docere, delectare,[98] movemus in
exordio, i.e. afferimus passionem aliquem animi in auditorem ut misericordiam,
indignationem, et hoc facimus in exordio, ubi captamus benivolentiam a persona
nostra. Aut commovemus odium in adversariorum inducendo ipsum in odium, i.e.,
contemptionem et invidias per regulas superius traditas, et in hoc convenit conclusio

---

[94]Voigt, *Risorgimento* vol. 2 (Florence, 1890) 383n.

[95]It is partly quoted in Sabbadini, *Storia* 22: Sabbadini uses the passage to show that Loschi and
the two Guarinos suspected the authorship of a passage in the *Ad Herennium*. Subsequent critics
have often mistaken this to mean that the three scholars suspected the authorship of the whole text.
See, for example, Woodward, *Vittorino da Feltre* 171, n. 1, a circumstance quite belied by Battista's
own automatic assumption—in the treatise Woodward translates—that the *Ad Herennium* was "the
Rhetoric of Cicero."

[96]MS Fc fols. 108v–109r.

[97]Om. Sabbadini.

[98]See J. Monfasani, "Lorenzo Valla and Rudolph Agricola," *Journal of the History of Philosophy*
28 (1990): 184–185.

cum ipso exordio quia etiam in conclusione movemus exercitando indignationem contra adversarium per amplificationem aut misericordiam erga nos per commiserationem. Est iste effectus in oratore ut doceat quidem quod potissimum sit in narracione ubi nos exponimus rem gestam et docemus auditorem quod gestum sit in quo quidem convenit etiam conclusio cum narracione quia et ipsa docet quando enumerat omnia predicta et sic summatim reducit in auditoris memoriam. Tertius est oratoris[99] effectus ut ipse delectet, quod potissimum fit in argumentacione cum audit locos suos ab oratore confirmari et adversariorum argumenta refelli in quo quidem et conclusio cum argumentacione ipsa convenit, nam in causa repetimus breviter argumenta materiamque; dum reservantur in auditoris memoria, ipse aliqua delectacione afficitur. Qui autem dicat conclusionem in conclusione posse fieri vel hoc pacto excusabitur conclusionem i.e. hunc effectum conclusionis posse fieri in conclusione, i.e. in illo loco ultimo orationis ubi est ipsa conclusio. Tamen videtur absurdum hunc textum esse hic ab Cicerone interpositum, nam cum fecerit triplicem conclusionis divisionem[100] sequebatur ut ipse primam partem exequeretur secundum ordinem et iste textus est interpositus, itaque non videtur esse Ciceronis.

Something of the medieval concern for the correctness of the authoritative text was blended here with a Renaissance sensitivity toward the interpolated, and above the whole debate loomed the authoritative figure of *Guarinus senior*. A comparable passage from another version of the gloss[101] suggests a *reportatio* of the lectures of the master himself:

In *quattuor locis*: quidam dubitant utrum iste testus sit Ciceronis et videtur quod non. Nam deviare videtur a proposito. Nihil est enim contrarius neque alenius[102] quam quod conclusio cadat in exordio ideo putatur hunc textum fuisse in antiqui codicis margine et librariorum inscitia depravatum atque Cice[f.76v]ronis testui insertum; sed tamen potest excusari non secundum verba sed secundum intellectum ut intelligamus aliquas proprietates constructionis[103] esse in exordio, ut commovere indignationem vel misericordiam quia in exordo sit quedam degustatio misericordie et indignationis ut dicit Quintilianus.[104] Sed in conclusione dicit liceat totos effundere effectus i.e. totum quod induci potest indignationis vel misericordie effundatur in conclusione. *In principio* i.e. in exordio. *Secundum*: post firmissimam argumentationem scilicet complexionem. *Enumeratio*: in conclusione per enumerationem non debet repeti nec exordium nec narratio ut ostendat illa non esse de essentia rei. Sola autem confirmatio et confutatio sunt de eius essentia ex quibus pendet tota victoria. Ut et in primo libro[105] dixit sciendum quod principium enumerationis debet summi a divisione. *Commonemus*: tangit utilitatem enumerationis breviter;

---

[99]Corrected from *auditoris*.

[100]MS: *divisionis*.

[101]Ms Fr (Version III) f.76r–v.

[102]= *alienus?*

[103]In the margin: *aliter conclusionis*.

[104]*Institutio Oratoria* 4.1.28.

[105]*Ad Herennium* 1.3.5 *et seqq.*

per hoc possumus intelligere quod debemus enumerare solum punctos principaliores
et non renovare totam orationem.[106]

There is space in the present chapter for only a few introductory remarks about
the versions of Guarino's commentary that are available to us. I intend by these
remarks to point to the interesting aspects of Guarino's commentary, aspects that
will, I hope, be addressed in future work on the subject. My remarks are designed
to raise rather than answer questions. I then indicate how Guarino's gloss differs
from the medieval *Ad Herennium* gloss, as far as can at the moment be determined.
Here I hope to introduce some important qualifications to the estimate of
Guarino's significance put forward by Jardine and Grafton, and discussed earlier.

Introductory Remarks

In this section I pose a series of questions. First, no antique, medieval, or
Renaissance commentary on the *Ad Herennium* or *De inventione* has survived
in as many manuscripts as has Guarino's commentary, even though little more
than a decade separated Guarino's death from the widespread adoption of the
technology of printing. What does this indicate?

Second, why did the popular medieval (12th-century) commentary (on the *De
inventione*) by Thierry of Chartres[107]—for example—survive in nine manuscripts,
yet in only one version?

Third, why is the incunabulum edition of Guarino's commentary on the *Ad
Herennium* never found (more or less exactly) in any manuscript (other than MS
G, copied after the incunabulum was printed and derived from it)? Who compiled
the incunabulum text, from what manuscript, and under what imperatives?

Fourth, why was there a tendency for what seem to be the later versions of
Guarino's commentary to make fewer references to the contemporary world of
the commentator and more extensive references to the classical world? The 14th-
century commentators made fairly frequent reference to their own day.[108] I provide
some illustrations from Guarino's commentary:

(i) From Version III:[109] "Et sunt hodie forte multi quorum hoc loco maxime re-
futandus est error. Nam dicunt fuisse ante artis inventionem multas oratores
et egregios viros sine arte in eloquentia valuisse." Only Version III makes reference
to "today."

---

[106]Here follows the passage cited in footnote 134.

[107]K. M. Fredborg, *The Latin Rhetorical Commentaries by Thierry of Chartres* (Toronto, 1988).

[108]For example, Bartolinus de Benincasa de Bononia (see Wertis, footnote 55) says at one point:
"Hodie nunc apud nos demonstrativi causa tractabatur sicut in Sancto Petro quando laudantur illi qui
conveniantur et interdum alibi secundum consuetudinem populorum; concionator est prolocutor, sicut
sunt sermocinatores, populus autem ibi auditor. . . ." Such references could easily be multiplied. See
S. M. Karaus (= Wertis), "Selections from the Commentary of Bartolinus de Benincasa de Canulo
on the *Rhetorica ad Herennium*," diss., Columbia University, 1970. Twelfth-century commentators,
too, frequently referred to contemporary canon-law cases and other aspects of their own day.

[109]MS Fr fol.7v.

(ii) From Version III:[110] "Exemplum: Dicunt aliqui in una civitate constituendum studium, quidam non; qui dicunt omnino faciendum, sic asserunt: 'non ego ex mercantia preciosas civitates vidi sed sapientia et litteris alias longe superare. Quantum autem interest inter pecuniam sive mercantiam et sapientiam sive scientiam tantum interest inter meam questionem et tuam.' " In the 1430s at Ferrara, Leonello d'Este had wanted to refound the studium and the subject must have been frequently discussed at court. Guarino himself, in fact, pronounced some four *prolusiones* in this connection during the 1440s.[111]

(iii) From Version III:[112] "Exemplum: Pompeius accepit uxorem, domum duxit, deinde ex ea liberos procreavit. Iste est mos. Sed esset contra morem si quis diceret filius pape constitutus est successor patris in pontificatu. Nam non est mos pontificis quod habeat filios et si hec sibi non succedat, sed eligitur per cardinales unus papa, alio deficiente. *Ut opinio* firma extimatio hominum de aliquo; exemplum: episcopus fecit magnas elymosinas et talis est opinio hominum. Homo unus libidinosus irrumpit domum virginis etc. *Ut natura*. Natura est vis quedam alicui ingenita. Exemplum: montes cecidisse est possibile et naturale, sed crevisse, non est verisimile. Sicut etiam si unus diceret nasci rosas mense ianuarii. Exemplum aliud non verisimile si quis diceret: ego navigavi Ferraria usque Hostiliam[113] servo flumine, cum sit certum quod flumina non revertuntur. . . ."[114]

Fifth, what relationship do the extant versions of Guarino's gloss bear to the different stages of his career? At present it seems possible only to make a few suggestions, based on selected passages.[115] For example:

---

[110]MS Fr f.16r, *Ad Herennium* 1.5.8 *ab rebus ipsis benivolum efficiemus . . . nostram causam laudando extollemus.*

[111]See footnote 115.

[112]MS Fr f.27r, *Ad Herennium* 1.9.16 *mos.*

[113]Ostiglia (Hostia, Hostilia) is a community situated upstream along the Po, halfway between Ferrara and Verona. Guarino must have passed through it many times on his travels.

[114]See also 4 and 5 in the following list. According to Grendler, *Schooling* 229ff, 233f, reference in lectures to daily life was characteristic of the more elementary, utilitarian teaching.

[115]Some lesser indications might include the dating of early versions by reference to the number of elementary or grammatical explanations included within them, the assignment of the versions with more references to the mature rhetorical works of Cicero to Guarino's later lecturing period (on the grounds that some of these works and the full text of others were known to the learned world only from 1422 onward), stronger links between some versions and the terminology and structure of the medieval *Ad Herennium* commentary, and possible links between the contents of some passages in the lectures and the *prolusiones* delivered in connection with the arts studium at Ferrara. In regard to this latter, compare, for instance, the preface to MS P with Müllner, "Acht inauguralreden" 296ff. The *prolusiones* that should be compared in detail with the rhetorical lectures, especially their prefaces, are four in number: the inauguration of the course of rhetorical lectures at Verona in 1419 (Sabbadini, *Scuola* 61ff., 66–67; Müllner, "Acht inauguralreden" 285–289, no. 1); the *praefatio in incohanda lectione rhetorices* that Müllner (it is his no. 5) dates to Ferrara 1436 but that Sabbadini dates to 1445; "la più solenne di tutte" (Sabbadini, no. 9 *Scuola* 67; Müllner, "Acht inauguralreden," no. 6, 298–302) delivered in 1442 to inaugurate, at the request of Leonello, the courses of the new *studio*

1. Passage 1 in the preceding list suggests that the version in question was nearer to the early days of Guarino's teaching, when he was attempting to establish, and profit from, the profession of *rhetor*.[116] Clearly, the commentator is acutely aware of those in his own day who argued (as indeed their kind did in antiquity[117]) that rhetoric was a natural attainment, not an art that could be usefully taught.

2. Passage 2 in the preceding list suggests that the version in question dates from Guarino's early lecturing at Ferrara.

3. Passage 3 suggests, likewise, early Ferrara days, perhaps, when Guarino was more sensible of his ties with Verona.

4. From Version III:[118] "Quam longe enim ceteros eloquentia excelluerit Latinos nec non Grecos minime latet. De numero autem librorum et de eius vita atque interitu, vitam nuper a Leonardo Aretino partim ex Plutarcho traductam, partim ex se et luculenter et copiose editam videre cupientibus percurrendam[119] relinquo." Only Version III provides this remark. Other versions suppress the details of Cicero's life as superfluous. This version explains them. *Nuper* in the letters of Guarino normally means "a few months ago" or at most "a year or two ago." Clearly the word cannot mean so short a time here, but it is still likely that Guarino's early lecturing had occasion to recall the impact upon contemporaries made by the *Cicero novus* of Leonardi Bruni. Bruni wrote his semitranslation, semicomposed life of Cicero "in the course of the year 1415–1416."[120] Guarino, as we have seen, had developed a close relationship with Bruni and Florence in the period just prior to this year, and his own translations from Plutarch seem to date from a similar period. Is it not likely, therefore, that his early lectures on the *Ad Herennium* would refer students to Bruni's "recent" "life"? Subsequently, perhaps, as Guarino moved further from the later medieval pattern of glossing, it may have seemed less relevant to bring up these details in his prefatory remarks: The humanists knew when to clutter their practical

---

generale at Ferrara *coram marchione Leonello et aliis famosis viris*; and, finally, the eulogy of the seven liberal arts delivered in 1447 to inaugurate the second *quinquiennium* of the Ferrara *studio* (Sabbadini's no. 10 and as discussed in his "Una prolusione").

[116]In an act of 1420, Guarino is described as *prudens vir magister Guarinus de Guarinis retoricus*: His first vocation seems to have been that of *rhetor*. See footnote 73 and the first *prolusione* noted at the end of footnote 115.

[117]See Quintilian's *Institutes of Oratory* 2.17.4.

[118]MS Fr f.1r. The subject of the sentence is Cicero.

[119]MS A: *parturendam*.

[120]Griffiths et al., *The Humanism of Leonardo Bruni* 36; see also 177ff. Fryde, "Humanism and Western Historiography" (1983, originally *English Historical Review* 95 [1980]: 533–552) 37, 39. Fryde, "Humanism" 51, citing the wrong folio of MS Fr, ascribes the remark to "Battista Guarini . . . in his lectures on Cicero delivered at Ferrara in the second half of the fifteenth century"; but this seems a mistake for MS Fc. See also H. Baron, ed., *Leonardo Bruni Aretino, Humanistisch-Philosophische Schriften, mit einer Chronologie seiner Werke und Briefe* (Leipzig, 1928) 113–114, 163–164, 184–190.

instruction with antiquarian detail, and when not to. Later medieval glossators were not so particular and, because they had few other professional involvements with Cicero, often adverted to his life in their prefaces. For how long after the year 1415/1416 would Bruni's *Cicero novus* have seemed *nuper*?

5. *memoria rerum*:[121] "ut velle recordari gesta aliquorum principum." All other versions used another example here. "Considerate fortunam quod ille imperator nuperrime in tanto erat honore et hodie sit in tanto periculo. Miseremini imperatoris eius qui cum esset nuper in tanto honore nunc fit in periculo capitis.[122] These two passages seem to point unmistakably to a controversial moment in Guarino's life connected with the meteoric fall from Venetian favor of the Count of Carmagnola, whose victory against the Milanese at Maclodio (near Brescia) had stimulated Guarino to write an *oratiuncula* in praise of the count, "la più famosa se non la più bella delle orazioni del grande umanista."[123] Guarino mentioned his *oratiuncula* (which *nuper edidi*) in a letter to his pupil Baptista Bevilacqua (Verona, 1428)[124] who had, as *equitum praefectus*, written a very full account of the battle on XV Kal febr. 1428 "litteratissimo et ornatissimo viro Guarino Veronensi," which Sabbadini[125] thinks Guarino must have known when he wrote his own panegyric for Carmagnola. Bevilacqua announced his reason for writing thus: "Quo, cum bellum hoc Mediolanense tuarum acumine litterarum fortasse scripturus ad id praelii perveneris, uti omni ex parte gestum fuerit, tuo facundissimo eloquio et oratione suavi abs te describi quam rectissime queat; eaque si non oratoris sed indocti hominis ingenio ad te delata sunt, te non indignabere quaeso sed potius, utcumque fuerint, tamquam ab amantissimo tuique observantissimo voluptatis loco sumito." Guarino replied by praising Bevilacqua's combination of learning, literature, and military activity, on the model of Caesar, Alexander the Great, and Brutus, in the past.[126] He went on to thank Bevilacqua for providing the material (*argumentum . . . materiam . . . calcar*) with which writers might prepare a history of the events in question but hinted that he lacked the "ingenii vires . . . dicendi auctoritas . . . et licentia vel securitas" to do the job himself—he would certainly have welcomed, otherwise, the opportunity to exercise his wits and permit the glory of his age to live on to later ages: "Sed

---

[121]*Ad Herennium* 1.2.3, from Version III, MS Fr f.7r.

[122]MS Fr f.57r, on *Ad Herennium* 2.14.22 *per conquestionem*.

[123]R. Sabbadini, "Guarino Veronese e la polemica sul Carmagnola," *Nuovo Archivio Veneto* 11, part 2 (1896): 327–361, offprint available in the Querini-Stampalia library, Venice, paginated 1–37. Quotation is from p. 3. Also see Sabbadini, *Epist.* vol. 3, 227–228. According to Sabbadini ("la polemica," 5) Guarino intended his panegyric to be read as a letter and sent it to Carmagnola with this in mind. Certainly many of the protagonists in the storm of controversy that the panegyric aroused between 1430 and 1438 took it to be a letter. A. Battistella, however, in his *Il Conte di Carmagnola* (Genoa, 1889) 511, says it was read publicly to Carmagnola at Verona after the peace of April 1428. On Carmagnola and the battle of Maclodio, see Norwich, *Venice* chap. 22.

[124]Sabbadini, *Epist.* vol. 1, 618.

[125]"la polemica" 5.

[126]See Sabbadini, *Epist.* vol. 1, 616–618 and "la polemica" 24–26.

ardua res est et humeris digna non imbecillibus memorabile bellum, magnas et
validas opibus civitates, ingentes apparatus oratione aequare,[127] copias navales
et terrestres duces inclitos, milites insignes pro dignitate consequi." You must
not forget, either (he went on), that history must be the "light of truth" "nihil ad
gratiam, nihil ad simultatem explicatura,"[128] seeking neither to flatter nor to
offend: You yourself may be the judge of how safely that can be effected. When
it comes to explaining the causes of war, morality, loyalty, probity, and virtue
have to be covered up, and their contraries placed in the limelight: "Quae cum
olim odiosa, hodie capitalia sunt." It is easy to see why would-be historians have
preferred to speak of the dead rather than of the living. After a paragraph of
chitchat about Giovanni Corvini, who had not returned a manuscript loaned to
him, Guarino slipped in a reference to the "oratiunculam quam cuperem multas
ob causas tuas ad manus obrepsisse, si forte Brixiam hoc tempore tibi visere
contigisset."

This exchange tells much about Guarino's attitude toward princely and gov-
ernmental authority. A panegyric he would write and did, but not history, despite
attention to history in his teaching curriculum and his own long essay on historiographical method.[129] How different the environment in Florence![130] Guarino's
panegyric spells his attitude out further. Praise for Venice and its leaders culmi-
nates in an impassioned appeal to Carmagnola to temper his military vigor by
allocating "studiis literarum et Musis otium tranquillitatemve . . . unum enim
illud tibi . . . praeque omnibus unum praedicam et repetens iterum iterumque
monebo ut literatis hominibus et scriptoribus faveas. Nulla enim tam ingens, tam
clara, tam admirabilis res gesta est quam non vetustas obscuret et oblivio nisi
literarum splendor et scribentium lumen accenderit." Born and bred in the land
of northern Italian tyrants and the autocratic republic of Venice, Guarino knew
which side his bread was buttered on: He would not be tempted into the writing
of history that would lead him into either falsehood or prison. Thus he eschewed
the larger tasks that rhetors of his day commonly set themselves, remaining a
letter writer, speaker, scholar, and teacher. The impact that Carmagnola's triumph
and subsequent disgrace had on Guarino, however, entitles us to consider that
he was alluding to the count's affairs in those passages from his rhetorical lectures
with which the present section of this chapter began.

---

[127]Compare Jerome, *Vita S. Hilarionis ut facta dictis exaequantur* (*PL* 23.29B).

[128]Cicero, *De oratore* 2.36 and 62; Guarino uses the same quotation, *ep.* 796, Sabbadini, *Epist.*
vol. 2, 461, lines 103–105.

[129]Compare footnote 3 and Woodward, *Vittorino da Feltre* 169. See now Mariangela Regoliosi
"Riflessioni umanistiche sullo scrivere storia" *Rinascimento* ser. 2 vol. 31 (1991): 3–37.

[130]Those rare glimpses we do have into Guarino's teaching at Venice suggest that even then his
princely and patrician loyalties counted for more than any commitment to free speech or unprincely
chronicling. See Hans Baron, *The Crisis of the Early Italian Renaissance: Civic Humanism and
Republican Liberty in an Age of Classicism and Tyranny* (Princeton, 1966) 68, but note Hankins as
cited in footnote 48.

6. Some versions of Guarino's commentary explain, in regard to the opening of the *Ad Herennium*, that a friend should not excuse himself from the obligation to help another friend because of preoccupation with his personal affairs. Yet it is exactly this excuse that Guarino himself offers when he finally got around to writing a reply (Ferrara, III *idus Apriles* 1437) to the letter of Isotta Nogarola: "Et accusante ira cur pro Guarino causam, Isota, non dicis et vel silentium meliorem in partem non acceptas? 'Guarinus, diceres, domesticis extraneis, suis alienis, familiaribus litterariis negotiis immortalibus irretitus aut nullum aut perrarum scribendi tempus nactus est, cum interim docens legens audiens, tantam familiam tot liberos regat, alat, educet erudiat, parvum quieti, minus somno, minimum cibo tempus impertiat. . . .' "[131] Either there was one rule for male rhetorical students on the spot and another for would-be female humanists living at a distance, or the lectures that made reference to the illegitimacy of the excuse of preccupation were delivered at a different time from that in which the preceding letter was written![132]

In fact, of course, one cannot usefully date the versions of Guarino's lectures because they do not represent any specific, authorized, and authorial production: Guarino never sat down, as Quintilian did almost 1400 years earlier, to prepare a fully worked up version of his ideas about rhetoric and education, to replace the notes that "boni iuvenes, sed nimium amantes mei . . . temerario editionis honore vulgaverant."[133] We have today, in fact, only such idea of Guarino's rhetorical lectures as his students were able to catch in their notes, "quantum notando consequi potuerant."[134] Guarino, we may presume, like the orator that he was,[135] delivered his lectures without the benefit of any formal written text.

---

[131]Sabbadini, *Epist.* vol. 2, 307. See also Voigt, *Risorgimento* vol. 1, 439; Rosmini, *Vita* vol. 2, 67ff; Sabbadini, *Vita* 122–123; and M. L. King and A. Rabil Jr., *Her Immaculate Hand: Selected Works by and about the Women of Humanist Quattrocento Italy* (Binghamton, 1983) 17.

[132]Compare also *ep.* 544, 1429, Sabbadini, *Epist.* vol. 2, 52: "Aures mihi eiulatibus et clamoribus puellorum occalluerunt, quae res litterarum fastidium ingenerarunt, ut neque scribendi neque legendi commoditas aut voluptas adsit. Libenter inservirem postulatis tuis super Servio, sed tot occupationes tot animi et corporis perplexiones implicant, ut litteras non secus ac scorpiones aspectem."

[133]Quintilian, *Institutes of Oratory* 1 pr. 7. George of Trebizond, however, was preparing his own original textbook of Ciceronian rhetoric about the time of Guarino's transfer from Verona to Ferrara (Sabbadini, *Scuola* 61; Monfasani, *George of Trebizond* 26; and see footnote 27).

[134]Quintilian, *Institutes of Oratory.* Compare such phrases taken from one version of Guarino's lectures as "*ut renovetur (Ad Herennium* 2.30.47) scilicet memoria. Unde putat Guarinus Veronensis deficere hic unum verbum scilicet memoria propter negligentiam librariorum (MS Fr f.76). . . . Rethoricorum feliciter recollecte (cf. Sabbadini, *Il Metodo* 43ff and *Scuola* 90ff) expliciunt sub Guarino quas recollectas transcripsit presbiter (********) de piscia pro se suisque successoribus anno domini MCCCCLXXXI (MS Fr f.149r) . . . *hac copia (Ad Herennium* 3.19.32) hac abundantia quam dico est credendum quod Cicero manu monstravit ut ait Guarinus (MS Fr f.100r). . . . sed eius expositio talis est secundum Guarinum" (MS Fr f.100v). Some of the omissions from version to version are curious. Only one student noted the reference to the *Moretum* (see footnote 160) that got caught up in the incunabulum edition; yet where the incunabulum says only "nam si fuisset materia altiloqua dixisset (Virgilius) 'Aureus occasum iam sol spectabat equosque pronum iter urgebat facili

Observations on the Relationship Between Guarino's Gloss and the Gloss of his Medieval Predecessors[136]

The first observation concerns length. In the first two chapters of the *Rhetorica ad Herennium* (for example), there are some 360 words. In the commentary by Thierry of Chartres,[137] written in the 12th century, the gloss on these two chapters occupies some 480 words. In the gloss by Bartolinus of Bologna,[138] written in the first decades of the 14th century, the gloss on these two chapters has come to occupy some 14,850 words. The incunabulum version of Guarino's gloss has reduced the commentary on these two chapters to some 4,072 words. Guarino has thus stripped away the greater part of the late medieval commentary but presents nevertheless a much richer gloss than that prepared for his contemporaries by, for example, Thierry of Chartres. The kinds of things that Guarino would have found in his medieval sources and has abandoned or much reduced include: citations from medieval authors, the *Rhetoric* of Aristotle, Isidore, St. Ambrose, and Victorinus on the *De inventione*; almost all the general definitions, etymologies, references to other arts such as dialectic and grammar; items of general education without particular reference to rhetoric;[139] references to the world of the commentator; and all the paraphrases, elementary explanations, and alternative words furnished in the Middle Ages to assist the student in grasping the original. It would have been possible, it seems to me, for Guarino to have completed a course based on the incunabulum version of his lectures in approximately 80 to 100 hour-long lectures, about the time I was allocated in 1968 (my first full-time year of teaching) to cover

---

transmittere cursum'," the MSS of Version I(b) tell us that the passage was written by Petrarch, as, indeed, it was (*Bucolicum carmen*, Ecl.2, vv.1–2, ed. Francesco Petrarca; *Il Bucolicum carmen e i suoi commenti inediti*, ed. Antonio Avena, 2 vols. (Padua, 1906 repr. 1969) vol. 1, 100). Further, we learn that a Florentine professor of rhetoric—Bartolomeo Fonzio—had expressed interest in the same passage (Francesco Petrarca *Epistolae de rebus familiaribus et variae*, ed. G. Fracassetti, 3 vols. [Florence, 1859–1863] vol. 3, 438–439; both references I owe to the kindness of Prof. and Mrs. Dennis Dutschke, of the University of California Padua office). Does this mean we should place Version I(b) closer in time to Guarino's Venice and Verona days, when his contacts with Florence were close? If so, how do we account for the relatively late date of some of the MSS within this group, and the fact that it is close to the text of the incunabulum?

[135]Compare the following passage from Guarino's rhetorical lectures: "*oratorem* (*Ad Herennium* 1.2.2) i.e. illum dicit qui exercet artem, non autem rhetorem nam sine memoria rhetor esse potest, quia libros habet unde doceri potest."

[136]The remarks that follow are based on some years of research into the medieval commentaries, but, in particular, on a close comparison made in Venice, earlier in 1991, between the early chapters of the incunabulum version of Guarino's commentary and the Correr museum manuscript of Bartolinus' commentary (on which see Wertis, as cited in footnote 55).

[137]See the edition by K. M. Fredborg cited in footnote 107.

[138]See Wertis, cited in footnote 55.

[139]For example, Bartolinus' comment on *memoria*, *Ad Herennium* 1.2.3: "Triplex est celula: una est per quam invenimus et ymaginativam informamus et ista vocatur fantastica; alia est per quam discernimus et rationem informamus et hec vocatur discretiva; tertia est per quam recordimur et hec vocatur memorativa."

a general introduction to the history of the Middle Ages. I do not think Guarino can be accused of inordinate or tedious length.

Second, Guarino has abandoned all the special terminology that was introduced into the art of rhetoric after the middle of the 12th century and that reached a high point of development in the commentary by Bartolinus.[140] Bartolinus' preface contains a number of terms Guarino will not use: *prologus ante rem* (much earlier in origin), *causa comparativa/positiva, exordium per positivum/absolutum, per comparativum (equaliter/inequaliter), causa agens (mediata/ immediata/ immediatior), materialis, formalis (forma tractatus/ forma tractandi [diffinitivus/ divisivus/ probativus/ improbativus/ exemplorum positivus]), formalis (operatoris/ operis)*.[141] Guarino has also adjusted much medieval vocabulary (for example, replacing *assentiabiliter* by *verisimiliter*).

Third and most significant, Guarino has abandoned the late medieval method known as *divisio*, used at every point to render the text of Cicero amenable to systematic commentation. Medieval commentators used *divisio* first as a rigorous method for structuring their gloss. I typify their procedure with the following summary:[142] First, the art is considered both extrinsically[143] and intrinsically.[144] Next, *descendum est ad libri divisionem*, that is, the *forma tractatus*, under which the *Ad Herennium* is divided into two parts, *prohemium* (*Ad Herennium* 1.1) and *tractatum* (*Ad Herennium* 1.2 et seqq.). The *prohemium* is subjected to a *divisio quo ad sententiam: secundum doctrinam/artem rhetoricae* (based on the doctrine announced later, at *Ad Herennium* 1.4.6 *ut adtentos, ut dociles, ut benivolos auditores habere possimus*), and to a *divisio quo ad textum, secundum sententiam/scienciam sive sensum litere seu testum* (= *demonstratio 'lemmatum'*: I *'benivolum'* = <u>*Etsi negotiis*</u>, II *'attentus'* = <u>*spe questus*</u>, III *'docilis'* = <u>*nunc ne nimium*</u>). I *'benivolum'* is then subdivided into (a) *a se*, (b) *ab auditore* (<u>*quod te non*</u>), (c) *a re* (<u>*non enim parum in se*</u>), and (d) *a persona adversariorum* (<u>*quas ob res*</u>). (a) *A se* is then divided into (i) *a se: ostendit se velle servire Gaio Herennio*, (ii) *causa quia vult servire* (<u>*ne aut tua*</u>), and (iii) *finem imponit* (<u>*et eo*</u>

---

[140]A very good example here is the development of the doctrine of *insinuatio* (*Ad Herennium* 1.6.9 *et seqq.*) on which I have prepared an extensive but unpublished paper. Compare also the terms coined or used—for example—in the passage cited in footnote 139 and my general remarks in O. Weijers, ed., *Méthodes et instruments du travail intellectuel au moyen âge. Études sur le vocabulaire* (Brepols, 1990) 20ff, 33, 60.

[141]See the text of Bartolinus' preface printed in Wertis, footnote 55.

[142]Illustrated with actual citations from the Bartolinus group of commentaries. In these quotations from the original Latin the lemmata (i.e., passages from the *Ad Herennium* presented in the text of the commentary to orient the reader) are given in underlined italics.

[143]"Eo quod extra et antequam ad doctrinam agendi perveniatur oportet ista praescire—scientia introductoria."

[144]"Intrinsecus vero artem appellant ipsam artem eloquendi." The distinction goes back to Victorinus and beyond. See J. O. Ward, "The Date of the Commentary on Cicero's *De inventione* by Thierry of Chartres (ca. 1095–1160?) and the Cornifician Attack on the Liberal Arts," *Viator* 3 (1972): 219–273.

124   WARD

studiosus). The commentary proper begins on (i) *a se: ostendit* and so forth, with
a literal gloss on the lemma *Etsi negotiis . . . conscriberemus*: *et hic est quod
littera dicit: possumus* (a) *construere literam ordine grammaticali* (i.e., according
to sense order) *aut* (b) *ordinare literam secundum ordinem libri* (i.e., according
to the order of words on the page of the original text of Cicero). This is known
as the literal gloss, the *glossa ad literam*, and consists of a strict paraphrase. It
is followed by a *glossa in extenso*, an *est notandum/aliqua sunt notanda* gloss,
in which larger comments are offered on various points arising out of the text.
These notes are often numbered and are frequently extensive, offering many
general observations far from the field of rhetoric narrowly considered.

   The second use made of *divisio* in the medieval commentary was to structure
every observation or comment on the text of "Cicero." Thus, on *alicuius certe
persone laudem vel vituperationem* (*Ad Herennium* 1.2.2) we find a division
into *communis* (*vituperatio/laudatio*), *ut 'vir[i] fortes in communi'* and *singularis
aut specialis* (*abusio [a bono] corporis, ut iste est pulcher vel deformis [tur-
pis]/ abusio [a bono] fortune ut iste est dives vel pauper/ abusio [a bono] anime
ut iste est sapiens vel insipiens*). On *imitatio . . . impellimur* (*Ad Herennium* 1.2.3)
we find a complicated *divisio*, into *impulsus* (divided into *realis sive exterior
quo impellimur corpore* and *intellectualis sive interior quo in mente movemur
et de isto inpulsu loquitur hic* [this latter being divided into *irrationalis* and
rationalis with the latter dividing into *inperfecte* and *perfecte* (the latter being
defined thus: *alio modo movetur intelligenter [aliter perfecte] quando diu cogi-
taverunt et recte intelligunt et isti sunt qui moventur ratione dilligenti i.e. perfecta
et de hac loquitur hic et ideo subiungit dilligenti*)]). This entire approach Guarino
has abandoned, perhaps as a pioneer.[145]

   For the medieval commentator a rigorous conformity had to exist between the
word and reality as the latter was thought to exist. Compare the explanation of the
lemma *dilligenti* in the passage just cited, or the following on *Ad Herennium* 1.1.1
si te unum illud monuerimus. Bartolinus says that when a superior teaches an
inferior, words such as *informare, docere, instruere* should be employed. When,
however, an inferior teaches a superior (*si potestas* [*=podestà*] *petteret conscilium
ab uno notario vel scolari*), words such as *monere* and *recolligere in memoria*
should be used. He then goes on to note the use of *monuerimus* at the beginning of

---

[145]A brief examination I have made of some commentaries contemporary with Guarino's lecturing,
located nowadays in the Biblioteca Communale Bergamo, suggests that Guarino was a pioneer in
his abandonment of medieval methods. Certainly Gasparino Barzizza (1360–1430), whom Kohl
(Rabil, *Renaissance Humanism* vol. 3, 15) calls "perhaps the last product of the older scholastic
education, with its set medieval authors and emphasis on Christian morality," seemed to have been
content for the most part to use older commentaries in his lecturing on the *Ad Herennium*. Grendler
(*Schooling* 208) incorrectly supposes that Barzizza commented on the *Ad Herennium*. In fact, only
a small part of his gloss is extant, dealing with style, and there is no evidence that he commented
further on the text himself. See G. W. Pigman III, "Barzizza's Studies of Cicero," *Rinascimento* 21
(1981): 128ff.

the *Ad Herennium* and explains *quia mayorem se docebat, scilicet Gayum, qui erat magnus philosophus et potens.* Another version of the Bartolinus gloss has *quia iste Gaius erat maximus Romanorum quasi et Tullius erat minimus quia erat depressa pars sua, scilicet Pompei(i) pro Cesare* (!!) In this last case the medieval commentator has deduced reality from the word: Who was Gaius Herennius? We do not know (even today), but he must have been an important person, because Cicero has used the word *monuerimus* instead of *docuerimus*! We do not find here research into the classical texts, but a theoretical deduction from them based on a presupposed conformity between word and reality. Such an approach has entirely disappeared from the commentary of Guarino in its final form.

Fourth, one no longer finds in the commentary of Guarino the references to the world of the *dictator* or *arrengatore* that occur not infrequently in the commentary by Bartolinus,[146] whom we know to have taught *dictamen* as well as advanced classical rhetorical theory. Although Guarino's letters were early included in dictaminal collections[147] he did not, it seems, perform the role of instructor in the vocational trades of *dictamen* and the *ars concionandi*, except insofar as he trained students to deliver set piece panegyrical or diplomatic orations for ceremonial occasions. Guarino taught the acquisition of *cortesia* and *civiltà f*or a narrow but cultivated group[148] who stood guard over classical culture and its influence and was in large part responsible for the fact that "by the second quarter of the fifteenth century, it was received opinion throughout Italy that the public correspondence of republics, princedoms, and the papacy should be managed by classically trained men of letters, and that a humanistic education was an essential part of an ambassador's training. It is significant that the 15th-century word for ambassador was *orator*."[149]

What do all these changes to the medieval pattern of commentation signify? The beginnings of a new world.[150] For Guarino, the text of Cicero should not be taken in such a way as to reflect a comprehensive and ordered system of universal

---

[146]Consider, for example, on *sine adsiduitate* (*Ad Herennium* 1.1.1), "assiduitas in rethorica est duplex: cum lite, sine lite, et sic est epistolaris sermo de quo non tractatur principaliter in hoc libro; si cum lite et sic est exercicium ratiocinandi sive concionandi sive sermocinandi et de hoc traditur in hoc libro."

[147]See footnote 3 and Sabbadini, *Epist.* vol. 2, 687ff; vol. 3, 516ff.

[148]See *ep.* 452 (1428), Sabbadini, *Epist.* vol. 1, 633, "vale igitur . . . et a litterario nostro coetu."

[149]Not, note, *arrengator* or *concionator*! Compare Griffiths et al., *Humanism of Leonardo Bruni* 7.

[150]See Griffiths et al., *Humanism of Leonardo Bruni* 7:

The chief gift of humanism to philosophy was to change by little and little its method and orientation in the study of philosophical authors. Gone was the scholastic method of cutting the *sententiae* of classical authorities out of context and weaving them into a closed and logically articulated system, most of whose premises had already been dictated by religious dogmata. Instead, the humanist approach to the text was philological and historical and consequently open-ended and non-systematic. It encouraged a spirit of free enquiry, which in the end led to a much more precise knowledge of the philosopher and his philosophy in its cultural and historical environment.

knowledge and disciplined reality. Behind the text, the *involucrum*, the *integumentum*,[151] the *visible* cover, we should not be seeking an invisible and systematic world. For Guarino, the classical text ought to speak for itself, as a privileged channel to a world worthy of imitation, a world that existed in time, a world that we can illustrate with other similar texts. It is for this reason that we find in the incunabulum of Guarino an almost exclusive preference for the works of Virgil,[152] Horace, Ovid, Terence, Cicero himself, Quintilian, Plutarch. We find ourselves, with this preference for the works of Virgil and Cicero, returned once more to the ambiance of the late antique commentator Grillius,[153] whose commentary relies heavily upon these two sources of illustration. Guarino has an awareness of the conditions of life and thought in the classical world that we do not find in Bartolinus, no matter how keen the medieval commentator was to retail the details of Cicero's life. For this reason, Guarino can correct the disdain the author of the *Ad Herennium* seems to express for the concept of *gloria*,[154] with a reference to the speech *Pro Archia*;[155] he can correct the disdain expressed toward the Greeks in the same chapter of the *Ad Herennium*, with a reference to Demosthenes, Theophrastus, and Aristotle, among others. He accepts that an orator must sometimes lie and illustrates with a reference to the *Pro Milone*; he does not accept the disdain for the sophists that we find in the medieval rhetors. On *imitatio*[156] he[157] can write: "Quos imitemur? Idoneos viros, non illos vetustissimos ut fuit Cato Censorinus quia adhuc non venerat in illum succum eloquentiae lacteum, neque modernos . . . sed Ciceronem ipsum qui idoneos est ac omnium ornatissimus, unde sit Quintilianus . . ."[158]

But for all his empathy with the classical Roman world, Guarino was a practical man, dedicated to producing students who could, in the courtly world of his day, work within its idiom. He recognized the sometimes obscured difference between *loqui* 'to speak as in unstructured daily life conversation' and *dicere* 'to practice the art of systematic discourse': "Loquimur a natura . . . sed dicimus solum ex arte," he says in the early pages of his *Ad Herennium* commentary. For him, the *Rhetorica ad Herennium* was an exact guide to the *ars dicendi* as Cicero practiced it, a guide worth all the attention he could devote to it, a guide both practical and authoritative, in that it derived (as he and his contemporaries believed) from

---

[151]See E. Jeauneau, *Lectio Philosophorum: recherches sur l'École de Chartres* (Amsterdam, 1973) 125ff.

[152]But see footnote 160!

[153]See Jos. Martin, *Grillius, Ein Beitrag zur Geschichte der Rhetorik* (Studien zur Gesch. und Kultur des Altertums, 14, Hft 2-3, Paderborn, 1927).

[154]*Ad Herennium* 1.1.1.

[155]11.26.

[156]*Ad Herennium* 1.2.3.

[157]That is, he or whoever took the *reportatio*.

[158]*Inst. Or.* 10.1.105ff; 10.2.25. See, too, Gundersheimer, *Ferrara* 110–111.

the pen of the great practitioner himself. For this reason, it seems, he eschewed the composition of his own independent rhetoric.[159]

We should not, finally, conclude that Guarino presents an absolute revolution in his commentary on the *Ad Herennium*. He derived much from his medieval predecessors and carried over many of their emphases. We may, indeed, speak properly only of a tendency in Guarino's commentary toward a reflection of the new humanist world of his day.[160] In this regard, it might be appropriate to draw an analogy with a work of art, located today not far from where Guarino would have stayed during his time in Venice, Biagio d'Antonio da Firenze's *Oltraggio di Lucrezia e suo suicidio*,[161] which portrays a scene palpably classical but presented in the manner of a dormition of the Virgin: The appearance is classical, but there remains still the savor of the medieval. The temple is truly Renaissance, the clothes are Renaissance, the countryside is Renaissance; but we do not find here an exact recreation of a classical monument, a classical episode.

It is thus, perhaps, with the commentary on the pseudo-Ciceronian *Rhetorica ad Herennium* by Guarino da Verona.

ACKNOWLEDGMENTS

A preliminary version of much of the present chapter was presented (in Italian) as a seminar for the Dipartimento di Antichità e Tradizione Classica, Università degli Studi di Venezia, in January 1991. For the opportunity of presenting this seminar and for so much help before, during, and afterward, I am greatly indebted to the kindness and friendship of Giancarlo Alessio of the University of Venice.

---

[159]See footnote 133.

[160]See, for example, Guarino's comments on *exercitatio* (*Ad Herennium* 1.2.3) "ut Virgilius fecit, nam priusquam publice aliquid scriberet scripsit *Moretum* et multa alia ut promptitudinem compararet" (incunabulum text). MS P f.10r has "nam priusquam publice aliquid scriberet prius se ipsum exercuit in quibusdam levibus materiis quia scripsit et alia pleraque opera ut promptior fieret." Among the MSS, only M makes mention of the *Moretum* of the incunabulum. Such reasoning about classical conditions and practices, of course, in the light of modern philological findings, which have labeled the *Moretum* a dubious or suppositious work of Virgil, represents an excess of zeal! See also footnote 42.

[161]Venice, Ca'd'Oro, Galleria Giorgio Franchetti.

Chapter 8

Ludovico Carbone on the
Nature of Rhetoric

Jean Dietz Moss
Catholic University of America

A product of the Jesuit College at Rome, probably during the second decade after its inception in 1551, Ludovico Carbone never became a Jesuit priest. He did, however, disseminate in a number of books much of what he learned there. The breadth of scholarship in his writings is remarkable even for a time when "Renaissance men" were not rare. His scope embraced logic, philosophy, theology, sacred oratory, and rhetoric. Among his published rhetorical works are a guide in the form of tables (*Tabulae*) to the popular text of Cipriano Soarez, seven books on various aspects of rhetoric, and two books on sacred oratory.[1] All of his books were published in the last two decades of the *quinquecento*, and the rhetoric texts in the space of 5 years.

We know little about the life of Carbone other than that he was a professor at the University of Perugia and died in 1597. What is obvious from reading his books is that he was a master pedagogue, familiar with scholastic doctrine, humanistic learning, and the doctrinal distinctions held and debated by the foremost scholars of his day. Above all he was clear and systematic in his exposition, and we do not find it hard to believe him when he voices the scholarly com-

---

[1] A list of Carbone's writings is provided in my essay "The Rhetoric Course at the Collegio Romano," *Rhetorica* 4 (1986): 146 n. 21. Marc Fumaroli treats Carbone's contribution to Jesuit rhetoric in his *L'Age de l'Eloquence* (Geneva: Librairie Droz, 1980) 182–186.

monplace that his pupils and admirers urged him to rush these volumes into print for the benefit of a larger public.[2]

Concerning the topic of this chapter, the nature of rhetoric, Carbone is particularly illuminating. Although the genre he chose for his examination of the subject, the disputation, is not especially congenial to the modern *mentalité*, it is a form eminently suited for probing every nuance of a subject and examining prevailing opinion on all of its elements. The *Tabulae* and *De arte dicendi* (*On the Art of Speaking*), bound with it, were probably intended for the instruction of students in the upper levels of the gymnasium, our junior college level.

Carbone's topic has not receded from scholarly concern today; it has been extensively explored in a recent book and an article by Brian Vickers. In these he has sought to return consideration to the essential meaning of the "art" of rhetoric and away from the current tendency to equate rhetoric with communication in general or the "tropics" of rhetoric in particular.[3] Carbone's disputations, surprisingly, treat some of the same tendencies to globalize or to contract rhetoric too narrowly.

The Renaissance pedagogue attempts primarily to find a satisfactory definition of rhetoric and to unfold its import in the first book of *De arte dicendi, libri duo* (1589).[4] The work was meant to be a companion piece to Carbone's guide to the rhetoric of the eminent Jesuit, Cipriano Soarez, *Tabulae rhetoricae Cypriani Soarii* (1589). *De arte dicendi* comprises two separate series of disputations; the second moves beyond the definition of rhetoric to examine the five canons or

---

[2]The comments are in the introduction to his *Tabulae rhetoricae Cypriani Soarii* (1589). He credits his professors at the Collegio Romano for inspiring these rhetorical works and notes that their lectures and exercises were of great benefit to him. Because much of the content of Carbone's logic texts has been demonstrated conclusively to have been drawn from the lectures at the Collegio of Paulus Vallius, we may conjecture that his rhetorical works also record the substance of Jesuit courses. The story of the Vallius discovery is told in the article just cited. I have also discussed Carbone's writings in "Aristotle's Four Causes: Forgotten *Topos* of Renaissance Rhetoric," *Rhetoric Society Quarterly* 17 (1987): 71–88; "Rhetorical Invention in the Italian Renaissance," *Visions of Rhetoric* (Arlington, TX: Rhetoric Society of America, 1987) 30–41; and in *Novelties in the Heavens: Rhetoric and Science in the Copernican Controversy* (Chicago: University of Chicago Press, 1993).

[3]Brian Vickers, "The Atrophy of Modern Rhetoric, Vico to DeMan," *Rhetorica* 6 (1988): 21–56; and *In Defence of Rhetoric* (Oxford: Oxford University Press, 1989). I have discussed the import of the nature of rhetoric for teachers of composition in "Is There a Place for Classical Rhetoric in the Teaching of Composition Today," *Kinneavy Festschrift* (forthcoming). The general tendencies are best exemplified in Sonia K. Foss, *Rhetorical Criticism: Exploration & Practice* (Prospect Heights, Ill.: Waveland Press, 1989) 4, where Foss says rhetoric is simply an "old term" for communication. The particularizing tendency has been in existence ever since rhetoric was equated with style. But it is most evident today in DeMan and in Hayden White's work on "The Tropics of History: The Deep Structure of the New Science," in Giambattista Vico's *Science of Humanity*, ed. Giorgio Tagliacozzo and Donald P. Verene (Baltimore: Johns Hopkins University Press, 1973) 65–85.

[4]The text of the work was published with the *Tabulae rhetoricae Cipriano Soarii* (Venice, 1589). I am grateful to my colleague Professor William A. Wallace for making his translation of much of this work available to me.

parts of the discipline. Although it, too, throws light on ancient and contemporary conceptions of the art, it might strain the patience of the reader to describe its exhaustive analysis. That will have to await a longer study of Carbone.

In the preface Carbone explains that his original intention was to write a comprehensive treatment of the art of speaking in one book, but he soon realized this would be impossible. Instead, he now sees he must write at least 10 more! The present work on the nature and parts of rhetoric, he views as the first and third parts of the new plan. In a second book he expects to treat the causes of eloquence, including a discussion of what is given by nature, what art can accomplish, and what can be effected by exercise and imitation. Another work would describe the offices of the orator, three would treat invention, one would deal with disposition, and three more would examine style. The last of these would discuss memory and pronunciation. Of this projected program, at least six of the works are extant.[5] Carbone does not mention his works on sacred oratory; these must have developed out of further recognition of the enormity of his mission.

ON THE NATURE OF RHETORIC AND ELOQUENCE

Given James J. Murphy's interest in reviving medieval and Renaissance texts, it seems appropriate for his Festschrift to provide a close look at what is seldom noted, the survival of the medieval genre of the disputation in Renaissance rhetorical literature. In order to convey the unfamiliar character of the disputation as an instrument of inquiry, an abbreviated paraphrase follows. Since the 96 folios treat the subject in exhaustive detail, only parts of the preliminary principles and the conclusions adduced in each of the disputations that prepare the way for the final definition are aired here. At the end of this epitome, some comments on the import of the work and of Carbone's contribution to rhetoric are offered.

Carbone's choice of the method of disputation for his analysis reveals his respect for the dialectical approach as a pedagogical tool. Despite the scholastic character of the format, the author manages to invigorate the subject through his own talent for illuminative exposition. The approach serves him well in examining the range of opinion on every aspect of the art of rhetoric without losing the focus of the discussion. In keeping with the traditions of disputation, he first exposes the issues, then surveys what authorities have asserted, lays out fundamental points that should be considered in developing opinions, next sees what conclusions can be hazarded, and, finally, entertains and refutes opposing positions.

---

[5]These texts are probably derived from the Jesuit courses at the Collegio, which seem to have been quite extensive. The text for the elementary course was *De arte rhetoric* (1568) by Cipriano Soarez. S. J. Carbone's students would have had the *Tabulae* to help them assimilate that work. He probably modeled his own teaching on the courses at the Roman College; thus, the disputations of *De arte dicendi*, which take up issues about the art, were probably intended for students who had completed the first course.

The first book of *De arte dicendi*, entitled "On the Nature of Rhetoric and Eloquence," is divided into ten disputations whose subtitles reveal the distinctions important to the author:

1. On the terms rhetoric and rhetor
2. On definitions of rhetoric
3. Is rhetoric a virtue?
4. Is rhetoric a wisdom, a science, or prudence?
5. Is rhetoric an art?
6. In what genus of art should rhetoric be located?
7. On the matter of rhetoric
8. On the end of rhetoric; is it to persuade?
9. What are the efficient causes of rhetoric, and how many?
10. Aristotle's definition of rhetoric is explained and defended, and a new description of eloquence is offered.

1. On the Terms Rhetoric and Rhetor

Carbone begins by citing the advice of various authorities—Socrates, Aristotle, Lucian, Cicero, and Epictetus among them—who tell us that "a knowledge of terms is the beginning of erudition." With that he looks at the etymology, usage, and genus assigned to the terms rhetoric and rhetor in order to arrive at those that are most apt and precise.

Rhetoric has been said to have had its origin in the Greek word meaning to flow, he says, citing Cicero's *Orator*: "but the art of speaking (*ars dicendi*) has nothing in common with the flow of a river." And Cicero has pointed out that since those who cultivated the art were eloquent the art came to be called eloquence. It would have been better, says Carbone, to have called the originators inventors and the art an inventive art. That is the reason Cicero and others entitled their books *On Invention* (1ᵛ–2ʳ). Some commentators have even called the art poetics, since poetics also is a faculty of speaking and a type of eloquence.

In order to clarify the terms to be defined, Carbone offers the following fundaments (*fundamenta*) or bases. The first of these is sought in etymology, which as a good Renaissance humanist he grounds in the Greek, the ancient Greek verb *rhion*, meaning to speak or elocute, and the terms associated with it, *rhetorike, rhetor, dictor*. The Greeks considered the act of speaking to be a "power" or "faculty" or "art" (2ᵛ). He notes in passing that Cicero renders *rhetorike* as *eloquens*, which leads to the second basis on the meaning of the term orator.

Citing Cicero, Livy, Virgil, and Plutarch, he says *orare* frequently means to speak or argue a case (*causa*). Orator sometimes denotes a legate; at other times, someone who is eloquent or who argues cases. The first is foreign to our usage; the second, closer to our needs; and the third is best suited.

In the third fundament Carbone mentions the variety of ways the art is characterized—as "an artifice, a prudence, a faculty, a virtue, a doctrine, a supply of things to say, an oratorical power" (5ᵛ). Likewise, rhetor gained different meanings—claimer, declaimer, patron. The Greeks speak of one who employs the art as a sophist and an ecclesiast, which in Latin becomes a conferencer (*concionator*, a preacher).

Taking into consideration the fundaments, Carbone next offers the positions (*positiones*) that can be accepted. He begins with the most elementary, that the proper manner of approaching the subject is with a definition of terms. The second, fourth, and fifth of these are worth quoting in detail:

> Second position: Properly, rhetoric does not mean the same thing as eloquence, or an oratorical faculty, or power, nor is a rhetor the same as an eloquent person or an orator, although the terms are frequently used interchangeably. For rhetoric means the art that teaches precepts, eloquence, an abundance in speech, and the latter is not necessarily found in those who know precepts. (7ᵛ)

> Fourth position: An eloquent person (*eloquens*) is not necessarily clear and methodical (*disertus*). The latter is able to speak to average people precisely and clearly, using the common opinions of men; the former is able to speak wonderfully and magnificently. (8ʳ)

> Fifth position: For convenience this faculty is called rhetoric by the Greeks and eloquence or oratorical power by the Latins. The terms are taken from the principal function of the art, and so are well adapted to it. (8ᵛ)

Carbone cites Aristotle and, most often, Cicero for these positions, particularly *De oratore*.

In the remainder of this disputation Carbone resolves difficulties posed by other names attributed to the discipline.

2. On Definitions of Rhetoric

Having sharpened the terms, Carbone moves on to the construction of a proper definition. Following Aristotle's advice that "we know a thing perfectly only when we understand its causes," he tries to get at the nature of rhetoric by looking first at its causes (9ʳ).

He notes that much has been said about causes by philosophers; but since rhetoric is the subject here, he prefers to turn primarily to Cicero's discussion. The Roman has explained that a cause is the power (*vis*) that creates effects. Carbone cites Cicero's *De natura Deorum* for discussion of the four kinds of causes: material, formal, end or final, and agent or efficient. According to this mode of thinking, the material cause is that from which something is made. In rhetoric it is the syllables that are expressed in the form of sentences and orations. The form is that through which a thing is what it is. Rhetoric is the form by which a rhetor is distinguished. End, called *telos* by the Greeks, is the "extremity, highest, and ultimate," as Cicero translates the term. It is "that to which all things look or that for which something is done," as to persuade is the end of rhetoric. The agent or efficient cause is that by which something exists, or by which something is produced. The result is called its effect, an event (*eventum*), by Cicero (10ʳ). The first two causes, material and formal, are said to be internal causes, while the last, end and agent, are said to be external. One of these, usually the formal cause, is expressed in a definition. Although this conception of causes is seldom taught today, the description of the process of defining that follows is similar to that found in many modern texts.

For the essentials of definition, Carbone again turns to Cicero, who says that a definition explains what a thing is, making clear what is obscure or unraveling something that is complex. Of the two kinds, nominal and real, he prefers the latter, observing that it should detail the genus and differentia of the thing defined. He draws from three different texts of Cicero to posit the remaining requirements for framing a good definition: "first, that it clearly explain the thing defined and make it manifest; second, that it apply only to the thing defined and be convertible with it, not transferable to something else; third, that nothing be lacking or be in excess" (10ᵛ).

Applying these elementary principles to the term rhetoric, he searches for some common ground among definitions offered by a number of authorities. Although the patience of modern readers may be taxed by Carbone's practice of prefacing each step of his inquiry with appeals to authority, most Renaissance readers would be comforted by doxographical certification for doctrinal assumptions.

Carbone draws upon Quintilian for part of the historical survey of opinion, sometimes acidly offering his own evaluations of these.

Aristo, the disciple of Critolas the Peripatetic, describes rhetoric as "the science of seeing and of acting on civil questions through speech of popular persuasion." Carbone argues against this view, maintaining that to say that rhetoric is a science is erroneous, as he promises to demonstrate later. He notes that Aristotle says that "those who treat it as a science destroy the nature of rhetoric." The gloss cites *Rhetoric* I.iv. Aristo errs also in contracting the faculty of rhetoric to civil questions, since Aristotle says it treats all things. Another error is Aristo's notion that a rhetor speaks only to a popular audience, for learned audiences can be addressed by rhetors as well (11ᵛ).

Theodorus Gadareus, described as "a servile kind of Sophist," the teacher of Tiberius Caesar and a senator, says that rhetoric is "an inventive, judicative, and enunciative art that can be persuasive in any civil matter." Carbone calls this a poor definition in that it defines through parts and functions, contracts the field too narrowly, and is unclear (11ᵛ).

Dionysius of Halicarnassus, "a famous professor under Caesar Augustus," says that it is "an artificial power of persuading reasonably in civil and political matters, whose end is to speak well." Carbone replies, "This author does not speak well himself, for he confuses its task with its end, and designates its matter improperly" (12ᵛ). Hermogenes erred as well in approving this definition.

And Quintilian himself does not escape Carbone's razor, for he too defines rhetoric as an art or doctrine of speaking well. The definition is too broad, for "philosophers, physicians, and other artisans can speak well on the matters of their disciplines. . . ." (13ʳ). Nor does Trapezuntius get it right. He says, "Rhetoric is a civil science whereby we say, with the assent of our hearers, what should be done in civil matters" (13ʳ).

Carbone next offers Aristotle's definition: "Rhetoric is the power of seeing (not of finding, as some translate it) what can be persuasive in any subject matter; or the power whereby one perceives what is probable [*probabile*] in any subject matter" (13ᵛ). He does not examine the definition at this point but does so in the final disputation. He does note, however, that both Quintilian and Hermogenes disagreed with it.

The final definition is one posed by the famous professor of rhetoric who taught at the Universities of Pisa and Padua, Franciscus Robertellus:[6] "Eloquence is a faculty, natural in the soul, of expressing those things conceived in the mind, aided by art and practice, accommodated to subject matter and to the form of speech, either continuous or interpolated and either adapted to the popular way of speaking or remote from it, but useful for teaching and persuading" (14ᵛ–15ʳ). Comments Carbone, succinctly, "Much can be criticized in this definition; I will say briefly that it is long-winded and obscure."

Before he discusses what can be garnered from the foregoing analysis, he provides various definitions of orator. M. Cato Cisorius, described as the first Roman to write about the art of speaking, defines an orator as "a good man expert in speaking." Quintilian, he says, defends this definition tenaciously and expands it. But the best authority, he says, is Cicero, who described the orator in a number of texts, which Carbone lists.

At this point Carbone pauses to summarize the positions that can now be accepted as propadeutic for a proper understanding of the nature of rhetoric. The first two again acknowledge the primacy in disputation of arriving at a definition and repeat the requirements for a definition. The third holds that if rhetoric is to be defined as eloquence, its "causes, parts and tasks" must be described as well (15ʳ⁻ᵛ).

The fourth position erected upon those previous tenders the congruous and qualified definition that rhetoric is "the art of speaking well."

In this definition one has included the genus and the differentia. The genus is art; the differentia, speaking well. And if we mean by art that which teaches the precepts

---

[6]Robertellus is listed on the rotulus of the University of Pisa as teaching Greek and Latin there in 1548; on the rotulus of the University of Padua he is recorded as teaching both rhetoric and humanities, Greek and Latin, for the years 1550 through 1557, and perhaps to 1564 when the position is listed as vacant. (The record omits some years.) He was succeeded by Ioannes Faseolus in 1568 and Antonius Riccobonus in 1571.

for speaking well, it describes rhetoric as an art and separates it from activity and from eloquence. If we mean by "art of speaking well" a power and a faculty, then it includes eloquence, and the ability to orate. . . . (16^{r-v})

This last position furnishes the nucleus for his own definition, presented in the tenth disputation. The fifth position summarizes what is required in a definition's differentia—an exposition of "the nature of this art, treating its principles, its causes, its parts, and its tasks. . . ." (16^v).

These preliminaries seem to us tedious scholastic make-work, but for Carbone they are essential in establishing rhetoric's status as an art and a discipline, which then entails a nature and a province worthy of examination. Such a foundation would provide his pupils with arguments to defend rhetoric against the opinions of those philosophers who consider rhetoric to be merely a knack, the result of natural gifts, or the practice of artifice and sophistry. He aims also to lay the groundwork for the moral and aesthetic responsibility implied by his definition. If it is an art, it contains principles and permits choices.

3. Is Rhetoric a Virtue?

Having disposed of the prerequisites, Carbone begins to unfold the implications of the proposed definition. He explains that in developing a working definition one has to look at the broadest limits of its subject, the genus. Many opinions have been expressed about the genus of rhetoric; one that is frequently suggested is that rhetoric is a virtue.

Carbone mentions that in deciding whether rhetoric is a virtue one must consider what constitutes a virtue. In his view, virtue means a power by which a man lives morally (*honeste*), but this he will explicate later. First one must take up the major authorities on the question.

The first opinion is one Quintilian notes, the view that rhetoric has been considered a vice, a bad habit (*kakotexnian*), or a bad art (*mataiotexnian*) or a "superfluous imitation of an art"; Carbone dismisses these, promising to argue against them in his disputation considering the usefulness of the art (18^{r-v}).

The second is the opinion of the Stoics and of Quintilian, who follows them, holding that rhetoric is a virtue.

Third is the view that it is neither a virtue nor a vice but a habit, what the Greeks call *adiaphorous* or indifferent, and that all cognitive skills are of this type. Both Cicero and Aristotle thought this, and it is "the common opinion of all teachers of speech." (Peter Ramus is also cited in the gloss.) Carbone says he will teach this as the "true opinion" (18^v).

In the section that follows he again posits some fundaments. First, he observes that a virtue can be conceived of as ordered to knowledge, and under that aspect it is a science, or it can be ordered to action, as in the case of temperance and fortitude. Someone who possesses the first kind is said to be knowledgeable, and one who has the second, good or zealous. And the contrary of this: if a person lacks the first, he is termed ignorant, and if the second, vicious.

Second, various meanings have been given for virtue by Latin authors. It is said to be a power by which something is accomplished, as when Quintilian speaks of the *virtus* of speed in a horse. (This he says is an improper attribution and perhaps not even correct Latin usage.) A more precise meaning: a virtue is any perfection of man that he acquires through "use and exercise." This perfection is found in the expert or one "who lives honestly and in accord with nature" (19ᵛ). Cicero understood it thus when he said that "virtue should be divided into two parts, and under this meaning are contained all of the habits of the arts and sciences." But the best and most proper conception is that granted by "good and approved authors, and especially among moral philosophers." They hold that by virtue is meant those perfections through whose use uprightness is acquired and a person is said to be "good in an unqualified sense" (19ᵛ).

Carbone develops the moral implication further in the third fundament when he mentions the four cardinal virtues: prudence, justice, fortitude, and temperance. He credits Cicero with teaching these in his writings.

In the fourth fundament he makes critical distinctions when he notes that virtue in regard to rhetoric can be given a number of interpretations. To say that rhetoric is to speak "well" (*eulegein*) may mean to speak uprightly, or aptly, or elegantly (21ᵛ). In a definition, then, the term "well" will have to be qualified.

By the end of this disputation Carbone arrives at conclusions of perennial significance. He establishes first that rhetoric is a *habitus* that pertains to reason. Moreover, it is a habit that enables one to do something in "expeditious fashion and without error" (21ᵛ). This statement concerns only acquired rhetoric, not natural rhetoric, "For the power of speaking well that one has by nature is not a habit [i.e., not something learned and acquired through repeated use]. . . ." (21ᵛ). He goes on to show as a consequence that rhetoric cannot be considered a bad habit and to argue against Quintilian's position that it is a moral virtue. And he thinks that Quintilian's attempt to find this view in Cicero is flawed.

Explicating the point further in the remaining positions, Carbone says that only if rhetoric is taken in the sense of a cognitive habit can it be called a virtue. He avers that it is an indifferent habit that can be put to good or bad use. Furthermore, it is not a simple habit; it contains five subsidiary habits: invention, arrangement, style, memory, and delivery. These are distinct habits, he adds, for a person can be seen to excel in one but not the other (23ʳ). But Carbone does not wish to exclude moral virtue from all consideration in the training of an orator, for he says to use rhetoric properly one must be trained in the moral virtues. Quintilian argued this well, for if he had not fortitude an orator could not oppose the efforts of evil men. Carbone adds that one could go on to show the appropriateness of the other virtues (24ʳ).

4. Is Rhetoric Wisdom, a Science, or Prudence?

Since he has already said that rhetoric is not a moral virtue but rather that it is an indifferent cognitive habit, Carbone now begins to distinguish the kind of cognitive habit it is. In this regard he looks at the five such habits differentiated by Aristotle: understanding, wisdom, science, art, and prudence. Each of these is defined in accord with Aristotle; but Carbone comments that the terms are used promiscuously, not only by Aristotle but even by Cicero.

After a preliminary discussion of wisdom, science, and prudence, Carbone finds that these are not the virtues of rhetoric. Instead, art is the habit most pertinent to rhetoric. As this will be the subject of the next disputation, he gives only a brief definition: Art is "a habit effective of the truth with reason." In summarizing, he notes that while "prudence directs human actions as they relate to morality and uprightness," art "moderates actions whose perfection is not judged on the basis of morality" (28ʳ). Here he warns his students against following Julius Caesar Scaliger, who persists in placing art in the will rather than in the reason, thus making it a moral attribute (28ᵛ).

In the positions he adduces, Carbone notes that rhetoric is not a science because by definition a science is concerned with certainty and what is universally true. Rhetoric, on the other hand, is concerned with human affairs, matters that are singular, doubtful in their outcome, and thus not subject to assured conclusions. Again he notes that rhetoric is not prudence, "for speaking well and living well are worlds apart" (30ᵛ). As for the other cognitive virtues, rhetoric is not understanding, that is, "a knowledge or power with which we are endowed by nature alone"; it is something gained by "artifice and exercise." Rhetoric considered as "perfect eloquence" contains intelligence within it and, thus, is "a certain kind of prudence" (30ᵛ).

5. Is Rhetoric an Art?

Carbone admits at the outset that this disputation is quite lengthy, and to avoid tiring the reader he divides it into six parts. I note only a few particulars of these.

Art has many meanings, he observes, but he settles on three. First, its aim is a product, getting something done. Second, it is an activity. Third, it includes not only making and doing but also knowing (32–34).

The properties of art concern him next. It should have some principles or rules, definite and stable ways of doing something. The precepts should be coherent and agree among themselves. These desiderata lead to his explication of Aristotle's definition of art: "a habit that is effective, with true reason" (35ᵛ). Habit means deliberate action, not the chance result of an action; and in this it has elements in common with other cognitive virtues. That it functions with "true reason" distinguishes it from *atechnia* or unskillfulness. That it is "effective" makes it different from simply knowing or acting, which "effects nothing." Quintilian points out that art strives for some end useful in life, a teaching also apparent in Aristotle's *Ethics* (36ᵛ). Surveying other definitions that provide more details, Carbone ends by stating that an art is "a constitution, or ordering, an agreement of perceptions exercised toward some end useful for life" (36ʳ). He then examines the philological bases for the terms of this statement, citing Aristotle, Cicero, Quintilian, and the Stoics.

In the passage that follows Carbone considers the meaning of method as it pertains to an art. The subject of method is one that preoccupied many Renaissance scholars. Carbone observes that it is "a way of proceeding from more common and better known things to those that are particular and less known" and adds that its aim is to teach "briefly and easily." He defines it finally as "the arrangement of materials that are to be treated in any discipline in a proper ordering from prior to posterior, as appropriate to the nature of the things to be treated or to the interests and capacity of the audience. . . ." (38ʳ).

In keeping with the protocol of disputation, he passes to the various opinions authorities have offered on this subject, from Socrates' view that rhetoric is a skill, to that of Antonius and Lysias, who thought it "a kind of observation," to those who held it to be a power or faculty (38ʳ⁻ᵛ). In regard to this last, he notes that some would assert its genus to be faculty and not art. Others would place it in the genus of art, which he says is the view of almost all teachers of the subject.

At the end of this section Carbone observes that in referring to the art of rhetoric one may mean only "the art that includes precepts for speaking well," or one may have in mind "the entire faculty of speaking well and of eloquence," which would include additional knowledge of other principles. The two conceptions "differ quite radically from one another" (39ʳ). These distinctions figure in the positions he outlines in the next part.

Finally, Carbone states the positions he holds with regard to the foregoing opinions. As these are somewhat surprising, they are noted here.

First, if by art is meant a discipline that contains certain knowledge, then rhetoric is not an art. This is the same as saying that it is not a science. (Science in the Aristotelian tradition meant certain knowledge.)

Second, if we define art following Aristotle, then it is not an art. For rhetoric is not "a reasoned way of effecting something, a finished product, as in painting, weaving, or building."

Third, if by art we mean method, then it is "truly and properly an art." "For the person who has it, definitely with reason, discovers and arranges, and distributes a speech into its parts and treats these in a way that conduces to persuasion, and in a manner that is easily grasped by his audience."

Fourth, if it is taken to be "a discipline that treats precepts for speaking well, it is truly and properly an art." This is the opinion he prefers and he cites "the authority of the most reliable authors," including Plato, Aristotle, Cicero, and Quintilian.

Fifth, if rhetoric is considered to be eloquence, "made up of the art itself and the science of many other things, then preferably rhetoric is to be located in the genus of art rather than in any other genus." He adds: "From this twofold knowledge one perfect art of speaking is formed . . . and this the artificial faculty we call eloquence; with it, one who is instructed can speak copiously and aptly persuade with true and right reason" (41ᵛ). Other conclusions support this view also.

Sixth, if rhetoric or eloquence is considered as it pertains to its subject matter, then it contains some imperfection, for it is concerned with the contingent affairs of men.

Seventh, even though rhetoric is an art, eloquence requires more than such an art to perfect it. These matters, he says, will be the subject of another book.

The last three positions are somewhat puzzling, for Carbone appears to have accepted the equation of rhetoric with eloquence that he was careful to distinguish in the first and second disputations. But on closer examination he seems to mean that rhetoric is the art, the teaching or doctrine, and eloquence the doing of it spectacularly well. Thus eloquence is a power formed by the art of rhetoric but going beyond it.

6. In What Genus of Art Should Rhetoric Be Located?

Now that he has placed rhetoric among the arts, Carbone follows up some of the distinctions made earlier to refine the kind of art rhetoric is. He returns to distinctions made in the third disputation regarding virtues of knowledge and of action and differentiates the concomitant two types of art: those related to knowledge and those to action. Among the latter type two varieties can be distinguished: doing and making.

The arts called *theoretikai* by the Greeks are the arts of knowledge such as metaphysics, physics, geometry, and astrology. These are properly referred to as sciences. The other genus, termed by the Greeks *praktikai* and the Latins, action or activity, is not concerned with knowledge alone. The arts in this genus may be divided into two varieties. Some are devoted to perfecting the agent; others are ordered to making something. The first, *praktike*, is governed by ethics and moral virtues, and the second, *poetike* (in Latin *ars effectionis* or *ars factiva*), is directed by the habit of the art (49–50ʳ).

Carbone next takes up other ways of differentiating the arts. One may speak of certain or "never failing" arts, those that always achieve the same results—architecture, weaving, and bridlemaking. Other arts make use of "certain conjectures of the mind to attain their ends," and one may refer to those as conjectural arts—medicine, agriculture, nautical and military arts. The first the Greeks call *orismenas* and the second, *soxasikas* (51ᵛ–52ʳ).

The arts can also be divided into those that treat of words, *sermocinales*, such as grammar; or others that employ reasoning, *rationales*, such as logic. Some arts are designed to treat only one side of a controversy and prove a point, whereas others dispute on both sides. These last are called by the Greeks *du-

nameis, that is, faculties. One also sometimes classifies arts into liberal or mechanical (54).

After these extensive observations, Carbone develops the following positions. He thinks, first of all, that rhetoric is not in the genus of knowledge and so is not a science, even though this is what Quintilian thought (56ʳ).

Likewise, opposing Quintilian again, rhetoric should not be classified among the arts of making or poetics. The Roman rhetor thought so because, as he said, "orators usually write their orations." But our sense of rhetoric is fundamentally different. Its intention is not to make a work of art, whereas the arts of making are designed to produce a work of art, and after their operation the artifact remains. At the end of its operation, on the other hand, rhetoric "does not leave behind a work of art, nor does the art of singing nor discoursing" (57ᵛ). It follows from this that one can imagine "a perfect orator who never wrote anything, but was content only with arguing cases." Carbone offers in support the hypothetical case of a Cicero who wrote nothing down but simply argued beautifully in the Forum. Would he then be less an orator because his speeches were not written?

In this Carbone does not seem to mean that rhetoric is concerned only with oral discourse. He appears, rather, to want to emphasize that rhetoric's primary aim is not to create a literary product, but to perfect the orator.

Carbone goes on to say that rhetoric is not simply an *ars sermocinalis*, an art of words, for it is *rationalis*, concerned with reasoning as well. It is also one of the faculties, because it teaches how to argue both sides of an issue. Certainly, it is among the liberal arts and should be termed useful—in fact, it is almost necessary in society (58ʳ).

Finally, he notes that it is an instrumental art, used by the science of politics to govern well. Aristotle taught this in the *Ethics*, noting that politics is an architectonic faculty that is served by both oratory and the military art (58ᵛ).

7. On the Matter of Rhetoric

In the seventh disputation Carbone first takes up the major opinions about the proper subject of rhetoric. Although most of these are familiar to us, the range of opinion he lists is remarkable.

One of the most common opinions is that rhetoric is concerned with both everything and nothing, that it can be applied to anything but has no particular subject matter. Quintilian was of this opinion. Gorgias and others said ornate words are the subject of rhetoric. Civil questions comprise the content said Dionysius of Halicarnassus; Hermogenes, Agricola, Trapezuntius, and many others agreed. Quintilian thought that it is concerned with human life and virtue, especially. Cornelius Celsus believed it to treat doubtful matters. Plato said that it is concerned with the soul, moving the souls of men. Still others, Cicero and Aristotle among them, taught that the orator is concerned with three types of cases (62ʳ–64ʳ).

Carbone concludes the list by saying that today there is no common opinion. Speaking of the views of some of the foremost commentators among his contemporaries, he cites professors of the University of Padua. He notes that Iacobus Zabarella, the eminent philosopher, assigns to rhetoric civil questions and uses Aristotle to support this. Antonius Riccobonus, the well-known teacher of rhetoric, opposes this and defends Aristotle's view that all questions are the subject of the art (64ᵛ).

In summary, these are the positions Carbone takes on the subject: that rhetoric does have a subject matter if it is understood either as an art or as eloquence; even if there is no determinate thing (*nulla certa res*) with which it is concerned, it still has content. If it is considered to be the art that teaches how to speak well, then, at the least, its matter is ornate or elegant speech (69ᵛ).

With regard to opinions claiming that rhetoric is solely concerned with virtue, or with civil questions, or the three kinds of cases, Carbone simply states that it is concerned with any matter at issue. He concedes that it does, however, treat civil questions more frequently then others, and so this is its more proper matter.

Nevertheless, Carbone emphasizes the point that rhetoric can concern any matter proposed. He mentions that "Aristotle taught this when he defined rhetoric as the power of perceiving whatever is 'persuasible' (*persuasibilia*) about any thing whatever; and concluding, wrote that 'concerning this we also say that this art is not contained in any definite genus' " (71ᵛ). The term "persuasible" is an unusual one; we find it mentioned in Riccobono, although Carbone does not cite him at this point.[7]

Finally, Carbone concurs with Plato that rhetoric treats of the souls of men, for it does effect persuasion by appealing to the soul.

8. On the End of Rhetoric, Is It Persuasion?

In this disputation the major opinions are again rehearsed by Carbone before he develops his own conclusions. First among the views surveyed is that of Quintilian, who opposed both Aristotle and Cicero, holding that speaking aptly in order to persuade is the aim of rhetoric. Carbone comments that many rhetoricians teach a refinement of this view, saying that the end of rhetoric is to persuade. Others distinguish two aims here, saying that rhetoric has "an intrinsic and an extrinsic aim." The first is that of speaking aptly and well, and this the orator can achieve himself. The extrinsic aim to persuade, however, "depends on the will of the auditor." On this score Quintilian emphasizes the intrinsic and Cicero, the extrinsic aim. A similar opinion cited is that of Marius Fabius Victorinus, the teacher of St. Jerome, who taught that "the aim of rhetoric is to persuade

---

[7]Riccobonus was a well-known scholar contemporary with Carbone who taught the humanities at the University of Padua from 1571 to 1599. Wallace discusses the significance of the term "persuasible" in this volume, chapter 9.

and that the orator always seeks this, even though he may not always accomplish it" (77^v).

In his concluding positions, Carbone agrees that rhetoric's aim is to persuade but adds that the distinction concerning two ends, intrinsic and extrinsic, should not be accepted. He disagrees also with Victorinus that persuasion is the sole aim, saying that this cannot be defended (83^v).

9. What and How Many Are the Causes of Rhetoric?

Although this subject was of great interest to classical and Renaissance scholars, it is of little concern today, so only the conclusions to which Carbone comes will be briefly noted. He sees nature, art, practice, and imitation as the efficient causes of rhetoric or eloquence (88^r). None of these by itself, he says, achieves perfect eloquence. One can reduce the causes to three if one considers imitation to be included in art. Besides these, other factors are helpful in attaining eloquence or in conserving it, in particular, reading the poets and historians.

10. Explanation and Defense of Aristotle's Definition

In the final and most important disputation in the volume, before Carbone introduces his own definition he returns to Aristotle's: "Rhetoric is the faculty of seeing, in any matter whatever, what is suitable for persuasion." He remarks that Quintilian, Hermagoras, and Hermogenes all opposed this position (91^r).

After considering their objections, Carbone stresses the following fundaments. First, rhetoricians are not as careful in making distinctions as are philosophers and dialecticans, and they need not be. But, as a consequence, their descriptions are not always perfect. They should take care, however, that their descriptions are congruent with what they attempt to explain and should distinguish the subject of the definition from other matter. At times rhetoricians define through effects, at other times through parts, properties, or attributes, sometimes with metaphors or with positive or negative statements (91^v–92^r). That is why the art has been defined in so many different ways by various authors.

Second, dialectic and rhetoric can be differentiated from other arts in many ways, but one characteristic is most important. Other arts may treat of contraries—virtue and vice, health and sickness—but these never argue on contrary sides of the same issue. Dialectic and rhetoric do. For this reason they are called *dunameis*, powers or faculties, as Aristotle teaches. Because they employ this power they are very powerful and free arts. The Latins refer to their essential property as "force (*vis*), faculty or power, and as Fabius [Quintilian] writes, virtue" (92^r).

Third, Aristotle's commentators are not in agreement in their interpretations of *dunameis*, or faculty. Some think it is a trait that brings honor to those who possess it. Others think that the term means that a speech can be done well or badly, and still others, such as Alexander of Aphrodisias, that its arguments are not certain but conjectural.

The commentators also debate the meaning of the term *to see* (*videre*), questioning whether it means invention alone and so excludes other parts of rhetoric, such as style.

Fourth, Carbone says that by faculty he thinks more is meant than "one simple faculty or habit, but rather one that arises from the knowledge of many things in a sort of cumulative way" (93ᵛ).

Following the airing of these fundaments Carbone states his positions. He maintains first of all and not surprisingly, that Aristotle's definition is the best. He then expatiates on each part of the Stagirite's definition. The fact that faculty is mentioned as the genus is defensible because it is the genus that comprises both rhetoric and dialectic. In this way the nature of the art is conveyed most clearly. By faculty Aristotle meant what was explained in the second and third fundaments, that it is an art treating both sides of a question.

Carbone further concludes that "when Aristotle says it is 'a faculty of seeing what is apt to persuade,' he is using its 'work' (*officium*) to explain its nature, and this is how it is discerned for any art." Thus, in this sense its end is to persuade, but Aristotle used the word *diaresai* 'to contemplate', and *idein* 'to see', in speaking of its task, which he says is "to see and intuit." So the work of rhetoric is to intuit the reason "why the things that people say generate conviction (*fides*)" (94ʳ).

By the phrase "in any matter whatever" Aristotle clearly meant that rhetoric could be applied to any subject, that is, any subject amenable to persuasion.

In his penultimate position Carbone states that the "persuasible" is the end of the art, "from which its work is to be gathered." One can understand why definition is important now, he says, for it explains what rhetoric is through "its proximate genus, its work, its matter, and its end, all of which stand in place of a differentia" (94ᵛ).

In his final position, Carbone holds that Aristotle certainly did not intend to exclude everything but invention from his definition, but that his definition would have become too lengthy had he stipulated all of rhetoric's parts. When he said "to contemplate" he meant invention, and this would entail inventing from all of the other parts as well. In support of this contention Carbone cites "his better commentators," meaning by them Victorius, M. Antonius Mairoragius, and Antonius Riccobonus (94ᵛ). He points out that the other parts of rhetoric are not extrinsic when one considers the speech itself, for all of them have to be accommodated to the audience. For this reason, he says, he differs from Robertellus, who holds that Aristotle did not include style but referred only to the act of invention.

Following this analysis Carbone casts his own definition, which he evidently expects will clear up many of the difficulties Aristotle's wording has generated for the commentators: "Rhetoric, or eloquence, is a faculty, fostered by nature, art, and exercise, whereby one speaks aptly on any matter proposed, ornately and copiously, to produce popular persuasion. [Rhetorica, seu Eloquentia est facultas natura, arte, et exercitatione comparata, qua de unaquaque re proposita, ornate et copiose ad popularem persuasionem apte dicitur.]" (95^v)

Carbone explains that in this he, too, has given the genus as a faculty. The other phrases are the differentia. Among these are a description of the efficient cause, "nature, art, and exercise"; the matter, "any matter proposed"; the activity or work (*officium*), "speaks aptly"; the form, "ornately and copiously"; and the end, "to produce popular persuasion." By "art," he adds, he does not intend solely the art of speaking with its five parts but, rather, implies all of the other arts, "since this faculty is not found except in a person who is skilled in the knowledge of all things."

Carbone says no more regarding his definition, evidently considering it self-explanatory. In the last two pages of the book he concludes his arguments for the superiority of Aristotle's understanding of the nature of rhetoric and his definition, referring to the essential attributes of a definition he has earlier marked. Aristotle's version cannot be called incomplete, because the terms used are sufficient to characterize the principal element, which embodies the rest, and the same terms cannot be applied to any other discipline.

Carbone points out again how much in error Quintilian was in placing speaking well as the principal end. To clarify the grounds for his difference with Quintilian, Carbone returns to the Greek of the *Rhetoric*, emphasizing that the proofs, *pithanon*, the persuasibles, or the things that can readily be refuted are in the power of both false sophists and honest disputers. The sophist, Aristotle notes, offers "captious arguments," but not because of the power that derives from the art of dialectic, which recognizes these as true or false arguments, but rather because of "the will," his desire to induce apparent arguments with the aim of deceiving the audience (96^{r-v}).

Thus does Carbone resolve the issue. Aristotle attributed the use of apparent proofs to the sophist not because it is the nature of the faculty of dialectic to see both true and false arguments, but because of the sophist's desire to lead people to believe falsehoods. The use of fallacious tactics, then, depends on the will of the orator and not on his knowledge and understanding of the arguments (96^v). In the same way some rhetoricians may have knowledge of enthymemes and examples both true and false and may not use the latter. Others may choose to do so. Unfortunately no separate term exists for these deceivers; they too are called orators.

CARBONE'S CONTRIBUTION

Looking back over the fruits of Carbone's labor, one must concede that he put order into several knotty problems, clarified and simplified, and reduced a mass of material to well-articulated positions. With consummate erudition he defended the definition of Aristotle, his major task.

But what of the definition he constructed as a clearer and more accurate alternative? In some ways it compares quite favorably to Aristotle's; however, it does not emphasize the intuitive character of the art, a matter of much discussion in his disputations. Perhaps he thought *faculty* or *art* conveyed that function as well. Yet he makes so much of Aristotle's use of the terms *diaresai* 'to contemplate' and *idein* 'to intuit' one would expect it in his definition.

The conglomerate of eloquence and rhetoric effected in Carbone's definition ignores the distinctions made in his first disputations and builds on the elision of the two developed in the fifth disputation. In collapsing the distinctions between rhetoric and eloquence and in omitting the focus on the inventive aspect in Aristotle's definition, he is revealed as a man influenced more by the spirit of his time than by the matter itself. In substituting for the element of *seeing*, the phrases *speaks aptly* and *ornately and copiously*, he has placed emphasis instead on the fifth part of rhetoric, style. That he does not explain the omission is unexpected, given the nuances Carbone exposes for almost every other element. Perhaps one should conclude from this that for him, as for Aristotle, the definition manifests what each thought to be most important in the nature of rhetoric.

That invention in the Aristotelian sense actually is important to him is made clear by his next book, which he devotes entirely to that subject. The manner in which he treats it is again in tune with the times. The title of the book identifies him as more humanist than scholastic, for dialectic was combined with rhetoric to create one art of invention: *De oratoria, et dialectica inventione, vel de locis communibus* (On oratory and dialectical invention, or the common topics). Yet it is not a mere elision of the two as in the writings of Agricola or Ramus, where dialectic lost its special province and rhetoric two of its parts: invention and disposition. This work simply focuses on the lore of the common topics and distinguishes the areas to which each are appropriate or in which they overlap. Carbone provides tables of the major systems of the topics in the preliminary matter of the book, including those of Themistius-Boethius, Cicero, and Agricola.

As I have explained at length in another essay, the book on invention may preserve for us a course given at the Collegio Romano (the Jesuit College at Rome), in the late 16th century.[8] It provides an explanation of the origin of the topics, seeing them as emerging from Aristotle's teachings on the nature of being and on the way we discourse about being—that is, from the predicaments as taught in the *Categories* and the predicables as described in the *Topics*. The two sources are distinguished carefully and clearly, with engaging illustrations.

In this later work, Carbone mercifully did not choose the disputation as a method of presenting the matter, preferring exposition instead, a mode far more agreeable in the print medium. Thus he avoided the repetitions of the disputation, which, in that oral genre, may have served to clarify successive points in extensive treatments by authorities, but which make for tedious reading. Readers do not

---

[8]See "The Rhetoric Course at the Collegio Romano," referred to in footnote 1.

need such frequent, broad reminders; they can, of course, leaf back through a work to confirm the thread of the arguments. Yet even in the later book, Carbone's training in dialectical method is evident in the manner in which he fully explains his views; he takes great care to cite those who thought similarly or who have arrived at different opinions. Perhaps the change of approach in the two works may result from two different aims and mindsets. The first text on rhetoric, which he anticipated would be conveyed in a classroom setting, seems to reflect a desire to preserve the format and content of his lectures for his students or other teachers, as he implies in the preface; the second work appears to be intended for a wider public, one that could expect to gain such knowledge through reading. The marked shift in approach also displays for us, who read these works four centuries later, Carbone's pedagogical versatility.

In conclusion we might observe that in all of Carbone's works we have seen, whether in rhetoric or in philosophy, he lives up to the ideal he set for himself in the preface—"not to attempt to be eloquent, but to use a simple style of writing, with no ornament or emotional appeals." In this he reveals himself more the philosopher than the rhetorician whose art he analyzes so copiously.

Chapter 9

Antonio Riccobono: The Teaching of Rhetoric in 16th-Century Padua

William A. Wallace
Catholic University of America

One of the little studied texts for the teaching of rhetoric in the late Renaissance is the Latin translation of Aristotle's *Rhetoric* published by Antonio Riccobono in 1579, with an accompanying commentary, also in Latin.[1] In this chapter, whose aim is to honor Professor James J. Murphy—himself an indefatigable teacher of rhetoric and translator of Latin rhetoric texts—I analyze Riccobono's views on the nature of rhetoric. These Riccobono presents in the first treatise of his commentary, a treatise he entitles *De natura rhetoricae*, where he is concerned not only with explicating Aristotle's views on the subject but also with treating rhetoric's relation to other disciplines in the curriculum of his day. Although

---

[1]The full title reads *Aristotelis ars rhetorica ab Antonio Riccobono Rhodigino i. c. humanitatem in Patavino gymnasio profitente latine conversa. Eiusque Riccoboni explicationum liber, quo Aristotelis loca obscuriora declarantur, et Rhetorica praxis explicatur in orationibus Ciceronis pro Marcello, et pro Milone, ac oratione Demosthenis ad epistolam Philippi ab eodem latina facta* (Venice: Apud Paulum Beiettum, Bibliopolam Patavinum, 1579). Also included in this edition is Riccobono's translation of Aristotle's *Poetics*, entitled *Aristotelis ars poetica ab eodem in latinam linquam versa. Cum eiusdem de re comica disputatione.* The last-named item, the treatise on comedy, has been reprinted, with notes, in Bernard Weinberg, ed., *Trattati di poetica e retorica del cinquecento*, 4 vols., Scrittori d'Italia n. 253 (Bari: Laterza, 1972) 3:255–276, 504–507.

With regard to Riccobono's *Rhetorica*, Paul D. Brandes notes that an earlier, partial edition containing only the translation of the first book was also issued (Padua: Laurentius Pasquatus, 1577). Subsequent printings of the complete edition appeared at Frankfurt in 1588, at Lyons in 1590, again at Frankfurt in 1593, at Vicenza in 1594, at Lyons in 1597, and at Avignon in 1599. See Paul D. Brandes, *A History of Aristotle's Rhetoric, with a Bibliography of Early Printings* (Metuchen, NJ: The Scarecrow Press, 1989) 88–89, 149–151.

courses at the University of Padua were then quite different from those now offered in an American university, I hope that the ideas of this 16th-century humanist prove of interest to readers acquainted with Professor Murphy's many explorations of the pedagogy of rhetoric in times before our own.

RICCOBONO THE RHETORICIAN

Riccobono was born in Rovigo, a city in the Venetian Republic close to Padua, in 1541. After completing his studies in Venice and Padua, where his professors included the eminent rhetoricians Carlo Sigonio and Marc Antonio Mureto, he was called back to his native city to teach humane letters there. This he did until 1571, when he received the *Doctor iuris* from the University of Padua. We know from a decree of the Venetian Senate that in 1571 he also was appointed to the second chair of humanities at that university—a position he was prevailed upon to accept, though he had intended to enter the legal profession because of its higher income. In the following year Riccobono succeeded to the first chair of humanities, a position he occupied until his death in 1599. An interesting folio of the *rotulus* of professors at Padua for 1592 lists his name under that of Galileo Galilei, who had just begun teaching mathematics there in that year. Whereas Galileo's assignment for the year as shown in the *rotulus* is unspecified (*ad libitum*), Riccobono's is indicated there as "interpreting" Demosthenes and Cicero's *De oratore*.[2]

Apart from his teaching, Riccobono was expert in Greek and Latin and a capable translator of one to the other. Though little known today, his translation of the *Rhetoric* was much appreciated and often reprinted in the latter part of the 16th century, apparently because it was better adapted than others to the needs of students in the university. At the time printing was invented the most accurate Latin translation of the *Rhetoric* from the Greek was that of the Dominican William of Moerbeke, which dates from the second half of the 13th century. With the onset of the Renaissance and the humanist revival of interest in classical thought, new translations began to appear. The first in the tradition that culminated with Riccobono's work was that of George Trapezuntius, printed at Paris between 1475 and 1477; this enjoyed some ten editions or reprintings down to 1544, when another translation appeared. This was that of Hermolao Barbaro, who taught at Padua and whose version was printed at Venice and Lyons in that year; this in turn went through several editions down to 1559. Next came the translation of Antonius Maioragius, who taught eloquence at Milan and whose first edition was printed there in 1550; it proved popular and effectively replaced Barbaro's version, being often reprinted down to the 1590s. At that

---

[2]The contents of the folio are reprinted in Antonio Favaro, *Galileo Galilei e lo Studio di Padova*, 2 vols. (Padua: Editrice Antenore, 1966) 2:113.

time the locus of activity shifted back to Padua, where new translations were prepared by Riccobono's two teachers, Sigonio and Mureto. The first of these had his translation printed in Venice and Bologna in 1565 and the second, in Rome in 1577. Mureto's work was reprinted only once, in Rome in 1585; but Sigonio's had six editions, the last at Brescia in 1584. Riccobono's partial translation made its appearance in 1577 and the full work, in 1579; the latter went through six editions, the last printed at Avignon in 1599, as indicated in footnote 1.[3]

Apart from his translations of the *Rhetoric* and the *Poetics*, between 1579 and 1591 Riccobono published paraphrases of both works. Later he translated Books 3 through 5 of Aristotle's *Ethics* under the title *Ethicorum ad Nicomachum tota illa pars quae est de principiis actionum humanarum et de singulis virtutibus moralibus* (Padua, 1593), and later still, Book 8, with the title *Doctrina de amicitia* (Padua, 1595); his translation of all ten books then quickly followed (Frankfurt, 1596). In 1596 he also published at Frankfurt an extensive comparison of Aristotle's rhetoric with that of Cicero. The year of his death, finally, saw the appearance of his extensive collation of Aristotle's *Poetics* with the works of Horace (Padua, 1599), which completed a study of Horace he had begun in 1591 and in which he aimed to show how that poet's work conformed strictly to the Aristotelian canons.[4]

Yet another side of Riccobono's career is seen in his historical writings. The first historiographer of the University of Padua, he published his *De Gymnasio Patavino commentariorum libri sex* in 1598. Years earlier, while still at Rovigo in 1568, he had written a treatise on history, *De historia commentarius*. But among Paduans he perhaps is best known for his epideictic rhetoric, particularly for the large number of orations he delivered at the university as eulogies and on special ceremonial occasions. Among these, Antonio Favaro makes extensive use of a funeral oration Riccobono preached on the death of Giuseppe Moletti, Galileo's predecessor in the chair of mathematics at Padua. We know from this and from his history of the university that Riccobono possessed detailed information about the curriculum in mathematics there in the latter part of the 16th century. Although little is available on his precise relations with Galileo, there are also indications that Riccobono was very enthusiastic about this young mathematician coming to Padua. He was in direct communication with Galileo and

---

[3]Brandes, *A History of Aristotle's Rhetoric* 69–160. This work includes many plates illustrating the title pages of these and other editions.

[4]Most of these details are found in Charles H. Lohr, *Latin Aristotle Commentaries II. Renaissance Authors* (Florence: Leo S. Olschki Editore, 1988) 384–386; and Weinberg, *Trattati* 3:504–505. Lohr also lists a monograph on Riccobono, C. Mazzacurati, *La Crisi della retorica umanistica nel Cinquecento (Antonio Riccobono)* (Naples, 1961), which I have not seen to date. Additionally, Weinberg makes many references to Riccobono's teachings in his classic study, *A History of Literary Criticism in the Italian Renaissance*, 2 vols. (Chicago: University of Chicago Press, 1961) ad indicem; see also later citations from this work in footnotes 34, 51, and 52.

conveyed the impression that it was Moletti's high regard for his work that led to his being called to replace his friend, who had only recently passed away.[5]

RHETORIC: AN ART OR A SCIENCE?

To turn now to Riccobono's treatise "On the Nature of Rhetoric," we can gain from it some idea of his ability to interpret Aristotle's text and his skill in communicating its contents to his students. In this connection a key interpretative and pedagogical problem relating to the *Rhetoric* is its proper situation within the Aristotelian corpus as a whole. Should it be included in the *Organon*, along with the *Analytics* and the *Topics*, and thus share the character of logical science; or should it be seen as the art of rhetoric, as an adjunct to Aristotle's *Politics* and thus primarily as the art of persuading people to political action? Riccobono gives a nuanced answer to this question, allowing for the possibility of its being both an art and a science, and, for the second alternative, showing precisely wherein its scientific character differentiates it from other disciplines treated in the *Organon*.

There are obvious problems in calling rhetoric an art, for it does not make anything, and also in calling it a science, because it is not concerned with necessary matters. But, Riccobono notes, if one takes the term *art* in a way broad enough to include all sciences and faculties and arts, both liberal and operative, each of which considers causes so as to obtain an end, then rhetoric can be put in the genus of art [201].[6] But this is not its proximate genus: rather, rhetoric is better seen as a faculty or power [*dunamis*], because, like the *Topics*, it has the ability to deal with both sides of a question [202]. So, taking faculty as rhetoric's genus, Riccobono would expose its nature by contracting that genus through appropriate differentiae, which he supplies by considering its end, its work or function, its subject matter, and the way in which it deals with that subject matter [204].

The end of rhetoric, for Riccobono, is to persuade. Quintilian contests this, he says, holding that its end is not to persuade but to speak well. But he departs from Quintilian here, arguing that "whatever is ordered to another is not an end, for an end is that to which all others are ordered and itself to no other. To speak well in the oratorical art is ordered to something else, namely, to persuasion. Therefore it

---

[5]Antonio Favaro, *Amici e corrispondenti di Galileo*, 3 vols. (Venice: Carlo Ferrari, 1914; Florence: Libreria Editrice Salimbeni, 1983) 3:1585–1656, especially 1630–1631.

[6]Page numbers in square brackets here and hereafter refer the reader to the 1579 Venice edition of Riccobono's *Rhetorica*. In some cases the pagination of this *editio princeps* is faulty; where this occurs I have corrected it to agree with the actual sequence of page numbers. In those instances where I make a direct citation of Riccobono's text in English translation, because the text itself is not readily available in the United States, I supply the Latin in notes. I hope that this procedure acquaints readers unfamiliar with the Latin of this period with some aspects of its usage in commentaries on Aristotle's *Rhetoric*.

is not an end. . . ."[7] Riccobono would introduce here a distinction regarding ends that derives from Galen, namely, that between the goal proposed, *ton skopon*, and the attainment of the goal proposed, *to telos*. For the rhetorician the first, the goal, is to persuade, whereas the second, the attainment of that goal, is actually to effect the persuasion. The orator does not always do the latter, effect the persuasion; and yet his end is always the former, namely, to persuade [205].

A more serious problem is that other arts and sciences persuade also, and so to persuade cannot be the proper end of rhetoric. Riccobono replies to this by again distinguishing: " 'persuade,' can be taken in two ways, one way in general, to include even that from the proper principles of an art [or science] for those who know them, and this is not the persuasion of rhetoric; the other in particular, when one is persuaded from probabilities and commonly conceded opinions, and this is proper to rhetoric."[8] How and why it does so he promises to explain later.

With persuasion as the end, Riccobono turns to the work or task or function of the rhetorician; the Greek for this is *ergon*, and Riccobono translates it with the Latin *munus*. He identifies this as seeking out what is able to persuade, namely, the causes that will enable the rhetorician to move or persuade his audience; on this understanding, rhetoric is the faculty of "seeing into [*theoresai*]" whatever is conducive to persuasion. This is not merely invention, as Quintilian took it, but includes arrangement and elocution as well, and anything else that can count as a means of persuasion [206].

THE SUBJECT MATTER OF RHETORIC

The subject matter of rhetoric offers more difficulty for Riccobono. On this, he writes, Aristotle is not completely clear: he seems to restrict its matter to civil questions, as Cicero interprets him, whereas Gorgias had thought it applied to everything, and Quintilian reads Aristotle as intending this wider extension also. Riccobono's famous colleague at Padua, the logician Jacopo Zabarella, held that "rhetoric looks to action, not to knowledge,"[9] thus restricting it to human affairs, such as are dealt with by the three types of rhetoric: deliberative, forensic, and epideictic. But Riccobono respectfully disagrees, and his reason is worth quoting in full:

> It is very true that the principal matter of rhetoric is things that . . . humans do, and that things we do are included among the types of rhetoric. . . . But Aristotle,

---

[7]"At, quod refertur ad aliud finis non est, nam finis est is, ad quem referuntur omnia, cum ipse nusquam referatur. Benedicere in arte oratoria refertur ad aliud, nempe ad persuasionem. Ergo finis non est . . ." [204].

[8]"Persuadere dupliciter accipi; uno modo in universum, etiam ex propriis principiis artium inter illos, qui ea tenent, quod non convenit Rhetoricae; altero modo in parte, cum persuadetur ex probabilibus et confessis, quod est proprium Rhetoricae" [205].

[9]"Rhetoricam spectare actionem, non cognitionem" [209].

speaking generally, does not seem to exclude other matters from the function of the orator, not even those that pertain to knowledge, provided the orator treat them in a way that is appropriate for common understanding. For, when he proves that the function of rhetoric is not proper to other arts, he says that medicine is concerned with health and sickness, geometry with the properties of extension, arithmetic with numbers, and likewise the other arts and sciences in their proper subject matters, but the rhetorician with any matter whatever, in a way that is appropriate for persuading; he does not exclude what is treated in other arts, but makes them all the province of rhetoric itself if their matters are treated in rhetorical fashion.[10]

Riccobono then goes on to elaborate on this broadness of scope of the rhetorical enterprise:

> Nonetheless Aristotle says at the beginning of the *Rhetoric* that rhetoric, together with dialectics, is concerned with matters of the type that belong to no definite science, and, when he treats of the persuasible, that the function of rhetoric is to deal with matters for which we have no art, and in this way he seems to exclude matters that pertain to other arts. Yet, from the same teaching, one can respond that, while it is not licit for rhetoric to treat matters pertaining to other arts by using enthymemes proper to those arts, nonetheless it is licit to use enthymemes taken from common topics and accommodated to common opinion. . . .[11]

Note that in this passage Riccobono introduced a new term, the "persuasible," in Latin, *persuasibile*, meaning by this what is able to persuade, which he will subsequently juxtapose to the "probable," in Latin, *probabile*, what is able to induce assent. He goes on:

> It is thus apparent that it is licit for rhetoric to use arguments drawn from common topics not only when dealing with civil matters, which deal with some proposed

---

[10]
Ac profecto illud tam verum est, quam quod verissimum, praecipuam Rhetoricae materiam esse res illas, de quibus consulamus, et quas agimus, et ex illis, quae pertinent ad agendum, genera caussarum, quae res definitas complectuntur: sed Aristoteles in universum loquens, cetera a munere oratorio non videtur excludere, nec ea quidem, quae pertinent ad cognitionem, si modo proprio, id est ad communem intelligentiam accommodato tractentur. Nam, dum probat munus Rhetoricae aliis artibus non convenire, dicit Medicinam versari in sanabili, et morboso; Geometriam in affectionibus, quae magnitudinibus accidunt; Arithmeticam in numero; similiter vero etiam artes, et scientias reliquas in rebus sibi subiectis. At Rhetoricam in quaque re modo apposito ad persuadendum; nec illis quidem exceptis, quae ab aliis artibus traduntur, et fiunt quodammodo propriae ipsius Rhetoricae, si oratorie tractentur. [210]

[11]
Tametsi enim initio [Aristoteles] dicat, Rhetoricam una cum Dialectica esse de talibus quibusdam rebus, quae nullius sunt scientiae definitae; et ubi agit de persuasibili, Munus Rhetoricae esse de talibus rebus, de quibus artes non habemus; et hoc modo res ad alias artes pertinentes excludere videatur. Tamen potest est eiusdem doctrina responderi, Rhetoricae quidem non licere res illas tractare, quae ad alias artes pertinent, enthymematibus propriis ipsarum artium, sed licere, enthymematibus sumptis ex communibus locis, et ad communem opinionem accommodatis. [210–211]

action, but also with natural science and indeed with any matter whatever. And this great utility of rhetoric was recognized by Aristotle, namely, that the other arts do not persuade everyone, since they use the formality of speaking that arises from the particular science; rhetoric on the other hand persuades all people, since it induces conviction and assent from common notions.[12]

One can only surmise whether or not this idea was known to Galileo. Jean Dietz Moss has made the point that Galileo was among the first to use rhetoric in his scientific discourse, and in some places he did so to persuade everyone, not merely scientists, so it is not beyond belief that he got the inspiration for this from his colleague Riccobono.[13]

Coming now to the rhetorician's way of treating his subject matter, Riccobono here sets up the parallel already referred to: "just as dialectics considers all matters insofar as they are probable (*probabile*), . . . so rhetoric considers the same matters insofar as they are persuasible (*persuasibile*)."[14] Again this offers him the opportunity to disagree with his more famous colleague Zabarella, who wrote that rhetoric takes its form of argumentation from logic and its subject

---

[12]

Apparet igitur ex his verbis, licere Rhetoricae argumentis ductis ex communibus locis agere non solum de rebus civilibus, quae propositam habent actionem, verum etiam de naturalibus, et de quacunque re. Quae Rhetoricae utilitas ab Aristotele agnoscitur maxima, ut aliae artes non persuadeant omnes, cum teneant eam dicendi rationem, quae a scientia proficiscitur; Rhetoricae vero persuadeat omnes, cum ex communibus ducat fidem, et rationem. [211]

Riccobono elaborates further on this point as follows:

So we can say, from his teaching, that the matter of rhetoric is twofold: one infinite, the other definite, one more common, which Quintilian noted, the other more proper, which Cicero noted. This also seems to be the opinion of Alexander [of Aphrodisias], when he writes as follows in the first book of the *Topics*: 'The orator, therefore, treats of all things, though not in the same way as the dialectician, and he is not concerned with any one definite species; so the orator also discusses medical matters, and likewise philosophical and musical matters, but particularly civil matters. And indeed we do not see why the term persuasion should not apply to knowledge, and particularly to popular knowledge, since it is more a kind of assent than a knowledge, in the sense that assent is given to those things that pertain to knowledge, and men are led to it by persuasion, that is, by the kind of conviction that is appropriate to common understanding.' Here therefore it is proposed to us that most broadly conceived the matter of rhetoric is all things, most narrowly, civil questions alone. [212]

[13]For details on this, see Jean Dietz Moss, *Novelties in the Heavens: Rhetoric and Science in the Copernican Controversy* (Chicago: University of Chicago Press, 1993). In this volume she makes the point that Galileo inaugurated not only a scientific revolution but also a rhetorical revolution when he wrote his famous *Letter to the Grand Duchess Christina* of 1615 and his *Dialogue on the Two Chief World Systems* of 1632. See also Jean Dietz Moss, "Galileo's *Letter to Christina*: Some Rhetorical Considerations," *Renaissance Quarterly* 36 (1983): 547–576; and Jean Dietz Moss, "The Rhetoric of Proof in Galileo's Writings on the Copernican System," *Reinterpreting Galileo*, ed. William A. Wallace (Washington, DC: Catholic University of America Press, 1986) 179–204.

[14]"Quemadmodum Dialectica considerat res omnes, quatenus sunt probabiles, . . . sic Rhetorica easdem contempletur, quatenus sunt persuasibiles" [213].

matter from political science. The subject matter, for Riccobono, is wider than civil questions, as we have seen; its form, he now states, it takes from its end, as follows:

> Since the end of rhetoric is to persuade, it should have its own proper mode of consideration, insofar as either all things or civil questions are persuasible. But the persuasible is indeed said to be proper to rhetoric not only in argumentation, or in oratorical demonstration, which it takes from logic, but also in its use of character and the emotions, which it takes from civil science. And this is what Aristotle teaches when he writes: "Artificial proof is threefold: character, the emotions, and [logical] demonstration."[15]

This gives Riccobono his full definition of rhetoric: "it is the faculty of seeing in any subject matter whatever happens to be persuasible,"[16] that is, whatever is able to persuade. But at this point another adversary arises, Antonius Bernardi Mirandulanus,[17] sometime professor of logic at the University of Bologna, who says that this very definition applies also to dialectics. Riccobono disagrees with him on the ground that the probable, with which dialectics is concerned, is not the same as the persuasible, and then, as he had promised, he launches into a detailed discussion of the difference between the two [214].

THE PROBABLE VERSUS THE PERSUASIBLE

There are many kinds of statements that are probable, Riccobono writes. Some gain assent from all "that the good is to be sought, and also health, life, and wealth"; some gain assent from many, such as "that wisdom is preferable to riches" and "that the soul is more important to the body"; some again gain assent only from the wise, such as "that from nothing, nothing comes"; some yet again gain assent from most of the wise, such as "that virtue is to be sought for its

---

15

Cum finis Rhetoricae sit persuadere, ipsa habeat proprium considerandi modum, quatenus res omnes, vel quaestiones civiles sunt persuasibiles. Ac persuasibile quidem proprium Rhetoricae positum est, non solum in argumentatione, vel demonstratione oratoria, quam ipsa sumit a Logica, verum etiam in moribus et affectibus quos a scientia civili, quod aperte docet Aristoteles, cum scribit: Fidem artificiosam esse triplicem, mores, affectus, demonstrationem. . . . [213]

[16]"Haec definitio Rhetoricae, ut sit facultas videndi in quaque re, quod continget esse persuasibile . . ." [214].

[17]As his name suggests, Mirandulanus was born in Mirandola, in March of 1502. He studied at the University of Bologna under Pietro Pomponazzi and Ludovico Buccaferrea, receiving his doctorate in 1533. From then until 1539 he was professor of logic and philosophy at the same university, and later he held various ecclesiastical offices, serving as bishop of Caserta from 1552 to 1554. He died in Bologna on June 18, 1565. His exposition of Aristotle's *Rhetoric* was published posthumously at Bologna in 1589.

own sake, that the number of worlds is not infinite"; and some, yet again, from the most outstanding among the wise, such as "that the soul is eternal."[18] All of these statements fall under the consideration of dialectics, for they can all be seen as topical questions, and it is possible to argue on either side of each.

The persuasible, Riccobono argues, is not to be equated with all probables of this type. Rather, as he puts it,

> The persuasible is the acknowledged probable, that is, not the probable in an absolute sense, which can even gain assent from some who are quite wise, as that contraries are the same, but the probable of this type, that either the all or the many assent to it. In this sense Aristotle mentions also the acknowledged good, and what is agreeable to the ordinary multitude of men, and it consists in a certain common sense or intelligence, and it is not examined, as Cicero says, with the steelyard of the artisan but with the scales of ordinary people. . . . Therefore the persuasible is not everything that is probable but definite matters that appear that way to the all or to the many.[19]

On this basis Riccobono is able to clarify a number of ways in which the probable differs from the persuasible, and thus in which the *Topics* differs from the *Rhetoric*. The first treats more of universal matters; the second, more of singulars. The first uses question and answer in the form of a disputation; the second, continuous speech directed to the popular mind. The first takes the probable as common and as more apt for philosophical discourse; the second, the persuasible as less common but more suited to common intelligence. But this leads him to an interesting comparison, which he puts in these words:

> But the first [i.e., dialectics], since it is concerned with the probable, embraces even the persuasible, insofar as a thing is probable to the extent that it will be approved by the all or the many; the latter [i.e., rhetoric], since its object is the

---

18

Probabilia primum esse, quae probantur omnibus, ut bonum esse expetendum, expetendam sanitatem, divitias, . . . ; deinde, quae probantur plurimis, ut sapientiam esse divitiis optabiliorem, animum esse praestantiorem corpore . . . ; praeterea, quae sapientibus omnibus, ut . . . ex nihilo nihil fieri; inde, quae sapientibus plurimis, ut virtutem per se expetendam esse, . . . infinitos non esse mundos; inde, quae sapientius clarissimis, ut animum esse aeternum. . . . [214]

19

Colligo persuasibile esse probabilem confessum, id est non probabile simpliciter, quod potest etiam probari sapientibus probatis, ut contraria esse eadem, sed eiusmodi probabile, quod omnes communiter, vel plurimi confitentur, quo sensu Aristoteles commemorat etiam bona confessa; et quod accommodatum est ad rudem hominum multitudinem, et consistit in communi quodam sensu, atque intelligentia, nec examinatur, ut inquit Cicero, artificis statera, sed quadam populari trutina. . . . Ergo persuasibile est, non omne probabile, sed definitum, quod omnibus, aut plurimis apparet. [215]

persuasible, looks also to the probable, not in an absolute way as does dialectics, but to the probable that is persuasible. For everything that is persuasible is probable, but not the other way around. Therefore no clearer differentiation can be made between dialectics and rhetoric, in our judgment, than that, since each of them argues from probables, the former seeks the probable in an absolute sense, the latter, the probable that may also be called the persuasible.[20]

Obviously, as a result of this analysis, the *Topics* and the *Rhetoric* have elements in common, even though there are differences between them. Before turning to the similarities, Riccobono spells out the differences in slightly more detail:

1. The probable differs from the persuasible in the way a genus differs from a species.
2. The probable involves only argumentation; the persuasible also involves character and the emotions.
3. The probable pertains to opinion; the persuasible, to belief and persuasion.
4. The probable is more argued than stated; the persuasible is more stated than argued.
5. The probable is treated by question and answer, the latter, by continuous speech, "for to argue is proper to dialectics, to speak, and even to speak clearly and eloquently, to rhetoric, as is apparent from the etymology of the two."[21]

THE RELATION OF RHETORIC
TO OTHER DISCIPLINES

Remaining to be discussed now are a number of expressions that Aristotle uses to compare rhetoric to other disciplines and that have challenged commentators. Riccobono tries his hand at clarifying them on the basis of his analysis to date. The expressions communicate that (a) rhetoric is a composite [*sunkeisthai*] of

---

[20]

Atque illa, cum versetur in probabile, complectatur etiam persuasibile, quod eatenus est probabile, quatenus omnibus vel plurimis probetur; haec cum propositum habeat persuasibile, spectet etiam probabile, non simpliciter, ut Dialectica, sed illud, quod est persuasibile. Nam omne quidem persuasibile est probabile; sed non e converso. Itaque nulla clarior distinctio Dialecticae et Rhetoricae afferri nostro quidem iudicio potest, quam quod cum utraque ex probabilibus disputet, illa quidem probabile simpliciter; haec vero probabile, quod vocatur persuasibile, persequatur. [216]

[21]"Nam disserere est proprium Dialecticae; dicere, et quidem diserte dicere, atque eloqui Rhetoricae, quod patet ex utriusque etymologia" [218].

analytics and politics; (b) it is akin [*paraphuesti*] to dialectics and politics; (c) it is similar [*homoian*] to dialectics and sophistics; (d) it is the counterpart [*antisrophon*] of dialectics; and finally (e) it is both a part of and similar [*morionti kai homoiōma*] to dialectics [219]. I look briefly at each of these in turn.

Rhetoric is said to be a composite in this text, Riccobono explains, because it is "composed of analytical science and of politics, which is concerned with ethics." He goes on:

> That is, [it is a composite] of that universal and common logic that makes use of the syllogism, and is said to be analytics from analysis, that is, the dissolution of a thing into that of which it is composed, because the syllogism resolves to its principles; and also of politics, which studies character and the emotions. In this way rhetoric has a twofold nature, one from logic, whence it takes argumentation, the other from politics, whence the emotions and character. For although in this text only character is named, yet emotions are related to character, . . . for emotions are considered in rhetoric as a type of character, to the extent that speech can be applied to them; they are differentiated from character by the way in which they are aroused by the speaker in the souls of the hearers.[22]

To show that rhetoric is akin to dialectics and to politics, Riccobono first describes how Alexander of Aphrodisias explains this in his commentary, then how Cicero understands the comparison. His own view is that "dialectics and politics are like large trees from whose roots rhetoric rises like a branch."[23] For him Aristotle here meant dialectics, not as it was understood by Plato, but only as the part of logic that treats of probable arguments, and he meant politics to include only treatises on character and the emotions as these relate to life in the republic.

The statement that rhetoric is similar to dialectics and sophistics comes next. According to Aristotle's text, rhetoric "conforms its precepts either to the truth or to what appears true"; thus, on the face of it, "to the degree that the rhetor seeks truth he is similar to the dialectician, to the degree that he appears to do so, to the sophist."[24] Riccobono does not attempt to show, as do many commentators, that sophistical persuasion is foreign to rhetoric in its proper sense. He

---

[22] Id est, [Rhetorica esse composita] tum ex illa universali, et communi Logica, quae syllogismum conformat, et dicitur Analytica ab analysi, id est rei dissolutione in ea, ex quibus ipsa constat, quia syllogismum dissolvit in ipsius principia; tum ex scientia civili, quae mores, et affectus exornat; ita ut Rhetorica duplicem habeat naturam, unam a Logica, unde sumit argumentationem, alteram a scientia civili, unde affectus, et mores. Nam tametsi hoc in loco nominantur tantum mores, tamen affectus ad mores referuntur . . . ; affectus enim in Rhetorica considerantur tamquam mores, quatenus ad eos accommodatur oratio; distinguuntur a moribus quatenus ab oratore excitantur in animis auditorum. [219–220]

[23] "Nam prope Dialecticam, et Politicam quasi magnas arbores ex earum radicibus tamquam virgultum ipsa Rhetorica orta est" [220].

[24] "Etiam ipse quatenus sequitur verum est similis Dialectico; quatenus id, quod apparet, Sophistae" [221].

simply admits that Aristotle "locates the nature of rhetoric not only in the persuasive but also in the apparently persuasive."[25]

That rhetoric is the counterpart of dialectics elicits an extensive discussion based on the interpretations of Alexander and Cicero and of two of Riccobono's contemporaries, Petrus Victorius,[26] a professor of Greek at Florence; and Marc Antonio Maioragius,[27] a professor of rhetoric at Milan. Riccobono himself prefers Aristotle's own explanation, "as we read in his text, for it is a kind of counterpart of, and similitude of, dialectics, just as we also said it takes its origin. For neither of them is a science with a definite subject matter, inquiring into its properties; rather both are kinds of faculties for preparing arguments."[28] So, for him, these disciplines are similar to each other in that they both are about common subject matters and run somewhat parallel in their treatments.

The final point of comparison, that rhetoric is said to be a part of, and similar to, dialectics, Riccobono attributes to rhetoric's concern with what he calls "oratorical demonstration." He explains this as follows:

> With respect to its matter this type of demonstration is contained under dialectical demonstration, and the persuasible is a kind of probable. So also rhetoric is a kind of dialectic and a counterpart of dialectic, just as the rhetorical persuasive is a counterpart of the dialectical probable. And it is a similitude of dialectics, because both dispute on the same matters, both from probables, both on either side, even if there is a certain dissimilitude in that the one, dialectics, disputes on all issues, the other, rhetoric, more on civil matters; the one from all probabilities, the other only from those that are persuasive; the one uses question and answer, . . . the other continuous speech.[29]

---

[25]"Naturam Rhetoricae constituit non solum in persuasibili, sed etiam in apparente persuasibili" [222].

[26]A Latin and Greek scholar of distinction, Victorius (Vettori) was born in July of 1499 at Florence. In 1538 he became professor of Latin at the university there, and in 1543 also professor of Greek; five years later he assumed the post of professor of moral philosophy. In addition to his commentary on the *Rhetoric*, which he published at Florence in 1548, he published commentaries on the *Poetics* (Florence, 1560), the *Politics* (Florence, 1576), and the *Nicomachean Ethics* (Florence, 1584). Several photographs of frontispieces and page-spreads of his works on the *Rhetoric* are found in Brandes, *A History of Aristotle's Rhetoric*. Victorius died in Florence on December 18, 1585.

[27]This author was born in Maioraggio, a town near Milan, on October 26, 1514. He studied rhetoric and mathematics at Milan, then taught rhetoric there from 1540 to 1542. From 1543 onward he served as professor of eloquence, doing so until his death on April 4, 1555. Like Riccobono, he was a Latin translator of Aristotle's *Rhetoric*; for a list of the editions of his translation, see Brandes, *A History of Aristotle's Rhetoric* 142–145.

[28]"Nam sic apud eum legitur: Est enim Dialecticae particula quaedam, et similitudo, quemadmodum etiam exordientes dicebamus. Neutra enim ipsarum est scientia de aliqua re definita, quaerens, quomodo se habeat; sed ipsae facultates sunt quaedam parandi rationes" [221].

[29]Nam quoad materiam huiusmodi [oratoria] demonstratio continetur sub Dialectica demonstratione; et persuasibile est probabile quoddam. Itaque etiam Rhetorica est Dialectica quaedam, et particular Dialecticae, quoniam persuasibile Rhetoricum est particula probabilis Dialectici,

This more or less completes Riccobono's exposition of the nature of rhetoric. There are two additional matters, however, to which he turns his attention toward the end of his essay. One concerns the significant amount of overlap, one might say, between rhetoric and logic; the other, a similar overlap that might be seen between rhetoric and ethics. Both overlaps have pedagogical implications, for it would seem that, in view of the common concepts treated in these disciplines, a student should first have extensive foundations in logic and in ethics before beginning the study of rhetoric. This idea runs counter to late 16th-century practice in the schools, for students were introduced to rhetoric at a fairly early age, usually long before they could study logic and ethics, say, in the university.

RHETORIC AND LOGIC

The problem with regard to logic focuses on the enthymeme, for, as Riccobono states, "the rhetorician's knowledge of enthymemes depends on the logician's syllogism" [225];[30] and thus, if he has no knowledge of the syllogism he will not be able to understand "oratorical demonstration" as this is set forth in the enthymeme. His reaction to this is the following:

> Now we do not deny that for the perfection of the orator not only would the knowledge of logic be relevant but also that of other disciplines; but we do not think it so necessary that one have completed all the books of the logic before being a rhetor, and that one could not understand rhetoric sufficiently without them to be able to persuade. For if rhetoric needs any matters from logic, it has those things translated for its needs, and it is sufficient to learn them from the *Rhetoric*. For without doubt Aristotle's intention was to consider the same matter in various disciplines, but to do so in different ways, and only as much as seemed sufficient for the particular discipline.[31]

To illustrate the point, Riccobono takes an example from Aristotle's *Ethics* and the relation of its books to a more theoretical treatment found in his *De anima*.

---

et similitudo eiusdem, quia ambae disputant de rebus omnibus, ambae ex probabilibus, amabae in utranque partem, etiam si in eo sit dissimilitudo, quod una aeque disputat de rebus omnibus, altera magis de rebus civilibus, una ex probabilibus omnibus, altera tantum ex iis, quae persuasibilia sunt, una utitur interrogatione et responsione, ... alter continuata oratione. [224]

[30]"Unde facile perspicitur, enthymematis Rhetorici cognitionem a syllogismi Logici notitia pendere ..."[225].

[31]
Nos quidem non negamus ad oratoris perfectionem pertinere non solum Logicae, sed aliarum etiam artium cognitionem; sed non putamus esse ita necessariam, ut Logicorum libri omnino pervolutandi sint, prius quam Rhetorum, et non possint hi sine illis intelligi satis, atque ad persuadendum accommodate. Nam profecto si quibus rebus Logicis Rhetorica indiget, eas ex Logica in ipsam translatas habet, sat est eas percipere ex Rhetorica. Atque sine dubio habet, Institutum enim Aristotelis est, eandem rem variis quidem in artibus considerare, sed modo diverso, et quantum sufficere artibus videatur. [225–226]

The student of politics should know all of this matter if he is to study his discipline properly, and yet it may not be practical for him to do so. Aristotle knew this, Riccobono says, and that is why he structured his treatises the way he did. As he explains it:

> Since the virtues arise from the powers of the soul, and for this reason one has to treat of these powers in the *Ethics*, it would be suitable for him to transfer this matter from the *De anima*, whose books he calls exoteric, to the first book of the *Ethics* and to consider it there not in detailed fashion but only to the extent needed for ethical understanding. . . . Similarly politics should have some knowledge of the soul. But it should have this for the sake of, and only needs as much as can be applied to, the matters it studies; for to inquire into more than is suitable would perhaps involve more work than anticipated. Some matters are said about the soul that are more fully treated in the exoteric disputations, but they are to be used in this fashion, that the student of politics have but a competent understanding, the student of *De anima* an expert knowledge, of them. . . . Therefore Aristotle did not wish to deter the student of ethics from learning about the powers of the soul, nor did he wish to restrict this study to natural philosophy; rather he wanted to include it in the moral disciplines as well. But he said that the latter should have a theoretical knowledge of the soul for the sake of moral matters, and only what is sufficient for such matters, since a precise knowledge of what he had already treated [in the *De anima*] was not required.[32]

Once one has understood this fairly complex relationship between the *Politics*, the *Ethics*, and the *De anima*, it becomes a simple matter to grasp the complementary relationships that hold between logic and rhetoric. This Riccobono now explains as follows:

> Just as in ethics, where the detailed manner of learning natural philosophy is not needed but only the things needed for an understanding of ethics, so in rhetoric, where one requires a less precise manner of knowing matters contained in logic and only those that are worthwhile for the knowledge of rhetoric. And concerning these matters there should be knowledge for the sake of, and only as much as can

---

[32] Cum virtutes a facultatibus animae proficiscantur, et hac de caussa in libris Ethicorum agendum esset de ipsis facultatibus, quae convenerunt, omnia ille transtulit ex libris de animo, quos appellat exotericos, in librum primum de moribus eaque consideravit non modo exquisito, sed quantum visum est sufficere morali contemplationi. . . . Igitur et Politico contemplatio habenda est de animo; habenda autem horum gratia, et quatenus satis esse potest ad ea, de quibus quaestio est. Exquirere enim plus, quam conveniat, laboriosius fortasse est, quam ea, quae proposita sunt. Dicuntur autem de ipso non nulla, quae satis sunt etiam in exotericis disputationibus, atque ipsis utendum est; quemadmodum unam quidem partem eius compotem esse rationis, alteram vero expertam, et quae sequuntur. Noluit igitur Aristoteles studiosos Ethicae facultatis deterrere, nec eos prius reijcere ad res naturales, quam admittere ad morales; sed dixit habendam esse contemplationem de animo rerum moralium gratia, et quatenus satis esse potest, cum antea tradidisset, non requiri exactam rerum cognitionem. [226]

be applied to, the question proposed: for example, what is a syllogism, an enthymeme, induction, an example; in what way an enthymeme is an imperfect syllogism and what is lacking to it; that an example is an imperfect induction, as part to part; how an enthymeme is concerned with persuasibles and is made from verisimilars and signs; what the verisimilar is and also the sign; what the topical places are; in what ways objections are raised. Although all these things are treated as if they were logic, they are always interpolated into the *Rhetoric* to the extent that they are needed there.[33]

Having thus made his point, Riccobono concludes on a more conciliatory note, bowing in this way to his powerful colleague Zabarella:

Although nothing more may be required, if there are those who are not content with this knowledge that is sufficient for rhetorical purposes, they can always go to the primary sources themselves and fill up their souls from them. But we do not wish to argue this point further, nor do we wish to condemn those who, for the sake of greater erudition, wish to study logic before rhetoric (especially considering that among our students there are those who are studying both together), provided it be conceded to us that the knowledge of logic is not so necessary that it cannot be attained otherwise. . . . For rhetoric considers demonstration in much the same manner as does dialectics, although there is a difference in the force put in it, namely, that dialectics takes up all kinds of probables in demonstrations, whereas rhetorics contracts its probables to those that are properly persuasive.[34]

33

Iam quemadmodum in Ethicis ubi exquisitus discendi modus non postulatur, sunt omnia Physica, quae pertinere ad Ethycorum intelligentiam existimantur; sic in Rhetoricis, quae minus exactum contemplandi modum habent, sunt omnia logica, quae ad Rhetoricorum cognitionem valent. Atque de illis habita est contemplatio horum gratia, et quatenus satis esse poterat ad propositam quaestionem; ut quid sit syllogismus, quid enthymema, quid inductio, quid exemplum, quemadmodum enthymema sit syllogismus imperfectus cui aliquid desit, et exemplum inductio imperfecta tamquam pars ad partem; quemadmodum enthymema versetur in persuasibilibus, et constet ex verisimilibus, ac signis, et quid sit verisimile, et quid signum; qui sint loci Topici, quot modis afferantur obiectiones. Quae dum traduntur tametsi citetur Logica, ita tamen citatur, ut semper res Logicae, quibus indiget Rhetorica, in ipsa interponantur. [226–227]

34

Ut nihil aliud citata auctoritas valeat, nisi ut qui ea cognitione contenti non sunt, quae satis esse ad propositam quaestionem potest, ad praecipua loca earum rerum se conferant, et animum expleant suum; sed de his longius non contendemus; nec damnabimus, si quis voluerit maioris eruditionis caussa prius versari in logicis, quam in Rhetoricis (cum praesertim auditoribus nostris auctores esse soleamus, ut Logicam cum Rhetorica coniungant) dummodo nobis detur, id non esse ita necessarium, ut etiam aliter fieri non possit. . . . Considerat ergo Rhetorica demonstrationem, quemadmodum etiam Dialectica; quam vis in eo posita differentia sit, quod Dialectica, quidem demonstrationem suam per omne probabile diffundit; Rhetorica vero ad id probabile contrahit, quod est proprie persuasibile. [227]

In this connection we may note that Riccobono sees in the Aristotelian corpus an affinity of logic not only with rhetoric but also with poetics. Bernard Weinberg translates a passage from his *Ars poetica* that explicitly makes this point:

RHETORIC AND THE EMOTIONS

With these matters understood, Riccobono then extends his discussion to show how rhetoric considers character and the emotions just as does politics, but for a different reason. "Politics," he says, "views them insofar as they lead man to happiness, rhetoric, insofar as they are instruments of persuasion. For that reason the former treats them in greater detail, the latter in lesser."[35] Just how they do so he then explains in a fairly lengthy discourse on the emotions and how they are not foreign, as some have held, to the nature of rhetoric.

Riccobono begins by noting a number of Aristotle's own statements that might lead one to think that there is no place in rhetoric for treating the emotions, because they are extraneous to the discipline and should be absent when one is striving to arrive at a correct and unbiased judgment. As previously, he turns to his colleague Zabarella for an expression of this view and goes on to quote him as follows:

> He [Aristotle] says that the oratorical art consists in argumentations and asserts that these make up the body of the oration. He reproves the rhetors of those times because, passing over the argumentative part, they taught only matters that are extraneous and foreign to the nature of this art, such as elocution and arousing the emotions, which are not permitted in a well governed city, as in the Areopago, though they are allowed because of the depraved customs of men. According to Aristotle, therefore, argumentation alone constitutes the nature of the rhetorical art; arousing the emotions is completely foreign to it, despite the fact that it is in use because of the corrupt morals of the citizenry.[36]

> For although it [the art of poetry] has many things which do not belong to logic, nevertheless it is sufficient that in some outstanding aspect it may be called logic; just as also is the case with rhetoric, which contains not only the demonstrative discourse through which it is assigned to logic but also character and passions and moreover language and the order of its parts; nevertheless it is said to be a part of logic because of one device of demonstration. Similarly poetry, in addition to sententia which it has in common with rhetoric, treats not only plot whose most important part, which is called recognition, needs the syllogism, but also character and diction and harmony and spectacle; nevertheless because of one form of reasoning which is employed in plot construction, and instruction in whose use is pertinent in the extreme to the plot itself, it seemed to the great philosopher Averroes and to others that it should be called a part of logic. (Weinberg, *A History of Literary Criticism* 1:583)

[35]"Nam Politica eos intuetur, quatenus ipsi hominem ad felicitatem perducunt; Rhetorica, quatenus sunt instrumenta persuasionis" [228].

[36]
Dicit [Aristoteles] oratoriam artem in argumentationibus consistere, quas etiam ipsius orationis corpus esse asserit. Rhetores autem suorum temporum reprehendit, qui pretermissa parte argumentativa ea solum docebant, quae extranea erant, et aliena ab huis artis natura, ut est elocutio, et perturbationum commotio, quae quidem in orationibus admittenda non essent, in civitate bene gubernata, quaemadmodum in Areopago non admittebantur; admittuntur tamen propter mores hominum depravatos. Quare apud Aristotelem sola argumentatio naturam oratoriae artis constituit; affectionum autem commotio ab ipsa penitus aliena est, licet in usu sit propter mores civitatum corruptos. [229–230]

With all due respect to Zabarella, and not so much to refute him as to arrive at a fuller appreciation of the truth, Riccobono offers "a few considerations that might induce one to hold that the emotions, in some way, are not foreign to the nature of rhetoric."[37] He does so first by calling attention to Aristotle's own practice in treating the emotions, and then by answering the various arguments that have led others to exclude them from the rhetorical art.

Aristotle himself, says Riccobono, identified his treatise on the emotions as a part of rhetoric and indeed gave over a large part of book 2 to their discussion. Aristotle also made clear that persuasion requires not only logical argument but also appeals to character and to the emotions. From what has been said earlier, it should be clear that rhetoric is "conflated of analytical science, that is, of matters that pertain to demonstration [i.e, logic], and of politics, that is, of matters that pertain to emotions and characters."[38] If this is so, then there are two principal parts of rhetoric: one is concerned with logical argument; the other is concerned with how the argument affects the judge who hears it and is influenced by the character of the one presenting it. The second part is just as necessary as the first. That is why Aristotle stated at the beginning of book 3 that the oration should treat of three things, which Riccobono summarizes as follows: "first, the matters from which belief is induced; second, elocution; and third, how the parts of the oration should be arranged."[39] He goes on to note that "this first part of rhetoric that induces belief is divided into demonstration, emotions, and characters."[40] The Aristotelian text on which Riccobono bases that statement is undoubtedly the following: "In all cases persuasion is the result either of the judges being affected in a certain manner, or because they consider the speakers to be of a certain character, or because something has been demonstrated" [1403b11–13]. From this he argues that the rhetorician must be just as concerned with emotions and characters as with logical argument.

Yet there are three arguments that might be brought against this interpretation, all based in varying degrees on the text of Aristotle. One is that inducing belief is a matter of logic, and it alone pertains to the art of rhetoric, all other considerations being extraneous to it. Another is that the enthymeme constitutes the body of belief, and apart from this nothing more is required. A third is based on the practice in the Areopago, where moving the emotions was prohibited; for the same reason, moving the emotions should be excluded from the art of rhetoric.

---

[37]"Non nulla in medium afferam, quibus existimare aliquo modo possit, affectus a natura Rhetoricae non esse alienos" [230].

[38]"Rhetorica esse conflata ex Analytica scientia, id est ex ijs, quae pertinent ad demonstrationem, et ex Politica, id est ex ijs, quae ad mores et affectus" [230].

[39]"Unum, ex quibus ipsa fides existat; alterum, de elocutione; tertium, quomodo conveniat ordinare partes orationis . . ." [230].

[40]"Prima pars Rhetoricae quae fidem continet, dividitur in demonstrationem, affectus, mores" [230].

Riccobono approaches the first argument by distinguishing various ways in which components might pertain to an art and thus be called *artificiosa* or "arte-factual." One way is to see a component either as intrinsic to the matter the art considers (*de re*) or as extrinsic to it (*extra rem*). Riccobono is willing to concede that belief or logical persuasion is artefactual in the first way, but he holds that moving the emotions is artefactual in the second. "That is the reason," he writes, "why Aristotle himself enumerated the emotions among the artefactual parts of belief, even though he thought them to be extrinsic."[41] Furthermore, the matter of the art can be considered in two additional ways: "either according to right reason and the way in which matters should be rightly understood, and thus by artefactual demonstration alone; or according to necessity and how it is referred to the audience, who are presumed to be uncultured (*rudi*), and thus by artefactual appeals to the emotions."[42] "Rhetoric," he goes on, "is always to be taken in the second way." That is why it is necessary to look not only to proof or belief, the subject of book 1, but to emotion and character, subjects treated respectively in books 2 and 3, as well. So he concludes: "Therefore the nature of rhetoric is made up of two components: things that are intrinsic, such as demonstrations, and those that are extrinsic, such as the emotions."[43]

Riccobono's reply to the second argument is similar to his response to the first and, indeed, may be seen as a further clarification of it. He does not wish to deny that the enthymeme constitutes the body of proof or belief; his position is simply "that the nature of rhetoric is concerned not only with the body of belief but with certain additions also."[44] So, when he used the expression *extrinsic* (*extra rem*), he did not intend that to mean 'outside the scope of rhetoric' (*extra rhetoricam*). Moving the emotions, in this sense, is "outside the case" (*caussa*) that is being presented; it is not "outside the rhetoric" being used to present it [231].

The final argument evokes from Riccobono an interesting distinction between two kinds of rhetoric, one of which he refers to as a rhetoric "in action" (*quae agit*), the other as a rhetoric "that gives precepts" (*quae praecepta tradit*) [231–232]. The distinction is of interest because effectively it is the same as that between *rhetorica utens* (rhetoric in use) and *rhetorica docens* (rhetoric teaching), mirroring that between *logica utens* and *logica docens*—a distinction known to

---

[41]"Quae fuit caussa, cur ipse Aristoteles inter partes fidei artificiosae affectus numeraverit, etiam si eos esse extra rem intelligeret" [231].

[42]"Vel materiam artis spectari modo secundum rectam rationem suam, et quatenus res se recte habeat; sic solam demonstrationem artificiosam; modo secundum necessitatem, et quatenus refertur ad auditorem, qui supponitur esse rudis; sic etiam affectus artificiosos . . ." [231].

[43]"Natura igitur Rhetoricae duo complectitur: tum ea, quae sunt de re, ut demonstrationes, tum ea, quae sunt extra rem, ut affectus" [231].

[44]"Dicimus naturam Rhetoricae versari non solum in corpore fidei, sed etiam in additamentis" [231].

Zabarella and much used by medieval and Renaissance logicians.[45] On the basis of this distinction Riccobono proceeds to argue:

> Emotions can sometimes be absent from a rhetoric in action, since an occasion might be given the orator in which there is no opportunity to move the emotions, but not from a rhetoric that gives precepts, for it must treat norms to which the orator should conform universally, such that, whatever the occasion that may be given, however he may wish to persuade, he may carry out his function in praise-worthy fashion.[46]

In the incidental case, therefore, it may not be necessary to make emotional appeals, but this is no reason for excluding them completely from the rhetorical art.

The problem posed by usage within the Areopago yields to solution in similar manner, though it has also been touched upon in Riccobono's answer to the first argument discussed earlier. He grants that the prohibition against emotional appeals in the Areopago would also rule out a large part of what he sees as legitimate rhetoric. In the Areopago, of course, such appeals would not be needed if, in the ideal case, all audiences were endowed with wisdom and sanctity. But these virtues are not found in audiences universally. Or, to put the matter somewhat differently, logic will suffice to convince those who are virtuous and well informed, but necessity may require using more than logic when presenting a case to those who are not. "There is no reason, therefore, to exclude emotions from the nature of rhetoric."[47]

These considerations move Riccobono to his final question, namely, whether it is licit to move the emotions. The problem arises because Aristotle holds that it is not licit to pervert the judge; and if this is so, it would follow that it is not licit to move the emotions. Riccobono denies the consequent of this argument, maintaining:

---

[45]For an explanation of the difference between *logica docens* and *logica utens* as well as that between *rhetorica docens* and *rhetorica utens*, see William A. Wallace, "Thomas Aquinas on Dialectics and Rhetoric," *A Straight Path: Studies in Medieval Philosophy and Culture*, ed. R. Link-Salinger (Washington, DC: Catholic University of America Press, 1987) 244–254. The difference between *docens* and *utens* was known to Galileo. Indeed, I structured my detailed study of his entire logic on the basis of that distinction; see William A. Wallace, *Galileo's Logic of Discovery and of Proof: The Background, Content, and Use of His Appropriated Treatises on Aristotle's "Posterior Analytics"* (Dordrecht: Kluwer Academic Publishers, 1992). This is a companion volume to William A. Wallace, *Galileo's Logical Treatises: A Translation, with Notes and Commentary, of His Appropriated Latin Questions on Aristotle's "Posterior Analytics"* (Dordrecht: Kluwer Academic Publishers, 1992).

[46]"Posse aliquando affectus abesse, cum offerri oratori possit occasio, in qua ei affectus movendi non sint; sed non ab ea, quae praecepta tradit, cum ad ipsam pertineat, oratorem in universum conformare eiusmodi, qui, quaecunque occasio offeratur, quomodo libet persuadendi, munus suum laudabiliter obeat" [232].

[47]"Non est igitur, cur a Rhetoricae natura affectus abijciamus" [232].

Either through the emotions one draws the audience to what is false, and then it is not licit, or to what is true, and then it is licit. Therefore if all audiences were of the type of the Areopagites, virtuous and wise, there would be no need for moving the emotions, for it would be sufficient to open up reasons and arguments showing the truth. But since those who hear are often reprobates and labor under great ignorance, for them demonstrations have greater force when they are conjoined with emotional appeals.[48]

His warrant for this conclusion is a passage from Quintilian, which he cites in its entirety:

What, therefore, is one to say? Is the truth to be obscured by moving the emotions? Not at all, for if the judge cannot be led to the truth otherwise, he should be led to it by moving them. Add to this that audiences are often led by these emotions because of their own wickedness and ignorance, and this leads them into error. Thus, if the same emotions are not removed from them, or if they were not impelled to contrary emotions, they would never be able to perceive the truth. It is necessary, therefore, to move the emotions so that the truth may better shine forth, and this should be undertaken out of necessity, since the emotions gain great strength from the depravity of the audience, as Aristotle himself testifies.[49]

RICCOBONO THE TEACHER

Even from this brief sketch of Riccobono's views on the nature of rhetoric it can be seen that he was very much a part of both the Aristotelian and the humanist traditions at the University of Padua. Although critically aware of Zabarella's views on the subject, he was not at all subservient to this philosopher who dominated that university in his day. He was able to see his own discipline as having ramifications with regard to nearly all the university curriculum, and yet

---

[48]

dicimus, aut per affectus trahi auditores ad id, quod falsum est, et tunc non licere; aut ad id, quod verum est, et tunc licere. Ergo si omnes auditores existerent, cuiusmodi erant Areopagitae, sanctissimi, et sapientissimi, affectibus minime opus esset; sufficeret enim eis, veritatem rationibus, et argumentis aperire; sed quoniam saepe, qui audiunt, improbi sunt, et rerum ignoratione laborant, idcirco ut demonstrationes apud eos maiorem vim habeant, cum affectibus coniungendae sunt. [232–233]

[49]

Quid ergo, dicet aliquis? obscuranda ne est veritas animorum commotione? Minime vero; sed si aliter ad veritatem perduci Iudex non potest, necessario per commotionem est perducendus. Adde, quod saepe auditores propter improbitatem, aut propter ignorantiam in ijs affectibus versantur, qui ipsos in errorem inducunt; ut nisi eiusmodi affectus ab eis amoveantur, vel etiam in contrarios affectus impellantur, nunquam veritatem perspecturi sint. Necessarium igitur est, affectus movere, ut veritas magis illuceat; et huius rei tamquam necessariae suscipienda cura est, cum affectus multum valeant propter pravitatem auditorum, ut ipse testatur Aristoteles. [233]

he taught it in such a way as to preserve its autonomy and integrity against attacks by his adversaries.

Some have criticized Riccobono's translation of the *Rhetoric* as not being faithful to Aristotle's text,[50] but a better evaluation would be that of Bernard Weinberg, who describes the principles behind Riccobono's translation of the *Poetics* in terms that suggest they were pedagogical in intent. These principles, it seems clear from what we have seen, would also apply to his translation of the *Rhetoric*. Of them Weinberg writes:

> I think that we may state thus Riccobono's principles for the translation: To achieve a Latin version simpler and more readable than those heretofore available; to adopt, by means of the translation itself, a firm stand on as many of the disputed questions of the text as possible; to render apparent the order, the parts, and the method of the original work.[51]

To achieve these objectives, Weinberg goes on, Riccobono "simplifies word order in such a way as to make it almost as simple as Italian word order; he eliminates all flourishes of style, all farfetched words, all useless attempts at variety and sonority; he adopts a uniform terminology which eliminates ambiguity and doubt."[52] This causes him to depart from precise word-for-word translation, and perhaps his Latinity suffers as a consequence, but the end result is a text that is more palatable to the Italian reader and is more suited to the needs of students. His virtues as a pedagogue thus outweigh whatever defects he may have as a translator. In taking a firm stand on disputed points, for example, Riccobono risks his translation becoming a kind of interpretation of the text, but he usually informs the reader of alternate views in marginal notes. Thus he gives students a clear idea of the way he himself reads Aristotle's text, while alerting them to the possibility of other readings. Further, he breaks up the text into short, numbered sections, thus enabling students to see at a glance the order and the method behind Aristotle's presentation. All of these devices achieve for him praiseworthy instructional goals, even though they cost him elegance in translation.

In sum, Riccobono was quite sensitive to the problems involved in teaching classical rhetoric to 16th-century university students. He knew that even in that century many of them would not have a sufficiently expert knowledge of logic to appreciate the intricacies of the enthymeme and the example as modes of argument. He was also aware that they lacked sufficient knowledge of the soul and its powers to understand fully how appeals to the emotions and to character are effective means of persuasion. Yet he would not dispense with any one of these—*logos, ethos,* or *pathos*—on the grounds that they were too difficult to teach or that others in the university community would be able to teach them

---

[50]Brandes, *A History of Aristotle's Rhetoric* 83 n.29.

[51]Weinberg, *A History of Literary Criticism* 1:584.

[52]Weinberg, *A History of Literary Criticism* 1:585.

better. Instead he saw in Aristotle's text a coherent and self-sufficient exposition of the art of persuasion, and he took on the task of making it intelligible to his students. His efforts can surely be a guide, and perhaps an inspiration, to others who would emulate him in the present day.

CONTINUITY AND CHANGE
IN 18th-CENTURY
RHETORICAL EDUCATION

A Minor Skirmish: Balthazar Gibert Versus Charles Rollin on Rhetorical Education

Barbara Warnick
University of Washington

During the early 18th century in France, a series of events in the life of Charles Rollin conspired to produce a work that would influence rhetorical pedagogy until well into the 19th century. Rollin was first elected Rector of the University of Paris in his late thirties, then reelected 20 years later; in the interim he served as principal of the Collège de Beauvais. He was forced to resign his offices, however, because of his Jansenist sympathies and his liaisons with prominent Jansenists.[1] In 1720 he retired, and he spent the last 20 years of his life writing and revising his treatise, *De la Manière d'enseigner et d'étudier les belles lettres par rapport à l'esprit et au coeur*.[2] Commonly known as the *Traité des études*, this work was first published between 1726 and 1728 and contained sections on the teaching of rhetoric and the practice of eloquence that formed a matrix of elements from neoclassical and belletristic rhetorical theories.[3]

Rollin's *Traité* was well received. It was favorably reviewed in the journals of the day and commended by the Assemblée de la Faculté des Arts at the

---

[1]On Rollin's life, see H. Ferté, *Rollin: sa vie, ses oeuvres* (Paris: Hachette, 1902) 3–96; and Albert C. Gaudin, *The Educational Views of Charles Rollin* (New York: Thesis Publishing Co., 1939) 1–8.

[2]Charles Rollin, *De la Manière d'enseigner et d'étudier les belles lettres, par rapport à l'esprit et au coeur, ou Traité des études*, 4 vols. (Lyon: Russand, 1819). This and all other translations from Rollin's works are mine. Hereafter cited as *Traité*.

[3]On the emergence of belletrism in the works of Fénelon, Boileau, Rollin, and Dubos and their influence on 18th-century Scottish belletrism, see Barbara Warnick, *The Sixth Canon: Belletristic Rhetorical Theory and Its French Antecedents* (Columbia: University of South Carolina Press, 1993).

University.[4] It appeared in twenty-seven French editions prior to 1882, six abridged editions, and seven editions of Rollin's collected works.[5] First published in English in 1734, Rollin's *Traité* subsequently appeared in ten editions at London, three at Edinburgh, and one at Dublin.[6]

The *Traité*'s favorable reception can be explained in part by Rollin's progressive views on the education of young people. His Jansenist leanings and his admiration of Port Royalist education led him to advocate instruction in the vernacular along with reading and study of contemporary French authors such as Fléchier, Bossuet, Massillon, and Malherbe. Like later belletrists, Rollin believed that one of the principal purposes of adolescent education was to form taste. In his *Traité*, Rollin noted that reading and study of great models of eloquence "are very suited to forming young people's taste. We must tell them that the surest means of succeeding in description is to consult nature, to study it well, to take it as a guide, so that each person feels in himself the truth of what he says, and finds in his own heart the feelings expressed in the discourse."[7] Rollin's emphasis on forming taste, emulating models of eloquence, and natural expression anticipated Adam Smith and Hugh Blair's *Lectures on Rhetoric and Belles Lettres* and was highly compatible with the views of his 18th-century successors.

Unfortunately, favorable reception of Rollin's work was not unanimous. Many of the *Traité*'s recommendations went against the grain of traditional rhetorical pedagogy, which emphasized careful composition on technical or specialized subjects and learning through direct prescription rather than through exposure to models. This school of thought had a powerful advocate in Balthazar Gibert, professor of rhetoric at the Collège de Beauvais and of theology at the Collège Mazarin. Gibert was also a former Rector of the University and author of *Traité de la véritable éloquence* (1703) and *Jugement des savants sur les auteurs qui ont traité de la rhétorique* (1713–1719).[8] He took exception to Rollin's entire

---

[4]Rollin refers to these accolades in his published response to Gibert, "Lettre de Mr. Rollin à Mr. Gibert, ancien Recteur de l'Université, au sujet de ses observations sur le Traité de la manière d'enseigner & d'étudier les Belles Lettres," *Opuscules de feu M. Rollin*, 2 vols. (Paris: Estienne, 1771) 1:198.

[5]For a publication history of the *Traité*, see Barbara Warnick, "Charles Rollin's *Traité* and the Rhetorical Theories of Smith, Campbell, and Blair," *Rhetorica* 3 (1985): 48–49.

[6]The title page of the English translation's 11th edition reads, *"The Method of Teaching and Studying the Belles Lettres, or, an Introduction to Languages, Poetry, Rhetoric, History, Moral Philosophy & c., with Reflections on Taste, and Instructions with regard to Eloquence of the Pulpit, the Bar, and the Stage.* The whole illustrated with Passages from the most famous Poets and Orators, Ancient and Modern, with critical remarks on them. Designed more particularly for students in the University. By M. Rollin, late Principal of the University of Paris, Professor of Eloquence in the Royal College, and Member of the Royal Academy of Inscriptions and Belles Lettres. Translated from the French. London: W. Wilson, 1810." English language editions appeared at London in 1734, 1737, 1742, 1749, 1758, 1761, 1798, 1804, and 1810; at Edinburgh in 1759, 1768, and 1773; and at Dublin in 1778.

[7]Rollin, *Traité* 2:201.

[8]*La grande encyclopédie*, 1st ed., s.v. "Gibert, Balthazar."

approach, and in 1727 he produced his 476-page *Observations addressées à Mr. Rollin ... sur son Traité. ...*[9]

Early in his work, Gibert explained his motivation for publishing a work so opposed to one of his *confrères*:

> Regarding the precepts of eloquence, I believe I can prove to you that there are great mistakes in your work which are all the more to be feared when they are mixed with so many good things. . . . But there is more. For what you teach on this point, you say you offer to instruct young professors and to show the public what the form-masters of the University teach. I belong to this group, and you see the consequence! Would it be suitable for me to recognize a doctrine that I have never taught, that I would be very displeased to teach, and whose errors I can demonstrate?[10]

With this disclaimer, Gibert accused Rollin of misrepresenting systematically the nature and method of rhetorical instruction at the University, and furthermore, he appointed himself to correct any erroneous impressions that Rollin's work might have caused.

Shortly after Gibert's response appeared, Rollin, then hard at work on the remaining two volumes of his treatise, wrote a brief response dealing only with the severest of Gibert's accusations, and Gibert responded with a second treatise.[11] Their exchange illuminated the issues that separated the old pedagogy from the new. For most of the students in the 18th-century colleges, the rhetoric class was the culmination of their basic education in grammar and composition.[12] For the rest, the course served as a transition between elementary instruction and subsequent study of logic, metaphysics, morals, and physics in the philosophy course. In either case, the rhetoric course was the linchpin in the student's academic development, and Gibert and Rollin painted very different pictures of what the rhetoric classroom ought to be like.

Gibert's classroom was a place where students learned the precepts of Aristotle and other classical rhetoricians by rote and applied them systematically to brief excerpts and *thèmes* designed by the instructor. Learning tasks were highly structured, and instruction was provided in Latin. Rollin, however, was more con-

---

[9]Balthazar Gibert, *Observations addressées à Mr. Rollin, Ancien recteur et professeur royal, sur son Traité de la manière d'enseigner et d'étudier les Belles-Lettres* (Paris: François-Guillaume l'Hermite, 1727). Hereafter cited as *Observations*.

[10]Gibert, *Observations* 13. This and all translations from Gibert's works are mine.

[11]Rollin's letter to Gibert is cited in footnote 4. See also the tract-length *Réponse de Mr. Gibert à la lettre de Mr. Rollin* (Paris: François-Guillaume L'Hermite, 1727), hereafter cited as *Réponse*.

[12]For descriptions of rhetoric as taught in late 17th- and early 18th-century classrooms, see Peter France, *Rhetoric and Truth in France: Descartes to Diderot* (New York: Oxford University Press, 1972) 13–29; Georges Snyders, *La Pédagogie en France au XVIIᵉ et XVIIIᵉ siècles* (Paris: Presses Universitaires, 1964) 111–128; and Henri Lantoine, *Etudes sur l'histoire de l'enseignement* (Paris: Hachette, 1919) 199–236.

cerned with forming taste through reading and explication of classical and contemporary models. Rollin's instructor would serve as a model and coach to his students rather than as a taskmaster. These two theorists' contrasting views of rhetorical education offer a snapshot of the change from 17th-century neoclassicism to 18th-century modernism, a microcosm of the intellectual milieu in which the two men worked. The controversy between them thus merits examination.

The first point on which Gibert takes issue with Rollin is the latter's theory of taste. Early in the *Traité*, Rollin had discussed at length the all-important concept of *le goût*. He observed that one of the principal ends of his work was to enable its readers to instruct the young in such a way as to form taste. "Good taste, which is based on unchanging principles, is the same in all ages, and it is the principal fruit that we must cause young people to gather from their reading of the ancients, who have always been viewed as the masters, the depositories, the guardians of sound eloquence and good taste."[13] Here Rollin speaks of *le goût* in a definite sense—that which is lasting, "*immuable*," which endures despite cultural proclivities and preferences.

This *goût immuable* can be intuitively sensed but defies precise definition. Rollin claims that the *goût immuable* is innate but can be developed through study of great models and learned application. This compromise between inborn, intuitive sense and a capacity that can be cultivated and developed also characterized the 18th-century views on taste of Alexander Gerard, David Hume, and Hugh Blair.[14] In his view of taste, Rollin shared these authors' faith in great works that, in Rollin's words, "draw the praise of persons of all ages and conditions, the ignorant as well as the learned."[15]

The *goût immuable* that brings about and responds to such works consults and follows nature, discerns the true from the false, detects faults or errors that lead us away from true art, and thus recognizes art of enduring value. Rollin claims that it is in the study of rhetoric that such taste is principally to be developed.

There is clearly yet another variety of taste in Rollin's aesthetic system; let us call it the *goût éphémère*. This is taste in the culture-bound sense, and Rollin believes that it can become corrupt, even depraved. This ephemeral taste is first discussed when Rollin argues that the *goût immuable* could not be totally eliminated or subdued by the *goût éphémère*. "However depraved taste might be, it does not perish entirely. There remain always in men points that are fixed, impressed deeply in their spirit in which they agree and join together."[16] Rollin furthermore believes that in some quarters of his own society a *goût corrumpu* prevails and tempts the naïve young with its sparkling floridity. "They want

---

[13]Rollin, *Traité*, 1:159.
[14]Warnick, *Sixth Canon* 96–116.
[15]Rollin, *Traité* 1:151.
[16]Rollin, *Traité* 1:151.

nothing but what is novel, showy, extraordinary, bold. They are attracted only to thoughts that are trivial and puerile or rash and exaggerated to excess. They affect a labored and florid style, and elaborate elocution that is only sound and nothing more."[17]

There is a tension here in Rollin's aesthetics between the *goût immuable* and the *goût éphémère*. Rollin offers the rhetoric course as a means of access for students to the *goût immuable*, but, at the same time, he believes that the orator must adjust his discourse to the taste of his auditors (*goût éphémère*). In praising Cicero in the first edition of the *Traité*, Rollin observed that "the orator must form his style according to the taste of those who hear him."[18] This is the point on which Gibert attacks Rollin. How, he asks, can we discover what a fixed rule of taste is to be and at the same time insist that the orator adjust his style to the audience's taste? "How have you not perceived that this principle, which is true, overthrows your project of *forming or fixing taste* and renders your work useless?"[19] Gibert gives two reasons why this requirement of audience adaptation is ill advised: first, audience taste may be corrupt or depraved and therefore should not be perpetuated by the orator; second, it is the orator's responsibility to set taste rather than to pander to it. Gibert, who believes in a fixed rule of taste, insists that "the orator thus forms his style according to the rules as reason requires, and not according to the taste of those who hear him. . . ."[20]

Rollin, who seemed largely unperturbed by this apparent circularity in his theory of taste, responded to Gibert in two ways. First, in his published response, he again insisted on the importance of adjusting one's discourse to audience taste because "one of the surest means of persuading is to please."[21] If the orator's purpose is to affect his auditors, he reasoned, then the orator neglects the *goût éphémère* only at his own peril. Second, Rollin, in his second and subsequent editions, carefully qualified the passage from the first edition that Gibert had selected for attack: "persuaded that the orator, *without deviating from good principles* can *to a certain point* form his style according to the taste of those who hear him (*it is understood that I do not speak here of a depraved or corrupt taste*). . . ."[22] In Rollin's view, then, one could suit one's style to audience taste yet conform to the appropriateness and judgment implied in the *goût immuable*.

The second major issue separating Rollin and Gibert involved the use of examples in pedagogy—in particular, the nature of the examples to be used and the use to which they were to be put. Rollin believed that exposure to appropriate and carefully chosen passages from ancient and modern writers was essential to

---

[17]Rollin, *Traité* 1:155.

[18]Cited from the *Traité*'s first edition by Gibert in his *Observations* (31). I was unable myself to consult the first edition of the *Traité*.

[19]Gibert, *Observations* 33.

[20]Gibert, *Observations* 42.

[21]Rollin, "Lettre de Mr. Rollin à Mr. Gibert," *Opuscules* 1:203.

[22]Rollin, *Traité* 2:275.

the forming of good taste, which, he said, should be the central purpose of instruction in rhetoric. He observed: "Rhetoric without the reading of good writers is a mute and sterile science . . . examples have infinitely more force than precepts. Indeed, rather than being satisfied with showing young people from afar the route that they must take, the sensible rhetor takes them by the hand and shows them the way."[23]

Rollin justified his use of lengthy and unabridged passages from ancient and modern authors in three ways. First, he said, because the original principles of rhetoric were drawn from observation of great eloquence in action, close reading of great orators and writers ought to enable students to discern similar principles.[24] Second, familiarity with great models allows students to comprehend the reasoning and justification behind the rules and precepts that accompany the examples.[25] And, third, reading lengthy examples provides students with the opportunity to compare various styles of discourse and even to detect defects in some.[26] The approach involves close reading of texts, commentary on the style, exposure of artifice in arrangement and invention, discussion of the text's arguments, and conclusions concerning the orator's or author's skill in effectively addressing his audience. This method, similar to *explication de texte* in literary studies, was recommended for rhetorical study in Rollin's source, the *Institutio Oratoria* of Quintilian.[27]

Rollin further believed that models and assigned topics for development should be within students' immediate experience and capacity to understand and reproduce. Additionally, Rollin recommended readings in the vernacular from contemporary authors (la Fontaine, Fontenelle, Bossuet, Massillon) in graduated order of difficulty. Rollin included extensive extracts from Cicero and Demosthenes, but his reliance upon the vernacular, although popular with the public, must have irritated and angered representatives of the "old guard" pedagogy such as Gibert.

Gibert's theory of learning differed noticeably from Rollin's. Midway through his response to Rollin, Gibert describes his own method. "After all, what do you think of those who first provide principles to open the mind and very brief examples to explain them? Who then provide a proposition for treatment and who question their students so that, guided by these principles, the students produce from their resources, not the work itself, but some ideas designed to get them started?"[28] Sample propositions for development into *thèmes* are provided by Gibert: "Nothing merits admiration more than eloquence." "Speak in favor or against Caesar's murderers." "Decide what should be done with the city of

---

[23]Rollin, *Traité* 2:2.
[24]Rollin, *Traité* 2:2.
[25]Rollin, *Traité* 2:4.
[26]Rollin, *Traité* 2:2.
[27]Quintilian, *Institutio Oratoria* 2.5.16, cited in Rollin, *Traité* 2:2.
[28]Gibert, *Observations* 135.

Carthage once it is taken."[29] The importance of set rules and precepts in these activities is stressed repeatedly by Gibert, who insists to Rollin: "We see only that your idea concerning the dryness of precepts is untenable, because the precept is the seed, which, sewn in good soil, develops and produces abundance."[30]

Many of Gibert's objections to Rollin's use of examples are well taken. Gibert notes that many of Rollin's long citations are virtually unaccompanied by precepts or commentary—all text and very little or no explication. How, Gibert asks, is a student to learn precise rules or precepts when he is exposed to long passages without commentary? Gibert was puzzled by Rollin's method, which proceeded "not only without the substance of rhetoric, but without even explaining well its examples by its principles, as if in order to instruct students in eloquence, one must only put before their eyes pieces of harangues to imitate."[31] Expecting students to learn to compose and speak eloquently through mere exposure to long passages from works is equivalent to expecting one to learn to sculpt by observing statuary, or to play an instrument by hearing an orchestra. It is evident that examples were much more closely tied to rules and precepts in Gibert's classroom.

Gibert furthermore observes that some of the finer treatises on rhetoric from antiquity—Aristotle's *Rhetoric*, for example, which Rollin approvingly cites— were composed primarily of precepts and nearly devoid of examples. "I point out to you only that this precise Rhetoric of Aristotle has produced great orators and teachers. Which shows that the preciseness of precepts dries up neither the mind nor the discourse."[32] It is clear that Gibert believed that command of principles of rhetoric was not only desirable but even necessary to the production of eloquent discourse.

The most serious indictment of Rollin's theory of rhetorical pedagogy comes when Gibert accuses him of misrepresenting Quintilian's position on the appropriateness of examples as a means of instructing students in eloquence. Gibert maintains that Quintilian endorsed the use of extensive examples only for more advanced students of rhetoric: "It is true that Quintilian in his second book boldly determines that *examples are more effective than precepts*: but for whom does he decide this? It is for advanced persons. There is the condemnation of your idea. For what he declares is proper only for already instructed minds, you present and put into practice for children who are not instructed."[33] If what Gibert maintains is correct, this is very damaging for Rollin, who did indeed suggest the use of extended examples in elementary rhetorical instruction.

In fact, Rollin's use of Quintilian is one of the few points on which Rollin bothers to respond directly to Gibert in his brief answer. Rollin defends his use

---

[29]Gibert, *Observations* 137.

[30]Gibert, *Observations* 110.

[31]Gibert, *Observations* 68.

[32]Gibert, *Observations* 106.

[33]Gibert, *Observations* 70–71.

of Quintilian, not only maintaining that his source recommends use of entire orations as models but, furthermore, claiming that "reading Demosthenes and Cicero will serve young people much better than all the corrected declamations that teachers can give to schoolboys to serve as models."[34] Gibert seems unwilling to give up this point, for, in his final refutation of Rollin's essay, he again accuses his opponent of misrepresenting Quintilian and misapplying his source's recommendations.[35] Consultation of Rollin's and Gibert's claims leaves the issue unresolved.

Careful consultation of Quintilian's *Institutio Oratoria*, books 2 and 10, indicates that Rollin's interpretation of Quintilian's position on the use of models in rhetorical instruction is much more accurate than Gibert's. First, Quintilian believes that rhetorical instruction should begin at a much younger age than it did in his day: "The custom has prevailed and is daily growing commoner of sending boys to schools of rhetoric much later than is reasonable. . . . Consequently, subjects which once formed the first stages of rhetoric have come to form the final stages of a literary education. . . ."[36] Second, Quintilian clearly believes that, even in the earliest stages of instruction in rhetoric, students should be exposed to extensive models of discourse and directed to use the method of *explication de texte*: "As we are discussing the elementary stages of a rhetorical education, I think I should not fail to point out how greatly the rhetorician will contribute to his pupils' progress, if he imitates the teacher of literature . . . and gives the pupils whom he has undertaken to train instruction in the reading of history and still more of orators."[37] Shortly thereafter, Quintilian precisely outlines the method to be used in studying long passages, and his recommendations are mirrored by Rollin. It is clear that Quintilian believed that formal rhetorical instruction should begin at an earlier age than was then customary and that it should consist of sustained study of entire passages from the works of orators and historians. One is hard pressed to understand why Gibert so assiduously pursued the lines of his argument that Quintilian felt *explication de texte* should be reserved only for advanced students, when Quintilian clearly took the opposite position. In any case, on other points at issue regarding his own use of sources and examples, Rollin declines to comment, evidently leaving it to the public to judge whose interpretations were the more faithful and responsible.

There are other, less significant points at issue in this dispute on which Rollin rather than Gibert has been supported. One of the more interesting is the question of the authorship of Fénelon's *Dialogues on Eloquence*, a source Rollin referred to frequently in his *Traité*. Gibert cites a passage from Fénelon's will repudiating all works not published during his lifetime and claims that authorship of the

[34]Rollin, "Lettre de Mr. Rollin à Mr. Gibert, *Opuscules* 1:202.

[35]Gibert, *Réponse* 11.

[36]Quintilian, *Institutio Oratoria* 2.1.1, 3. English translation from the Loeb edition, trans. H. E. Butler (London: Harvard University Press, 1958), 1:205.

[37]Quintilian, *Institutio* 2.5.1. Translation from Butler, 1:247.

Dialogues is questionable. And, even if the work were Fénelon's, Gibert argues, it is a work of questionable quality: "It is certainly a work of his youth, which he himself did not give to the Public. He had it suppressed indefinitely, or at least until he could correct it. And he did need to correct it. . . ."[38] In response to Gibert, Rollin placidly notes that the *Dialogues* were published by the Marquis de Fénelon, the prelate's nephew, to whom the manuscripts had been given. "A fact of this sort," Rollin concludes, "is soon cleared up."[39]

Rollin was exonerated, not only by the facts themselves but also by the subsequent opinion of his colleagues and peers. As Ferté informs us, the interchange between these two prominent theorists and pedagogues caused quite a stir in the University community.[40] Rollin was seconded because of the veracity and quality of his critical observations and recommendations; he was also supported because of the recriminatory, ill-spirited, and haughty tone of Gibert's work. Rollin has been historically vindicated as well, because his ideas and recommendations have been subsequently cited with approval by the encyclopedists and the Scottish belletrists, among others.[41]

This exchange between two 18th-century Parisian professors could be characterized as insignificant in its own right, but it has a sign relationship to larger trends in Enlightenment thinking. Post-Renaissance classical rhetorics had shunned innovation, seeking to recover and resituate the ancient *techne* for instructional purposes. Rollin's ideas, although not revolutionary, were innovative. To teach in the vernacular, to provide extensive excerpts from contemporary models of eloquence, to assign *thèmes* on topics close to the students' experience, and to move in graduated, sequenced orders of difficulty to advanced composition promoted a different kind of learning from that practiced in Gibert's classroom. Ideally, the graduate of Rollin's rhetoric course could think for himself, write good French prose, judge works with a well-formed taste, and emerge from his rhetoric training prepared to negotiate his way in an increasingly literate society. Rollin's emphasis on models of discourse and on forming taste contributed to his popularity among 18th-century *philosophes* and common sense theorists, whereas Gibert's work was consigned to obscurity.

---

[38]Gibert, *Observations* 407.

[39]Rollin, "Lettre de Mr. Rollin à Mr. Gibert," *Opuscules* 1:201.

[40]Ferté, *Rollin* 286.

[41]Rollin is cited by Voltaire in his article on "Eloquence" in the *Encyclopédie* (Paris: Briasson, David, Le Breton, Durand, 1755) 5:530. Also, for an account of Rollin's influence on later rhetorical theories, see Warnick, "Charles Rollin's *Traité*," cited in footnote 5.

Chapter 11

Hugh Blair's Use of Quintilian and the Transformation of Rhetoric in the 18th Century

S. Michael Halloran
Rensselaer Polytechnic Institute

A widely held view of the 18th-century Scottish rhetorics emphasizes their discontinuity with classical rhetoric. W. S. Howell's influential *Eighteenth-Century British Logic and Rhetoric*, for example, states flatly that "British writers on rhetoric in the second half of the eighteenth century regarded Ciceronian rhetoric as an anachronism" (441) and goes on to articulate the idea of a "new rhetoric" rooted in philosophical empiricism and French belletrism. According to Howell's analysis, the new rhetoric is exemplified in the lectures and treatises of Adam Smith, George Campbell, David Hume, John Lawson, Joseph Priestley, Hugh Blair, and John Witherspoon. While recognizing that there are important differences among these writers and acknowledging that they drew in certain ways upon classical rhetoricians, Howell nonetheless sees them as unified in a "discordant consensus" that turned its back on the classical tradition.

Howell had at his disposal previous work on 18th-century British rhetoricians by scholars such as Vincent Bevilacqua, Lloyd Bitzer, Herman Cohen, Douglas Ehninger, and James Golden, as well as more general studies of enlightenment thought by Ernst Cassirer, Walter John Hipple, Samuel Monk, George Saintsbury, and many others. Although few of these scholars are as categorical as Howell in distinguishing between 18th-century and classical modes of thought, all of them place some emphasis on the differences. And among the many works on 18th-century rhetoric subsequent to Howell's, I am aware of none that challenges the idea of a new rhetoric that is sharply distinct from the old. For example, in explaining what moved her to undertake the study that resulted in *The Sixth Canon: Belletristic Rhetorical Theory and Its French Antecedents* (1993), Barbara Warnick notes:

"The belletrist framework seemed to have transformed the agenda of neoclassical Renaissance rhetorics into something entirely different. . . . This book examines this belletrist transformation of rhetoric, and in particular its French antecedents" (xi). The phrase "something entirely different" suggests a conscientious effort to avoid the term "new rhetoric," and for whatever reasons Warnick eschews the term throughout her book. The underlying idea of a sharp discontinuity between 18th-century and classical/neoclassical rhetorics is nonetheless a premise of her work, and she devotes no attention to what the Scottish belletrists took from the classical tradition.

Warnick's use of "transformation" recalls Kenneth Burke's use of that term to point out that in any historical sequence, "the position at the start can eventually be seen in terms of the new motivation encountered enroute" (1969, 422). Gregory Clark and I argue in *Oratorical Culture in Nineteenth-Century America* (1993) for a historiography that uses this Burkean notion of transformation to situate changes in the theory and practice of rhetoric firmly in the larger context of cultural change, and thus to discover the interplay of continuity and change in the history of rhetoric. Such a historiography privileges neither origins nor end points; it seeks to avoid both narratives of decline and fall and narratives of rise and triumph. Its ultimate purpose is to uncover an ongoing dynamic through which "culture constructs discourse and discourse constructs culture" (248). From such a historiographical perspective, Howell's opposition between new and old rhetorics is a powerful trope figuring a narrative of rise and triumph. It is a narrative curiously at odds with recent studies of 19th-century rhetoric by scholars such as James Berlin (1984) and Sharon Crowley (1990), whose works tend to feature 18th-century belletrism prominently in a tale of rhetorical decline and fall. That two groups of scholars could see Scottish belletrism in such different ways suggests both the magnitude of the transformation that took place in the western rhetorical tradition during the 18th and 19th centuries and the difficulty of understanding it.

This chapter is part of a larger effort to understand this transformation in the context of the British colonies that became the United States. My immediate purposes are more modest: first, to point out that there was continuity as well as discontinuity between neoclassical rhetoric and 18th-century "new rhetoric"; second, to discover something of "the new motivation encountered enroute" from Renaissance neoclassicism to 18th-century Scottish belletrism. I focus specifically on the appropriation of ideas from Quintilian's *Institutio Oratoria* in Hugh Blair's *Lectures on Rhetoric and Belles Lettres* (1783), a text that must figure prominently in any effort to understand American rhetoric of the 19th century.

As James J. Murphy points out in the introduction to *Quintilian on the Art of Writing and Speaking*, the third major period of Quintilian's influence in western education extended from the early Renaissance through the mid-19th century (1987, xliv–xlv). The 18th century witnessed the publication of at least three Latin editions (1738, 1758, 1792) and two English translations of *Institutio Oratoria* (tr. W. Guthrie 1756; tr. J. Patsall 1774) at London. The French belletrist Charles Rollin—cited by Howell, Warnick, and others as a major influence on 18th-century

British rhetoric—edited a Latin text of the *Institutio* that served as the basis for the 18th-century British editions just cited, and he cited Quintilian frequently in his own *De la maniere d'enseigner et d'etudier les Belles Lettres*. The auction catalogue of Blair's personal library includes two editions of *Institutio Oratoria* in Latin, as well as numerous other works in classical rhetorical theory and practice (Amory 1973, 176–177). It is thus clear that Hugh Blair worked in an intellectual milieu that valued Quintilian and that he had access to *Institutio Oratoria*. The evidence I present suggests that Blair may have been partly responsible for extending Quintilian's influence well into the 19th century, in that his *Lectures* endorsed and transmitted Quintilian's ideas on rhetoric, albeit in a truncated form. What Warnick calls "the belletristic transformation" shows important traces of a classical tradition reshaped by a "new motivation" whose outlines I attempt to uncover.

Hugh Blair lectured on rhetoric at the University of Edinburgh from 1759 to 1783, from 1762 as Regius Professor. He published his *Lectures on Rhetoric and Belles Lettres* in the year of his retirement, partly because their apparent popularity had led to the circulation of numerous unauthorized copies based on students' notes. An American edition of the *Lectures* was published in 1785, just 2 years after the work appeared in London and Edinburgh; it quickly became one of the most influential books on the study of English language and literature in both Great Britain and the United States. Numerous editions were published through the 19th century, and it is generally agreed that it was the most widely used textbook on rhetoric at colleges in the United States through at least the midpoint of the 19th century, a period in which rhetoric was a central element of the college curriculum.

In addition to the French belletrists, Blair drew heavily on the work of such contemporary British rhetoricians as Adam Smith and George Campbell, but on the evidence of a simple tally of citations he seems to have regarded the *Institutio Oratoria* as the most important existing manual on the art of rhetoric. He cites it more frequently than any other single work, ancient or modern, using it as an authoritative source on numerous specific precepts, and offering the following general evaluation:

> Of all the Ancient writers on the subject of oratory, the most instructive and most useful, is Quinctilian. I know few books which abound more with good sense, and discover a greater degree of just and accurate taste, than Quinctilian's Institutions. Almost all the principles of Good Criticism are to be found in them. He has digested into excellent order all the antient ideas concerning Rhetoric, and is, at the same time, himself an eloquent Writer. Though some parts of his work contain too much of the technical and artificial system then in vogue, and for that reason may be thought dry and tedious, yet I would not advise the omitting to read any part of his Institutions. To pleaders at the Bar, even these technical parts may prove of some use. Seldom has any person, of more sound and distinct judgement than Quinctilian, applied himself to the art of Oratory. (lect. 34, v. 2, 244–5)[1]

---

[1]In this and all subsequent quotations from Blair's *Lectures*, I observe the spelling, mechanics, and pagination of the 1783 London edition, as reproduced photographically in the 1965 Southern Illinois University Press edition.

The *Lectures* contain no endorsement of any other work approaching, in strength, this statement on Quintilian.

By "the technical and artificial system then in vogue," Blair means the classical method of *inventio*, which he had discussed briefly in an earlier lecture, dismissing it as "superfluous" but then allowing that "if any think that the knowledge of [loci or topics] may contribute to improve their invention, and extend their views, they may consult Aristotle and Quinctilian, or what Cicero has written on the head, in his Treatise De Inventione, his Topica, and the Second Book *De Oratore*" (lect. 32, v. 2, 182). Howell makes the rejection of artificial invention a major point in concept of the new rhetoric, and Warnick in a more subtle way makes the decline of classical invention a key element in her conception of belletristic rhetoric. It is thus worth noting that Blair's position on this issue is in fact qualified: He allows that topical invention may be of some use, particularly to practitioners of forensic rhetoric. And, as Sean Patrick O'Rourke shows in a recent paper, on the one documented occasion when Blair engaged in the practice of forensic rhetoric, he made use of the classical system of invention. O'Rourke shows convincingly that the brief Blair prepared in the Douglas case makes abundant use of the classical topics, classical forms of organization, and the Ciceronian method of controversial reasoning. O'Rourke estimates that the un-dated manuscript brief, now housed in the National Library of Scotland at Ed-inburgh, was composed in 1767 or 1768, several years after Blair had begun lecturing on rhetoric but a decade and a half before he undertook to publish his *Lectures*.

A second major point in Howell's interpretation of Blair as a new rhetorician is that "he recognized and rejected the ancient doctrine of three major styles, and he indicated that he was going instead to follow Adam Smith's teachings upon this matter, as those teachings had come to him from Smith's manuscript treatise on rhetoric" (653). As with the treatment of topical invention, a look at Blair's actual discussion of classical doctrines on style, including the doctrine of the three *genera dicendi*, reveals something more complex than Howell's categorical distinction between old and new rhetorics.

After summarizing briefly the views of Dionysius, Cicero, and Quintilian on the plain, middle, and grand styles, Blair says, "These divisions, and the illus-trations they give of them, are so loose and general, that they cannot advance us much in our ideas of Style. I shall endeavour to be a little more particular in what I have to say on this subject" (lect. 18, v. 1, 370–371). In a footnote several pages later, he acknowledges taking from a manuscript treatise by Adam Smith "several ideas" concerning the "general characters" of style, in particular the plain and the simple characters and the application of these categories to certain English authors (v. 1, 381 n.). But he cites Quintilian no fewer than twenty-five times in the ten lectures devoted specifically to style, concluding with this advice on forming one's own style: "On these heads of composing, correcting, reading, and imitating, I advise every student of oratory to consult what Quinctilian has delivered in the Xth book of his Institutions, where he will find a variety of excellent observations and directions, that well deserve attention" (lect. 19, v. 1, 406).

Blair thus did find the doctrine of the plain, middle, and grand styles too general for his purposes. And he did emphasize, as Adam Smith had, the idea that style should flow "naturally" from the character of the writer, the nature of the subject, and the writer's attitude toward the subject. But in supporting this view he cites classical authorities, including Quintilian, who emphasized the need for appropriateness to speaker and occasion in the employment of figures. And in developing a taxonomy of stylistic characters more complex than any the classical rhetoricians had offered, his rationale is simply to become "more particular." Blair thus seems to have understood himself to be extending and refining the classical theory of the three styles rather than rejecting it. The debt he owes to Adam Smith, by contrast, appears to be confined to ideas on stylistic "plainness" and "simplicity," certain critical views of Swift and Shaftsbury, and possibly the emphasis on "naturalness" as a virtue of style.

As the quotation from lecture 19 indicates, Blair held up "the Great Roman Critic" Quintilian as a major authority on the analysis and formation of style (v. 1, 407). And when he turned to the meticulous criticism of Addison's style in several of the *Spectator* essays that remains one of the major points of interest in the *Lectures*, Blair again turns to Quintilian for authority. "It is, indeed," he says, "my judgment that what Quinctilian applies to Cicero, 'Ille se profecisse sciat, cui Cicero valde placebit,' may with justice be applied to Mr. Addison; that to be highly pleased with his manner of writing, is the criterion of one's having acquired a good taste in English Style" (lect. 20, v. 1, 409).

The sorts of general and possibly ceremonial commendations quoted here are not the most typical citations of Quintilian to be found in Blair's treatment of style. More often he cites the *Institutio* in support of specific precepts, as in this example:

> As long as sounds are the vehicle of conveyance for our ideas, there will be always a very considerable connection between the idea which is conveyed, and the nature of the sound which conveys it. Pleasing ideas can hardly be transmitted to the mind, by means of harsh and disagreeable sounds. The imagination revolts as soon as it hears them uttered. "Nihil," says Quinctilian, "potest intrare in affectum quod in aure, velut quondam vestibulo statim offendit" (lect. 13, v. 1, 247–248).

In this instance Blair translates the passage in a footnote: "Nothing can enter into the affections which stumbles at the threshold, by offending the ear," but his practice on translations is inconsistent. Sometimes he quotes in English and gives the Latin in a footnote, sometimes he offers a translation in the text immediately following a quotation in Latin, and sometimes he quotes in Latin with no translation. A check of some of the student copies of Blair's lectures held in the University Library at Edinburgh indicates that English translations were offered considerably less often when the lectures were dictated in class. Many translations were added to the published version of the *Lectures*, apparently as a concession or a convenience to the broader public audience they would reach in printed form. Blair expected his students to understand Quintilian in Latin and to apply his precepts in the development of their own style in English as well as in Latin.

The other subject regarding which Blair draws quite heavily on Quintilian is the analysis and composition of orations. Although, as noted earlier, he deemphasizes the classical method of invention and refers to it as "superfluous," the section of the *Lectures* devoted specifically to oratory is nonetheless strongly classical, and he cites Quintilian frequently as an authority on precepts.

This section of the *Lectures* takes up roughly the first half of volume 2. It begins with two lectures on the history of eloquence, by which Blair means oratorical practice: one lecture (25) on Greek oratory featuring Demosthenes as the principal figure and one lecture (26) on Roman through modern oratory featuring Cicero. He offers here and in other places the opinion that modern eloquence falls short of ancient eloquence, and I will return to his argument on this point. Next come a lecture on the eloquence of popular assemblies illustrated by lengthy extracts in English from the Phillipics and the Olynthiacs of Demosthenes (lecture 27) and a lecture on the eloquence of the bar illustrated by a precis and extracts from Cicero's *pro Cluentio*, again in English but in this case with some of the Latin given in footnotes (lecture 28). Blair defends the choice of *pro Cluentio* over *pro Milone* on the grounds that it "comes nearer the strain of a Modern Pleading" and is "one of the most chaste, correct, and forcible of all Cicero's judicial Orations" (v. 2, 86). These are followed by a lecture on the eloquence of the pulpit (29) and a separate lecture (30) analyzing a sermon by Bishop Atterbury. Next come two lectures (31 and 32) on "Conduct of a Discourse in all its Parts," organized as a slight variation on the classical canon of dispositio: Introduction, Division, Narration, and Explication in one lecture and The Argumentative Part, The Pathetic Part, and The Peroration in the second. The sequence concludes with a lecture (33) on delivery and a lecture (34) on "Means of Improving in Eloquence." The remainder of volume 2 comprises a lecture on the relative merits of ancient and modern writers, on which subject Blair takes a middle ground, and twelve lectures on various nonoratorical forms of writing—history, philosophy, dialogue, poetry of various kinds, and drama.

Blair invokes the authority of Quintilian repeatedly in most of the lectures on oratory, particularly those tracing the "Conduct of a Discourse" according to the classical parts. Yet in the two lectures devoted to the eloquence of the pulpit he makes no reference to Quintilian or any other classical author, citing instead Bruyere and George Campbell on points of theory, and a number of French and British preachers by way of illustration. The striking absence of classical citations in Blair's discussion of preaching is perhaps accounted for by his taxonomy of rhetorical kinds. He records the classical division into demonstrative, deliberative, and judicial rhetoric and acknowledges both the wide acceptance and the soundness of this taxonomy in both ancient and modern times, but then he continues,

> It will, however, suit our purpose better, and be found, I imagine, more useful, to follow that division which the train of Modern Speaking naturally points out to us, taken from the three great scenes of Eloquence, Popular Assemblies, the Bar, and the Pulpit; each of which has a distinct character that particularly suits it. This division coincides in part with the ancient one. The Eloquence of the Bar is precisely the same with what the ancients call the Judicial. The Eloquence of Popular Assemblies, though mostly of what they term the Deliberative Species, yet admits also of the Demonstrative. The Eloquence of the Pulpit is altogether of a distinct nature, and cannot be properly reduced under any of the heads of the ancient Rhetoricians. (lect. 27, v. 2, 47)

When in lecture 29 he comes to the discussion of preaching as a genre, he raises the question whether it is properly regarded as a part of the art of eloquence, given that eloquence is a human study. His answer is that the objection would hold if eloquence were "an ostentatious and deceitful art"; but given that "true eloquence is the art of placing truth in the most advantageous light for conviction and persuasion," preaching does properly belong to the art of eloquence (v. 2, 104). Blair is thus somewhat ambivalent on the relationship of preaching to the classical tradition of rhetoric. On the one hand, he argues for its place in the art of eloquence, situates his discussion of it within a discussion of the classical modes of oratory, and asserts that "to all three, Pulpit, Bar, and Popular Assemblies, belong in common, the rules concerning the conduct of a discourse in all its parts" (v. 2, 47). On the other hand, he insists on its uniqueness as a kind of eloquence and invokes no classical authorities for any precepts on preaching.

As noted earlier, Blair concludes his two lectures on the history of eloquence with an extended discussion of the inferiority of modern public speaking to that of the Greeks and Romans (lect. 26, v. 2, 37–45). He cites France and Great Britain as the two countries where modern eloquence has achieved some distinction, noting further that the "free and bold genius" of Great Britain together with the nature of its legislative system might have been expected to produce "a more conspicuous figure in Eloquence." Yet, owing to the "accuracy and closeness of [modern] reasoning," the "phlegm and natural coldness" of the British character, the more exacting standards of modern legislative and judicial forums, and the modern practice of reading sermons from prepared texts, modern eloquence has failed to rise to the heights of ancient practice.

Blair develops this argument without citing a single contemporary British orator, and it is worth noting that he lived in the age of Edmund Burke, William Pitt, and the revolutionaries of the North American colonies. Even granting the arguable claim that none of these orators measured up to the standard of eloquence set by the ancient Greeks and Romans, there were contemporary British speakers worthy of Blair's notice, if only to illustrate his claims about their inferiority. He shows no aversion to discussing contemporary writers of other genres: he devotes four full lectures to close analysis of the style of Addison and one to an analysis of an essay by Swift; and he mentions Pope, Fielding, Richardson, Voltaire, Young, and a number of other modern writers in the lectures devoted to nonoratorical genres. And in these discussions he does not hesitate to make negative critical comments. It would thus be consistent with his practice in discussing other rhetorical kinds for him to comment on contemporary British orators, if only to point out their defects. Yet no reference to a British secular orator appears anywhere in the *Lectures*.

The explanation for this striking absence is to be found, I believe, in the audience and purpose of the *Lectures*, and here we may begin to discern "the new motivation encountered enroute" from neoclassicism to Blair's version of Scottish belletrism. Scotland in the 18th century was a province striving for acceptance in the mainstream of British society, and Blair's *Lectures* were motivated in significant part by that effort. He says as much in a footnote to one of the critical lectures on Addison:

> If there be readers who think any farther apology requisite for my adventuring to criticise the sentences of so eminent an author as Mr. Addison, I must take notice, that I was naturally led to it by the circumstances of that part of the kingdom where these Lectures were read; where the ordinary spoken language often differs much from what is used by good English authors. Hence it occurred to me, as a proper method of correcting any peculiarities of dialect, to direct students of eloquence, to analize and examine, with particular attention, the structure of Mr. Addison's sentences. Those Papers of the Spectator, which are the subject of the following Lectures, were accordingly given out in exercise to students, to be thus examined and analized; and several of the observations which follow, both on the beauties and blemishes of the Author, were suggested, by the observations given to me in consequence of the exercise prescribed. (lect. 21, v. 1, 430n.)

Blair was in the business of helping young provincials rid themselves of the linguistic habits that would mark them as such and bar them from the upper reaches of British society. His emphasis on correct syntax and diction is one consequence of this purpose.

Another is his neglect of contemporary oratory. Encouraging students to argue controversial issues in the public forum would have been contrary to the purpose of enabling them to fit comfortably into an established social order. The models of political and forensic oratory offered by the *Lectures* are thus safely distanced from the social world of the students. The eloquence of the bar and of popular assemblies becomes, in effect, a form of literature, equivalent to lyric poetry or the novel, to be appreciated for its beauty and strength. But it is not a social practice in which students are learning to participate. In the lecture devoted to "Means of Improving in Eloquence," Blair recommends participation in certain

"Meetings or Societies" where students can become practiced in appropriate forms of public discussion. He cautions strongly, however, against:

> those public and promiscuous Societies, in which multitudes are brought together, who are often of low stations and occupations, who are joined by no common bond of union, except an absurd rage for Public Speaking, and have no other object in view, but to make a show of their supposed talents. (lect. 34, v. 2, 240)

The oral eloquence students were developing was to be noncontroversial and addressed exclusively to "polite" society.

The lectures devoted to nonoratorical genres similarly ignore the rich contemporary literature of controversial essays and pamphlets. For his analysis of Swift's style, for example, Blair chooses a passage from "A Proposal for Correcting, Improving, and Ascertaining the English Tongue" rather than one of the controversial essays. On England's conflict with the North American colonies—a subject of clear rhetorical interest, given a classical or neoclassical understanding of rhetoric—the *Lectures* are altogether silent. Blair is preparing members of another colonized society for entry into the colonizing social order, where any hint of political controversy might call attention to their marginal origins. As Blair's friend Samuel Johnson is supposed to have said to Boswell, Scotland was a good place to be *from*, and Blair's *Lectures* would enable students to get as far as possible from Scotland, even as they continued to reside in Edinburgh.

This motive produced a relationship to Quintilian (and to classical and neoclassical rhetoric generally) that was somewhat bifurcated. In volume 1 of the *Lectures*, which is devoted to such general topics as taste, grammar, style, and criticism, Quintilian is treated as a living authority throughout. In volume 2, which is devoted to analysis of particular kinds of discourse, Quintilian becomes a voice from the past, an authority on kinds of discourse worth reading but no longer worth producing. In general, Blair seems to emphasize those aspects of the *Institutio Oratoria* having to do with composing prose and judging completed works of prose according to standards of propriety and elegance. He ignores or deemphasizes those aspects meant to help students make arguments on controversial subjects.

An interesting contrast is provided by Blair's University of Edinburgh classmate John Witherspoon, who as president of what is now Princeton University, from 1768 to 1794, delivered lectures on moral philosophy and eloquence that are regarded as articulating the first complete theory of rhetoric written in America. Unlike Blair, Witherspoon was a ready participant in political controversies. While in Scotland he had written a satirical pamphlet that got him into hot water with church authorities, and not long after his arrival in America he was deeply involved in revolutionary politics. And although his lectures draw upon many of the same classical and enlightenment sources as do Blair's, they develop an understanding of rhetoric in which oratory and writing on controversial public issues figure much more prominently. Witherspoon assumes, as Quintilian does and Blair does not, that his students are being educated for life in the public forum, that the ability to persuade a "promiscuous public assembly" on controversial issues will be essential to them. Like Quintilian, Witherspoon sets up as an ideal the man (it seems to be, for both Quintilian and Witherspoon, a man specifically and not a generic human being) who combines virtue and broad learning with eloquence and applies these qualities to civic concerns. Witherspoon calls this ideal "the compleat orator," Quintilian, the "vir bonus dicendi peritus."

Blair articulates no character ideal as such, but he clearly implies one: the person of taste, who is fully sensitive to the beauties and blemishes of nature and art. As Warnick points out, this emphasis on taste is part of a broader shift in rhetoric from the classical emphasis on production of discourse to a belletristic concern with "receptive competence" (xi and passim). Once an art through which speakers and writers learned to adapt to audiences, rhetoric was acquiring a new and perhaps even more important role as an art through which audiences learned to adapt to texts.

Although Blair himself taught only young men and, like the classical rhetoricians, emphasized "manly" virtues and "masculine" style, his move away from the vir bonus ideal and its focus on the production of discourse in the public forum helped open the door for an eventual regendering of rhetoric. Women had been excluded from public speaking platforms since ancient times, and so long as the traditional public forum remained the primary scene of eloquence, women would have difficulty achieving rhetorical stature. But taste could be exercised as readily in the polite society of drawing rooms, and the person of taste could thus be a woman as easily as a man. Adam Smith went so far as to suggest that the highest standard of language is illustrated by "the conversation of the ladies" (2). The great popularity Blair's *Lectures* and his notion of taste achieved in the United States during the 19th century may thus reflect or even help account for the cultural transformation that made space for such women as Sarah Josepha Hale, Margaret Fuller, and Jane Addams.[2]

Although he did not adopt the vir bonus ideal as such, Blair accepted the classical association of rhetorical excellence with moral virtue and in fact tied the two together even more intimately than had Quintilian. In the classical view, moral virtue was a prerequisite to true eloquence, but presumably one could be virtuous without achieving eloquence. For Blair, the exercise of taste was both a means of forming virtue and a manifestation of it sufficiently clear to suggest that tastelessness was equivalent to a want of virtue:

> To be entirely devoid of relish for eloquence, poetry, or any of the fine arts, is justly constructed to be an unpromising symptom of youth; and raises suspicions of their being prone to low gratifications, or destined to drudge in the more vulgar and illiberal pursuits of life. . . . I will not go so far as to say that the improvement

---

[2]See the essays by Nicole Tonkovich, P. Joy Rouse, and Catherine Peaden in Clark and Halloran, *Oratorical Culture in Nineteenth-Century America*, for studies of Hale, Fuller, and Addams in terms of our notion of transformation.

of taste and of virtue is the same; or that they may always be expected to coexist in equal degree. More powerful correctives than taste can apply, are necessary for reforming the corrupt propensities which too frequently prevail among mankind. Elegant speculations are sometimes found to float on the surface of the mind, while bad passions possess the interior regions of the heart. At the same time this cannot but be admitted, that the exercise of taste is, in its native tendency, moral and purifying. (lect. 1, v. 1, 12–13)

Nowhere does he suggest the contrary idea that "inelegant speculations" can float on the surface where good passions possess the heart. And when we recall Blair's motivation of "correcting any peculiarities of dialect" and otherwise socializing his Scottish students to English ways, this moralized concept of taste takes on disturbing implications. The peculiarities of dialect and taste that Blair's students brought with them from home and family were precisely the "low gratifications" and "inelegant speculations" they were now learning to regard as signs of a morally low character.

An economic and social hierarchy was thus transformed into a moral one, and the symbolic markers of class were transformed into signs of moral worth. In learning Blair's rhetoric, Scottish students could gain access to an English social hierarchy, but quite possibly at the exorbitant cost of learning to despise their cultural origins and to suspect any impulse of taste or expression that might spring from those origins. (I should acknowledge here that Blair did not disdain all things Scottish; he was a highly vocal champion of the Ossian hoax and, in his later years, befriended and admired the young Robert Burns.)

Transplanted to the newly independent United States, where a similarly moralized notion of taste was developing in the form of what Gregory Clark calls the "oratorical poetic" of Timothy Dwight (Clark and Halloran, 57–77), Blair's rhetoric became part of a middle-class ethos that began to undermine the exclusiveness of the old aristocracy of hereditary privilege, replacing it with a new hierarchy that was inherently unstable and shifting. Wallace Douglas calls the new hierarchy a meritocracy. The ideal of taste contributed a rationale for the belief that more was at stake in the constant rising of the middle class than economic and social power, that the merit of that meritocracy was not just intellectual and social, but moral and spiritual as well. And although neither Blair's rhetoric nor the explicitly moralized concept of taste would survive into the 20th century, the virulence of our debates over canons, curricula, and "the politics of virtue" suggests that we retain a considerable vestige of the cultural unease they inspired.

To return to the more technical issue with which this chapter began, there is an important sense in which both Hugh Blair and his classmate John Witherspoon are "new" rhetoricians. They drew upon intellectual currents that were fresh in their own time, including common-sense realism and French belletristic thought. But it is misleading to portray them as part of a consensus, even a "discordant" one, that rejected classical rhetoric. Such an account neglects the important ways in which they drew upon classical rhetoric, appropriating it for ends peculiar to their own contexts and transforming it into something that would serve those ends. Blair himself chose to downplay the new aspects of his rhetoric by foregrounding his debts to Quintilian and other classical writers. Perhaps he wished to conceal the Burkean "new motivation" for his transformation of the tradition. But we cannot understand the full complexity of his relationship to that tradition unless we recognize what he took from it as well as what he may have contributed to it.

This same point can be made more generally. Every rhetoric is inevitably both old and new. New in the sense that it is addressed to the concerns of the historical moment and the social context in which it is written. Old in the sense that merely by using terms like "rhetoric," "style," "argument," and "eloquence," it places itself in some relationship to the tradition from which those terms derive. The more important question about a rhetoric may not be whether it is old or new but, rather, how it situates itself in relation to both the rhetorical tradition and the concerns of its own time, how it transforms what tradition offers into symbolic instruments for dealing with the present.

ACKNOWLEDGMENTS

Research for this chapter was supported by the Undergraduate Research Program and the Paul Beer Trust of Rensselaer Polytechnic Institute. The author was assisted by Cynthia Haller and Medhavi Reddy.

WORKS CITED

Amory, H. (Ed.). (1973). *Poets and Men of Letters* (Vol. 7), *Sale Catalogues of Libraries of Eminent Persons*, A. N. L. Munby (Gen. Ed.) London: Mansell with Sotheby Parke Bernet Publications.

Berlin, J. A. (1984). *Writing Instruction in Nineteenth-Century American Colleges.* Carbondale: Southern Illinois University Press.

Blair, H. (1965). *Lectures on Rhetoric and Belles Lettres* (2 vols.), Harold F. Harding (Ed.). Carbondale: Southern Illinois University Press. (Original work published in 1783).

Burke, K. (1969). *A Grammar of Motives.* Berkeley: University of California Press. (Original work published in 1945).

Clark, G., & S. M. Halloran (Eds.). (1993). *Oratorical Culture in Nineteenth-Century America: Transformations in the Theory and Practice of Rhetoric.* Carbondale: Southern Illinois University Press.

Crowley, S. (1990). *The Methodical Memory: Invention in Current-Traditional Rhetoric.* Carbondale: Southern Illinois University Press.

Douglas, W. (1976). "Rhetoric for the Meritocracy: The Creation of Composition at Harvard." In Richard Ohmann, *English in America: A Radical View of the Profession.* New York: Oxford University Press.

Howell, W. S. (1971). *Eighteenth-Century British Logic and Rhetoric.* Princeton: Princeton University Press.

Miller, T. P. (Ed.). (1990). *The Selected Writings of John Witherspoon.* Carbondale: Southern Illinois University Press.

Murphy, J. J. (Ed.). (1987). *Quintilian on the Teaching of Speaking and Writing.* Carbondale: Southern Illinois University Press.

O'Rourke, S. P. "Hugh Blair in the *Douglas* Cause: An Essay on the Theory and Practice of Legal Rhetoric." Presented at the 1994 Conference of the Speech Communication Association in New Orleans, LA.

Smith, A. (1971). *Lectures on Rhetoric and Belles Lettres: Delivered in the University of Glasgow by Adam Smith, Reported by a Student in 1762–63,* John M. Lothian (Ed.). Carbondale: Southern Illinois University Press. (Original work published 1963).

Warnick, B. (1993). *The Sixth Canon: Belletristic Rhetorical Theory and Its French Antecedents.* Columbia: University of South Carolina Press.

Chapter 12

An 18th-Century Greek
Triplex modus praedicandi Treatise

Thomas M. Conley
University of Illinois

The manuscript entitled *Skiagrafiai*, found in *Cod.Ath.*1196 in the National Library in Athens, offers a fascinating glimpse into the cross-cultural activities of late 17th- and early 18th-century Greek intellectuals. *Skiagrafiai*, attributed by V. Bombou-Stamate and S. Harakas to Vikentios Damodos (1700–1752), contains a graded series of instructions and exemplars designed to provide Orthodox clergy with a systematic approach to sermon composition. There are in all, twelve "sermon sketches" (a fair rendering of the Greek title) provided, each on a different sermon theme, in which Damodos (if he was in fact the author—on this, more in due course) gives step-by-step directions on how to construct, compose, and deliver sermons of various types: "In order to begin, you must . . ."; "After you have given the first argument, make a transition as follows . . ."; "Turn now to the audience and say . . ."; "Now, to bring your sermon to a successful close. . . ." These represent very explicit prescriptions to the aspiring preacher.[1]

---

[1]This treatise was brought to my attention by Rev. Stanley S. Harakas, Archbishop Iakovos Professor of Orthodox Theology at Holy Cross Greek Orthodox School of Theology in Brookline, MA, in the fall of 1990. Harakas was at the time preparing a translation of the *Skiagrafiai* for publication. He first wrote of it in *Proclaiming God's Word: Preaching Concerns in the Greek Orthodox Archdiocese of North and South America* (Minneapolis: Light and Life Publishing Co., 1989) 55–70. In attributing this work to Damodos, Harakas follows Bombou-Stamate, "Ho Vikentios Damodos: Biografia-Ergografia, 1700–1752" diss., Athens, 1982, 209–212. I am grateful to Prof. Harakas for allowing me to examine this treatise and for his assistance in preparing this chapter.

In what follows, I outline a few of the sketches provided by Damodos to give the reader some idea of how they work. These are not very detailed (for obvious reasons of space) but are, I think, sufficient for present purposes. After those outlines and some observations on their significance, I discuss briefly the milieu in which Damodos may have composed this unusual treatise.

PART ONE

Here are the outlines of three of the sermon sketches in *Skiagrafiai*. The following does not contain detailed page references to the manuscript. The curious mix of directions and examples provided in these sketchings makes it difficult to attach much significance to the relative amount of space devoted to different matters of form and content. Two observations may, however, be in order: The sections of *prooimia* are almost uniformly about two and a half pages long; and the amount of space devoted to *Meros B'* (Part Two) is in most cases much less than that devoted to *Meros A'* (Part One). This relative distribution is consistent with the actual sermon practices that lie behind the instructions given in the treatise.

First Skiagrafia (fol. 2–8^v = pp. 2–16)

Teaching: On the Torments and Sufferings Sinners Receive From God.

Theme: That the suffering given to a sinner is a blessing from God and that the punishment and discipline of God is his happiness.

Sermon text: "Come and see." (John 1:46)

I.   The Organization and Composition of the Introduction: The introduction (*prooimion*) must harmonize the four parts of which it is composed: the opening statement (*protasis*), support (*kataskeuē*), explanation (*adoposis*), and statement of the theme (*basis*).

The *basis* of this sermon: that affliction in the life of a sinner is a blessing from God *and* [his] happiness is in the punishment and discipline of God.

II. Demonstration (*apodeixis*):
A.   Of the first part of the theme: that affliction is a blessing.
1.   Take your first argument from the commonplace (*koinos topos*) "from the final cause": "Affliction has as its purpose benefit to mankind."
a.   State the demonstration as a syllogism.
b.   Explain in the common idiom.
c.   Address the audience directly.
[Amplify and elaborate each step.]
2.   Take your second argument from the [*topos* of] "consequence": "The result of affliction is repentance."
a.   Proofs from Scripture.

      b. Paraphrase (in common idiom).

      c. Draw the conclusion explicitly.

      [Amplify and elaborate at each step.]

    3. [From "equivalence"]: "Suffering is salvation."

      a. Argument from Scripture.

      b. Argument from a paradigm case (the parable of the Prodigal Son).

      c. Argument from personal experience/testimony.

  B. Demonstration of the second part of the *basis*: that man's happiness is in the punishment and discipline of God.

    1. First argument: from the *topos* of contraries.

    2. Argument from circumstances (*peristaseis*).

    3. Draw conclusion explicitly; amplify.

III. Part Two: "The preacher must say in the second part (*deuteros meros*) other things that have some connection with what was said in the first part (*protē meros*)." In this case:

  1. Get your audience to reflect.

  2. Explain any matters still obscure.

  3. Move the emotions of the audience.

[Summary]: "This present sketch was presented in full since it will serve as a pattern (*kanōn*) for other sketches and for the manner (tropos) of rhetorical composition (*rhetorikē synthesis*)."

Sixth Skiagrafia (fol. 32ᵛ–38 = pp. 63–76)

Theme: Saint Katherine overcame idolatry with heavenly wisdom. She conquered tyranny with incomparable courage. She was victorious over the pleasures of the world with undefiled virginity.

Sermon Text: "Who shall find a courageous woman?" (Prov 31:10)

I. Organization and Composition of the Introduction.

  [Same four parts (*protasis, kataskeuē, apodosis, basis*) as in first Skiagrafia. The *basis* is the same as the theme, given earlier.]

II. [Demonstration (*apodeixis*) of the *thema*.]

  A. *Apodeixis* of the first heading (*kephalaion*): She was victorious in her debate with pagan philosophers.

    1. Narration (*diēgēsis*) of the debate, in which Katherine converted them by a new teaching (*didaskalia*) that was above nature (*hyper physin*), above knowledge (*hyper gnōsin*), and above thought (*hyper ennoian*).

    2. Demonstration that this teaching was of necessity heaven-sent.

    3. Conclusion that her victory was immeasurable (*hypermetros*), full and complete (*plerestatē*), and exceedingly marvelous (*hyperthaumatos*).

   B. *Apodeixis* of the second heading: She conquered tyranny with incomparable courage.
1. *Diēgēsis* of tortures she endured, including:
   a. Vivid and detailed enumeration.
   b. Comparison (*synkrisis*) with tortures of St. Peter.
   c. Draw to conclusion, amplifying with repetition.
   C. *Apodeixis* of third heading: Her greatest victory was that over the pleasures of the world:
1. Argue *a minore*: If victory over enemies or animals is great, how much greater that over the pleasures of the world?
2. Support by bringing in examples (*paradeigmata*) of David and Sampson.
3. Give an account (*diēgēsis*) of her burial on Mount Sinai, famous for the six miracles (which are enumerated).
III. [Recapitulate, amplifying again on the three victories.]

Twelfth Skiagrafia (fol. 78–84ᵛ = pp. 153–169)

Teaching: On the Sinner's Confidence Before God

Theme: That sinners should not lose hope because of their many sins.

Sermon text: "And when Jesus saw their faith he said to the paralytic, take heart, my son, your sins are forgiven." (Matthew 9:2)

I. Organization and composition of the Prologue.
[Standard four parts, as earlier; here a less mechanical set of directions, amply exemplified. *Basis*: Sinners should not lose heart because of the multitude of their sins.]
II. Part One:
   A. The "showing" (*phanerōsis*) of God's mercy.
1. God's mercy is without limit (repeated and supported by numerous citations from *Psalms*).
2. Move into the "moving" (*kinēsis*) of the audience, ending with "If you repent, you will immediately (*eutheōs*) be forgiven, immediately healed, immediately worthy of heaven."
   B. "The other argument" (*allo epicheirema*): Despair is unjustified (a preview cast in the form of a syllogism is set out here).
1. "Then (*tōra*) show extensively (*kata platos*)" that God is always prepared [support of "minor" by means of several Scriptural citations].
2. ["The other part (*allo meros*) of this proof"]: that sinners are responsible for repentance.
   a. An argument based on an exegesis of the meaning of "repentance" (*metanoia*).

       b. An argument "from impossibility."

III. Part Two:

    [C]. An objection (*mia aporia*) by a sinner and the response: a brief "dialogue."

       1. The sinner's argument is inconsistent.

       2. A passage from John's *Apocalypse* shows the sinner's objection to be contrary to God's word.

    [A brief epilogue is recommended.]

The language of *Skiagrafiai* is in the main neo-Greek, that is, the literary idiom designed to approximate the demotic. Passages from Scripture are quoted in their original Septuagintal for Old Testament citations and in *koinē*, the dialect of the New Testament. There is in these sketchings a great deal of technical vocabulary that betrays the influences of Hermogenes and Aphthonios and of the Byzantine commentary traditions connected with them. Thus, for example, standard Hermogenean terms are used throughout: *epicheirēma* for *argument* or *argumentation*. Modes of argument such as "by comparison" (*synkrisis*, which is also a standard exercise in the *progymnasmata*), "by appeal to examples" (*dia paradeigmatōn*) are used, with commonplaces (*koinoi topoi*) such as "from impossibility," "from circumstances" (*peristaseis*), or "from opposition" (*ex enantiōn*). The most striking Hermogenean feature is the insistence in all of the sketchings on the four-part *prooimion* (compare Hermogenes, *Peri heureseōs* 1.5, pp. 106–108 Rabe; and, e.g., *Anon. in Heur.* 7:1. 68.19–70.9; 7:2. 713ff. Walz; "Planudes" *in Heur.* 5.381f. Walz), although the definition of *kataskeuē* in the first *Skiagraphia* ("the firming up [*bebaiōsis*] of the *protasis*") is more immediately reminiscent of Aphthonios at *Progymn.* 6 (1.77f. Walz). Also Hermogenean is the continued emphasis on amplification (*auxēsis, exergasia, platynein*, etc.); and the recommendation of various schemes and tropes for achieving amplification and ensuring its impact on the hearers, as in *perittologia* ('excess' or 'overstatement'), *epanalepsis, synonomia*, or *paraphrasis*, all of which are treated in the many handbooks composed in the Byzantine tradition.[2] The term I have translated "organization" is *oikonomia*, which here refers to the pattern or arrangement of the sermon: *prooimion* plus the division of the *thema* into two or three parts, each of which may be developed in turn along three lines—of which more later. This is not a term found in Hermogenes, but it has a long history in Byzantine rhetoric going back (at least) to Basil of Caesarea.[3]

Another feature of the *Skiagrafiai* that cannot be found in Hermogenes is the interest manifested by the author in syllogistic form as it came through the

---

[2]See, e.g., my "Byzantine Teaching on Figures and Tropes: An Introduction," *Rhetorica* 4 (1986): 335–374.

[3]On *oikonomia* and *taxis*, often taken to mean the same thing, see G. Kustas, "Basil and the Rhetorical Tradition," *Basil of Caesarea: Christian, Humanist, Ascetic*, 2 vols., ed. P. J. Fedwick (Toronto: Pontifical Institute of Medieval Studies, 1981) especially 228ff.

Aristotelian tradition. Thus, the author recommends that the *apodeixis* of the first part of the *thema* in the first *Skiagraphia* be cast in the form of a syllogism; and in the twelfth *Skiagraphia*, he makes the same recommendation for the *apodeixis* of the second part of the *thema*. Such recommendations show up in other sketchings, too—as in, for example, the ninth *Skiagraphia*, where the *apodeixis* of the first part of the theme of "Love thy neighbor" is explicitly set up as a syllogism in which first the major and then the minor premises are supported. So there is evidence of some important influence if not of Aristotle's *Rhetoric* then certainly of his *Analytics*. At the same time, however, "*apodeixis*" is used both in the strict Aristotelian sense and in the more common Byzantine sense not of a rigorous proof but of "showing" more loosely conceived. Such a conflation is not unusual in later Byzantine sources, as in Planudes, at a time when Byzantine writers were for the first time getting interested in the argumentative potential of formal syllogistic reasoning.[4]

On the whole, the technical vocabulary is rooted deeply in the Greek rhetorical tradition, mainly the Hermogenean tradition so important in Byzantine rhetorics but also the Aristotelian tradition that was grafted onto it between the 14th and 16th centuries by such scholars as Barlaamos of Calabria or Gennadios Scholarios.

There is one crucial feature in the *Skiagrafiai* that has no roots in the Greek, Patristic, or Byzantine rhetorical traditions: the method of three-way division in the disposition of sermon headings and subheadings in the *ergasia* of the sermon theme. Such three-part treatment is evident in the outlines sketched previously. There seems to be a single standard (but not inviolable) basic pattern to the sermons in *Skiagrafiai*:

I.   *Prooimion.*
II. Part One (*meros A'*):
     A. First *apodeixis* of the *thema*.
     B. Second *apodeixis* of the *thema*.
III. Part Two (*meros B'*):
     [C]. Third *apodeixis* of the *thema* (which includes functions of the *epilogos*).

Variations on this scheme can be detected in the sermon outlines we have seen and are evident as well in the other sketchings. In all of the following, the

---

[4]That interest in syllogisms was nothing if not untraditional. The anathemas pronounced against, for instance, John Italos in the late 11th century had become a regular part of Orthodox liturgy; John's trial is fully discussed in J. Gouillard, "Le Synodikon de l'Orthodoxie: édition et commentaire," *Travaux et Mémoires* 2 (1967): 1–316. It will be recalled that one of John's students, Eustratios of Nicaea, had been condemned specifically for holding that Christ "syllogized in an Aristotelian fashion" (*syllogizetai aristotelikōs*); see the text published by P. Joannou, "Eustrate de Nicée: trois pièces inedits," *Revue des Études Byzantines* 10 (1952): 24 (no. 24).

prooimion develops the four parts prescribed in the first *Skiagrafia*. The headings are developed as follows:

> 2: "On Greed": [(I) *Prooimion*.] (II) *Meros A'*: The theme ("that the foolishness of the covetous person is indescribably great") should be supported by means of a syllogism: (a) support of major, (b) support of minor, (c) conclusion. (III) *Meros B'*: Major, minor, and conclusion of teaching.
>
> 3: "On the Crucifixion of Christ": *Basis*: "that God's love was great. . . ." (II) Meros A': Three *epicheirēmata* showing the magnitude of God's love, each supported by three arguments. (III) *Meros B'*: The "fruit (*karpon*) of the teaching" laid out as a three-part ("syllogistic") argument.
>
> 4: Panegyric to St. Stephen: The *basis* lays out three virtues (courage, faith, love of Christ), and these are treated in turn.
>
> 5: Panegyric of St. Spyridon: *Basis* lays out two lines of argument: "from virtues" and "from consequences," both of which are worked out in three parts.[5]
>
> 7: "On Prayer": Three-part *basis*: *Meros A'* covers the first *kephalaion*, which is supported by a three-part *apodeixis*; *Meros B'* divided into two subheadings, each of which is subdivided further into two, covering the remaining two *kephalaia*.
>
> 8: "On the Last Repentance": Two main divisions, each of which is developed in three parts.
>
> 9: "On the Love of One's Neighbor": *Basis* lays out three evils as the main headings. *Meros A'* takes up the first two, supporting the first with four arguments (all of which are subdivided into two parts) and the second with one long one; *Meros B'* is arranged in three parts.
>
> 10: "On Mercy": *Meros A'*: three *epicheirēmata* supporting the first *kephalaion*: *Meros B'*: two headings, the second of which is subdivided further into two subheadings.
>
> 11: "On the Saving Passion of Christ": *Meros A'*: two headings, the first developed in one argument, the second in two, each with two subdivisions; *Meros B'*: one *epicheirēma*, worked out in two parts.

This three-part armature bears a closer resemblance to the prescriptions in Western *artes praedicandi* than to anything in the Byzantine Greek tradition. That tradition began perhaps with the sermons of Bernard of Clairvaux; continued down through the 13th century in the *artes* of Alexander of Ashby and [Ps-]Bonavetura; continued into the 14th in such treatises as Jean de Chalons'

---

[5]These two, like the other panegyric in the collection (6) have no *Meros B'*. It is still possible, however, to see their three-part structures.

Ars brevis, which assimilated the *triplex modus praedicandi* to syllogistic form; persisted in the 15th-century sermons of Bernardin of Siena and Jean Gerson; and appears regularly in manuscripts produced in the 16th and 17th centuries of the *artes* of Fusignano and J. U. Surgant, famous for their visual depictions of the ideal sermon plan in the image of a tree.[6]

If this is the case, then we see in the *Skiagrafiai* a hybrid of Byzantine and Western rhetorical traditions. Yet we need not imagine that the author of these sketches had read—or even needed to read—Hermogenes and, for instance, Jean de Chalons. As we see in this chapter, the author of *Skiagrafiai* was heir to a more recent set of contributions to sermon theory and practice. Having said that, let us turn to a consideration of the identity of the author and the milieu in which he worked.

PART TWO

Vikentios Damodos makes a brief appearance in all the standard histories of neo-Greek literature,[7] but none of the lists of his work include *Skiagrafiai*.[8] Damodos was born in 1700 (not 1678/1679, as was previously believed)[9] in Charviata on Kefallinía, the largest of the Ionian Islands, off the west coast of Greece. Damodos' family was one of many Greek families who sent their sons

---

[6]On the medieval *artes praedicandi*, see the survey in J. J. Murphy, *Rhetoric in the Middle Ages* (Berkeley: University of California Press, 1974) 303–344. On Bernard, see J. Leclercq, *Recueil d'études sur Saint Bernard et ses écrits* 3 (= *Storia e Letteratura* 114 [Rome, 1969]) 13ff, 105ff. For Bernardin of Siena and Gerson, see *Miscellanea franciscana* 80 (1980): 385–424; and *Six sermons français inédits de Jean Gerson*, ed. L. Mourin (Paris: J. Vrin, 1946). On Surgant, see D. Roth, *Die mittelalterliche Predigttheorie* (Basel: Helbing & Lichtenhahn, 1956); and O. Dieter, "*Arbor picta*: The Medieval Tree of Preaching," *QJS* 51 (1965): 123–144.

[7]See, for example, C. Dimaras, *Histoire de la littérature néo-hellénique* (Athens: Collection de l'Institute Français, 1965) 122f; B. Knös, *L'histoire de la littérature néo-grecque*, Studia graeca Upsaliensia 1 (Stockholm, 1962) 348f. Damodos' philosophical interests are discussed briefly by G. Henderson, *The Revival of Greek Thought: 1620–1830* (Albany: SUNY Press, 1970) 29–33. The fullest treatment to date is that in G. Podsalsky's magisterial *Griechische Theologie in der Zeit der Türkenherrschaft: 1453–1821* (Munich: C. H. Beck, 1988) 337–342, with numerous references.

[8]See, for example, E. Papanoutsos, *Neoellenikē filosofia A'*, Basikē Bibliothēkē 35 (Athens: J. Zacharopoulos, 1953) 120. A number of manuscripts of theological works by Damodos in the library of the monastery of Vatopedi are listed in S. Eustratiades, *Catalogue of Greek Manuscripts in the Library of the Monastery of Vatopedi on Mount Athos, Harvard Theological Studies* 11 (1924; rpt. 1969) 27, numbers 99–102. No *Skiagrafiai* is listed there. K. Kourkoules, "Hē ekklesiastikē rhetorikē eis ta heptanēsa apo tou (15th) mekhri tou (19th) aionos," *Parnassos* 6 (1964): 323–340, notes (330f) that a volume published in Korfu in 1763 contains Damodos' *Rhetorikē* (first published in Venice in 1759), his *Praxeis kata syntomian eis tas rhetorikas hermeneias* (published separately in 1815, in Pest), and an untitled brief work on rhetoric that contains, at the end, a *skiagrafia* exemplifying the composition of a sermon (*didachē*) evidently drawing from the sermons of Elias Miniatis (*Logos* 9, ed. B. Tatakis, *Basikē Bibliothēkē* 8 [Athens, 1953] 198ff). The *Rhetorikē análysis didachōn tinōn tou Meniatou* listed by Papanoutsos does not seem to be our *Skiagrafiai*. On the debt of the author of *Skiagrafia* to Miniatis, see later discussion.

[9]See the evidence from the Venetian Archives in K. Dimaras, "Chronologika tou Vikentiou Damodou," *Praktika tritou panioniou Synedriou*, vol. 2 (Athens, 1969) 15–21.

to Italy to be educated (such opportunities were largely lacking in Greece proper during the *Tourkokratia*); and so Vikentios attended the Flanginian Academy in Venice and then the University of Padua, where he took a double Juris doctor degree in 1721.[10] On completing his studies, he returned to Kefallinía to teach and write until his death in 1752. None of his works was published during his lifetime. Evidently, he left a library of about 4,000 volumes that still exists in the town of Lixouri on Kefallinía.[11]

At the Flanginian Academy (sponsored by the Metropolitan of Venice), Damodos studied not only Greek literature and rhetoric—including Aristotle's *Rhetoric* and the works of Aphthonios and Hermogenes, along with the *Technē rhetorikē* of Frankiskos Skoufos (1681)—but also Latin (including Cicero's *Brutus* and the *Ad Herennium*) and Italian. The curriculum also included a heavy dose of theological study, mainly of the works of Greek Patristic and Byzantine writers.[12] At the Orthodox church of St. George, Damodos could have heard a number of famous preachers, many of whom preached not only to the Greek community in Venice but also abroad—in Crete or even Constantinople itself, or in Bratislava or Vienna, to Orthodox congregations there. At Padua, long a center of Aristotelian studies, he may have studied the works of scholastic commentators and of the neo-Aristotelian Theofilos Korydaleus (1565–1646), along with those of Aristotle himself, and he may have engaged in further theological and legal studies.[13] Scholastic influence is clear in Damodos' *Logic*; and that of Aristotle (and Augustine) in his *Synopsis of Ethics*. Another indication of works he found important can be seen in his précis of systematic dogmatics, where he seems to approve of the methods of Denis Petau (d. 1652), the famous Jesuit scholar and theologian.[14] Damodos' study of canon law must have been conducted under

---

[10]G. Ploumidis, "Hai praxeis engraphes tōn hellenōn spoudasmatōn tou panepistemiou tēs Padouēs (Meros B'), Legisti 1591–1809," *Epeteris Hetaireia Byzantinōn Spoudōn* 38 (1971): 84–195; 137, number 1236; his brother's name appears at number 1337, "Class of 1728." Ploumidis has provided statistics on the geographical distribution of the places of origin of Greek students at Padua for this period in "Gli Scolari greci nello studio di Padova," *Quaderni per la storia dell' Università di Padova* 4 (1971): 127–141.

[11]See M. Manousakas, "Ekthesis peri tōn en Kefallinia kai Zakyntho bibliothekōn kai archeion meta tous seismous tou 1953," *Deltion tēs Historikēs kai Ethnologikēs Hetaireia tēs Hellados* 11 (1956): 43–58.

[12]See, on this subject, A. Karathanasis, *Hē Phlangineios scholē tēs Venetias* (Thessalonkie: Hydrima meletōn, n.d. [after 1965]) 31ff, 192–201.

[13]On the contents of the philosophical and theological curricula, see G. Chassiotis, *L'instruction publique chez les grecs* (Paris: E. Leroux, 1881) 75–78, 91–119; and, more recently, G. Fabris, "Professori e scolari greci all' Università di Padova," *Archivio Veneto*, ser. 5, 30 (1942): 121–165.

[14]See I. Tsiamalenga, "La méthode théologique chez Denys Petau," *Ephemerides Theologicae Lovanienses* 48 (1972): 427–478, especially 444–446. The prologue to this work was published by G. Metallinos, "Theologia dogmatikē kata syntomian: hen agnoston ergon tou Bikentiou Damodou," *Theologia* 41 (1970): 645–654 (text on 652–654). In a review of Metellinos' Cologne dissertation, "Vikentios Damodos (1679/1700–1752): Theologia dogmatikē ētē syntagmation theologikon," *Orientalia Christiana Periodica* 48 (1982): 215–217, Podskalsky reminds us that great care is needed in assessing Orthodox attitudes toward scholasticism and its 17th-century critics.

Nikephoros Comnenos Papadopoulos, who was professor of canon law from 1713 to 1738. (Papadopoulos was a member of the Jesuit order from 1670 to 1686. His nephew, Andreas, a near contemporary of Damodos, was a Jesuit also.) His reading at Padua, in short, was extensive.

If we cannot reconstruct Damodos' intellectual formation with much precision, we can yet perceive some clear general influences on the composition and contents—and, indeed, the ecclesiastical politics—of the *Skiagrafiai*. The one that perhaps interests us most here concerns the *triplex modus* patterns we saw earlier in the outlines of the various *Skiagrafiai*. Looking at the *Skiagrafiai* against the background I have sketched, the ideal sermon the author had in mind looks a great deal like those of Elias Miniatis (1669–1714). When we consider the selections from Miniatis' *Didachai*, published by Tatakis,[15] this becomes abundantly clear.[16] Although it may be that such structural arrangement can be traced back to 12th-century Latin treatises on sermon composition, the more palpable influence on Miniatis was exercised by literary conventions not nearly as remote—the Italian (Jesuit) preacher Paolo Segneri (1624–1695) and the great Bossuet (1627–1704), whose influence spread far to the east of the court of Louis XIV.[17]

---

[15]In "Skoufos, Miniatis, Voulgaris, Theotokis," *Basikē Bibliothēkē* 8 (Athens, 1953) 127–238. It may be an indication of how marginalized Modern Greek studies have been that I cannot find a copy of any complete version of Miniatis' *Didachai* in this country. I have been able to consult the 1775/1776 St. Petersburg Russian translation (*Ilias Minijati: Pouchenija v raznyja nedeli*, dedicated to Catherine the Great), one of many versions to be found in the microfilm collection of 18th-century Russian books in the University of Illinois Library. My meager Russian makes such judgments difficult, but it looks as though the author of *Skiagrafiai* did not borrow his sample passages from Miniatis.

[16]See, for instance, the texts published by Tatakis, such as number 4, "On Faith": (I) 148–149.7, (II) 149.8–154, (III) 155.1–156; number 8, "On the Nature of Sin": (I) 189–190.4, (II) 190.5–195.25, (III) 195.6–197.

[17]For Segneri, see the sermons included in *Trattatisti e narratori del seicento*, ed. E. Raimondi (Naples: R. Ricciardi Editore, 1960): for example, "Predica 5," where the transition between the *exordium* and Part One (not indicated as such in the text) occurs at 658.14ff; "Predica 10," transition at 675.31–676.2; "Predica 15," 695.12ff. On the argumentative functions of the three-part format in Segneri, see G. Marzot, *Un Classico della Controriforma: Paolo Segneri* (Palermo: G. Palumbo Editore, 1950) 160f. The same format is evident in Bossuet. See the edition of B. Velat, *Bossuet: Oraisons funèbres panégyriques* (Paris: Librairie Gallimard, 1951): for example, *Oraison funèbre du révérend Père François Bourgoing* (1662), 36.12ff; *Oraison funèbre de Henriette-Anne d'Angleterre* (1670) 99.20ff. To my knowledge, J. Truchet was the first modern scholar to notice this feature in Bossuet's sermons; see "La division en points dans les sermons de Bossuet," *Revue d'Histoire littéraire de la France* 52 (1952): 316–329. As Truchet points out, La Bruyère was very critical of the practice. Earlier 17th-century French examples of this format can be seen in the *Homélies des États généraux* of J.-P. Camus; compare the analytic tables in the edition of J. Descrais (Geneva: Librairie Droz, 1970) 99–110. In Greek, we find this format used in the first decades of the century by the Patriarch Kyrillos Loukaris, who had of course studied at Padua (a century before Damodos); see the edition of Keetje Rozemond (Leiden: E. Brill, 1974) and G. Hoffmann, "Patriarch Kyrillos Lukaris. Einfluss abendländischer Schriften auf seine Predigten," *Orientalia Christiana Periodica* 7 (1941): 250–265. I say more about Loukaris later.

The influence of Miniatis is evident also in the variety of linguistic registers found in the *Skiagrafiai*. There are at least three: the *koinē* Greek of the New Testament (or Septuagintal, in the case of the Old), the atticizing Byzantine Greek of the church Fathers quoted in the sample sermon passages, and the neo-Greek of Damodos' own day. The use of the vernacular ("vulgar," in the nonpejorative sense of the word) was more than a mere literary decision—in both Miniatis and Damodos.

As this is an important issue in the assessment of the significance of the *Skiagrafiai*, it may be worth a brief digression. Champions of the Reformation saw a potential ally against Rome in the Orthodox Church, early on. Pope Gregory XIII took this seriously enough to mandate the establishment in 1576 of the College of St. Athanasius in Rome, whose main mission was to train Greeks to take the Counterreformation back to Greece and other Orthodox regions in the East "per confutar poi universalimente gl' errori heresie e scisma de'Greci," as the Rule of 1584 put it.[18] In this project, it is almost needless to say, the Jesuits played a conspicuous role. For their part, Lutheran and Calvinist proselytes to the Orthodox Church conceived of a strategy to do for Greeks what had been done for the German, French, and English laity: produce and distribute translations of Scripture into the vernaculars, so as to allow each individual to have access to it. Protestant attempts to gain a foothold among the Orthodox intensified particularly after the foundation of the Congregatio Propaganda Fide in 1622. In 1628, Cornelius Haga was sent as ambassador from Calvinist Holland to approach the Ecumenical Patriarch himself, Kyrillos Loukaris (1620–1638), in whom they saw a potential ally after the publication in Geneva of the Patriarch's "Confessio fidei" in 1625. The result was a crisis for the Orthodox Church at large, the generation of a three-sided factionalism among the faithful in which traditionalists tried to protect the Church from outside contaminating influences from both the Protestants and the Church of Rome and from the rekindling of controversies already hundreds of years old within Orthodoxy itself—chiefly the Hesychast/Palamite struggle that went back at least to the end of the 13th century.[19]

With Loukaris' approval and the support of the States General of the Dutch Republic, a neo-Greek version of the New Testament appeared in 1638 in a

---

[18]See E. Legrand, *Bibliographie hellénique ou description raisonnée des ouvrages publiés par les Grecs au XVIIᵉ siècle*, 5 vols. (Paris, 1894–1903) (= *BH* XVIII) 3:512.

[19]See the account of Loukaris' career and these events in Podskalsky, *Griechische* 162–180. Especially useful on the controversies over vulgar translations in the Orthodox Church is A. Argyriou, "La Bible dans l'Orthodoxie grecque du XVIIᵉ siècle," *Revue des Sciences Religieuses* 64 (1990): 141–168. See also T. Xanthopoulos, "Traductions de l'Écriture sainte en néo-Grec avant le XIXᵉ siècle," *Échoes d'Orient* 5 (1902): 321–332 (the first part of which discusses tentative attempts at such translations before Loukaris). The authenticity of Loukaris' "Confessio" has been a matter of enormous controversy, as the only extant version is the Latin one published in Geneva by Mitrophanis Kritopoulos. On Haga's relationship with Loukaris and on the Jesuit mission to Constantinople, see also A. De Groot, *The Ottoman Empire and the Dutch Republic* (Leiden/Istanbul: Nederlands Historisch-Archaeologisch Instituut, 1978) 200–207.

translation by Maximos of Gallipoli, whose preface argued that such a version would prove both "useful" and "necessary."[20] Shortly after the publication of this translation, however, Loukaris died; a new Patriarch was installed within a day—Kyrillos II Kontaris, who had received his education from the Jesuits; and the new version was utterly and completely suppressed.[21]

The Jesuits may have had a hand in engineering the suppression of the vulgar text; but in fact there was not a great deal of support for a vernacular version of Scripture among Orthodox theologians at the time. A translation by Maximos the Peloponnesian of Psalms had appeared in Venice in 1610; and another by Athanasios Pateloros had appeared in 1626 in Valachia. What conservative Orthodox clergy found suspect in these was not that they were in a vernacular dialect (besides, Psalms is part of the Old Testament), but that the dialect itself—neo-Greek—was, in their view, a concoction by Western intellectuals, that is, Uniate Greeks and their Jesuit masters, and in no way a genuine language suitable for expressing God's word.[22]

Nevertheless, it was argued, many Orthodox congregations, particularly in mainland Greece, were not able to understand (much less read) either the language of Scripture, the traditional Byzantine Greek in which the commentaries on Scripture were composed (hence the neo-Greek version by Maximos the Peloponnesian of a commentary on *Apocalypse* by Arethas), or the Greek spoken by the preachers themselves. So there was a pragmatic need for a level of language suitable for the audiences the Gospel was meant to save. As a result, a compromise seems to have been reached, for we see during the 17th century, after 1638, the emergence of a large body of sermon literature in neo-Greek and rhetorical textbooks in that dialect, as well. However, the sermons preserve the *koinē* text of Scripture in citations of the Evangelists and St. Paul, and when they quote the Church Fathers, they quote the atticizing Greek in which the Church Fathers wrote.

This is the reason for the multiple linguistic registers found in the *Skiagrafiai*. The author's instructions and the sample passages he provides to the reader are in neo-Greek. When the sermon text includes either a passage from Scripture or a quotation from Chrysostom or Basil (or indeed Augustine, who is often cited—in Greek), the author instructs his reader to "paraphrase, stating the point in the vernacular." The instruction, "Now state plainly (*haplōs*)," is in fact almost

---

[20]The text of the preface can be found in Legrand, *BH* XVII 1:365–370. Argyriou (154) speculates that the contents of this preface were in fact dictated by Antoine Léger, a scholar who traveled to Constantinople as part of Haga's entourage.

[21]There are still many historians, such as C. Tsourkas, "Les premières influences occidentales dans l'Orient orthodoxe," *Balcanica* [Bucharest] 6 (1943/1944): 333–356, who believe that Loukaris was assassinated by agents of the Jesuits, who then installed their stooge on the patriarchal throne.

[22]Jesuits scholars published over 40 books in neo-Greek between 1628 and 1677, including glossaries and grammars, as part of their Eastern strategy. See Z. Tsirpanlis, "I libri greci pubblicati della 'Sacra Congregatio de Propaganda Fide'," *Balkan Studies* 15 (1974): 204–224.

formulaic in the *Skiagrafiai*.[23] In this, as in the case of the three-part format, it might be added, the author follows the example of the sermons of Miniatis—as well as of all 17th-century Orthodox (and Uniate!) Greek preachers. It might also be added that Segneri, for instance, preached in Italian but quoted Scripture always from the Latin. So perhaps here, too, we are seeing Western influence at the same time we can document influences on the author of *Skiagrafiai* by his Greek Orthodox predecessors.[24]

Finally, returning to the matter of the work's technical vocabulary, for all the apparent influence, indirect and direct, of the West on the author, his manner of talking about matters of rhetorical art is largely Greek—Hermogenean, to be more specific—in its inspiration. His emphasis on syllogistic form, however, seems at first to have been yet another Western element in his thinking, as Aristotle was not traditionally respected by (Byzantine) Orthodox authorities— recall the reading of the anathemas against John Italos during Orthodox Sunday (first Sunday in Lent) services. Of course, as I noted, Damodos lived in an age when Orthodox thinkers—including authors of rhetorics—found much in Aristotle to be admired. So, for instance, the *Ekthesis tēs rhetorikēs* of Korydaleus and the *Technē rhetorikē* of Skoufos (1681), who in turn deeply influenced Miniatis, are thoroughly Aristotelian in their approach to the art.[25] Their rhetorics, however, like that of Aristotle, provide little in the way of practical advice (this is less true of Skoufos than of Korydaleus) on two crucial matters in preaching: organization and amplification. On these, Hermogenes and the commentary tradition on his works had much to offer, and presumably, readers of *Skiagrafiai*,

[23]Citations of passages from Augustine and Ambrose are not uncommon in 17th- and 18th-century sermons. Interest in the Latin Fathers goes back to the late 13th century, as evidenced by the translation of Augustine's *De trinitate* by Maximos Planudes—who was, incidentally, given honorary citizenship by the Venetians in 1296—and, in the next century, of Augustine's *De libero arbitrio* by Prochoros Kydones. In fact, there is some evidence that Greek translations of "Ambrose's" *Expositio fidei* and of Gregory the Great's *Regula pastoris* were in circulation before the 9th century. See, for instance, M. Rackl, "Die griechischen Augustinusübersetzung," *Miscellanea Fr. Ehrle*, vol. 1 (Rome, 1924) 10ff; A. Pertusi, "Le antiche traduzione greche delle opere di S. Ambrogio e l' *Expositio fidei* a lui falsamente attribuita," *Aevum* 18 (1944): 184–207; E. Dekkers, "Les traductions grecques des écrits patristiques latins," *Sacris Erudiri: Jaarboek voor Godsdienstwetenschappen* 5 (1953): 193–233.

[24]A further factor may well have entered into our author's practice, namely, the condemnation and burning of a reedition of Maximos' neo-Greek rendering of the New Testament that was produced in London in 1704 with the support of Anglican clergy. The decree by the Patriarch Gabriel III called it "superfluous . . . and useless (*perittēs . . . kai anōphelous*)"; the text can be found in M. Gedeon, *Kanonikai Diataxeis*, vol. 1, Subsidia byzantina 7 (Constantinople, 1888; Leipzig, 1970) 106–108.

[25]Korydaleus' *Ekthesis* mentions Hermogenes (e.g., 67.11ff, 79.26ff on *pithanotēs*, 81.41ff on *pistis*, 85.25f) in Papanoutsos, *Neoellenikē filosofia A'*, but only in passing. What Korydaleus has to say about *prooimia* (71f) simply paraphrases Aristotle's *Rhetoric* 2.1, 1378a6ff, on the elements of effective *ēthos*. The format of the *Technē* of Skoufos (abridged text in Tatakis, 44–124) more nearly resembles 16th- and 17th-century western rhetorics. Skoufos' influence on Miniatis is demonstrated in some detail in A. Papadopoulos, "Epidraseis tēs Technēs Rhetorikēs tou Fr. Skoufou epi tōn Didachōn tou Elia Miniate," *Parnassos* 7 (1965): 305–318.

like its author, had read Hermogenes (and Aphthonios) in schools like the Flanginian Academy. Hence, a mixture of Aristotle and Hermogenes such as the one we find in *Skiagrafiai* should not come as any great surprise.[26]

On the other hand, although much in *Skiagrafiai* has counterparts in the rhetorics of Korydaleus and Skoufos, it should be stressed that those systematic treatises, in addition to their strong Aristotelian bent, do not concern themselves with homiletics as such. That Skoufos influenced Damodos is certain; but that influence is clearest not in the *Skiagrafiai* but in the *Technē rhetorikē* Damodos composed (unpublished in his lifetime, recall), particularly in the similarities between their respective discussions of tropes (Skoufos 99–103 Tatakis// Damodos 314–322) and figures of diction and thought (Skoufos 103–122// Damodos 322–352). Aside from the fact that some of the schemes recommended in *Skiagrafiai* are discussed also in Damodos' *Technē* (e.g., *paralepsis, apostrophē, periphrasis*), however, there are few comparisons one can make between the two works. At the textual level, in other words, there exist scarcely any grounds for relating *Skiagraphiai* to Damodos' *Techē*. Of course, a detailed stylometric test might turn up textual evidence for attributing the two to the same author, should anyone have the energy to produce such an analysis.[27] But on the face of it, there seems to be no compelling reason for doing that. In short, aside from considerations of the milieu Damodos shared with predecessors such as Skoufos and Miniatis, it is hard to say confidently that this treatise can be attributed to him.

The question of authorship, therefore, is for the time being moot. But that diminishes neither the significance of the treatise nor the need for further study of the complex multicultural milieu that produced it. If nothing else, the existence of works like *Skiagrafiai* shows beyond a reasonable doubt that the *triplex modus praedicandi* flourished well beyond the end of the Middle Ages, that the history of Byzantine rhetoric did not come to an end with the fall of Constantinople, and that the study of Renaissance and early modern rhetorical theory can no longer ignore what was occurring east of the Adriatic at the time.

---

[26]It might be suggested that another source for the *Skiagrafiai* may have been George of Trebizond's *Rheticorum libri quinque (RLV)*. Trebizond's theological tracts were widely read in the 17th and 18th centuries (cf. Legrand *BH* XVII, index, *s.n.*), but *RLV* evidently was not. I have suggested a reason for the sudden disappearance of this work, in Thomas M. Conley, *Rhetoric in the European Tradition* (Chicago: University of Chicago Press, 1994) 117f.

[27]Bombou-Stamate's arguments are impossibly circumstantial, given that they turn on references to and parallels in technical vocabulary that was widely shared among Greek writers on rhetoric at the time. The five textual parallels she exhibits (Bombou-Stamate, "Ho Vikentios Damodos" 211) between the *Skiagrafiai* and Damodos' *Technē* are unfortunately not as persuasive as she seems to think.

Part IV

RHETORIC AND CULTURE
FROM THE RENAISSANCE
TO THE PRESENT

Chapter 13

International Humanism

Kees Meerhoff
University of Amsterdam

> *Inter nos colemus amicitiam et ex literis et in literis vivemus suaviter.*
>
> J. Sturm, 1565

The title of this chapter is a tautology. But some things, though self-evident in principle, need to be said time and again: The essential feature of humanism has been its crossing of national boundaries, a crossing facilitated by an international language, a refined Latin. There has been no conflict between the transnational nature of humanist communication and nationally defined local interests; on the contrary, one observes a constant fertilization of national grounds by international thought and practice. This is precisely what was called culture, the enrichment of local artistic practice, of locally rooted philosophy and literature, by the Greek, Latin, and Hebrew monuments of artistic and linguistic communication, both of the past and of the contemporary period. Thus, the foundation of the Collegium Trilingue in Louvain and the creation of the Collège des Lecteurs Royaux in Paris have been landmarks in the national cultures of the Low Countries, of France and of the surrounding countries, which were all more or less in the process of becoming, often for the first time in their history, a national unity proud of their difference. The example that comes to mind immediately is the Pléiade, a group of poets who played a major part in the development of national French culture. The education they received in Parisian colleges like the Collège de Coqueret and the Collège de Boncourt was exclusively classical; hardly any attention was paid to the contemporary vernacular culture. And yet it was Jean Dorat, the learned headmaster of Conqueret, who opened the famous manifesto of the young and very ambitious poets, *La Deffence et Illustration de la langue françoyse*, published in Paris by Joachim Du Bellay in the year 1549 with an epigram in Greek. Characteristically, Dorat's first line is a quotation from Homer in which Hector expresses his ardent patriotism just before attacking the Greeks (*Iliad*, XII, 243); the quotation echoes Du Bellay's own remarks in his dedicatory letter to a high-ranked relative, where he speaks of the essentially patriotic motives that lay behind his enterprise: "l'affection naturelle envers ma patrie." The open manifestation of a multilingual perspective in presenting a defense of the French national tongue is coherent with the basic aim of the manifesto, which is to show that there is only one adequate way to defend the national language and literature. This unique and quite paradoxical method was meant, as is well known, to avoid any imitation of national, vernacular models and to turn exclusively to classical, neoclassical, and modern Italian model authors for imitation.

Of course, the expression of this idea already puts into practice the very theory it wanted to present. Indeed, the kind of imitation that the Pléiade poets both defended on the theoretical level and put into practice in their poetry[1] is clearly an imitation of Cicero's own theory and practice with regard to the Greeks. This is also why we find a remarkable number of strict Ciceronian Latinists converted to the defense of their own mother tongue (Cardinal Bembo in Italy, Longueil and Dolet in France, for example); they were simply following the example of their radiant model, as expressed in the *Academica*, the *De finibus*, and elsewhere.

The crossing of borderlines in time and space did not have the same impact all over Europe. For instance, the return to the Greek and Roman past was experienced quite differently in Italy, where in a large measure the rediscovery of antiquity was

---

[1]It is very significant that Du Bellay, alongside the manifesto, published his first collection of sonnets, the *Olive*, under the same royal privilege, thus appearing at the same time as his theory of imitation and a sample of its results. Equally significant is the fact that the *Olive* opened with a Latin epigram by the same Jean Dorat, in which the latter revealed Du Bellay's major source of inspiration, Petrarch's *Canzoniere*. Dorat underlined the emulative nature of Petrarch's poetry and, by the same token, the process of imitation as virtually indefinite, even though it was clear that in fact his imitative interest did not go beyond the *scripta vetusta* of the Greeks and Romans. In short, this small poem is to be considered a reader's guide to humanist vernacular poetry: it offers a theory of imitation in a nutshell and a key to the very complex imagery that links the beloved Lady with the natural environment and with ancient mythology (Olive—tree—Minerva, reproducing a similar Petrarchan string of associations):

> Sola virûm nuper volitabat docta per ora
>   Laura, tibi Thuscis dicta, Petrarcha, sonis:
> Tantaque vulgaris fuerat facundia linguae,
>   Ut premeret fastu scripta vetusta suo.
> At nunc Thuscanam Lauram comitatur Oliva
>   Gallica, Bellaii cura laborque sui.
> Phoebus amat Laurum, glaucam sua Pallas Olivam:
>   Ille suum vatem, nec minus ista suum.

See J. Du Bellay, *Oeuvres Poétiques*, vol. 1, ed. H. Chamard, repr. and completed by Y. Bellenger (1908; Paris, 1982) 4.

a return to the "national" roots, and in France, where the earlier presence of the Romans was often felt as a humiliation inflicted by a foreign occupying force. But here again, nothing is simple, because all experience was tied to local historical developments. For one thing, Italy was not a national unity before the end of the 19th century (those who have read *La Chartreuse de Parme* will remember that Stendhal's hero is constantly crossing borders), Sicily's history—with its impressive Greek remains—differs greatly from that of Venice, and so on. In France, the past felt different in Lyon, the former capital of the larger part of Roman Gaul, center of worship of Roma and Augustus, in Marseille, which Du Bellay calls "a second Athens" because of the city's excellent Greek schools during the imperial period, and in the village where Asterix and Obelix so bravely resisted Caesar's superior numbers. Small wonder, then, that one observes a profoundly ambiguous attitude toward Greco-Roman antiquity in a key text like the *Deffence et Illustration de la langue françoyse*, where Du Bellay develops, alongside his famous theory of imitation of ancient model authors, a kind of mythology of the Gallic "national" past. I have shown elsewhere that this myth of glorious Gaul even affected the evolution of Ramist rhetoric in the second half of the 16th century; and it would be easy to draw up a long list of very erudite works of epic poetry or history in which the Gallic myth continues to play a major part, often seasoned with tales about the Trojan origins of the Gallic ancestors. This was so well into the 17th century, in spite of the fact that these tales had been very effectively destroyed by 16th-century humanist scholarship.[2]

But it goes without saying that these nationalistic mythologies never really affected the educational system or the imitative practice of writing. The result was that the authority of Greek and Roman culture remained unchallenged, even though the study of the classical texts was accompanied by occasional complaints about the unfortunate habit of the druids of giving only oral instruction, so that no written proof of their undoubtedly profound wisdom was available. Here again, Ramus acted in an emblematic way, for he expressed his regrets concerning the loss of Gallic educational source material in a Latin closely imitated from Cicero and Quintilian. What else was there to be done than to envy Socrates for having had his Plato?

Ramus' Gallic infatuation is perhaps all the more amusing due to his own intellectual origins. As is well known, Ramus received his education in the humanistically oriented colleges that lay in the orbit of the newly founded Collège des Lecteurs Royaux, in Paris, which he came to after a very modest childhood in Cuts, a small village near the city of Noyon in Picardy (northern France),

---

[2]K. Meerhoff, *Rhetorique et poétique au XVIᵉ siècle en France. Du Bellay, Ramus et les autres* (Leiden, 1986); and G. Huppert, "The Origins of the Nation," *The Idea of Perfect History* (Urbana, 1970). It is noteworthy that Lyon was celebrated by Pontus de Tyard, one of the more philosophical poets of the Pléiade group, as "la Cité par Plance *restaurée*" (2:25), Plancus being the founding father of Lyon. See also the nicely illustrated work, F. Beck and H. Chew, *Quand les Gaulois etaient romains* (Paris, 1989).

where John Calvin was born some years before him. I recently tried to demonstrate that Ramus was influenced in a decisive way by three German professors, all of whom were dedicated followers of fashion and, as such, disciples not only of Erasmus but also of R. Agricola and, perhaps first and foremost, of Luther's second man in Wittenberg, Philip Melanchthon.[3] In other words, the patriotic Ramus, ironically enough, far from being brought up within the Gallic or even the French tradition, was mainly shaped by educators coming from abroad. This brings us back to the central issue of this chapter, international humanism.

In the summer of the year 1571 a booklet appeared in Strasburg, written by a certain Johann Ludwig Hauvenreuter, containing an outline of the didactic system that had given the city's Latin school international fame. This outline, which consists of a series of bracketed schedules, is entirely based upon two of Johann Sturm's educational works, the *Classicae Epistolae* (1565) and the *Academicae Epistolae* (1569). The booklet itself is called simply *Schola Argentinensis*, School of Strasburg, and the author's debt to Sturm is willingly admitted on the front page. The rector himself has honored his disciple's industry with a dedicatory letter, as is mentioned on the same front page, composed by the school's regular printer Rihel.[4]

This letter is remarkable in more than one respect. It shows Johann Sturm as a leading authority in the field of humanist education. As such, it is important evidence of the institutionalizing of the humanist movement, that is, of the evolutionary process "from Humanism to the Humanities." As is appropriate to the wise and indulgent helmsman he had become, Sturm casts a panoramic glance around him, comparing his ideas and his school with others, looking across the border and back in time, inviting his readers to do the same.

His first move is from Protestant Strasburg, the Free City that was a part of the German Empire, back to the capital city that he had left more than 30 years ago at the instance of Strasburg's Reformer Martin Butzer. "This outline of yours," he writes to his former pupil, "reminds me of a similar endeavour made in the old days in Paris (*olim Lutetiae*) by a colleague of mine, James Omphalius, who tried to make an abstract of the entire *Institutio Oratoria* of Quintilian; I hope the result will be somewhat more rewarding to you than it was to him; in any case, I like your diligence, and I appreciate your kindness towards me, or rather, towards our school."[5] So, right from the start, Sturm invites his readers to cross the border between the Empire and the kingdom of France nearby, and to remember the great days of humanist attacks upon the strongholds of "me-

---

[3]K. Meerhoff, "Logic and Eloquence: A Ramusian Revolution?" *Argumentation* 5 (1991): 357–374.

[4]See reproduction in Fig. 13.1.

[5]I give a paraphrase of the text of which an abstract is reproduced in the Appendix to this chapter.

I do not want to go into the virtually anti-Ramistic implications of Sturm's comments on Omphalius' efforts: "It neither seemed as if Quintilian had very much to say, nor that he himself had accomplished a great deal."

SCHOLA ARGEN=
TINENSIS.

Hoc est,

EPISTOLARVM IOANNIS
STVRMII CLASSICARVM ET
Academicarum χυικτισμοί, confecti

A

IOANNE LVDOVICO HAVVENREVTERO.

Cum præfatione Ioannis Sturmij.

ARGENTORATI EXCVDEBAT
Iosias Ribelius,
M. D. LXXI.

SCHOLA

ΣXHMATIΣMOΣ generalis, complectens summatim docendi modum
in classibus vsurpandum.

Explicatio-
nem perspi-
cuam &
B R E-
V E M.

Cognitio-
ne: quæ re-
quirit

Memori-
am firmam.
Hæc compa-
ratur par-
tim

Omnis classi-
um doctrina
consistit in præ-
ceptionum
Grammatica-
rum, Rhetori-
carũ, & Dia-
lecticarum

Si inchoetur in singulis: constituatur in
omnibus.

Renouatione et repetitione traditorum
QVOTIDIANA.

Oratorum.
Poëtarum
Historica-
rum.
} um { Græcorum.
Latinorum.

Aliena. Re-
soluendis &
ad artis loca
referendis
scriptis.

Exercita-
tione & v-
su: qui est
in opere
vel

Scriptione QVOTIDI-
ANA.

Nostra. Si aliosimi
tentur tum scriben-
do , tum commen-
tando: quæ æmula-
tio perficitur exerci
tatione styli: in qua
opus est

Operæ præceptoris : vt præceatin
ijs, quæ cognita nõdum sunt; sub-
sequatur in ijs, in quibus erratũ
est, idq; non voce solum: sed scri-
ptura etiam in tabula.

FIGURE 13.1. Frontispiece and general outline of the Sturmian school system, in *Schola argentinensis*, Strasburg, J. Rihel, 1571, ff. [A1ʳ] and [A3ᵛ]. (Rott, no. 106; Ritter, no. 1075).

dieval" scholasticism in Paris. It was in these days that both Omphalius and Sturm taught Ramus, like many others who became in turn heralds of the New Learning. Both had come from Louvain, where Sturm already gained fame by printing a number of Greek texts in association with Rutger Rescius and in close contact with the Collegium Trilingue. Once in Paris, they first settled down in the Collège de Lisieux, associated with leading Parisian printers and, in order to establish their reputation as modern humanist scholars, published their first rhetorical analyses of classical authors (Cicero especially), which became the trademark of the new movement.[6] Sturm, moreover, wanted to maintain his fame as a specialist in Greek studies; he wrote a preface to a translation of Galen in which he violently attacked the "barbarian" scholastics. These men certainly knew how to handle their public relations, as did another young German who joined them in Paris, Bartholomaeus Latomus from Arlon. He turned out to be the most successful of them all, at least in the French capital. Latomus first taught at the Collège de Sainte Barbe, already famous for its humanistically oriented program of studies, and soon won the race against his colleague at Sainte Barbe, a specialist in rhetoric like himself named James L. Strebaeus, to become the first professor of Latin eloquence at the newly founded Collège des Lecteurs Royaux. One of the main reasons for his success was undoubtedly his great skill in analyzing Cicero's orations; it was a quality he had in common, as we have seen, with his fellow countrymen Omphalius and Sturm. Latomus took a concrete approach toward texts which was much more appealing to a young audience than reading the theoretical works of the Roman orator as his opponent preferred. So, whereas Strebaeus taught the *Orator*, Latomus, Omphalius, and Sturm lectured on *Pro Milone* and other exciting texts that they approached in the very methodical way they had inherited from Agricola and Melanchthon. Ramus, like so many other young students, attended the classes of these Germans, who carried the day in Paris in the early 30s. Had he listened more carefully to the young professor with whom he had so much in common (for one thing, a very modest origin in northern France; Estrebay (< Strebaeus) is even smaller than Cuts), Ramus just might have shown a little more moderation and insight in his attacks on the theoretical works of Cicero or Quintilian, attacks that James J. Murphy is republishing.[7] The nickname of *usuarius* that Ramus gained because of his teaching methods finds its explanation in this context: As disciples of Agricola, of Erasmus, and especially of Melanchthon, Ramus' German professors held that theory is only a tool to enable a person to analyze and to create texts. According to them, theory should be a method, that is, an easy way (*compendiaria via*) leading toward the text. Ramus' own "natural" rhetoric and dialectic would be just that: methods constructed on an experimental basis, by way of observation of the outstanding practice that came down to him from monuments of ancient eloquence and literature. Never in the history of philosophy had logic come so close to

---

[6]See Meerhoff, "Logic and Eloquence."
[7]See J. J. Murphy and C. Newlands, 1986 and 1992.

literature. This fundamental principle that links theory to practice to the extent of subjecting the latter to the former is as much Ramistic as it is a distinctive feature of Northern Humanism. We would naturally expect to find it in Sturm's preface and in the schedules of the *Schola Argentinensis*.

Johann Sturm's nostalgic return to the good old days in Paris is not unique; he often refers to this vital period of his life in other texts, in prefaces, and of course in his correspondence with Omphalius and Latomus.[8] But there may have been a more direct reason for this reference to Paris: Exactly 2 years before, Peter Ramus had written in person to Sturm in order to obtain a position in Strasburg's famous school. Ramus, indeed, wanted to escape from the civil wars that were ravaging his country. One year earlier, he had visited Strasburg, where Sturm and his colleagues honored him with a splendid banquet, "drei Tisch voll" (three tables packed with professors), according to a contemporary report. Ramus did not go after all; but only a few months before Sturm started to write his preface, he received another letter from Ramus in which the latter refers once again to the difficult political situation in Paris: the eve of St. Bartholomew's Day was not so far away.[9]

Sturm's short walk down memory lane is followed by some bitter remarks about the present lack of interest in his pedagogical ideals, and about a recent slanderous attack against his person, probably launched by the Lutheran theologian J. Marbach. The rector points to his lifelong struggle for a better education and to a series of writings in which, as he proudly assures us, his basic assumptions have always remained the same. One of Sturm's chief merits is, indeed, that he never changed his mind.

After these remarks, Sturm modestly compares the aims of his own school with those of the three major schools in Athens: the Academy, the Lyceum, and the Stoa. But after that, he casts another glance across the border and focuses on Paris once again. This time, it is a newly founded institution that gains his attention; indeed, according to the rector, his own dreams have come true not only in his own *schola argentinensis*, but also—although only quite recently—in

---

[8]See W. Friedensburg, "Der Briefwechsel zwischen Bartholomaeus Latomus und Johann Sturm von Strasburg im Jahr 1540," *Archiv für Reformationgeschichte* 30 (1933): 103–130. In an appendix, the author publishes a letter from Sturm to Omphalius written in 1539, in which the theme of the Parisian friendship between the three humanists recurs quite explicitly.

[9]C. Schmidt, *La vie et les travaux de Jean Sturm* (1855; Nieuwkoop, 1970) 151; C. Waddington, *Ramus: sa vie, ses écrits et ses opinions* (1855; Geneva, 1969) 195, 432, based on manuscript source material dated September 8, 1568 (banquet); July 16 and 30, 1569 (application); February/March, 1571 (letter). It was at least the second time that Sturm had tried to attract a celebrity to his school: he had done so before with regard to Philip Melanchthon at the end of the year 1556. In the *Classicae Epistolae* and elsewhere, Sturm expressed his gratitude toward the scholar of Wittenberg, *parens multo maximae partis literatorum hominum; in Philippo Melanchthoni cum alia fuerunt multa praeclara, tum illud etiam adulescentulo mihi valde placuit et fuit perutile, quod in omnibus quae docuit, idoneis et quae doctrinam sapiunt usus est exemplis.* After Melanchthon's death (April 1560), Sturm organized an official commemoration, *Argentinensis schola in Melanthonis funus*: compare Schmidt, *La vie* 119, 120; J. Rott, ed., intr., transl., *J. Sturm, Classicae Epistolae* (Paris, 1938) 86, 100.

this new French academy. We will soon see that with this academy, we are back with the Pléiade poets mentioned in the first part of this chapter and also with Peter Ramus, who was closely associated with its founding father. In fact, it was Ramus who, just one year before his journey to Strasburg, had pleaded the cause of the Academy before the Queen of France.

The new institution is no other than the famous Academy of Poetry and Music, the "chequered life" of which coincides, according to Frances Yates, "with the darkest period of the struggle between Catholic and Huguenot in France. Founded in 1570 during a short outbreak of peace between wars, the first event of horror which came to shake it was the Massacre of St. Bartholomew in 1572. And it disappears from view after the the last and most terrible recurrence of the 'troubles' in 1585."[10]

To this gloomy description by Yates we may add that right from the start, J. Sturm had been very actively implicated in these affairs, often acting on the highest diplomatic level. It is hardly surprising, then, that the details in the information he gives concerning the new institution all prove quite accurate. This is what he writes:

> I am told that a new Academy has been founded in Paris, in which all the disciplines are not only taught, but put into practice as well. . . . Even military science and music are taught in the same, active way. . . . The King and princes of France are so pleased with this new endeavour that they plan to send their children to it, and even do so already. The King, and also the Queen, has offered permanent financial support; the other princes plan to do the same. This corresponds exactly to my own schemes and to my own endeavours! In Italy this kind of academic gathering also exists; but as it seems, things will be organized more lavishly in France. . . . Providing all these rumours we heard of just a day or two ago, are true!

After this enthusiastic account, he stresses once more the essential didactic bond between his school in Strasburg and the new academy in Paris: Both institutions not only teach theoretical matters, but also require from their students daily practice and exercise as well. It is quite obvious that Sturm has in mind the "general outline" that summarizes his own teaching method and shows his allegiance to the basic principles of Northern Humanism. It also shows the fundamentally oratorical bent of the whole movement, based on the daily study and imitation of ancient texts, much more than on mere theory. It is needless to add that Ramus is part of the same tradition![11]

---

[10]F. A. Yates, *The French Academies of the Sixteenth Century* (1947; Liechtenstein, 1968) 69; compare Yates, *The French Academies* 210–211 concerning the eve of St. Bartholomew's Day, Catherine de' Medici, and Ramus.

[11]See the reproduction of this diagram, after *Schola Argentinensis*, f° Aiii^{vo} in Fig. 13.1 and compare Ramus on *usus*: "To become a musician we do not want to know only the rules of music, we want to hear other musicians playing, and we want to play music ourselves!" (*Pro philosophica parisiensis Academicae disciplina oratio*, 1551). One could easily add many other examples, by which he gained his reputation of *usuarius*.

In her magnificent study, *The French Academies of the Sixteenth Century* (London, 1947), otherwise so marvelously well documented, Frances Yates does not quote this testimony from abroad. The information Sturm gives about the scope of the new academy fully corroborates all her basic claims. For instance, the academy founded at the end of 1570 by a prominent member of the Pléiade, Jean-Antoine de Baïf—an esteemed poet, son of one of France's greater humanists—and by the musician Joachim Thibault de Courville in reality had encyclopedic ambitions, rooted in Neo-Platonic thought. These ambitions went well beyond those of a simple arts school and corresponded to fundamentally ethical, and even political, aims. Sturm is quite correct in stating that all the *artes* are taught in this school, including military discipline. Indeed, Sturm's contemporary testimony entirely confirms the detailed account given some 50 years later by the learned Father Marin Mersenne, one of Yates' star witnesses, in his *Quaestiones celeberrimae in Genesim* (Paris, 1623).

> When Jean Antoine de Baïf and Joachim Thibault de Courville laboured together to drive barbarism from Gaul, they considered that nothing would be of more potency for forming the manners of youth to everything honourable than if they were to recover the effects of ancient music and compose all their songs on the models of the fixed rules of the Greeks. Wherefore they wished so to provide that nothing should be lacking in the Academy which should make it suitable for the perfecting of a man, both in mind and body. Therefore they appointed to this Academy men most skilled in every kind of natural sciences, and instituted a prefect of it who should be called the Head Teacher. I leave out the other masters, of sciences, of tongues especially, of music, of poetry, of geography, of the various parts of mathematics, and of painting, who promoted the good of the mind, and the military prefects who taught all those things which are useful for military discipline and for the good of the body. There were also others appointed over domestic affairs, such as clothing, gardening, food, money, and such like.[12]

Other texts written by an acquaintance of Mersenne, the equally learned Guillaume Colletet, author of the important *Lives of the French Poets*, fully confirm Sturm's story of the financial support given by the French Court.[13] Did the king,

---

[12]Yates, *The French Academies* 24; Latin text from Yates, *The French Academies* 325.

[13]

I once saw some pages of the manuscript book of the institution of this noble and famous Academy in the hands of Guillaume de Baïf, son of Antoine de Baïf, who had rescued them from the shop of a pastrycook to whom the natural son of Philippe Desportes, who did not follow in the glorious footsteps of his father, had sold them together with other learned and curious manuscripts. An irreparable loss which I felt very deeply indeed. And all the more so since in the book of this institution, which was a very fine vellum book, one could see what the king Henri III, the Duc de Joyeuse, the Duc de Retz, and the greater number of the lords and ladies of the court had promised to give for the establishment and upkeep of this Academy.

Yates concluded quite correctly that in the mind of Colletet and others, "the academic activities of the two reigns [Charles IX and Henry III] are merged to the point of confusion" (Yates, *The French Academies* 28, 29).

Charles IX, really believe in the moderating force of those *vers mesurés*, that is, French poetry composed according to the rules of classical prosody and actually sung with musical accompaniment? Frances Yates makes a strong claim in favor of this idea, strange as it may seem to us; she shows that "the hope of the religious reunion of Christendom" was still widely entertained in the 16th century, even—or maybe especially—in the hopeless era of the civil wars. She also points to the previous efforts made by Philip Melanchthon and Cardinal Contarini to work out a "scheme of reconciliation": "The intense spiritual aspirations of many early sixteenth-century Neo-Platonists contained within them the double purpose of reform of the Catholic Church and compromise with the Protestants."[14] This is the very idea that we find back in the Academy's official Letters Patent. "It is of great importance for the morals of the citizens of a town that the music current and used in the country should be retained under certain laws, for the minds of most men are formed and their behaviour influenced by its character, so that where music is disordered, there morals are also depraved, and where it is well ordered, there men are well disciplined morally."[15]

It is well known that the poetic and political ideal of the *vers mesurés* is already present in Du Bellay's *Deffence et Illustration* (vol.1, 9); Frances Yates states quite correctly at the beginning of her chapter concerning the "external history" of the French academies that it is "impossible to separate the origins of Baïf's Académie de Poésie et de Musique . . . from those of the poetic movement . . . known as the Pléiade. Sixteenth century French academism takes its rise in the group round Dorat at the Collège de Coqueret which was also the well-head of the Pléiade."[16]

But it may still be less well known that the poets of the Pléiade shared this particular ideal with Peter Ramus, who, as we may assume, handed it down to none other than Johann Sturm. For one thing, Baïf and Ramus were friends. They were both in favor of a radical reform of French spelling, and they were both interested in ancient rhythm and in the writing of poetry measured "à l'antique." I have already mentioned that Ramus pleaded in favor of the foundation of an Academy before Catherine de' Medici, Queen of France. Comparing Cosimo de' Medici's Florence with the Paris of his own day, Ramus stresses the great tradition of patronizing the arts and sciences in the queen's illustrious family: "You see, therefore, Madame, the deeds of your family, which I propose to yourself, namely, to use their power and wealth liberally to fill their country with great benefits, to found Academies, build palaces to the Muses, give due rewards to learned men, and not only profit mankind in these praise-worthy ways, but inspire other princes to do likewise. . . ."[17] In the year of his death, Ramus

---

[14]Yates, *The French Academies* 199; compare 76. See Yates, *The French Academies*, chapter 10, "The Religious Policy."

[15]Yates, *The French Academies* 23; French text in Yates, *The French Academies* 319.

[16]Yates, *The French Academies* 14; compare 52.

[17]P. Ramus, *Prooemium mathematicum* (Paris, 1567), translated from the Latin dedication to the Queen by Frances Yates, *The French Academies* 20, n 4; Meerhoff, *Rhetorique* 302, n 34, compare 306, n 40 (Baïf and Ramus).

still praises the *vers mesurés* composed by another member of the Pléiade, Etienne Jodelle, in the second edition of his French Grammar (1572). But it is most curious to observe that the *vers mesurés* even found their place in the Latin rhetoric that Ramus entirely rewrote after the death of his major collaborator and friend Omer Talon. Most curious, because it is in the section concerning poetry that Ramus made his most radical changes in the text in order to fit in his ideas, evidently inspired by his study of Gallic civilization and the nonclassical origins of both ancient and modern verse. This is a very complicated, though exciting, story that I have told elsewhere. It is also very revealing to see that Johann Sturm, in person, took over Ramus' (and the Academy's) ideas about measured vernacular poetry in another preface introducing a German grammar written in Strasburg (1573).[18]

Clearly, then, there was a considerable circulation of ideas among learned poets and humanistic schoolmen. There was intense communication, on both a national and an international level. Modern scholarship should continue to cherish the old concept of imitation and seek its inspiration in the kind of crossing of boundaries that made 16th-century humanism so surprisingly vital. For instance, the splendid tradition of Anglo-Saxon scholarship in the field of French intellectual history and culture, so brilliantly illustrated by Frances Yates, should be kept alive at all costs. Until now, this tradition has fortunately been very much alive and is as prestigious as ever. The person we honor today with an international Festschrift is one further living example of this great tradition in intellectual history.

ACKNOWLEDGMENTS

I would like to thank Roger Moss for correcting my English.

REFERENCES

Beck, F., & Chew, H. (1989). *Quand les Gaulois étaient romains*. Paris.
Bolgar, R. R. (1973). "From Humanism to the Humanities," in *Twentieth Century Studies* 9, 8–21.
Chamard, H. (1939–1940). *Histoire de la Pléiade* (4 vols.) Paris.

---

[18]Meerhoff, *Rhetorique* 276–316 (Gallic rhetoric and Ramus' theory of poetry); K. Meerhoff, "D'étranges gymnastiques: poétiques et philosophie à la Renaissance," Histoire Epistémologie Langage 12 (1990): 103–122 discusses Sturm's preface to Oelinger's *Underricht der hochTeutschen Spraach* (Strasburg, 1573); (J. Rott, "Bibliographies des oeuvres imprimées du recteur strasbourgeois Jean Sturm (1507–1589)," *J. Rott—Investigationes Historicae*, vol. 2, ed. M. de Kroon and M. Lienhard [Strasburg, 1986] 319–407, no. 115) and the striking similarity between Ramus' and Sturm's ideas concerning the ideal of *vers mesurés*. Among other things, Sturm wrote approvingly that "poetas Gallos (!) et Italos videmus rhythmos similiter desinentes atque cadentes reliquisse et poeticum quendam invenisse numerum," where *rhythmi* are vernacular verses and *poeticus numerus* is poetry written according to the rules of quantity, that is, patterns of long and short syllables. For Ramus' ideas that Sturm clearly took over, see in particular the outlines in Meerhoff, *Rhetorique* 303, 316; and the relevant text of the *Rhetoric* quoted on p. 306.

Chamard, H., (Ed.) (1970). J. Du Bellay, *La Deffence et Illustration de la langue françoyse* (1549), Paris.

Chamard, H., (Ed.) (1982). J. Du Bellay, *Oeuvres Poétiques* (Vol. 1), repr. and completed by Y. Bellenger (1908), Paris.

Chartier, R., Compère, M. M., & Julia, D. (1976). *L'éducation en France du XVIe au XVIIIe siècle*, Paris.

Demerson, G. (1983). *Dorat en son temps. Culture classique et présence au monde.* Clermont-Ferrand.

Frémy, E. (1887). *L'Académie des derniers Valois, d'après des documents inédits*, Paris.

Friedensberg, W. (1933). "Der Briefwechsel zwischen Bartholomaeus Latomus und Johann Sturm von Strassburg im Jahr 1540," in *Archiv für Reformationsgeschichte* 30:103–130 [= 247–274].

Grafton, A., & Jardine, L. (1986). *From Humanism to the Humanities. Education and the Liberal Arts in Fifteenth and Sixteenth Century Europe*, London.

Huppert, G. (1970). *The Idea of Perfect History. Historical erudition and historical philosophy in Renaissance France*, Urbana.

Huppert, G. (1984). *Public schools in Renaissance France*, Urbana.

Lefranc, A. (1893). *Histoire du Collège de France depuis ses origines jusqu'à la fin du premier Empire*, Paris.

Meerhoff, K. (1986). "Rhétorique et poétique au XVIe siècle en France. Du Bellay, Ramus et les autres," in *Studies in Medieval and Reformation Thought* (Vol. 36). Leiden.

Meerhoff, K. (1990a). "Mélanchthon lecteur d'Agricola: rhétorique et analyse textuelle," in *Réforme—Humanisme—Renaissance* 30:5–22.

Meerhoff, K. (1990b). "D'étranges gymnastiques: poétique et philosophie à la Renaissance," in *Histoire Epistémologie Langage* 12:103–122.

Meerhoff, K. (1991). "Logic and Eloquence: A Ramusian Revolution?" in *Argumentation* 5:357–374.

Meerhoff, K. (1994). "The Significance of Philip Melanchthon's Rhetoric in the Renaissance," in P. Mack, (Ed.), *Renaissance Rhetoric*, London, New York. 46–62.

Murphy, J. J. (1981). *Renaissance Rhetoric—A Short-Title Catalogue*, New York.

Murphy, J. J. (Ed.) (1983). *Renaissance Eloquence. Studies in the Theory and Practice of Renaissance Rhetoric.* Berkeley.

Murphy, J. J., & Newlands, C. (Eds.), intr. and transl. (1986). *Arguments in Rhetoric against Quintilian. Translation and Text of Peter Ramus'* "Rhetoricae Distinctiones in Quintilianum" *(1549)*. DeKalb, IL.

Murphy, J. J., & Newlands, C. (Eds.), intr. and transl. (1992). *Peter Ramus's Attack on Cicero. Text and Translation of Ramus'* "Brutinae Quaestiones." Davis, CA.

Ong, W. J., S. J. (1958). *Ramus and Talon Inventory.* Cambridge, MA.

Ritter, F. (1937–1955). *Répertoire bibliographique des livres du XVIe siècle qui se trouvent à la Bibliothèque Nationale et Universitaire de Strasbourg* (4 vols.). Strasburg.

Rott, J. (1986). "Bibliographie des oeuvres imprimées du recteur strasbourgeois Jean Sturm (1507–1589)," in M. de Kroon & M. Lienhard (Eds.), *J. Rott—Investigationes Historicae*, Strasburg (Vol. 2), 319–407 [471–559].

Rott, J. (Ed.), intr. and transl. (1938). *J. Sturm, Classicae Epistolae*, Paris/Strasburg.

Schindling, A. (1977). *Humanistische Hochschule und freie Reichsstadt. Gymnasium und Akademie in Strasburg, 1538–1621*, Wiesbaden.

Schmidt, C. (1855). *La vie et les travaux de Jean Sturm*, Reprint Nieuwkoop, 1970.

Sharratt, P. (1972). "The Present State of Studies on Ramus," in *Studi Francesi* 16:201–213.

Sharratt, P. (1987). "Recent Work on Peter Ramus (1970–1986)," in *Rhetorica* 5:7–58.

Sharratt, P. (Ed.) (1991). "Ramus." Special issue of *Argumentation*.

Vocht, H. de (1951–1955). *History of the Foundation and the Rise of the Collegium Trilingue Lovaniense, 1517–1550* (4 vols.), Louvain.

Waddington, C. (1855). *Ramus: sa vie, ses écrits et ses opinions.* Paris. Reprint Genève, 1969.

Yates, F. A. (1947). *The French Academies of the Sixteenth Century Studies of the Warburg Institute*, F. Saxl (Ed.) (Vol. 15). London. Reprint Liechtenstein, 1968.

APPENDIX
An Abstract of J. Sturm's Letter to J. L. Hauvenreuter,
July 1, 1571

Ioannes Sturmius Ioanni Ludovico Havvenrevtero S. P. D.

Quod Epistolas meas constituisti Classicas atque Academicas contrahere, et quasi in tabulis figurare, vereor ne tibi accidat, quod olim Lutetiae Iacobo Omphalio, qui cum in angustum Quintiliani Rhetoricas institutiones coëgisset, id assecutus est, ut neque Quintilianus multa tradidisse, neque ipse rem magnam fecisse videretur. Sed tamen mihi placet industria tua Ioannes Ludovice, et grata mihi est tua erga me benevolentia, vel potius studium erga scholas nostras, quod si in aliis fuisset, aut esset in quibus esse deberet, minus gymnasium nostrum annos iam quatuor et amplius detrimentorum accepisset; nunc vero ut Prophetarum scripta, sic istae in patria neglectae iacent.

Scripsi multa de scholis instituendis, et de emendandis studiis philosophiae, ut de amissa dicendi ratione, ut de ludis literarum aperiendis, ut de Lavingano gymnasio, ut de nobilitate literata, quae omnia inter se discrepare non arbitror, neque ab his duobus generibus epistolarum dissidere existimo, neque ab ullo unquam sensi reprehendi; certe publice nemo vituperavit, praeter unum, si quis sit, Tragopithecum. Doctis enim scribo, talium hominum calumnias contemno; neque quod factu opus est iubeo aut mando, sed indico et demonstro, quod mihi optimum genus Academiae esse atque fuisse videatur. Sed etiam ego pecco, cum mihi disciplicent quibus ista non placent; veruntamen etiam isti errant, qui haec, quia non placent neque intelligunt, irrident, ut Horatius ait solenniter.

Meum certe institutum difficile et arduum est, et quod cum Atheniensium tribus gymnasiis contendere de gloria videatur, Academiae, Lycaei, Stoae, vel potius quod ex his tribus compositum sit, et excellentius aliquid videatur promittere, si recte intelligantur, quae his duobus generibus epistolarum comprehendi; praesertim si alteri duo accessissent libri epistolarum, quos in lucem edere constitueram, nisi nescio quae me impedissent.

Dum ergo nos cessamus, ab aliis antevertimur, et laudem inventionis amittimus, et illos sinimus immortalem consequi gloriam.

Audio enim Luteciae Academiam institui, in qua omnes artes atque disciplinae non solum doceantur, verum etiam exerceantur, nullaque hora vacua sit toto die, quae suis careat magistris et ludis liberalibus. Militaris etiam ars, et Musica ita tradantur, ut quasi exercitati pedites atque equites, et musicorum omne genus ex eo ludo copiosissime expectentur.

Atque hoc audio institutum ita placere Regi, atque Galliae principibus, ut liberos suos ad hoc Collegium mittere constituerint, quidam etiam iam mittant. Rex etiam atque Regina stipendia perpetua contribuerint, et alii principes idem propositum habeant facere. Haec ipsa mea ratio fuit, meumque institutum. In Italia etiam Academicas habent συζητήσεις, sed Gallia magnificentius aliquid videtur promittere, si vera sunt, quae superioribus hisce diebus audivimus. Nostrae certe συζητήσεις, etiam ut novi in Gallia Academici, non solum Theoremata continent, verum ἀσκήσεις καὶ μελέτας requirunt quotidianas. Quamobrem Gallicani isti viri, tametsi inventione nos non anteverterint, tamen actione atque exercitatione antecurrunt. Licebit tamen nobis cum illis contendere; multa enim illis, ut etiam nobis desunt, quae sunt invenienda . . . (&c.)

Argentorati Calendis Iulii Anno 1571
From: *Schola Argentinensis*, f° A2^{r–v}

Note: Sturm refers to the following works: *De amissa dicendi ratione* (Strasburg, 1538); *De literarum ludis recte aperiendis* (Strasburg 1538); *Nobilitas literata* (Strasburg, 1549); *Classicae Epistolae* (Strasburg, 1565); *Scholae Lavinganae* (Lauingen, 1565); *Academicae Epistolae* (Strasburg, 1569). See Rott, "Bibliographie" nos. 28, 29, 56, 87, 89, 100. Reprinted by F. A. Hallbauer and published at Jena in 1730; partially reprinted by R. Vormbaum in volume 1 of the *Evangelische Schulordnungen des sechszehnten Jahrhunderts* (Gütersloh, 1860). See Rott, *l. c.*, "Bibliographie" 387, 388.

Chapter 14

Diego Valadés and the Origins of Humanistic Rhetoric in the Americas

Don Paul Abbott
University of California-Davis

In 1579 the Tuscan printer Jacopo Pretruccio issued the *Rhetorica Christiana*, written by a Franciscan friar, Diego Valadés.[1] The publication of this work was a remarkable event in the already long history of rhetoric. Valadés was born in the New World, and his *Rhetorica Christiana* was almost certainly the first book written by a native of Mexico to be published in Europe. More important for its place in the rhetorical tradition, the *Rhetorica Christiana* is the first rhetoric that is not exclusively European in conception and execution. Not only was Valadés born in Mexico, but the work graphically reflects his Mexican origins and experiences.

The *Rhetorica Christiana* is an extraordinary combination of old world erudition and New World anthropology. In its pages Valadés transmits the literature of the Greeks and Romans and records the customs of the Mexicas and the Chichimecas. The *Rhetorica Christiana*, although very much a product of European humanism, is not an entirely conventional rhetoric of its time. It is a treatise that departs in significant ways from the accepted norms of Renaissance rhetoric.

---

[1] *Rhetorica Christiana: ad concionandi et orandi vsvm accommodata, vtrivsq facvltatis exemplis svo loco insertis; qvae qvidem ex Indorum maxime deprompta svnt historiis. Vnde praeter doctrinam, svma qvoqve . . . delectatio comparabitvr* (Perugia, 1579). I have used the Spanish-Latin edition: *Retórica cristiana*, intro. Esteban J. Palomera, trans. Tarsicio Herrera Zapién (Mexico: Universidad Nacional Autónoma de México; Fondo de Cultura Económica, 1989). This edition includes reproductions of the original Latin text with the Spanish translation on facing pages. All citations of the *Rhetorica Christiana* are to the original pagination of the Latin text. Subsequent references to the *Rhetorica Christiana* are abbreviated *RC* and cited parenthetically in the text. (Unless otherwise noted, translations from Spanish are mine.)

When Valadés deviates from the dominant idiom of 16th-century rhetoric he does so, almost invariably, because of his life as a teacher and preacher in the New World. Thus many of the distinctive features of Valadés' rhetorical theory derive from his mastery of European erudition, his understanding of Amerindian culture, and his attempt to integrate the two into a coherent theory of rhetoric. The *Rhetorica Christiana*, then, conceived in Mexico, written in Europe, reflects the recognition that the rhetorical tradition must transcend the boundaries of the Old World.

DIEGO VALADÉS: THE EDUCATION OF A RHETORICIAN

Perhaps more than any other Renaissance rhetoric, the *Rhetorica Christiana* is as much the memoirs of a man's life as it is a rhetorical treatise. Valadés was born in 1533 in the city of Tlaxcala, east of the Mexica capital of Tenochtitlán. His father, also named Diego Valadés, was a conquistador who had arrived in New Spain in 1520 with the expedition of Pánfilo de Narváez. The conquistador's father, Alonso Valadés, had fought the Moors in the Spanish war of reconquest. Thus the Valadés family had a long tradition of converting nonbelievers, a tradition the younger Diego would continue in more peaceful ways. Diego's mother was a now anonymous Tlaxcalan Indian. There is no convincing evidence that the birth was other than illegitimate.

At an early age Valadés came under the tutelage of Pedro de Gante, or Peter of Ghent, who is generally regarded as the initiator of European education in New Spain. Gante founded the school of San Francisco in Mexico City, adjacent to the chapel of San José de los Naturales. This institution served as a primary school for the education of Indian children, teaching them reading, writing, arithmetic, music, and fine and practical arts. Instruction was conducted almost exclusively in Nahuatl, using the Latin alphabet rather than pictographs as the written basis of the language. Although liturgical Latin was also taught, it apparently did not serve as a language of daily instruction. It is likely that Valadés received his primary education at Pedro de Gante's school for Indian elite. In the *Rhetorica Christiana* Valadés praises the Flemish friar as "a man of singular religion and piety, who taught the Indians all the arts; he was ignorant of none of them" (*RC* 222).

The young Valadés must have attracted the attention of his Franciscan teachers, for he was admitted to the order sometime between 1548 and 1550. The Franciscan authorities in New Spain presumably suppressed the illegitimacy of his birth and his mixed parentage from the order's hierarchy in Europe. For although the early Franciscan missionaries were committed to a native clergy, there was considerable opposition from other elements of the Church to the ordination of Mexican priests. Valadés was one of a very small number of *mestizos* allowed to enter religious orders before such entrance was prohibited by official policy. The synod of 1555 formally forbade the ordination of *mestizos*, Indians, and Negroes.[2] This policy of excluding natives from the clergy would have significant consequences for the church, ensuring that it would be a colonial, rather than a Mexican, institution. As Ricard concludes, "this error prevented the Church from striking deep roots in the nation, gave it the appearance and character of a foreign institution, and kept it strictly dependent on the mother country."[3] Valadés, as a *mestizo*, occupied an exceptional position in the church in New Spain and in Europe.

After joining the Franciscans, Valadés presumably continued his education in one of the order's educational institutions, most likely at the Colegio de Santa Cruz de Tlaltelolco. Founded by the Franciscans in 1536 to provide humanistic education to the sons of *caciques*, this *colegio* may well be considered the first European institution of higher education in North America. The first professors were the elite of the Franciscan missionaries; these were later joined by natives who had themselves been trained at Tlaltelolco. The curriculum represented an approximation of Renaissance education: grammar, logic, rhetoric, philosophy, music, together with the herbal medicine of the Mexicas. Rhetoric, as well as philosophy, was taught by Fray Juan de Gaona, who had been educated at Paris. It appears probable, then, that the first students of rhetoric in the New World were natives of that world. The University of Mexico, an institution for the education of the sons of Spaniards, was founded in 1553, nearly two decades after the college at Santa Cruz was founded. The teaching of rhetoric at the university began on July 12, 1553 under the professorship of Francisco Cervantes de Salazar.[4]

The holdings of the library at Tlaltelolco reflected the extent to which European humanism penetrated the Valley of Mexico. By 1572 the library contained some 71 volumes, including the following rhetorical works: Cicero's orations and his *De oratore* as well as Quintilian's *Institutio oratoria*. The library at Tlaltelolco also included works by such authors as Aristotle, Plato, Martial, Juvenal, Virgil, and Livy and Renaissance works by Erasmus, Juan Luis Vives, and Antonio de Nebrija. Tlaltelolco also possessed at least one book of Mexican origin: Fray Alonso de Molina's study of the Nahuatl language, *Diccionario en castellano y mexicano*.[5]

Clearly the intent of the *colegio* was to educate the sons of native nobility in a manner comparable to that available to the children of privileged Europeans. In this ambitious undertaking the Franciscans were at least partially successful.

---

[2]Robert Ricard, *The Spiritual Conquest of Mexico*, trans. Lesley Bird Simpson (Berkeley: University of California Press, 1966) 230.

[3]Ricard, *Conquest* 235.

[4]*Life in the Imperial and Loyal City of Mexico in New Spain*, trans. Minnie Lee Barrett Shepard (Austin: University of Texas Press, 1953) 7.

[5]Francis Borgia Steck, O.F.M., *El primer colegio de América: Santa Cruz de Tlaltelolco* (Mexico: Centro de Estudios Franciscanos, 1944) 34–35; and Pious J. Barth, "Franciscan Education and the Social Order in Spanish North America (1502–1921)," diss., University of Chicago, 1945, 243–244.

In his chronicle, Cervantes de Salazar, the Dominican professor of rhetoric at the University of Mexico, mentions a "college for the Indians, who are taught to speak and write in Latin. They have a teacher of their own nationality, Antonio Valeriano, who is in no respect inferior to our own grammarians. He is well trained in the observance of Christian law and is an ardent student of oratory."[6] Another contemporary Spanish source admitted that Valeriano "spoke Latin with such propriety and elegance that he equaled Cicero or Quintilian."[7] In Mexico, as in Europe, comparisons with the ancients were inevitable and essential.

It is difficult to know just how many of the Indian's students really rivaled Cicero in Latinity, but Valadés' *Rhetorica Christiana* provides evidence that the Franciscan's system was capable of creating true humanistic scholars. Although Valadés is, of course, exceptional, the *colegio* did train a generation of copyists and translators who proved to be valuable collaborators in the effort to Christianize the indigenous population.[8] The college at Tlaltelolco was, however, greatly vitiated by the civil and ecclesiastical opposition to a native clergy, a position that deprived the *colegio* of its reason for being. In the mid-16th century the *colegio* entered a period of decline, and in 1576 the student body was decimated by the plague. In the early 17th century the college was reduced to an elementary school. Eighteenth-century proposals to revitalize the school were never realized, and the *colegio* and its buildings at Santa Cruz de Tlaltelolco slowly disintegrated.

In its early years, at least, the *colegio* demonstrated the possibilities of replicating Renaissance learning in the Valley of Mexico. The *colegio* was predicated upon the assumption that natives should be educated in a manner that corresponded as closely as possible to the European curriculum. Although this educational experimentation imposed an almost exclusively European model of learning on the native youth, it did nevertheless provide for the intensive schooling of those youths. In the increasingly conservative post-Tridentine climate, the education of native children was less and less a possibility.

Valadés was no doubt regarded as an exemplar of the Franciscan educational experiment; his education appears to have completely Europeanized him. Despite his birthplace and parentage, Valadés is very much a missionary who never identifies with the natives; they are always Indians, always the other. With his education completed by about 1556, Valadés would devote many years to his mission among the natives of New Spain. In the *Rhetorica Christiana* he remarks that he spent some 20 years preaching and hearing confessions in three native languages: Mexican (Nahuatl), Tarascan, and Otomi (*RC* 184). From 1558 to 1562 he participated in the evangelization of the nomadic and warlike Chichimecas in the northern frontier provinces of Durango and Zacatecas. After his return

---

[6]*Life in the Imperial and Loyal City of Mexico* 62.
[7]Cited in *Life in the Imperial and Loyal City of Mexico* 62n.
[8]Ricard, *Conquest* 223–224.

from the North, Valadés taught in Franciscan schools—probably the very ones in which he had been educated. He probably taught painting and engraving at Gante's school at San José de los Naturales. Such an assumption is given credence by the elaborate engravings that illustrate the *Rhetorica Christiana* and are indeed the book's best known feature.

After almost 40 years in his native Mexico, Valadés was called to Europe by his order, and in 1571 he left New Spain for old. From 1575 to 1577 he served in Rome as the Procurator General of the Franciscan Order—a position that combined the duties of a chargé d'affaires, agent, and attorney. In 1579 Valadés was in Perugia to supervise the printing of the *Rhetorica Christiana*. The final years of his life were spent in Italy; he was never to return to Mexico. The probable year of his death is 1582.

THE *RHETORICA CHRISTIANA*: CICERO MEETS THE MEXICA

Much like Luis de Granada's *Ecclesiasticae rhetoricae* (1576), Valadés' *Rhetorica Christiana* was one of the Catholic rhetorics written "upon the heels of the revival of preaching and missionary activity encouraged by the Council of Trent."[9] Thus one of Valadés' chief concerns is to create the Christian embodiment of the Ciceronian ideal orator, an orator who would truly deserve to be called, in the manner of Quintilian, "the good man speaking well" (*RC* 51).

The obvious Ciceronianism of Valadés would seem to foretell a rather conventional rhetorical treatise. And although the *Rhetorica Christiana* shares much with Granada's *Ecclesiasticae rhetoricae* and other Tridentine rhetorics, Valadés' work was not a typical Renaissance rhetoric. A brief summary of the *Rhetorica Christiana* conveys the scope of Valadés' treatise. It is a work divided into six parts. Part 1 was devoted to the qualities and properties required to create the Christian orator. In part 2 Valadés defines rhetoric and discusses its constituent parts: invention, disposition, memory, and elocution. All four are discussed briefly, with the exception of memory, which receives a detailed treatment. Part 3 is devoted to an explication of the Scriptures, the primary source of the Christian orator's message. *Pronuntiatio*, which Valadés had earlier omitted as a part of rhetoric, receives detailed attention in this section. Part 3 concludes with a consideration of how to move the sentiments of the audience. Part 4 begins with a discussion of the three *genera* of oratory: demonstrative, deliberative, and judicial. Following a discussion of demonstrative oratory, Valadés embarks on an account

---

[9]Debra Shuger, *Sacred Rhetoric: The Christian Grand Style in the English Renaissance* (Princeton: Princeton University Press, 1988) 76. For Shuger's discussion of "The Tridentine Rhetorics (1575–1620)," see 76–80. For a comparison of Valadés' *Rhetorica Christiana* and Granada's *Ecclesiasticae rhetoricae*, see Palomera, "Introducción," *Retórica Cristiana* xxi–xl.

of the natives of the New World. He then returns to the remaining two genres of oratory. This, in turn, is followed by an additional account of indigenous customs and practices. Part 5 treats the structure of a discourse. In the sixth part of the *Rhetorica Christiana* Valadés considers, "as briefly as possible," the figures and tropes. The *Rhetorica Christiana* concludes with Valadés' commentary on the *Book of Sentences* of the 12th-century theologian, Peter Lombard.

The *Rhetorica Christiana*, although attentive to traditional subjects, also contains some obvious departures from the standard rhetorical lore. Indeed, the difference between Valadés and other Renaissance rhetorics is apparent from even the most cursory inspection of the volume. The reader is immediately confronted by a series of elaborate engravings drawn by Valadés himself.[10] Valadés explains that these engravings have not been included simply for the amusement of the readers but, rather, are designed to assist the reader in retaining the content of the *Rhetorica Christiana* (*RC* preface). The illustrations are an integral part of the book, and their presence in the *Rhetorica Christiana* signals the importance that visual imagery will have in Valadés' conception of rhetoric. These illustrations are the best known feature of the *Rhetorica Christiana* and have overshadowed Valadés' theory of rhetoric.

The work is distinguished not only by Valadés' engravings but also by his narrative of the natives of New Spain. Much like the illustrations, many of which portray native life, this chronicle of indigenous and colonial customs has obscured the greater portion of the book. Indeed, the *Rhetorica Christiana* is often treated as if it were an account of the natives with a brief rhetoric appended, when it is more the other way around. Moreover, much of Valadés' account is rhetorical in nature; that is, he focuses on the conversion of the Indians and the methods used by the Franciscans to achieve this conversion. It is, therefore, necessary to consider his account of the indigenous culture before turning to Valadés' theory of rhetoric.

RHETORIC AND CHRISTIAN CIVILIZATION

One of the principal purposes of the *Rhetorica Christiana* is to provide a testament to the triumphs of the Franciscan missionary endeavors. In his preface, Valadés promises to provide:

> examples of the successes of the Indies, among whose inhabitants we not only lived, but we were also in charge of them; we believe that this not only served their enjoyment but that it was also beneficial, for ultimately they clearly appreciated the principles, the development, and the practical application of rhetoric, as Cicero

---

[10]These engravings are discussed by Francisco de la Maza, "Fray Diego Valadés, escritor y grabador franciscano del siglo XVI," *Anales del Instituto de Investigaciones Estéticas* 3 (1945): 15–44. See especially 35–41.

attested when he said "There existed a time when men, in the manner of beasts, roamed the earth and struggled for life, and they had neither justice nor virtue of reason but only force. None were legitimate nor knew with certainty who were his children. Then, an excellent man, impelled by some higher motive to unite the men dispersed across the plains and hiding in the woods, converted the fiery savages into peaceful and gentle men." I say that the admirable effects of this influence, is no place more clearly apparent than in the pacification of the Indians of the New World of the ocean sea. (*RC* preface)[11]

In invoking the Ciceronian vision of the creation of civilization, Valadés is calling on one of the most ubiquitous themes in Renaissance rhetoric. This passage from *De inventione* is quoted or paraphrased in the prefaces and introductions to numerous 16th-century rhetorical treatises. For Europeans writing about the New World, however, Cicero's vision was more than a commonplace, it was a promise that European civilization could be recreated in the New World. More important, citing this passage enlists Cicero in the endeavor to legitimize European intervention in the affairs of the natives of the New World. Thus the Ciceronian account of civilization's rhetorical origin is invoked not only by rhetoricians but also by the various chroniclers and historians of New Spain and Peru.[12]

For Valadés, both a rhetorician and a chronicler, Cicero's words assume a special prominence. In New Spain Valadés and his fellow Franciscans assume the role of Cicero's "wise man," bringing the civilizing power of logos to the untamed Americans. Thus in the *Rhetorica Christiana*, Valadés both presents general principles of preaching and records the particular preaching of the Franciscans in Mexico. For Valadés, Cicero's affirmation of rhetoric's civilizing power is more than a convenient rationale for humanistic study; it is a justification of his own actions and a reflection of his own experience.

That experience was gained by 20 years of preaching among the natives of the New World, a career that gave Valadés a very real appreciation of the power of the spoken word. Valadés attributes much of the success of the Franciscans to their mastery of native languages. Valadés, accomplished in Nahuatl, Otomi,

---

[11]See Cicero, *De inventione*, trans. H. M. Hubbell, Loeb Classical Library (Cambridge: Harvard University Press, 1968) I.i–ii. Cicero had himself borrowed this idea from Isocrates. In *Antidosis* Isocrates says "because there has been implanted in us the power to persuade each other and to make clear to each other whatever we desire, not only have we escaped the life of wild beasts, but we have come together and founded cities and made laws and invented arts; and, generally speaking, there is no institution devised by man which the power of speech has not helped us establish." See Isocrates, *Antidosis*, trans. G. B. Norlin, Loeb Classical Library (Cambridge: Harvard University Press, 1962) 254–256.

[12]For a discussion of the prevalence of the view, among European commentators on the New World, that eloquence created human communities, see Anthony Pagden, *The Fall of Natural Man: The American Indian and the Origins of Comparative Ethnology* (Cambridge: Cambridge University Press, 1982) 20–21. Pagden identifies Cicero as the most common source of this idea (20 n. 25).

and Tarascan, recalls that once the Franciscans had learned the native languages, they then proceeded to teach the inhabitants of New Spain "to speak correctly, to write, and to sing" (*RC* 184, 226). As linguistically adept as many of the Franciscans undoubtedly were, Valadés recognizes that the power of words is not without limits. Not all friars mastered the native languages, and some even persisted in preaching in Latin to Indians untrained in that language.

Because of the difficulties inherent in attempting to communicate across great cultural barriers, Valadés advances the advantages, indeed the necessity, of augmenting verbal with visual communication. In doing so, Valadés is validating what was apparently a common Franciscan pedagogical practice. The Franciscans resorted to the extensive use of illustrations to supplement sermons and to assist teaching. According to Valadés the Franciscans were the first to employ such visual methods in educational endeavors. He therefore felt compelled to include several of these illustrations in the *Rhetorica Christiana* as examples of the Franciscan's pedagogical methods (*RC* 95). The preachers made use of large illustrated screens (*lienzos*, literally linens) as a backdrop to the sermons, which allowed the speaker to point to the particular concept or event being addressed. The best known illustration in the *Rhetorica Christiana* portrays a preacher addressing the Indians and pointing to a series of screens depicting the passion of Christ.[13] Valadés reports that various aspects of Christian doctrine, including the lives of the apostles, the Decalogue, and the seven deadly sins, were demonstrated in this manner (*RC* 95). Valadés also includes in the *Rhetorica Christiana* illustrations that were used to graphically represent ecclesiastical and civil themes in addition to theological issues. He presents, for example, elaborately stylized trees or organizational charts, designed to show Catholic and Spanish hierarchies to their native charges. In each case the Pope or Emperor is at the top of the chart, lesser luminaries occupy the lower branches, and the Indians are at the bottom (*RC* following 180).

A similar visual method was used to teach the Roman alphabet to the Mexicas, an oral people with a pictographic writing system. Valadés presents an elaborate two-page chart in which letters of the alphabet are portrayed together with similarly shaped physical objects in order to facilitate the natives' retention of these unfamiliar symbols. These representations are often rather arbitrary and stylized, but no more so than the letters with which they are equated. The letter *A*, for example, is represented by a compass and a ladder. *B* is represented by a mandolin. *C* is represented by a horseshoe and a horn, and so on for the entire alphabet. Valadés says that vivid and familiar images ensure that the letters will be retained in the native's memory. He also presents a somewhat different system, although

---

[13]An obvious copy of this engraving was used by Juan de Torquemada as the frontispiece of his *Monarchia indiana* (1615). More recently, Valadés' preacher appears as the jacket illustration of James J. Murphy, ed., *Renaissance Eloquence* (Berkeley: University of California Press, 1983).

illustrated in a similar manner, which is based on sounds rather than shapes. Thus *A* is equated with the face of a man named Antonio, *B* with Bartolomé, and so on. By such methods Valadés and his Franciscan colleagues undertook to teach a phonetic alphabet to a people to whom such a symbol system was very foreign (*RC* 100–101).[14] For Valadés the use of pictorial representations proved to be a "graceful and fruitful" way to present the word of God to an indigenous audience (*RC* 94–96).

Visual communication was a fruitful method, in Valadés' estimation, not only because the Latin alphabet was alien to the natives but also because the natives were by nature and by tradition receptive to ideas conveyed by images. As evidence, Valadés cites the elaborate paintings that the Mexica and other peoples employed as a means of communication (*RC* 94). Although the Mexica were a predominantly oral culture, they did possess books that corresponded closely to books in the European sense. Although very few of these preconquest codices remain, prior to the Spanish arrival books were sufficiently numerous among the Mexica to require libraries (*amoxcalli*). These books were made of paper derived from the amate tree and other materials and folded together rather like a fan or map. The Mexicas also recorded information on larger sheets made of cotton and other fibers very similar to the *lienzos* employed by the Franciscan preachers. These books and screens were written in the complex glyphs of the Mexica symbol system. This system combined numerical, calendrical, pictographic, ideographic, and phonetic glyphs in a very versatile system.[15] With this combination of glyphs the Mexicas could record a great deal of information. Says Miguel León-Portilla:

> It is clear that the Nahuas could write in an unequivocal manner the date, in precise years and days, of any event. Furthermore, with their phonetic system of representation, they could point out the place where each event occurred as well as the names of those who participated in it. They also indicated pictographically numerous details about the event whose record was being committed to paper. Last they were capable of reducing abstract concepts about their religious doctrines, myths and legal ordinances to symbols with their ideographic writing.[16]

---

[14]Alphabets like those presented by Valadés appeared in several Renaissance memory treatises including Jacobus Publicius, *Oratoriae artis epitome* (Venice, 1482); Johannes Romberch, *Congestorium artificiose memoria* (Venice, 1520); and Lodovico Dolce, *Dialogo nel quale si ragiona del modo di accrescere et conservar la memoria* (Venice, 1521). See Francis Yates, *The Art of Memory* (Chicago: University of Chicago Press, 1966), especially chapter 5, "The Memory Treatises," 105–128. Maza contends that Valadés alphabet is a copy from Dolce's *Dialogo*, "Fray Diego Valadés, escritor y grabador" 39. Although Valadés and the Franciscans did not originate these relatively common Renaissance memory devices, they did adapt them to the teaching of alphabetic literacy in the New World.

[15]Miguel León-Portilla, *Aztec Image of Self and Society*, ed. Jorge Klor de Alva (Salt Lake City: University of Utah Press, 1992) 44–45.

[16]León-Portilla, *Aztec Image* 69–70.

This system, although highly developed, was not without certain deficiencies. León-Portilla continues:

> Those schematic pictures—calendrical-astronomical, doctrinal, or historical—frequently required further explanation. It was not easy (and often impossible) for the Nahuas to indicate in writing the causes of an event, the moral features of a person, or, the countless nuances and modalities that are necessary to narrate or understand fully the doctrines, events, and varieties of human acts and motivations.[17]

It was thus necessary to complement this written record with the oral traditions of the Mexicas.

Young men, particularly those intended for the priesthood, in the process of learning "good discourse" in the *Calmecac*, would therefore be taught to comprehend and explicate the books. In his *General History of the Things of New Spain*, Bernardino de Sahagún says of these students: "Carefully were they taught the songs which they called the gods' songs. They were inscribed in the books. And well were all taught the reckoning of the days, the book of dreams, and the book of years."[18] This knowledge of books was extremely important in maintaining the traditions of the Mexicas. Those who mastered the books did not read these texts, in the European sense, but did engage in difficult interpretive acts. The sequence of pictures and glyphs revealed a complex narrative of traditional events and beliefs. The oral tradition of the Mexicas, preserved in their songs, poems, and *huehhuehtlatolli*, was actually the product of a combination of verbal and visual elements. Thus Valadés' approach of combining sermons with pictures corresponded with the Mexicas' respect for paintings and the shared belief that illustrations could be the keys to important concepts.

Valadés believes the Franciscans' campaign of Christianization was successful and that their success was in large measure attributable to the use of methods congenial to the native mind. For Valadés, the efficacy of the Franciscans' methods is apparent in the sincerity of those converted to Christianity by the friars. He vigorously and indignantly challenged the charge that the conversion of these new Christians was insincere and that their apparent learning was merely imitation of their masters, much like that of monkeys (*RC* 186). Valadés argues that the conversion of the Indians of the New World was far more successful than the coercive conversion of the Spanish Muslims in the previous century. This is so because, in the first place, the Indians' conversion to Christianity was done with great care, by ministers using the natives' own tongues. Moreover, says Valadés, the Indians are by nature more tractable than are the Moors (*RC* 185). Although Valadés admits that the Indians are not saints, he argues that they were serious

---

[17]León-Portilla, *Aztec Image* 70.

[18]Bernardino de Sahagún, *Florentine Codex: General History of the Things of New Spain*, trans. Arthur O. J. Anderson and Charles Dibble, 12 parts (Sante Fe, NM: School of American Research and University of Utah, 1950–1969) 4:65.

about their Christian responsibilities, including communion and confession (*RC* 184, 188). Valadés leaves little doubt that he regards the Franciscans' missionary efforts as largely successful. These achievements were due to the sacrifices of the Franciscans, their methods of preaching and teaching, and, of course, divine assistance.

In addition to his accounts of the proselytizing and educational aspects of the Franciscan experience in the New World, Valadés includes descriptions of the Indians' deities and religious practices. Although the *Rhetorica Christiana* offers fewer details of native life than other works that were strictly chronicles, Valadés nevertheless provides some important information, much of it in the form of illustrations, that is unavailable from other sources. Nevertheless, the *Rhetorica Christiana* is of less importance as a chronicle of the Indies than better known works like Sahagún's *General History*. This does not diminish the significance of the *Rhetorica Christiana*, because it is not intended as a comprehensive chronicle of 16th-century Mexico but is, rather, a book about rhetoric. And it is rhetoric that occupies the central position in the *Rhetorica Christiana*.

IMAGERY AND MEMORY
IN THE *RHETORICA CHRISTIANA*

The *Rhetorica Christiana* has long been recognized as an important source of information about the Spanish experience in the New World and as an invaluable pictorial account of the great conversion. These aspects of Valadés' endeavor have obscured the importance of the *Rhetorica Christiana* as a treatise on rhetoric. Yet the work is a rhetoric; Valadés' primary goal is to address the needs of the Christian speaker, not only in New Spain, but wherever preaching is required. As a work of rhetoric, the *Rhetorica Christiana* is indebted to the standard classical and Renaissance authorities. But even without Valadés' accounts of indigenous customs and his handsome engravings, the *Rhetorica Christiana* would be a distinctive rhetorical treatise. For although Valadés' work is comprehensive and often conventional, it nevertheless departs in significant ways from the mainstream of Renaissance rhetoric.

What sets Valadés apart from other Renaissance rhetoricians, in addition to his account of New World customs, is the importance of memory in his theory of rhetoric. Valadés regards memory as the most important of the traditional parts of rhetoric, and it is this elevation of memory that is a defining characteristic of Valadés' theory of rhetoric. The work was written in Italy at a time of great interest in memory in the peninsula. But the tendency in the late 16th century was to exclude memory from rhetoric. Indeed, the large number of Renaissance memory treatises may be a result of the independence of memory from its traditional association with rhetoric. Certainly, the tendency among rhetorical theorists was to deny that memory was a constituent part of rhetoric. Juan Luis Vives, for example, in "De corrupta rhetorica," a part of his encyclopedic *De disciplinis* (1531), explicitly divorces memory from rhetoric, claiming that memory, as a part of nature, belongs equally to all the arts.[19] Granada's *Ecclesiasticae rhetoricae* includes a reference to memory as one of the five parts of rhetoric but omits any extended treatment of memory.

Valadés, by making *memoria* central to the *Rhetorica Christiana*, departs not only from the norms of 16th-century rhetoric, but also from those of classical rhetorical theory. He does so primarily because memory is essential to the creation of the Christian orator. The educational program Valadés advocates emphasizes Christian theology but also expects mastery of all the seven liberal arts. The knowledge Valadés considers essential for the preacher is nothing short of encyclopedic. He almost certainly had in mind some of the early Franciscans like Pedro de Gante and Martín de Valencia, who combined courage and piety with great erudition. The wide knowledge needed to be an effective Christian orator requires a prodigious memory because memory is "the treasury of the sciences" (*RC* part 3, chap. 24). In his preface, Valadés promises that he will "demonstrate the art of memory cultivation, so long desired by all men." Thus, before any of the other traditional five parts of rhetoric are introduced, Valadés elevates memory to a privileged position, a position it will occupy throughout the treatise.

Valadés describes memory as "a firm perception of the soul, of words, and of things, and their placement" (*RC* 97). Memory, then, is an intellectual process that transcends simple recollection. As such, it is "exceedingly necessary for the orator, is the treasury of invention, and the custodian of all the parts of rhetoric" (*RC* 97). In Valadés' plan, memory not only precedes invention but also assumes many of the functions more typically assigned to invention.

There are, says Valadés, two genres of memory, natural and artificial. Natural memory is a gift of God and is not susceptible to human improvement. However, artificial memory, which is Valadés' concern, is available to virtually all human beings and may be improved by theory and practice. Valadés' conception of artificial memory is almost entirely visual. It consists, he says, of places and images (*RC* 89). Memory, then, is the creation of a "place," an imaginary room, a chamber, or, as Valadés suggests, a temple, in the mind of the speaker. This place is then filled with vivid images. The speaker "travels" through this space, encountering images that prompt the appropriate portion of the speech.

Valadés' conception of artificial memory is derived almost entirely from the *Rhetorica ad Herennium*.[20] The *Ad Herennium* is the only surviving ancient treatise that contained a detailed treatment of the classical conception of memory, and as such it exercised considerable influence on the memory treatises of the Renaissance. [21] Valadés believes the ancient system derived its effectiveness from

---

[19] Juan Luis Vives, *Obras completas*, trans. Lorenzo Riber (Madrid: Aguilar, 1944–1948) 2:459.

[20] *Ad C. Herennium*, trans. Harry Caplan (Cambridge; Harvard University Press, 1954) 3.28–40.

[21] For a discussion of memory in the *Ad Herennium* and its influence in the Renaissance see Yates, *The Art of Memory* 1–49.

the virtually universal power of visual imagery. This visual memory system was first systematized by the ancients, and Valadés observes that the natives of the New World had independently developed a similar approach to memory. He further claims that the Indians' innate capacity for images ensured that such a system worked for them as surely as it did for Europeans.

Valadés' elevation of memory to the primary position among the traditional five parts of rhetoric naturally had significant consequences on the analysis of the remaining four. In particular, memory assumes virtually all of the functions typically assigned to invention. Memory is the beginning point of the oration, where all materials are held and drawn out into discourse. Given this function of memory, invention is necessarily truncated. Valadés does devote part 5 of the *Rhetorica Christiana* to invention, but this is the shortest of the six parts of the work. More significantly, Valadés' discussion of invention really bore little similarity to the standard account of argument, *topoi*, *stasis*, and all the usual apparatus of classical *inventio*. Instead, invention becomes synonymous with the structure of discourse. Although the terminology Valadés employs is that of *dispositio*, he claims that such matters belong to invention: "Invention comprises the six parts of the discourse, they are: exordium, narration, digression, division, confirmation, and conclusion" (*RC* 228). Invention, as the discovery of arguments, is thus replaced by invention as the management of discourse.

Although he removed arguments from the inventional process, Valadés does ultimately discuss argumentation at some length. Arguments, seemingly banished from invention, return in the guise of *elocutio*. Although Valadés had promised in the preface to treat elocution as briefly as possible, he ultimately devotes more attention to it than to any other part of rhetoric, including memory (*RC* 249–275). He begins with a discussion of the figures, which, he says, are "like the clothing and the ornament of discourse" (*RC* 249). The discussion of figures is followed, not surprisingly, by the discussion of tropes, "the efficacious modification of a word or discourse so that its proper signification is altered" (*RC* 272).

After this rather traditional discussion of figures and tropes, Valadés turns to schemes, which he distinguishes from both tropes and figures. Schemes, says Valadés, "are certain figures and modes of speaking rhetorically. If they are used to illuminate sentences, they are rhetorical ornaments, but if they are formed in order to prove, they pass into the denomination of argumentation or reasoning" (*RC* 278). These schemes include ratiocination, syllogism, induction, and enumeration. Thus Valadés recognizes what had been implicit in rhetoric, that there is a close, and often overlapping, function between argument and ornament.

After discussing devices that have both an argumentative and a stylistic function, Valadés turns to what he calls simply "arguments." By arguments Valadés means *stasis*: the issues of conjecture, constitution, and quality. The consideration of issues is followed by an enumeration of the places or topics of argument. In his treatment of arguments and *topoi*, Valadés is no longer concerned with the stylistic dimension but instead returns to the typical argumentative approach he had earlier abandoned. Argumentation thus remains important to Valadés, but it no longer has a function early in the process of constructing discourse. Instead, the early stages in the creation of discourse is assigned by Valadés to memory. Invention, occurring later in the compositional process, operates much like elocution: It embellishes discourse rather than creates it. Thus Valadés covers the key elements of rhetoric but in an unconventional manner. Memory, usually one of the last of the parts of rhetoric to be invoked, becomes the first; invention, at least in name, becomes disposition; and argument becomes a subspecies of the figures.

Valadés' unusual division and recombination of the traditional parts of rhetoric and the intermittent narrative of indigenous culture combine to give the *Rhetorica Christiana* a rather disjointed quality. And, indeed, the structure of the treatise is often confusing. There is, however, a certain unity to Valadés' work that may not be initially apparent. Indeed, the aspects of the *Rhetorica Christiana* that make it distinctive are also those features that provide it a certain coherence. Valadés' theory of rhetoric is guided by a belief in the primacy of memory in human discourse. Valadés' conception of memory is, in turn, founded upon a view of the mind that makes mental images central to retention and expression. The emphasis on visualization and mental imagery also reflects the attempt to convert the Indians, a conversion that was facilitated by pictorial as well as verbal persuasion. But Valadés does not recommend an imagistic approach solely for the Mexicas. Rather, the ability of the Indians to apprehend visual images underscores the universal appeal of those images. This visual orientation, in turn, required Valadés to illustrate his treatise, in order to appeal to his readers and to ensure that they remembered his rhetoric. Thus the very elements that separate the *Rhetorica Christiana* from other Renaissance rhetorics and that, at first glance, make the work appear rather disorganized are, in fact, the very aspects of Valadés' work that unify the book.

All of the elements that make up the *Rhetorica Christiana* reflect the conventions of European humanism, but the European antecedents of the work are affected in important ways by Valadés' life in the New World. This is almost certainly the case with regard to the place of memory in the *Rhetorica Christiana*. In an age when many theorists excluded memory from rhetoric, Valadés makes memory more central to rhetoric than ever before. That Valadés should contradict the dominant approach of his time suggests that he had good reasons to do so. A major motivation was his experience among a preliterate people for whom memory was absolutely essential.

Similarly, the visual elements of Valadés certainly were highly influenced by European models, especially the artist Albrecht Dürer.[22] Even the Indians in his engravings had a highly Romanized appearance. And certainly, rhetoricians had

---

[22]For a discussion of Dürer's influence on Valadés see Maza, "Fray Diego Valadés, escritor y grabador," especially 36–39.

long extolled the virtues of imagery that could make the audience see what the speaker was describing. Before Valadés' *Rhetorica Christiana*, however, illustrations had never been so integral to a work on rhetoric. The emphasis on illustration in *Rhetorica Christiana* is no doubt in part due to Valadés' exceptional artistic ability. But in addition, his New World experience had convinced him that actual images must be joined with mental images for persuasion to be more effective. Again, among the Indians the screens used by the Franciscans were more than clever devices; they were essential to the rhetorical process. They worked where words alone could not.

So, too, the accounts of the Mexicas and Chichimecas are not so anomalous as they at first appear. Although much of Valadés' rather lengthy account of indigenous customs may not be directly relevant to rhetorical theory, a considerable portion of that account of life in Mexico does illustrate or reinforce Valadés' conception of rhetoric. It is perhaps not simply faulty organization that causes Valadés to insert much of his treatment of the Indians in part 4, otherwise dedicated to the three genres of oratory. Valadés' account of native life occurs immediately after the treatment of demonstrative oratory. This is surely no coincidence because the chapters that follow constitute an encomium on the virtues of the Indians. The account of the Indians is, therefore, not simply informative; it is also an example of the principles of demonstrative oratory that preceded it. Valadés intersperses his accounts of the Indians among rhetorical subjects not because of organizational ineptitude but because his observations regarding the life of the natives is truly inseparable from his conception of how rhetoric operates.

It is most improbable that the *Rhetorica Christiana* could have been written the way it was without the long years Valadés spent in New Spain. There is, of course, nothing particularly unique about the treatment of many of the individual subjects included in the *Rhetorica Christiana*. Other manuals of preaching, other memory treatises, other chronicles of the Indies were printed in the 16th century. But there is almost certainly no other Renaissance treatise that more effectively combines all of these elements into a coherent whole. Valadés stresses the elements he does because of his insights gained over more than 20 years of preaching among the Indians of Mexico. Although Valadés thought of himself as a European and, therefore, a missionary among the Indians, he could not entirely escape his remarkable dual heritage. The *Rhetorica Christiana* is thoroughly in the European rhetorical tradition, and yet it is also a rhetoric that is, for the first time, cognizant of "the New World of the Ocean Sea."

Chapter 15

Shakespeare and the *Ars Rhetorica*

Heinrich F. Plett
University of Essen

PROLEGOMENA

Rhetoric has long failed to receive the critical attention it justly deserves. The reasons for this neglect are obvious. One of them is that the knowledge of Elizabethan rhetoric was comparatively poor. Though its major representative, Thomas Wilson's *Arte of Rhetorique* (1553), was made accessible again as early as 1909 in G. M. Mair's thorough, though by present-day standards not entirely satisfactory edition, this was to remain an isolated landmark for several decades.[1] A lack of source-texts did not, however, prove to be the only reason for the lasting disinterest in rhetoric. Of equal, if not greater, importance were the contempt and disrepute into which this discipline had fallen under the sway of idealistic philosophy. Ever since Plato's criticism of sophistic rhetoric, it was reputed to be a technique of illusion and delusion, a notion that has been transmitted by Kant, Hegel, and their followers up to the present time. But not enough that this technique (*techne, ars*) was discredited as such; it was also reduced, at first to stylistics and then to the so-called rhetorical figures, the totality of which

---

[1] The situation is aptly described in James J. Murphy's programmatic essay "One Thousand Neglected Authors: The Scope and Importance of Renaissance Rhetoric," *Renaissance Eloquence: Studies in the Theory and Practice of Renaissance Rhetoric*, ed. James J. Murphy (Berkeley: University of California Press, 1983) 20–36. His pioneering bibliography *Renaissance Rhetoric* (New York: Garland, 1981) points out a large number of source-texts still waiting for editorial treatment and critical comment.

was regarded as a rather random compilation. Thus in the first half of the 20th century, Shakespeare criticism still tended to be philosophically and psychologically biased, and it generally excluded rhetorical or stylistic perspectives and categories. Even publications on the history of Renaissance criticism like those by Joel E. Spingarn (1899), Charles Sears Baldwin (1939), or J. W. H. Atkins (1947)[2] did not restore rhetoric to its ancient rights but, rather, referred to it incidentally as an antecedent to poetics.

Thus it is small wonder that it was only at a fairly advanced stage of historicism that rhetorical criticism entered the scene of Shakespearean scholarship. Its first noteworthy contribution is Hardin Craig's article: "Shakespeare and Wilson's *Arte of Rhetorique*: An Inquiry into the Criteria for Determining Sources" (1931).[3] The very title of this study reveals its methodological perspective. The problem under consideration is whether Shakespeare knew and to what extent he used a specific rhetorical textbook. The dangers inherent in such a positivistic cause-and-effect approach are obvious: the constraint of source hunting, the difficulty of verifying certain influences, and a total disregard of the aesthetic qualities of the text. In spite of the evident deficiencies of this approach, it is, even from the present-day viewpoint, entitled to claim certain merits, for it opens up historical outlooks and furthermore demonstrates the applicability of rhetorical theories to Renaissance drama. This statement above all holds true for T. W. Baldwin's two-volume *William Shakspere's 'Small Latine & Lesse Greeke'* (1944), which not only traces the history of Elizabethan education but also displays the entire range of rhetorical knowledge that was available to cultivated persons in the English Renaissance. In this positivistic stage of methodology, rhetorical interpretations of Shakespeare are exceptions.

The second stage of the rhetorical criticism of Shakespeare can be termed encyclopedic as well as systematic. In being encyclopedic, it refers back to positivism; in being systematic, it points ahead to structuralism. This approach is manifested by Sr. Miriam Joseph's study *Shakespeare's Use of the Arts of Language* (1947), in which she draws up a highly complex achronic system of rhetoric that she illustrates by as many examples from Shakespeare's plays as she is able to discover. The result is a reference work that, by means of a carefully elaborated index, guides its reader toward the diversity of Shakespeare's rhetorical categories. Cruder successors to this manual are to be found in a number of alphabetical compilations of rhetorical categories, illustrated sometimes by Shake-

[2]Joel E. Spingarn, *A History of Literary Criticism in the Renaissance* (New York: Columbia University Press, 1899; rpt. with a new introd. by Bernard Weinberg, New York: Harcourt, Brace & World, 1963); Charles Sears Baldwin, *Renaissance Literary Theory and Practice: Classicism in the Rhetoric and Poetic of Italy, France, and England 1400–1600*, ed. Donald Lemen Clark (New York: Columbia University Press, 1939; Gloucester, MA: P. Smith, 1959); J. W. H. Atkins, *English Literary Criticism: The Renascence* (London: Methuen, 1947; New York: Barnes & Noble, 1968).

[3]Hardin Craig, "Shakespeare and Wilson's *Arte of Rhetoric*: An Inquiry into the Criteria for Determining Sources," *Studies in Philology* 28 (1931): 618–630.

speare's plays and sometimes also by the works of others (Taylor, Oyama, Lanham).[4] A methodologically updated version of Joseph's approach is Keir Elam's book *Shakespeare's Universe of Discourse* (1984), which, by employing semiotic, communication, and linguistic categories, aims at establishing a taxonomy of Shakespeare's language games and which includes many rhetorical phenomena as well.

Whereas the positivistic and encyclopedic/systematic strains generally refrain from rhetorical interpretations of Shakespeare's plays, the one tracing out sources, the other categorizing and compiling phenomena, a third approach aims at elucidating rhetorical structures and functions in a text.[5] This task is performed partly on a very formalist basis (M. B. Kennedy, M. Trousdale) and partly on a more functional basis (W. Clemen, B. Vickers). Topics include the analysis of a whole play (e.g., *Romeo and Juliet* by R. O. Evans); of a particular speech type (e.g., the hero's dying speech by R. Böhm); and, most of all, of certain stylistic devices such as alliteration (U. K. Goldsmith), ambiguity (J. L. Halio), antithesis (G. I. Duthie), apostrophe (M. R. McKay), word play (M. M. Mahood), or proverb (H. Weinstock). The structuralist concept is broadened, whenever it includes sociopolitical ideas and events as well (W. G. Müller). As is demonstrated by these studies, rhetorical criticism has by now established itself firmly in the field of Shakespeare scholarship.

The following exploration combines the structuralist point of view with that of the history of ideas, for it focuses on Shakespeare's image of the orator, or, more precisely, on his attitude toward the *ars rhetorica*.[6] Three possible attitudes can be postulated: (a) *demonstrare artem*, or the rhetoric of "good order"; (b) *celare artem*, or the rhetoric of dissimulation; (c) *negare artem*, or the rhetoric of denial. As the English explications of the Latin formulae suggest, these views of the rhetorical *ars* allow aesthetic as well as ethical evaluations. Each can be interpreted in a positive and a negative way. Their various modes of combination result in a fourfold typology of the orator:

Type 1: A figure who is a good orator and a good character as well.

Type 2: A figure who is a good orator but a bad character.

---

[4]Warren Taylor, *Tudor Figures of Rhetoric* (Whitewater, WI: Language Press, 1972); Toshiko Oyama, *English Rhetorics* (Tokyo: Shinozaki Shorin, 1956); Richard A. Lanham, *A Handlist of Rhetorical Terms* (Berkeley: University of California Press, 1969).

[5]For greater bibliographical details on the authors and their works, see H. F. Plett, "Shakespeare, William," *Englische Rhetorik und Poetik 1479–1660: Eine systematische Bibliographie* (Opladen: Westdeutscher Verlag, 1985) C. 798.1–187.

[6]On rhetoric as an art, see George Kennedy, *The Art of Persuasion in Greece* (Princeton, NJ: Princeton University Press, 1963) 321–330; Josef Martin, *Antike Rhetorik: Technik und Methode*, Handbuch der Altertumswissenschaft, II/3 (Munich: Beck, 1974) 4–7; A. D. Leeman and H. Pinkster, *M. Tullius Cicero: De Oratore libri III—Kommentar* (Heidelberg: C. Winter, 1981) 1:190–194; Jonathan Barnes, "Is Rhetoric an Art?" *darg newsletter* 2/2 (1986): 2–22. On the English Renaissance image of the orator, see the essay by Brian Vickers, " 'The Power of Persuasion': Images of the Orator, Elyot to Shakespeare," in Murphy, *Renaissance Eloquence* 411–435.

Type 3: A figure who is a bad orator but a good character.

Type 4: A figure who is a bad orator and a bad character as well.

The first type evidently represents the ideal orator, but an examination of Types 2 and 3 seems more rewarding. For these embody a conflict between art and morals that not only gives rise to highly dramatic situations but also may lead to the destruction of individuals and even entire commonwealths. Compared to these types, the last one is, both rhetorically and ethically, of minor interest here and hence is omitted from the ensuing argument.

As each of the aforementioned types is realized in communicative situations, some of the factors defining the communicative process must be considered: first, *decorum*, that is, the appropriateness of the communicative factors (speaker, audience, message, etc.) that warrants the success of the speech act as a whole; second, truth, that is, the conformity of the rhetorical message with the reality it refers to; and third, the code, that is, the stylistic level (grand, ornate, plain) of the message. Illustrative material is drawn mainly from Shakespeare's tragedies of state: *Richard III, Julius Caesar, King Lear*, and *Coriolanus*.

DEMONSTRARE ARTEM, OR THE RHETORIC OF "GOOD ORDER"

Classical rhetoric defined the ideal orator as *vir bonus dicendi peritus*, meaning "a (morally) good man being capable of speaking (well)." This unity of ethical and rhetorical perfection marks the origin of human civilization. Thomas Wilson, the early middle-class humanist and secretary of state to Elizabeth I, paraphrases in the preface to his *Arte of Rhetorique* (1553) the *locus classicus* of this concept, the first chapter of Cicero's early rhetorical work *De inventione* (I.i.1 ff.), on the first human beings:

> And althoughe at firste, the rude coulde hardelie learne, & either for straungenes of the thing, would not gladlye receyue the offer, or els for lacke of knoweledge could not perceyue the goodnes: yet being somewhat drawe[n] and delighted with the pleasauntnes of reason, & the swetenes of vtteraunce: after a certaine space, thei became through nurture and good aduisement, of wilde, sober: of cruel, gentle: of foles, wise: and of beastes, men. Suche force hath the tongue, and such is the power of eloquence and reason, that most men are forced euen to yelde in that, whiche most standeth against their will.[7]

This shows that neither reason nor rhetoric alone can turn men into social beings but only the synthesis of both. The unity of *eloquentia* and *sapientia* or, in a

---

[7]Thomas Wilson, *The Arte of Rhetorique*, The English Experience 206 (1553; Amsterdam: Theatrum Orbis Terrarum/Da Capo, 1969) Aiijᵛ.

play on words, of *oratio* and *ratio*[8] engenders social harmony—what Wilson calls "good order." Its mythical ancestor appears in the shape of the Gallic Hercules who did not slay the barbaric aborigines with his club but, rather, bridled their fierce instincts with the golden chains of his persuasive speech.[9] Cultural heroes such as the Gallic Hercules, Orpheus, and Amphion are, to the humanists, optimistic emblems of the ordering, even creative power of the word. They appear as the legendary founders of cities and commonwealths and, in short, make possible the rise of civilization. Wilson offers a theological interpretation of this concept by entitling the preface to his rhetoric as follows: "Eloquence first geuen by God, after loste by man, and laste repayred by God agayne."[10] Seen in this light, the Fall of Man and his loss of eloquence are identical events. The restitution of *oratio* and *ratio* causes the reversal of postlapsarian chaos and anarchy. Supported by God-sent "ministers," mankind, according to Wilson, finds once more its way back to "good order," that is, social harmony.

Another dimension of the *oratio-ratio* theorem is the political and ideological one. Rulers such as Henri IV, King of France, loved to be celebrated as a Gallic Hercules or as a second Orpheus and made ample use of this panegyrical iconography in order to strengthen their official roles as founders and guardians of social harmony.[11] In England, Henry Peacham explicitly refers to Hercules and Mercurius in his exhortation in *The Complete Gentleman* (1622): "Much, therefore, it concerneth princes not only to countenance honest and eloquent orators, but to maintain such near about them as no mean props, if occasion serve, to uphold a state, and the only keys to bring in tune a discordant commonwealth."[12] Here mythology provides maxims for a political praxis.

Which kind of rhetoric is required to serve the purpose of establishing "good order"? Certainly not one of Nature, that is, of inborn talent, but one of Nurture

---

[8]On this concept, see Etienne Gilson, "Eloquence et sagesse chez Cicéron," *Phoenix* 7 (1953): 1–19; J. E. Seigel, *Rhetoric and Philosophy in Renaissance Humanism* (Princeton, NJ: Princeton University Press, 1968) 3–30; Alain Michel, "Rhétorique et philosophie dans les traités de Cicéron," *Aufstieg und Niedergang der römischen Welt*, ed. Hildegard Temporini (Berlin: de Gruyter, 1973) I/3, 139–208; Siegmar Döpp, "Weisheit und Beredsamkeit: Gedanken zu ihrer Relation bei Cicero, Quintilian und Augustinus," *Information aus der Vergangenheit*, ed. Peter Neukam (München: Bayerischer Schulbuch-Verlag, 1982) 37–63; K. S. Frank, "Augustinus: 'Sapienter et eloquenter dicerre'," *Strukturen der Mündlichkeit in der römischen Literatur*, ed. Gregor Vogt-Spira, ScriptOralia 19 (Tübingen: Narr, 1990) 257–269.

[9]On this mythologeme, see, among others, M.-R. Jung, *Hercule dans la littérature française du XVIe siécle: De l'Hercule courtois à l'Hercule baroque* (Geneva: Droz, 1966); John M. Steadman, *The Hill and the Labyrinth: Discourse and Certitude in Milton and His Near-Contemporaries* (Berkeley: University of California Press, 1984) 146–163.

[10]Wilson, *Arte* A.iijʳ.

[11]See, for instance, Corrado Vivanti, "Henri IV, the Gallic Hercules," *Journal of the Warburg and Courtauld Institutes* 30 (1967): 176–197, and his *Lotta politica e pace religiosa in Francia fra Cinque e Seicento* (Torino: Einaudi, 1963) 74–131.

[12]Henry Peacham, *The Complete Gentleman*, ed. Virgil B. Heltzel (Ithaca, NY: Cornell University Press, 1962) 18.

or Art. For Art produces an order that reflects, as it were, the order of a commonwealth. To the humanists the orderly character of rhetoric appears, above all, in the *dispositio*, the art of structure. Thus Wilson, in his chapter on *dispositio* headed "Of disposicion and apte orderyng of thynges," justifies the necessity of a well-proportioned oration in the following manner:

> And the rather I am earnest in this behaulfe, because I knowe that al thynges stande by order, and without order nothyng can be. For by an order wee are borne, by an order wee lyue, and by an order wee make our end. By an order one ruleth as head, and other obey as members. By an order Realmes stande, and lawes take force. Yea by an order the whole worke of nature and the perfite state of al the elementes haue their appointed course.[13]

And he closes with the words: "So an Oration hath litle force with it, and dothe smally profite, whiche is vtterde without all order."[14] According to the principle of *analogia entis*, the order of speech is expressive of the order of being. The orator who ensures this verbal and consequently also social order is a second Gallic Hercules. The power of his words can settle disturbances in the social harmony and thereby revitalize the process of civilization.

Communicative situations to illustrate such a process can be found in Shakespeare's *Julius Caesar, Othello,* and *Coriolanus.* In the first Roman play, a populace enraged to the utmost presses Brutus to justify the murder of Caesar. The crowd acts like Thomas Wilson's barbaric man; a relapse into a pre-social mode of existence is imminent. Brutus counters this situation like the Gallic Hercules. His speech unites wisdom and eloquence, *ethos* and *logos*, moral conviction and rational argumentation. Its structure is so skillfully contrived that it could serve as a schoolbook *exemplum* of the rhetorical system. It is patterned on the regular *dispositio* model of *exordium, argumentatio,* and *peroratio*; it fulfills the three major requirements for the *exordium* (to convey information, to procure attentiveness, and to engender a favorable disposition). But, above all, it is arranged in elaborate parallelisms, antitheses, and gradations:

> There is tears, for his love;
>> joy, for his fortune;
>> honour, for his valour;
>> and death, for his ambition.
>>> (*Julius Caesar* III.ii.28–29)[15]

---

[13]Wilson, *Arte* 83^{r-v}. On the ideology of order, see, among others, Michel Foucault, *The Order of Things: An Archaeology of the Human Sciences* (London: Tavistock, 1970).

[14]Wilson, *Arte* 83^v. Compare Stephen Hawes, *The Pastime of Pleasure,* ed. W. E. Mead, *Early English Text Society,* original series, 173 (London: Oxford University Press, 1928 [for 1927]) vv. 820–903, especially vv. 862–889.

[15]Citations from Shakespeare follow the numbering in the respective volumes of the *Arden Edition.*

Here plain style and plain character form a convincing unity. Therefore, the plebeians, for the time being, leave off their seditious tumult and return to civilized conduct. In this communicative situation Brutus appears as a type (*figura*) of Hercules Gallicus restoring Rome to "good order"—indeed, a *vir bonus dicendi peritus*.

Othello's fate resembles Brutus' to a certain degree in that he, too, is accused of a crime, the seduction of Brabantino's daughter by means of magical practices. He, too, has to justify himself, not in front of a "many-headed multitude" (*Cor.* II.iii.16–17) but in front of the signoria of the city-state of Venice. Due to Iago's machinations, senate and town are in a state of extreme emotional uproar. Called upon to defend himself against the accusations uttered, Othello delivers a speech that follows strictly the rhetorical precepts for the *genus iudiciale*. Like Brutus he begins with a very formal address:

> Most potent, grave, and reverend signiors,
> My very noble and approv'd good masters.
> (*Othello* I.iii.76–77)

Like Brutus he structures his *defensio* according to the classical *dispositio* rules (I.iii.76–89: *exordium*; 90–94: *propositio*; 128–168: *argumentatio [narratio]*; 169–170: *peroratio*); like Brutus he prefers the moderate affections of *ethos* to the vehement emotions of *pathos*. The straightforwardness of his utterance matches the candid honesty of his character. Thus his promise, "I will a round unvarnish'd tale deliver" (I.iii.90), is not an empty *topos* of sincerity but indicative of, in Iago's words, "a free and open nature" (I.iii.397). This *decorum* of speech and speaker convinces the judges to such an extent that they acquit Othello without any further ado.

While the content of Brutus' speech is conveyed by plain logic, the proof of Othello's innocence is presented in the form of a narration. Here the orator adopts the guise of the historian; his trustworthiness is based not on the power of argument but on the vivid presentation (*evidentia*) of autobiographical details. *Sub specie rhetorica*, it is only a small step from the orator-historian to the orator-poet, that is, a speaker who strengthens his argument by fictions. This is the role of the senator Menenius Agrippa in Shakespeare's *Coriolanus*. His narrative fiction is the well-known parable of the insurrection of the parts of the body against the belly, meaning the fight of the plebeians against the senate. This parable had been a favorite *exemplum* in humanist circles to illustrate irrational and rational behavior. Thomas Wilson annotates it in a marginal gloss: "Fables how nedeful they are to teache the ignoraunte."[16] In Shakespeare's play it is employed as the argumentative part of a speech that is to secure senate rule. Menenius Agrippa adopts the role of the Gallic Hercules who restores social harmony.

---

[16]Wilson, *Arte* 105ᵛ.

Each of the three specimens of a rhetoric of "good order" arises from a sociopolitical situation that proves extremely dangerous to the commonwealth. It is the speaker's obligation to prevent, by means of his oration, a relapse into a state of the *homo homini lupus*. Congruent with this task, his speech is marked not by (irregular) Nature, but by (regular) Art; not by (stirring) *pathos*, but by (soothing) *ethos*; not by the elevated (emotional), but by the plain (rational) style. The *oratio-ratio* topos undergoes multiple variations, depending on the person of the speaker: Brutus appears as orator-logician, Othello as orator-historian, and Menenius Agrippa as orator-poet. The final link in this chain is the figure of Prospero who—no longer orator but poet—uses the magic of his creative imagination (Ariel) in order to civilize the creatures of chaos (Caliban) and the agents of human barbarity (Antonio, Alonso, Sebastian).

Measured in terms of persuasive success, the representatives of the rhetoric of order appear questionable. Brutus and Menenius Agrippa are successful with their *defensiones*, but only for a short time; then crafty demagogues—Antonius, the tribunes—take over. Othello does win his case against Brabantino but loses the one against Iago, for whose rhetoric he is no match.[17] Even the poet-magician Prospero cannot enjoy an untainted success; Caliban resists Nurture (*ars*) and presumably returns to (mere) Nature. Shakespeare obviously thinks little of the possibilities of the rhetoric of order to consolidate the state of social harmony for an extended period of time. Representatives of a subversive rhetoric—revolutionaries, demagogues, intriguers—are often better adapted to situations of crisis. This superiority results, according to contemporary notions, from the susceptibility of man to the vagaries of moods. In 1619, Samuel Purchas can therefore condemn rhetoric as "poison" for church and state; for

> it knowes the Arts of Adulation, of Hypocrisie, of malicious Slaundering, of AEqui-uocations; of all sorts of Iuggling, and Lying; it makes Men see with others Eyes, with strange Glasses, which make things seeme bigger, or lesse, or double, or not at all; it is Master of Mens furious Passions, and leades them (so *Hercules* was pictured) by the Eare (as Beare-wards their Beares, by the ringed Snowts) to any Out-rage.[18]

Here the humanist *oratio-ratio* ideal is questioned radically. In this new perspective the Gallic Hercules is no civilizing agent but an agitator and revolutionary; he transforms his audience not into rational men but into brutish beings that he can manipulate at will. Representatives of this figure in Shakespeare are Jack Cade in *2 Henry VI* (IV.iii–x), the tribunes in *Coriolanus*, and Iago in *Othello* (in the scenes of nightly unrest: I.i; II.iii; V.i). Their perverted rhetoric

---

[17]On Iago's rhetoric, see H. F. Plett, " 'Action is eloquence': Zur rhetorischen Aktionstypik in Shakespeare's *Othello*," *Germanisch-Romanische Monatsschrift* 32 (1982): 1–21; and, from another point of view, Sidney R. Homan, "Iago's Aesthetics: Othello and Shakespeare's Portrait of an Artist," *Shakespeare Studies* 5 (1969): 141–148.

[18]Samuel Purchas, *Microcosmus, or The Historie of Man*, The English Experience 146 (1619; Amsterdam: Theatrum Orbis Terrarum/Da Capo, 1969) 537–538.

is successful, because the humanist ideal of the orator-philosopher no longer has an equivalent in reality. Brutus in *Julius Caesar* is the tragical exception.

CELARE ARTEM, OR THE RHETORIC OF DISSIMULATION

To conceal art does not mean its renunciation but, on the contrary, its highest consummation, for in this case, the art is so perfect that one no longer perceives its artificiality but can surrender oneself entirely to the illusion of the natural—art as second nature (*altera natura*). Such a postulate presupposes two things: (a) the art to control art perfectly (*difficulté vaincue*), and (b) a culture based less on an objective rational order than on a personal aesthetic experience. Therefore the cavalier poet Robert Herrick can entitle a poem "Delight in Disorder" and close it with the words:

> A carelesse shooe-string, in whose tye
> I see a wilde civility:
> Doe more bewitch me, then when Art
> Is too precise in every part.[19]

The theoretical foundations of this paradox of an artful artlessness were laid in Baldassare Castiglione's *Il libro del cortegiano*, of which an English translation was published by Sir Thomas Hoby in 1561.[20] Its theoretical core, the concept of *sprezzatura*, refines the rhetorical *celare artem* into a codex of courtly behavior that was still to mould the gentleman, the *honnête homme*, and the dandy. The fair semblance of artistic lightness implies a habitual irony of dissimulation that is manifest in the pretense of an as-if-not, that is, in permanent role fictions. Thus it is not surprising that in his courtly poetic *The Arte of English Poesie* (1589), George Puttenham ascribes the same artistry "to dissemble his arte" (III.xxv) to the poet and the courtier alike and prescribes for both, as their "chiefe profession," "beau semblant."[21]

Perfect courtiers who follow this norm of speech and behavior can hardly be found in Shakespeare. In the historical reality of the 16th century, Sir Philip

---

[19]Robert Herrick, *The Poetical Works*, ed. F. W. Moorman (London: Oxford University Press, 1947) 28.

[20]See, among others, Wayne A. Rebhorn, *Courtly Performances: Masking and Festivity in Castiglione's "Book of the Courtier"* (Detroit, MI: Wayne State University Press, 1978); *La Corte e il "Cortegiano,"* ed. Carlo Ossola and Adriano Prosperi, 2 vols. (Rome: Bulzoni, 1980); *Castiglione: The Ideal and the Real in Renaissance Culture*, ed. Robert W. Hanning and David Rosand (New Haven: Yale University Press, 1983). Further literature in Lorenz Böninger, "Neuere Forschungen über Castiglione," *Wolfenbütteler Renaissance Mitteilungen* 9 (1985): 85–89.

[21]George Puttenham, *The Arte of English Poesie*, ed. Gladys Dodge Willcock and Alice Walker (Cambridge: Cambridge University Press, 1970) 158, 298–307. On the courtly contexts of this theorem, see, among others, Daniel Javitch, *Poetry and Courtliness in Renaissance England* (Princeton, NJ: Princeton University Press, 1978); H. F. Plett, "Aesthetic Constituents in the Courtly Culture of Renaissance England," *New Literary History* 14 (1982–1983): 597–621; Frank Whigham, *Ambition and Privilege: The Social Tropes of Elizabethan Courtesy Theory* (Berkeley: University of California Press, 1984).

Sidney was regarded as its ideal embodiment; his works—the sonnet cycle *Astrophel and Stella*, the pastoral romance *Arcadia*, the poetological essay *An Apology for Poetry*—demonstrate the accomplishments as well as the problematic nature of such a norm. In his plays, Shakespeare stresses above all its fragility. Great is his number of affected courtiers who miss the ideal through an overabundance of art. Their range includes Benedick and Beatrice in *Much Ado About Nothing*, Orlando in *As You Like It*, Malvolio in *Twelfth Night*, and Osrick in *Hamlet*. In *Love's Labour's Lost*, the artificiality of speech and behavior is the central topic. Berowne speaks for the whole courtly society at Navarra when he renounces "painted rhetoric" (IV.iii.236) at the end of his purification process:

> Taffeta phrases, silken terms precise,
> Three-pil'd hyperboles, spruce affection,
> Figures pedantical; these summer flies
> Have blown me full of maggot ostentation:
> I do forswear them. . . .
>   (*Love's Labour's Lost* V.ii.406–410)

Such an ornamental rhetoric that exhausts itself in the "ostentation" of artificial ruses is absurd and ridicules the speaker. The comic catharsis, which redeems from the bonds of a fantastical oath, includes the *affectatio* 'affection' in language, too.[22]

The ethical problem inherent in a rhetoric of the *celare artem* is illustrated by Proteus in *The Two Gentlemen of Verona* and by Don John in *Much Ado About Nothing*. These characters follow the practices of the corrupt Italian courtiers whom Puttenham declares to have witnessed: "to seeme idle when they be earnestly occupied & entend to nothing but mischieuous practizes."[23] The courtier as dissembler separates *res* and *verba*. Therefore Puttenham allows the courtly poet "to be a dissembler only in the subtilties of his arte. . . ."[24] Yet he does not ignore the problem of the aesthetically disguised lie; an English paraphrase of the trope of allegory ("the Courtly figure") is: "the figure of [*false semblant or dissimulation*]."[25] Thus rhetorical role playing can be fair as well as deceptive semblance. The latter lacks substance and essence; it has no identity but is a process of permanent change. Its mythical name—in Shakespeare and elsewhere—is Proteus.[26]

---

[22]On the themes of *ars* and *natura*, see William C. Carroll, "Living Art," *The Great Feast of Language in "Love's Labour's Lost"* (Princeton, NJ: Princeton University Press, 1976) 167–204, 265–267.

[23]Puttenham, *Arte* 301.

[24]Puttenham, *Arte* 302.

[25]Puttenham, *Arte* 186.

[26]See Richard in *3 Henry VI* III.ii.191–193:

> I can add colours to the chameleon,
> Change shapes with Proteus for advantages,
> And set the murderous Machiavel to school.

On Proteus as an actor ("comédien"), see Noël le Comte (= Natalis Comes), *Mythologie* (Lyon: Frelon, 1607) 842–848, here: 846 (VIII.viii.)

In this negative evaluation the courtly rhetoric of dissimulation is in concert with two other traditions. The older one is based on the late medieval morality plays, in which Dissimulation personified, a variant of the Vice figure, tries to seduce Man through clever deceptive speeches. The more recent tradition refers to the 18th chapter in Niccolò Machiavelli's *Il Principe* in which the author advises the politician to act not only the lion but also the fox in order to ensure success: "But it is necessary to know well how to color this nature, and to be a great pretender and dissembler."[27] In Shakespeare's plays the three traditions of dissimulatory rhetoric are still discernible. Marc Antony embodies, in his forum speech, the Machiavellian variant. Iago's successful plots against Roderigo, Cassio, and, above all, Othello are grounded in the Vice tradition. Richard III practices all three facets of a rhetoric of deceit: the courtly one in his courtship scene (I.ii), the theological (Vice-related) one in his feigned religious exercises (III.vii), and the Machiavellian one in several council scenes (I.iii; II.i; III.iv).[28] Each time Richard acts as a plain, ingenuous person who is incapable of rhetoric and deception.

A rather neglected instance of this rhetoric is Edmund in *King Lear*. As in the case of Iago, the Vice figure is one of his literary ancestors, but he acts like a courtier bent on promotion and pursues his Machiavellian aims ruthlessly. His advancement is based on a successful rhetorical feat. It consists in the deft application of *negatio*, which is a rhetorical figure of dissimulation. Abraham Fraunce defines it in his *Arcadian Rhetorike* (1588) as "a denial or refusall to speake, as, I will not say that which I might, I will not call you, &c. when neuerthelesse we speake and tell al."[29] When Edmund meets his father Gloucester, he addresses him in the following way:

Glou. Edmund, how now! What news?
Edm. So please your Lordship, none.
 Putting up the letter.
Glou. Why so earnestly seek you to put up that letter?
Edm. I know no news, my Lord.
Glou. What paper were you reading?

---

[27]Niccolò Machiavelli, *The Prince*, trans. Harvey C. Mansfield, Jr. (Chicago: University of Chicago Press, 1985) 70. Italian text: Niccolò Machiavelli, "Il Principe," *Tutte le opere*, ed. Mario Martelli (Firenze: Sansoni, 1971) 283: "Ma è necessario questa natura saperla bene colorire, ed essere gran simulatore e dissimulatore."

[28]See the interpretations by Wolfgang G. Müller, "The Villain as Rhetorician in Shakespeare's *Richard III*," *Anglia* 102 (1984): 37–59; Russ McDonald, "*Richard III* and the Tropes of Treachery," *Philological Quarterly* 68 (1989): 465–483; Betty A. Schellenberg, "Conflicting Paradigms and the Progress of Persuasion in *Richard III*," *Cahiers Elisabéthains* 37 (1990): 59–68. On Richard, Iago, and other representatives of hypocrisy, see Brian Vickers, "Shakespeare's Hypocrites," *Returning to Shakespeare* (London: Routledge, 1989) 89–134.

[29]Abraham Fraunce, *The Arcadian Rhetorike*, ed. Ethel Seaton, Luttrell Reprints 9 (Oxford: Basil Blackwell, 1950) 13.

Edm. Nothing, my Lord.
Glou. No? What needed then that terrible dispatch of it into your pocket? The
quality of nothing hath no such need to hide itself....

(*King Lear* I.ii.26–34)

Such a chain of feigned suppressions of information actually intended to be
disclosed presupposes, in order to be effective, are acted masterly with naturalness
of rhetorical delivery so that no doubts as to the honesty of the speaker arise.
Gloucester believes Edmund, who accuses Edgar of planned parricide. He falls prey
to Edmund's "inventions" (I.ii.20)—a rhetorical term—and commits the fatal error
of changing the "nothing" into something. The courtly spectacle of oratorical
naturalness here discloses its profound moral and epistemological ambivalence.
Everyone who practices the *celare artem*—courtier, politician, artist—is subject to
it. Possibly the most impressive study of the rhetoric of fair/false semblance in
Shakespeare is Hamlet—he, too, is courtier, politician, and artist and hence
combines in his person the triad of qualities that are fused in Castiglione's
Cortegiano.

NEGARE ARTEM, OR THE RHETORIC OF DENIAL

In Francis Bacon's *Advancement of Learning* (1605) we can find, as so often in
Renaissance literature, a rendering of the myth of Orpheus; but this one, unlike
the familiar versions, closes with a significant *volta.* Here the Greek bard performs
his art in a theatre in which animals of all kinds are assembled. As long as they
listen to him they manage to bridle their savage instincts; but as soon as he has
ended his song, they resort to them without delay, which makes Bacon comment:

> wherein is aptly described the nature and condition of men; who are full of savage
> and unreclaimed desires, of profit, of lust, of revenge, which as long as they give
> ear to precepts, to laws, to religion, sweetly touched with eloquence and persuasion
> of books, of sermons, of harangues, so long is society and peace maintained; but
> if these instruments be silent, or that sedition and tumult make them not audible,
> all things dissolve into anarchy and confusion.[30]

This mythic exegesis manifests a fundamental scepticism toward the humanistic
ideal of a rhetoric of order. Similar apprehensions had already been voiced in
Cicero's early treatise *De inventione* (I.iii.4). In it the dissociation of wisdom and
eloquence is made responsible for the decline of civilization. As a result, unprinci-
pled orators emerge who, by their unscrupulous conduct, bring eloquence into
disrepute and contempt. From the viewpoint of Christian humanism, Thomas
Wilson interprets this event as the Fall of Rhetoric and foresees, as an impending
danger, mankind's relapse into a pre-societal existence. Fifty years later, at the turn
of the century, Wilson's worst fears had, at least psychologically, come true. An

---

[30]Francis Bacon, "The Advancement of Learning," *Works*, ed. James Spedding, 14 vols.
(Stuttgart-Bad Cannstatt: Frommann, 1961–1963) 3:302.

all-encompassing *fin de siècle* pessimism put everything in doubt: God and man, society and culture—in short, any belief in a preestablished "good order." It is a time that produced the melancholic, the stoic, and the empiricist. It is the time of Donne's, Hall's, and Marston's satires, which disclaim any positive values for the present. It is also the time of the critics of language and rhetoric, of the shift from the abundance of words and things to linguistic brevity and terseness. Ciceronian *copia* is superseded by Senecan and Tacitean *brevitas*. The ornate style gives way to the plain style. The battle cry is now *tot verba quot res*—'as many words as there are things', the future programme of the Royal Society.[31] In other words, it is the time of the "Counter-Renaissance" (Hiram Haydn).

Shakespeare's attitude toward the *oratio-ratio* theorem had been tinged by scepticism early on. This is evident in the eventual failure of those figures who stand for a rhetoric of social harmony—Brutus, Menenius Agrippa, Othello. It becomes even more pronounced in Shakespeare's new oratorical type: the anti-rhetorician. Anti-rhetoric does not mean here a total renunciation of rhetoric in the sense of an idealistic rejection of all things rhetorical, but instead a specific kind of rhetoric itself. Its distinctive mark is the intentional violation of the *decorum*, that is, of the prevailing social norm of communicative behavior. This kind of *indecorum* allows for several variations that are reducible to two basic types: the radical code-shift and its *ultima ratio*, silence. In both cases the anti-rhetorician places himself deliberately outside the current system of communication and hence outside the social order of which it is a part.

Shakespeare's dramatic figures so often violate verbal and nonverbal *decorum* that one could deduce from them a sociology of conflict. Of the multitude of instances, of which T. McAlindon's useful study *Shakespeare and Decorum*[32] examines comparatively few, two plays may serve as illustrations: *Coriolanus* and *King Lear*.

Coriolanus' tragedy begins with his refusal to keep to the *decorum* of political canvassing. In this he opposes the will of his mother Volumnia, who takes a decidedly contrary position. She says about herself:

> I would dissemble with my nature where
> My fortunes and my friends at stake requir'd
> I should do so in honour.
>   (*Coriolanus* III.ii.62–64)

---

[31]On this subject, see A. C. Howell, "*Res et Verba*: Words and Things," *Journal of English Literary History* 13 (1946) 131–142; Robert Adolph, *The Rise of Modern Prose Style* (Cambridge, MA: MIT Press, 1968); G. A. Padley, "The Seventeenth Century: Words versus Things," *Grammatical Theory in Western Europe, 1500–1700: The Latin Tradition* (Cambridge: Cambridge University Press, 1976) 111–153; Brian Vickers, "The Royal Society and English Prose Style: A Reassessment," *Rhetoric and the Pursuit of Truth: Language Change in the Seventeenth and Eighteenth Centuries*, ed. Brian Vickers and Nancy Struever (Los Angeles, CA: William Andrews Clark Memorial Library, University of California, 1985) 1–76.

[32]T. McAlindon, *Shakespeare and Decorum* (London: Macmillan, 1973).

And she advises her son to talk to the plebeians:

> [. . .] with such words that are but roted in
> Your tongue, though but bastards and syllables
> Of no allowance to your bosom's truth.
> (III.ii.55–57)

Thus she recommends a rhetoric of dissimulation that only looks for oratorical success. The price for this is the dissociation of word and truth that calls into question the code of honor that Volumnia proclaims. Yet Coriolanus refuses to play the Machiavellian fox. He counters the agitatory speeches of the tribunes with passionate invectives. His anti-rhetoric is founded on the conviction that an eloquence that degenerates into mere spectacle ("only fair speech" [III.ii.96]) no longer has any social legitimation. In contrast to his friends and enemies, he knows how to preserve his personal integrity.

A more diversified spectrum of anti-rhetoricism is to be found in *King Lear*. Kent's use of it is marked by the code-shift from elevated to plain style (and vice versa). In the scene in which Lear divides his empire, Kent at first addresses Lear in the elevated style demanded by the courtly *decorum* from any subject:

> Royal Lear,
> Whom I have ever honour'd as my King,
> Lov'd as my father, as my master follow'd.
> (I.i.138–140)

But when he finds he is not listened to, he resorts to the plain style to restore the king to his senses after all:

> [. . .] be Kent unmannerly,
> When Lear is mad. What would'st thou do, old man?
> Think'st thou that duty shall have dread to speak
> When power to flattery bows? To plainness honour's bound
> When majesty falls to folly.
> (I.i.144–148)

Change of style here is equivalent to the violation of *decorum*. The *indecorum* amounts to a lèse-majesté to be punished in diverse ways according to the courtly code: imprisonment, banishment, execution at worst. The "plainness" of Kent appears in two forms: in his style and in his character. Where the traditional rhetoric of order has lost its validity, only the anti-rhetoric of the plain style can bridge the chasm between *oratio* and *ratio*.[33] This anti-rhetoric is practiced by Kent a second time in order to expose the vain courtier Oswald in front of

---

[33]Compare Emily W. Leider, "Plainness of Style in *King Lear*," *Shakespeare Quarterly* 21 (1970): 45–53; Sheldon P. Zitner, "*King Lear* and Its Language," *Some Facets of "King Lear": Essays in Prismatic Criticism*, ed. Rosalie L. Colie and F. T. Flahiff (London: Heinemann, 1974) 3–27; Norman R. Atwood, "Cordelia and Kent: Their Fateful Choice of Style," *Language & Style* 9 (1976): 42–54.

Gloucester's castle. The Duke of Cornwall, to whom he justifies this *indecorum* with his "plainness," demonstrates by his reaction (II.ii.92–101) that courtly rhetoric has degenerated so far that the professed negation of art is considered an especially subtle form of dissimulation, which is hypocrisy—the more so as Kent's playful shift into the elevated, though hyperbolically distorted, style demonstrates that he indeed masters the courtly register.

What remains, when all rhetorical codes fail? Silence. Of course, silence can indicate several things: linguistic deficiency, prohibition of speech, introversion, overwhelming emotions, stubbornness, discretion, protest. The historical gamut runs from the mystical silence of Harpocrates or Hermes Trismegistos to the speechlessness of Vladimir and Estragon in *En attendant Godot*.[34] Shakespeare's plays give evidence of such an abundance of instances that as early as 1929, Alwin Thaler could publish a treatise on *Shakespeare's Silences*.[35] What is of particular interest here is silence understood not as passive speechlessness but as "eloquent silence," signifying protest against "false speech." The most promi-nent representative of such an anti-rhetoricism in Shakespeare is Cordelia, who has to enter into speech competition with her sisters, when their father is dividing up his empire. Unwilling to surpass their epideictic rhetoric of excess through hyperbolic expressions of her own, she answers Lear's question of what she has to say to attain her share of the heritage, simply with: "Nothing, my lord" (I.i.86). In so doing, she is in no way conforming to typical female role expectations as contemporary conduct books prescribe them. Consider, for example, Thomas Becon (1560–1564): "Let her kepe silence. For there is nothinge that doth so much commend, avaunce, set forthe, adourne, decke, trim, and garnish a maid, as silence."[36] Barnabe Rich, in *The Excellency of Good Women* (1613), wrote: "The woman of modesty openeth not her mouth but with discretion, neither is there any bitternes in her tongue: shee seemeth in speaking, to hould her peace, and in her silence shee seemeth to speake."[37] And Richard Brathwait wrote, in *The English Gentlewoman* (1641): "Silence in a *Woman* is a mouing Rhetoricke, winning most, when in words it wooeth least."[38] This kind of silence is embodied

---

[34]Recent general studies on this subject are, for example, Bernard P. Dauenhauer, *Silence: The Phenomenon and Its Ontological Significance* (Bloomington, IN: Indiana University Press, 1980); Christian L. Hart Nibbrig, *Rhetorik des Schweigens* (Frankfort: Suhrkamp, 1981); and Niklas Luhmann and Peter Fuchs, *Reden und Schweigen* (Frankfort: Suhrkamp, 1989).

[35]Alwin Thaler, *Shakespeare's Silences* (Cambridge, MA: Harvard University Press, 1929); see also Laura Catherine Keyes, "Silence in Shakespeare," diss., State University of New York, Buffalo, 1981; Harvey Rovine, "Shakespeare's Silent Characters," diss., University of Illinois, Urbana-Champaign, 1985; Philip C. McGuire, *Speechless Dialect: Shakespeare's Open Silences* (Berkeley: University of California Press, 1985).

[36]Cited in Suzanne W. Hull, *Chaste, Silent & Obedient: English Books for Women, 1475–1640* (San Marino, CA: Huntington Library, 1982) 220.

[37]Barnabe Rich, *The Excellency of Good Women* (London: Thomas Dawson, 1613) 29.

[38]Richard Brathwait, *The English Gentlewoman* (1631; Amsterdam: Theatrum Orbis Terrarum/Da Capo, 1970) 90. On the context, see Catherine Belsey, "Silence and Speech," *The Subject of Tragedy: Identity and Difference in Renaissance Drama* (London: Methuen, 1985) 149–191.

in Virgilia, who is greeted by Coriolanus as "my gracious silence" (II.i.174).[39]
Such is, however, not Cordelia's attitude (or that of other educated Renaissance
women). Her silence signals neither meekness nor submissiveness but, rather, a
protest against a rhetoric of false semblance:

[. . .] I want that glib and oily art
To speak and purpose not, since what I well intend,
I'll do't before I speak. . . .

(I.i.223–225)[40]

The word is no longer reliable, only the deed. Cordelia's maxim is: "Love, and
be silent" (I.i.61). Only the moral deed can redeem the world from its rhetorical
fall.[41] The means of attaining this redemption are suffering and death, as the
several tragedies of *King Lear* demonstrate.

The drama of *King Lear* thus starts with a twofold paradox. The representatives
of evil conform to the rules of *decorum*, practice a rhetoric of "good order" and
fair semblance, and are rewarded for it. On the opposite side, the representatives
of good violate the *decorum* act as anti-rhetoricians and are punished for it. The
resolution of the play repeals this absurdity by revealing the emptiness of "fair"
words and of the *decorum* that validates them, thus radically questioning the
prevailing order. Rhetoric is the indicator of this development.

EPILEGOMENA

The foregoing remarks sketch roughly, and in an exemplary manner, a rhetorical
typology. It rests on three different attitudes to the *ars rhetorica*: its demonstration, dissimulation, and negation. Typologies are usually marked by a simplification of complex phenomena. This is done with the intention of providing such
discovery procedures as can integrate the rather fortuitous observations of an

---

[39]On Coriolanus' silence, see Carol M. Sicherman, "*Coriolanus*: The Failure of Words," *Journal of English Literary History* 39 (1972): 189–207.

[40]See the provocative remarks by Paolo Valesio, " 'That Glib and Oylie Art.' Cordelia and the Rhetoric of Antirhetoric," *Versus: Quaderni di studi semiotici* 16 (1977): 91–117.

[41]Cordelia is by her upbringing not a bad orator. She deliberately changes into one for two reasons. On the one hand she protests against the misuse of rhetoric by her sisters; on the other she wants to preserve a *decorum* of a different kind, that of her personal integrity. This, not surprisingly, finds its expression in the plain style that is the traditional medium for the statement of facts. Like Brutus she uses parallelisms and gradations for her defense:

You have begot me, bred me, lov'd me: I
Return those duties back as are right fit,
Obey you, love you, and most honour you.
(I.i.96–98)

Here speaks the orator-logician who has a greater confidence in the force of rational argumentation than in the elaborate devices of courtly rhetoric.

object of inquiry into a prestructured system of relations. There are two ways of developing the suggested typology, one with reference to Shakespeare's plays and another with reference to Renaissance culture at large.

Other dramatic figures than the aforementioned could be assigned to one of the three types. Yet this would only add to the list of illustrations. In a further stage, dramatic configurations and situative interactions could be subjected to a speech-typological examination. The result could be put down in a rhetorical score, separately for each drama. This score would notate which element dominates in a speech act and which is suppressed. The same score could also indicate in which way the rhetorical attitude of a character changes in the progress of the drama.[42] To describe such evolutionary processes adequately one needs, of course, additional methodological (ethical, ontological, epistemological) tools. This is evident from the discussion and illustration of the three types. Rhetoric, after all, is not an abstract technology but a social factor whose complexity requires a perennial effort of differentiation.

The presentation of the three rhetorical concepts of art started with the authors Thomas Wilson, George Puttenham, and Francis Bacon. This sequence, which may at first appear fortuitous, proves rather significant on a closer inspection. For the three names not only stand for three kinds of rhetoric but—in my concluding hypothesis—denote three cultural paradigms that follow each other in the Renaissance: the humanist, the courtly, and the rationalistic. This sequence does not mean that the emergence of a new paradigm makes the older one disappear; rather, there are phases of simultaneity and of retardation. The humanist paradigm dies out in England in the 17th century, the rationalistic one reaches its climax as late as the 18th century, and the courtly one survives in manifold forms up to the 20th century. Rhetoric can thus be regarded as the indicator of those paradigms and their changes. But with these remarks we are already in the midst of cultural speculations and far from the point of our departure: the rhetoric of "good order," the rhetoric of dissimulation, and the rhetoric of denial.

---

[42]Othello, for instance, participates in all the kinds of rhetoric described in this context. He first introduces himself as a representative of the rhetoric of "good order." But when he falls victim to the insinuations of Iago, he adopts the dissimulatory rhetoric of his seducer (e.g., in the brothel scene). He even changes into an anti-rhetorician who violates *decorum* (e.g., in the embassy scene). Finally, having recovered from his delusions, he reverts to the rhetoric of "good order" (in his dying speech). Thus the application of the typology is subject to many variations.

Chapter 16

The Borromeo Rings:
Rhetoric, Law, and Literature
in the English Renaissance

Richard Schoeck
University of Colorado

The Borromeo family was a powerful one in the area to the south of Switzerland in the north of Italy centering in Milan; but it is not of that family itself that I wish to discuss. Rather, I want to borrow an emblem associated with their coat of arms, the Borromeo rings, which were three rings so designed that they interlocked and no one could be detached without breaking one of the other two rings.[1] You will agree that it is a fine symbol of interconnectedness, and I want to use that emblem as a model for my thesis that during the Renaissance period law, rhetoric, and literature were so interconnected that we detach one from the others only at the risk of breaking relationships and of making it difficult to see the original working even of the one ring that we might be studying. My essay is largely historical, rather than theoretical, so far as rhetoric and literature are concerned; and to offer critical readings evincing legal structures and embodying concepts of justice must lie beyond its scope.

Whether we are studying Thomas More, whose daily life was filled with the multifarious activities of the law—at the time of writing his *Utopia* he complained of the demands of appearing in court, arranging arbitrations, making judgments, handling wills, and other such activities—or another busy common lawyer and

---

[1]On the three rings, see R. J. Schoeck, "Mathematics and the Languages of Literary Criticism," *Journal of Aesthetics and Art Criticism* 26 (1968): 370–371. See R. J. Schoeck, "Rhetoric and Law in Sixteenth-Century England," *Studies in Philology* 50 (1953): 110–127; and R. J. Schoeck, "Lawyers and Rhetoric in Sixteenth-Century England," in *Renaissance Eloquence: Studies in the Theory and Practice of Renaissance Rhetoric*, ed. J. J. Murphy (Berkeley: University of California Press, 1983) 274–291.

one who also became a Lord Chancellor, Francis Bacon, we do well, I urge, to think of the quotidian involvements of such men and to ask how the law shaped their thinking or contributed to their writing. In Tudor England it is no surprise to discover that the common lawyers were most active in writing about rhetoric and even in presenting new systems or theories of rhetoric; and they were prodigiously active in writing drama, poetry, various prose forms, and in making translations from a number of languages. Law, rhetoric, and literature constituted the Borromeo rings of the English Renaissance, especially of the 16th century.

Rhetoric and its tradition of teaching are likely to be more familiar to my readers than legal training and practice, for we all call our students' attention to the role of rhetoric in the idealized trivium. Further, we have all made use in varying ways of T. W. Baldwin's *Small Latine & Lesse Greeke* for its important (though largely unreadable) investigation of school curricula in Tudor England; and some of us have drawn on or written on and discussed the studies of M. W. Croll, W. S. Howell, J. J. Murphy, W. J. Ong, Brian Vickers, and others in the fields of Renaissance rhetoric.[2] But law is likely to be another matter, and I therefore begin with some generalizations about law and our study of it in the 20th century.

First, I consider the study of law from a large-scale view, looking both at the Continent and its traditions of the civil (or Roman) law, and at England with its traditions of the unique common law of the realm.[3] Lawyers, as I recently observed,[4] not only reflected but also contributed to the growth of a secular attitude: among the lawyers, revisionary discussions of the correct method for studying the law led

---

[2]The works referred to are: Thomas W. Baldwin, *William Shakespeare's Small Latine & Lesse Greeke* 2 vols. (Urbana, IL: University of Illinois Press, 1944), J. Max Patrick, Robert O. Evans, J. M. Wallace, & R. J. Schoeck, eds., *Morris W. Croll, Style, Rhetoric and Rhythm—Essays by Morris W. Croll* (Princeton: Princeton University Press, 1966); Wilbur Samuel Howell, *Logic and Rhetoric in England, 1500–1700* (Princeton: Princeton University Press, 1956); J. J. Murphy, ed., *Renaissance Eloquence* (Berkeley: University of California Press, 1983); J. J. Murphy, *Renaissance Rhetoric—A Short-Title Catalogue* (New York: Garland, 1981); Walter J. Ong, *Ramus, Method and the Decay of Dialogue* (Cambridge: Harvard University Press, 1958); Walter J. Ong, "Tudor Writings on Rhetoric, Poetic, and Literary Theory," *Rhetoric, Romance, and Technology* (Ithaca, NY: Cornell University Press, 1971); and Brian Vickers, *Classical Rhetoric in English Poetry* (London: Macmillan, 1970).

Winifred B. Horner, ed., *The Present State of Scholarship in Historical and Contemporary Rhetoric* (Columbia: University of Missouri Press, 1983) contains a survey of Renaissance rhetoric by Don Paul Abbott.

An indication of the classical roots of our triad of related fields can be found in C. J. Classen's investigation of Cicero's rhetorical strategies in *Recht-Rhetorik-Politik* (Darmstadt, Wissenschaftliche Buchgesellschaft, 1985); and Kathy Eden, *Poetic and Legal Fiction* (Princeton, NJ: Princeton University Press, 1986) cuts across much poetic and rhetorical theory and reveals how much legal proof resides in Aristotelian concepts of recognition, thereby illuminating in an important way Sidney's *Defence of Poetry* and Shakespeare's *Hamlet*.

[3]See R. J. Schoeck, "Humanism and Jurisprudence," *Renaissance Humanism*, ed. A. Rabil, 2 vols. (Philadelphia: University of Pennsylvania Press, 1988) 3:310–326.

[4]Schoeck, "Humanism and Jurisprudence" 311–312. There I indicate my indebtedness to the work of Gilmore, Kisch, Maffei, Kelley, and others.

Previous researchers have noted the roots of that scholarship in the medieval study and teaching of rhetoric.

some to be more receptive to the reformers than was the case with other professions— for, after all, the lawyers set about studying Christian texts in the same way in which some of them were studying the *corpus juris*: in effect, modern textual scholarship was largely born in the law schools of northern Italy at the end of the 15th century.[5] To these generalizations I might add that some of the authority of the medieval priest was shifted to the lawyers, and there was a steady growth of anti-lawyer sentiment that paralleled the older anti-clericalism—I speak here of England, where common lawyers were not clerics. I would add too that the study of ancient texts is necessarily interdisciplinary: Witness, in that interdisciplinary Society of Anti- quaries, the key role of common lawyers for the rediscovery of Anglo-Saxon in 16th-century England.[6] One final note: the fraternity of legal scholars in England (now speaking primarily of civilians and canonists) was indeed international, for several kinds of connections were made in Doctors Commons, as well as at court and elsewhere, between Englishmen trained at home in the Inns of Court and those trained abroad in canon and civil law, and between Englishmen and foreigners who were staffing innumerable posts in England by virtue of their expertise in canon and civil law.[7] Thus legal writings in 16th- and 17th-century England touched all aspects of human experience, as Shakespeare knew well in having his Portia (in *The Merchant of Venice*) tap one very small part of that vast literature[8] in northern Italy by making use of the influential form known as the *consilia*.[9]

---

[5]See R. J. Schoeck, "The Humanistic Concept of the Text: Text, Context, and Tradition," *Proceedings of the Patristic, Medieval and Renaissance Conference, Villanova* 7 (1982): 13–21.

[6]On the rediscovery of Anglo-Saxon during the 16th century (as it has been thought until recently), see R. J. Schoeck "Anglo-Saxon Studies in Sixteenth-Century England," *Studies in the Renaissance*, 5 (1958), 102–110.

To speak of the interdisciplinarity of the study of ancient texts is to introduce the concept of intertextuality, which was not born in the 20th century but was familiar to Erasmus and others; see R. J. Schoeck, *Intertextuality and Renaissance Texts* (Bamberg: Kaiser Verlag, 1984); and R. J. Schoeck, " 'In loco intertextuantur': Erasmus as Master of Intertextuality," *Intertextuality*, ed. H. F. Plett (Berlin: Walter de Gruyter, 1991) 181–191. I also have commented on the role of the rhetoric canon (which changed of course during the 15th and 16th centuries) in R. J. Schoeck, "Intertextuality and the Rhetoric Canon," *Criticism, History, and Intertextuality*, ed. Richard Fleming and Michael Payne (Lewisburg, PA: Bucknell University Press, 1988) 98–112.

[7]See R. J. Schoeck, "Canon Law in England on the Eve of the Reformation," *Mediaeval Studies* 25 (1963): 125–147.

[8]Some very rough estimates of the vastness of neo-Latin legal literature in the 16th century are offered in R. J. Schoeck, "Neo-Latin Legal Literature," *Acta Conventus Neo-Latini Lovaniensis*, ed. J. IJsewijn and E. Kessler (Munich: Wilhelm Fink Verlag, 1973) 577–588.

[9]On consilia, see Guido Kisch, *Consilia—Eine Bibliographie der juristischen Konsiliensammlun- gen* (Basel-Stuttgart: Helbing and Lichtenhahn, 1970); the term, one might add, was often used in the 16th century in an extended sense, meaning something beyond a counsel's opinion. See, further, Peter R. Pazzaglini and Catharine A. Hawks, eds., *Consilia: A Bibliography of Holdings in the Library of Congress and Certain Other Collections in the United States* (Washington, DC: Library of Congress, 1990), with its admirably succinct definition: "The term, little known among most practicing American lawyers, refers in its simplest aspect to analyses of certain points of law by medieval and Renaissance jurists, most often in answer to questions put to them by judges deciding a case" (vii).

In order to provide a more immediate context for my discourse, let me offer here a sketch of the institutions of the law and something of the sociology of lawyers in Tudor England.

On the continent the law schools or faculties were part of the universities. Not so in England, for the four Inns of Court (Inner and Middle Temples, Gray's Inn, and Lincoln's Inn) were all located in London and were quite independent of the universities—though by the end of the 16th century the four Inns of Court together came to be known popularly as England's Third University.[10] On the continent the civilians and canonists all shared with theologians and philosophers a common education in the liberal arts, including, of course, rhetoric. This was not the case in medieval or early Renaissance England, and only in the mid-16th century did the custom begin to grow of young men attending Oxford or Cambridge first before studying at the Inns—as Thomas Elyot and Coke recommended, and as Thomas More and a growing number of leading common lawyers had done.[11] In England and on the Continent, thousands of young men spent several years of their lives—during a formative period, from 15 or 17 to nearly 30—studying the law and living in a legal atmosphere. There were well-established legal families of wealth, power, and influence, and within this society there was much intermarrying. Thomas More was one of more than two dozen males in his family who followed the law, and a majority of them were members of Lincoln's Inn. There is the later example of George Puttenham, author of the influential *Arte of English Poesie* (1589): Himself a lawyer, Puttenham was related to the Elyots (he was in fact a nephew of Sir Thomas Elyot), to Sir James Dyer, the noted judge and legal writer, and to the Throckmorton family, with its numerous lawyers and judges. George Puttenham was at the Middle Temple in the late 1550s, when the Inns of Court were the chief center of literary activity in England.

Three-fourths of the members of the first Elizabethan Society of Antiquaries (which has found its historian in Joan Evans) were members of the Inns of Court,[12] and there were more translators in the Inns during the 16th century than at either Oxford or Cambridge. And then, there is the astonishing achievement of the Inns of Court plays: I refer first to the largely Senecan tragedy of Norton and Sackville, whose *Gorboduc* was performed in 1562 (but not printed until 1565), and to the collaborative work of Kinwelmarsh and Gascoigne, the *Jocasta*

[10]See R. J. Schoeck, "Thomas More and Lincoln's Inn Revels," *Philological Quarterly* 29 (1950): 126–130; and R. J. Schoeck, "Early Tudor Drama and the Inns of Court," *American Society for Theatre Research Newsletter* (November 1957): 1–15.

Several substantial historical studies of the Inns of Court have now been collected in J. H. Baker's volume, *The Legal Profession and the Common Law: Historical Essays* (London: Hambledon Press, 1986), notably "The Inns of Court in 1388," and "The English Legal Profession 1450–1550."

[11]See R. J. Schoeck, "Thomas More and the Law," *Thomas More: Action and Contemplation*, ed. R. S. Sylvester (New Haven: Yale University Press, 1972) 15ff.

[12]Thus R. J. Schoeck, "Elizabethan Society of Antiquaries and Men of Law," *Notes and Queries* n.s. 1 (1954): 417–421.

(1566), followed by others like *Gismond of Salerne in Love* (1567–1568), by Christopher Hatton (later Lord Chancellor and chancellor of Oxford University) and Robert Wilmot. Francis Bacon, as is well known, had a hand in the *Misfortunes of Arthur* acted by gentlemen of Gray's Inn before the Queen in early 1588, when Bacon was 27 years of age. These important early efforts in tragedy had involved the Inner Temple and Gray's Inn, but there were also entertainments and some dramatic activities at Lincoln's Inn and the Middle Temple. The plays were by no means mere antiquarian efforts: In *Gorboduc*, for example, there is the highly relevant warning to the Queen against divided sovereignty and against possible anarchy. These are not merely amateur efforts to be sneered at—as did Tucker Brooke in writing that "it was still true that Senecan tragedy could be produced only when it could draw upon the amateur ambitions of the Inns of Court and count on the Queen's Palace for a theatre" (462). The stakes were too high for mere amateurism. For ambitious law students and young lawyers to have thrown themselves into such dramatic efforts tells us much about the milieu of the Inns themselves and helps to explain why so much Elizabethan writing came out of these institutions. One of the Inns was even among the earliest of institutions to patronize the publication of a learned book, Minsheu's *Guide into the Tongues*, a book that is far more than a curiosity and merits respect as a monument in the history of English philology.

One final kind of evidence of learning and literary interest is to be found in the libraries, both the libraries of individual lawyers and the collegiate libraries. In 1962 I observed that lawyers were among the earliest builders of private libraries in the English Renaissance.[13] Great libraries like that of Edward Coke, for instance, clearly demonstrate a breadth of learning that was frequent enough in a profession that had its several Bacons and Cecils and their peers. It is well known that earlier in the century such common lawyers as Christopher St. Germain in England and Busleiden and Budée on the Continent had built great private libraries. The libraries of the civilian lawyers at Oxford and Cambridge (from which many books have found their way into the library of All Souls College, Oxford) have been relatively little studied; but we know from the library catalogue of Coke's extensive library (well edited by Thorne and Hassall in 1950) that there were the rhetorics of Aristotle and Quintilian, some Cicero, several grammars and books of logic, a "Fiore della Retorica" of 1560, a book of elocution, as well as much history and literature in several languages. Although Quintilian was not often specified in school curricula (we know from Baldwin),

---

[13]See "The Libraries of Common Lawyers in Renaissance England: A Provisional List," *Manuscripta* 6 (1962): 155–167. A comparison of lawyers' libraries with those of other professions may be made through the studies of Pearl Kibre, "The Intellectual Interests Reflected in Libraries of the Fourteenth and Fifteenth Centuries," *Studies in Medieval Science* (London: Hambledon Press, 1984); and of N. R. Ker, "Oxford College Libraries before 1500," and "Oxford College Libraries in the Sixteenth Century," *Books, Collectors, and Libraries* (London: Hambledon Press, 1985).

he was widely read, and Puttenham recorded the following anecdote, which is worth recounting at length:[14]

> And though grave and wise councillors in their consultatins doe not use much superfluous eloquence, and also in their judiciall hearings do much mislike all scholasticall rhetoriks: yet in such a case as it may be (and as this Parliament was) if the Lord Chancelour of England or Archbishop of Canterbury himself were to speake, he ought to doe it cunningly and eloquently, which can not be without the use of figures: and neverthelesse none impeachment or blemish to the gravitie of their persons or of the cause: wherein I report me to them that knew *Sir Nicholas Bacon* Lord keeper of the great Seale, or the now Lord Treasorer of England [Pawlet?], and have bene conversant with their speeches made in the Parliament house & Starrechamber. From whose lippes I have seene to proceede more grave and natural eloquence, then from all the Oratours of Oxford or Cambridge, but all is as it is handled, and maketh no matter whether the same eloquence be naturall to them or artificiall (though I thinke rather naturall), yet were they knowen to be learned and not unskillfull of th'arte, when they were yonger men and as learning and arte teacheth a schollar to speake, so doth it also teach a counsellour, and aswell an old man as a yong, and a man in authoritie, aswell as a private person, and a pleader [lawyer] aswell as a preacher, every man after his sort and calling as best becometh: and that speach which becommeth one, doth not become another, for maners of speaches, some serve to work in excesse, some in mediocritie, some to grave purposes, some to light, some to be short and brief, some to be long, some to stirre up affections, some to pacifie and appease them, and these common despisers of good utterance, which resteth altogether in figurative speaches, being well used whether it comes by nature or by arte or by exercise, they be but certaine grosse ignorants of whom it is truly spoken *scientia non habet inimicum nisi ignorantem.* (139–140)

These two rather massive periodic sentences are then followed by Puttenham's description of the Lord Keeper with his copy of Quintilian in hand: "I have come to the Lord Keeper Sir Nicholas Bacon, & found him sitting in his gallery alone with the works of Quintilian before him, in deede he was a most eloquent man, and of rare learning and wisedome, as ever I knew England to breed" (140). Sir Nicholas Bacon was not the least learned or eloquent of Tudor lawyers: It was an age that venerated the classics, read rhetorical models, and practiced the making of speeches.

The language of only a few of the Tudor lawyers has been studied—as with Fortescue, for example—and the results are most interesting; but we now need to study their learning as well, including, of course, their rhetorical theory and practice. Much remains to be done with charges to juries, arguments in court, lawyers' epistles, and that unique series of volumes which until the mid-1530s

---

[14]Quoted in "Lawyers and Rhetoric in Sixteenth-Century England," *Renaissance Eloquence*, ed. J. J. Murphy (Berkeley: University of California Press, 1983) 274–291.

recorded the actual speech and arguments of lawyers and of judges sitting in court.[15]

Learning is in large part a function of education, which generally also provides the techniques or tools of learning. What is known about education in the Inns is frustratingly little, for there are no curricula that have come down to us, as have the educational statutes of Oxford and Cambridge. We have no book prescriptions for the Inns, and few documents to indicate how the teaching (other than the governance of the moots and bolts) was done. There is in fact no documentary evidence even to indicate that rhetoric was taught within the four Inns of Court, although there is a convergence of probabilities that it was so taught.[16]

But what we do know—as I observed in "Lawyers and Rhetoric" (1983)—tells us several immensely important things about education in the Inns. The first is that all practicing lawyers took part in that education during their own years of practicing law, and that this intriguing learning-teaching relationship came to an end only with the promotion of a lawyer to serjeant, at which time he withdrew from his Inn and became a member of Serjeants' Inn. Second, we know a fair amount about the teaching method of the Inns by inference: there was a great stress on argumentation and upon the special forms of moots and bolts; and law students were expected to attend actual arguments in the law courts several mornings a week. It is this practical stress that leads almost ineluctably to the conclusion that there must have been rhetorical training somewhere along the line: at university, surely, if the student had gone there first; or in one of the subsidiary Inns of Chancery, where he would certainly have gone had he not attended university and which he probably would have attended even with one or more years of university education—although these generalizations have more force for the earlier decades of the century than they do for the latter. It is indeed possible that there was rhetorical training within the Inns of Court, even though it seems likely that there should have been some trace in the records if that had been the case, but there are great gaps that we know of in the extant records of the Inns.

I would therefore stress the continuing education from student at an Inn of Chancery through the half dozen and more years as a student in one of the four Inns of Court, to continuing participation in the teaching as a young lawyer, leading ultimately to the lawyer's own presentation of readings on individual statutes—a parallel, if you will, with advanced lectures at the universities (but nothing has been done to analyze these readings as rhetorical explication).

---

[15]Two important studies of the Yearbooks are reprinted in A. W. B. Simpson's *Legal Theory and Legal History* (London: Hambledon Press, 1986): "The Source and Function of the Later Year Books," and "The Circulation of Yearbooks in the Fifteenth Century." The Yearbooks are unique in reproducing the verbatim argument of pleaders before the judges, and for that reason they are of inestimable value in studying legal and judicial rhetoric.

[16]See, further, R. J. Schoeck, "Rhetoric and Law in Sixteenth-Century England," *Studies in Philology* 50 (1953): 110–127; and R. J. Schoeck, "Lawyers and Rhetoric" (cited in footnote 15).

To take one notable example of the continuing education of which I speak and to anchor it to the use of legal books: Louis A. Knafla has studied the annotations in one lawyer's books and from them has drawn valuable conclusions about the methods during successive phases of study and legal development and the uses to which that study was put. The lawyer was Sir Thomas Egerton, Lord Ellesmere (1540–1617), and Knafla's article appeared in the *Huntington Library Quarterly* (1969). Knafla also studied the implications of Egerton's studies of the classics and civil law in his *Law and Politics in Jacobean England* (Cambridge, 1977), especially chapter 1. Egerton has also been studied as a patron of learning by Virgil B. Heltzel in "Sir Thomas Egerton as Patron" (1948). A fruitful field for future study is that of the commonplace books of law students, which exist in some numbers at Cambridge University Library and the Folger Shakespeare Library; and one should here note the habit of a number of legal printers of printing late 16th-century books with folded-in blank pages to allow for annotation and commentary *in extenso*. Perhaps John Rainolds borrowed the concept from legal printers when he had his copy of the 1562 Paris edition of Aristotle's *Rhetoric* bound with blank pages between the printed ones, whereon he wrote his celebrated Oxford lectures on rhetoric.[17]

The many regulations of the Inns for both students and lawyers required participation in the learning exercises, which were dialectical, formalistic, and highly traditional. These regulations were peculiar to the Inns, but they were analogous to the university regulations governing the conduct of scholastic disputations, which required participation by all arts students over the period of their residence. Indeed, comparisons between serjeants at law and doctors at the universities, and between readings and disputations, occur in more than one treatise. These legal exercises obviously developed great skill in marshaling arguments pro and refuting those contra, and at the heart of their technique was the great use of rhetorical *division*. I take this skill to be the force behind Sir Thomas Smith's mid-century exclamation over the demonstration of young common lawyers that he had witnessed—the learned Sir Thomas (1513–1577, public orator at Cambridge and D.C.L. Padua) was trained in the civil law, not the common law. The following passage was given at Cambridge, not in the Inns.

> In an inaugural lecture at Cambridge Sir Thomas Smith, Professor of Roman Civil Law (who was a contemporary of Plowden as Master of the Bench at the Middle Temple), exclaimed upon the skill in disputation shown by the students of English law at the Inns of Court. Their skill extended to matters of philosophy and theology:

---

[17]These lectures have been edited and translated by L. D. Green in *John Rainolds' Oxford Lectures on Aristotle's Rhetoric* (Newark, DE: University of Delaware Press, 1986). The text of Rainolds' lectures is in Latin and Greek, and the lectures are found in Bodleian MS. Auct. S.2.29; and pointedly, Green observed that Rainolds "assumed his audience was familiar with, or had a copy of, the appropriate passage for each lecture" (91). One of the points of interest in Rainolds' lectures is his stress on the entire art of rhetoric as "a theory of teaching" (97).

"Etiam cum quid e philosophia, theologiae depromptum in quaestione ponatur, Deus bone! quam apte, quamque explicate singula resumunt, quanta eum facilitate et copia, quantaque cum gratia et venustate, vel confirmant sua, vel refellunt aliena! Certe nec dialecticae vim multum in eis desideres, nec eloquentiae splendorem."[18]

From an eccentric point of view, Abraham Fraunce in his *Lawiers Logike* (1588)—he was M.A. Cambridge 1583, then barrister at Gray's Inn—gave us yet another sense of the close relationship between law, rhetoric, and logic. There is much of literature in his translations and adaptations, as well as his ample quotations from Sir Philip Sidney.

I trust that even this rapid survey has suggested the atmosphere in the Inns of Court during the 16th century, for it was a world in which rhetoric and literature were at home with the law itself. That a Shakespeare should write with one eye for the lawyers and law students in his composite audience, and even write one or more of his plays specifically for presentation at the Inns of Court, should not now surprise us, nor should it be thought surprising that lawyers would be that much interested in the rhetoric (as well as the content and entertainment) of all his plays.

In one of the most celebrated and most long-lived books of the English common law, Christopher St. Germain's *Doctor and Student* (published at least as early as 1528), there is a cunning use of deliberative rhetoric in arguing the case for change within the law and concerning the vexatious question of the jurisdiction of canon and common law. In spite of the glaring professionalism or technicality of so much of the work, on a first reading, it is of equal interest with respect to significant aspects of Renaissance thought and letters.

The full title of St. Germain's work was *Dialogus de fundamentis legum Anglie et de conscientia*, and it was first published in Latin (of which the 1528 is the earliest extant edition); it was then printed in many English editions down to 1875. Although this work is called a dialogue (as I commented in a 1987 essay on St. Germain's rhetorical strategies[19]), it is strikingly different from the dialogues of contemporary Renaissance humanists both on the Continent and in England. That is to say, it differs strikingly from the *Utopia* of Thomas More and from the *Colloquies* of Erasmus (published from 1518 onward). The differences, one may assume, must have been deliberate, and in place of humanistic dialogue it is more likely that St. Germain had as his model something like

---

[18]Quoted in R. J. Schoeck, "Lawyers and Rhetoric" 282.

[19]R. J. Schoeck, "The Strategies of Rhetoric in St. Germain's *Doctor and Student*," *The Political Context of Law—Proceedings of the Seventh British Legal History Conference, Canterbury 1985*, ed. Richard Eales and David Sullivan (London: Hambledon Press, 1987) 77ff.

I am richly aware that the philosophical and technical aspects of St. Germain's treatise are far more complex than is indicated by the rhetorical dimension to which I have called attention: See, further, S. E. Thorne, "St. Germain's *Doctor and Student*," *Essays in English Legal History* (London: Hambledon Press, 1985).

William of Ockham's *Dialogus*. The introduction of character by St. Germain is thus perfunctory and non-Ciceronian; there is little attention to the mechanics of oral conversation (a point on which More was later to chastise St. Germain, his opponent in two of his polemical works, the *Apology* and the *Debellation*, both of which turn on conflicts between the canon and the common law); and there is little interest in the usual humanistic setting or contrived occasion—no gardens for leisurely conversation, no dinners to reward the devoted discussants. Each chapter of St. Germain's work is set up in a scholastic mode, following the principles of disputation rather than of Renaissance dialogue; and for models and dialectical resources surely we must also look further to the *questio disputata* of the scholastics as well as to the dialectic forms of the common law, the moots and bolts.

I cannot discuss the rhetorical strategies of St. Germain more fully here (I refer to my 1987 essay already cited), but the conclusions can be simply stated. Even while citing canon law authorities frequently enough, St. Germain quite neatly bypassed the authority of the canon law. It is impressive that a common lawyer should display such competence in the rival canon law, which was so different in so many ways from the common law; few of his common law contemporaries could have produced such a piece of work, and fewer still had anything like his influence. More than any other, it was St. Germain (to quote from J. W. Allen) who "expressed most clearly the nature and implications of the change that the Tudor government was bringing about and in fact seems to have been a bellwether of much of that change."[20] Nearly 70 when the *Doctor and Student* was published, St. Germain became increasingly radical in his thought and writings that followed. The force of St. Germain as an example, then, is to demonstrate the interlocking workings of law, rhetoric, and literary interests even in so unexpected a quarter.

Yet more than a dozen years before the publication of *Doctor and Student*, More had published his *Utopia*, which was recognizably part of a Renaissance humanist tradition of rhetorical treatments in dialogue and other genres of legal and political problems. The role of the legal systems and lawyers for providing justice and in making much-needed change possible is explored in book 1 with little satisfaction; and in book 2 Hythloday gives short shrift to lawyers themselves

---

[20]J. W. Allen, *A History of Political Thought in the Sixteenth Century*, 2nd ed. (London: Methuen & Co., 1941) 165; and "Strategies of Rhetoric" (cited in footnote 20) 79n.

The force of St. Germain's revolt against the authority of the canon law, which is implicit in *Doctor and Student* and made explicit in later writings, can be paralleled effectively in the career and writings of William Tyndale, whose translation of the Latin New Testament in the 1520s ran athwart the interests of churchmen: His translation of the New Testament was condemned in 1526. His 1528 book on *The Obedience of a Christen Man* laid down a double principle: the supreme authority of Scripture in the church and that of the king in the state. His arrest on the Continent in 1535 was on grounds of heresy, and he was executed by officials of the Holy Roman Empire. See my forthcoming essay on Tyndale: "Church Councils and Canon Law in William Tyndale."

by reporting that Utopians have few laws and that for laymen, access to justice is far simpler than in his European world. *Utopia* has been much studied, of course, but usually from 20th-century perspectives. I would suggest more emphasis on its fundamental opposition to the obscurantism and hyperprofessional aspects of the common law—the rigidity of a system structured on cases and writs, the isolating effect of Law-French, and other features—made it largely inaccessible to the layman, especially before the wave of printed books in the 16th century opened up areas or procedures of the until then obscure and arcane science of the law. Hythloday's presentation parallels in a most interesting way the Protestant Reformers' anti-scholasticism and their emphasis on the ability of the individual layman to read and interpret the Bible in the vernacular; yet More objects vehemently to St. Germain's analogous attacks on the canon law and its authority. Further, more attention needs to be paid, as I have urged elsewhere, to the letter of Guillaume Budé, a French humanist, lawyer, and pioneer in humanistic jurisprudence (whose letter appears in the Paris edition of More's *Utopia*); for he vigorously and directly calls for a better understanding and following of the natural law. Law, rhetoric, and literature interlock conspicuously and deeply in More's highly rhetorical and fundamentally justice-oriented little book.[21]

Further study needs to be done as well of Sir Thomas Elyot's *Book of the Governour* for its twinning of law and rhetoric; I have made a modest contribution toward such a study, but not enough. As well as in *The Book of the Governour* there is more of philosophy and rhetoric in Elyot's *Banquet of Sapience* and his Platonic dialogues, and likewise with William Baldwin (another member of the Inns of Court) in his *Treatise of Moral Philosophy*. To be sure, in later life both Thomas More and Thomas Elyot moved outside the world of the Inns of Court; but they had lived in and had been in important ways formed by that atmosphere. The Inns of Court plays of the 1560s still have not received the full and synthetic treatment they merit; nor has even that much-studied curiosity, *The Mirror for Magistrates*: a fortiori, this relative neglect is true for the Inns as a cultural institution. For in the Inns of Court the lawyers—and others who were their guests—were deeply concerned with both rhetoric and literature, and the major part of what they wrote is imbued with this interdisciplinary and sometimes trilingual approach.

Richard Hooker looms large in Elizabethan literature, and it is a happy thing that the Folger-Harvard-MRTS edition of the Works of Richard Hooker is now

---

[21] See R. J. Schoeck, "The Ironic and the Prophetic: Towards Reading More's *Utopia* as a Multidisciplinary Work," *Quincentennial Essays on St. Thomas More*, ed. Michael J. Moore (Department of History, Appalachian State University, Boone, NC: Albion, 1978) 124–134; also R. J. Schoeck, "On Reading More's *Utopia* as Dialogue," *Moreana* 22 (1969): 19–32. There is further exploration of these legal dimensions in R. J. Schoeck, "*Utopia*: A Humanistic Masterpiece," *Thomas Morus Jahrbuch*, ed. H. Boventer (Düsseldorf: Triltsch Verlag, 1989) 139–151. On humanism and jurisprudence see my essay cited in footnote 4.

complete. As part of the editorial work, close attention has been given by A. S. McGrade and other scholars working on this great edition to the legal dimensions of Hooker's great *Laws of Ecclesiastical Polity*. I echo the unqualified statement of Kermode and Hollander that "Hooker was the greatest of Elizabethan prose writers."[22] Difficult though that prose is for 20th-century students, the fault is in our students and their weak training (linguistic, rhetorical, cultural), not in Hooker—nor is it in other writers now thought difficult: Browne, or even Burton. For Hooker, one must accept the conviction that the foundation of an ecclesiastical polity (i.e., of the Church of England) is to be found in the hierarchy of divine-natural and human law; and thus the fundamental importance of book 1, with its closely reasoned discussion of the law of Nature. In one seminar I have spent an hour analyzing one sentence of Hooker's, demonstrating first his full panoply of rhetorical skills, the management of his complex thought with all of its distinctions and qualifications and its magnificent vision of a celestial hierarchy of law, and finally the persuasiveness of that writing. It is a prose which at times captures the plangency of the Book of Common Prayer: a prose which offers a superb exemplar of the reasoning that the Renaissance systems of thought could make possible—embracing more than discarded images, and including a fundamental understanding of the kinds of law and their interdependency—to the end that Hooker's book 1 becomes "a great meditation on natural, human, and divine law" (*Oxford Anthology*, vol. 1, 1424). A vital part of Hooker's education is to be found in his years as a student and then lecturer in Corpus Christi College, Oxford, with its unique twinning of Erasmian humanism and patristic theology, for there he mastered rhetoric along with Greek and Hebrew.[23] Hooker's six years as master of the Temple played a significant role in his continuing development, for the atmosphere of that Inn of Court may be seen to echo in much of his thought and writing in book 1.

A 20th-century man of letters or students of the Renaissance should reread Bacon's Essays from time to time; they offer, for the pleasures of rereading, the opportunity of testing our own changing responses to Bacon's "flinty nuggets of worldly wisdom by a worldly and ambitious man"[24]—an Elizabethan common lawyer and a most learned one. These essays might serve as a starting point for helping the 20th-century undergraduate to begin to understand the complex nature of the rhetorical prose of the period (one wonders, indeed, that it can be ignored, as the legal dimensions of Cicero cannot be slighted). Let me also remind the

---

[22]In *The Oxford Anthology of English Literature* (New York: Oxford University Press, 1973) 1:1424.

[23]I detail this development and Hooker's indebtedness to Bishop Jewel in *From Erasmus to Richard Hooker*, now in progress. One of the themes of this forthcoming work is the strong emphasis on rhetoric at Corpus Christi College as well as Hooker's study of rhetoric under John Rainolds, his tutor at Corpus.

[24]Hyder E. Rollins and Herschel Baker, *The Renaissance in England* (Boston: Heath, 1954) 903. So, too, one might add, were the *Essais* of another Renaissance lawyer, Montaigne.

reader of the ending of the essay "Of Studies": "If he be not apt to be over matters, and to call up one thing to prove and illustrate another, let him study the lawyers' cases . . ." (906).

We turn, by one or another kind of association, from Bacon to Shakespeare; and I would offer *Merchant of Venice* and *Measure for Measure* as two prime cases for demonstrating Shakespeare's knowledge (though not a professional one) of legal ideas together with the rich resources of Renaissance rhetoric and his engendering of them in his own dramatic work. I do not pursue the matter beyond wondering why commentators on the *Merchant of Venice* have not gone more deeply into the cross-currents of Tudor legislation against usury, and that in particular a 1594 legal commentary is not better known. I refer to *The Death of Usury, Or the Disgrace of Usurers, With Explanation of the Statutes now in Force Concerning Usury* (Cambridge, 1594); there were several contemporary cases that enunciated the doctrine further, and Norman L. Jones has explored the Tudor usury laws in a 1987 study.[25]

In exploring interrelations between law, rhetoric, and literature in the Tudor period, we may move to Spenser, who in book 5 of *The Faerie Queene* (and especially canto 7) offered a coherent theory of justice—albeit one rather steel-handed for our present ideals. The important point is that Spenser could not conceive of the complete knight who did not have more than a glimmering of a sense of justice in his total moral and intellectual armament: a full concept of justice was then (as now) much needed for the complete knight, or citizen.

And so to Ben Jonson and his many confrontations with issues of law, equity, malpractice, and the like in his plays—as in those of Webster and others—and beyond the 18th century (which took for granted the interminglings of law and rhetoric in its literature), to the many works of Dickens, Trollope, and Browning, in which law as an entity or institution, and constituent concepts of justice and equity, were an integral part of the structures of their narrative or poetic visions. One must stress the ordinary Elizabethan citizen's (and especially the land-owner's) familiarity with the law; Renaissance drama as a whole bears this out, but obviously there is no way of proving such a statement. One can only illustrate it in a number of ways: the plethora of legal references and situations; the use of fairly detailed legal knowledge; and the embodying of a goodly number of legal concepts.

How, indeed, can we not give consideration to law in a full and continuing study of English, or, I could add, American literature? The little volume of essays recently edited by Carl S. Smith, John P. McWilliams, and Maxwell Bloomfield (*Law and American Literature*, 1983), serves admirably as an introduction.

Much more needs to be said about and done with a number of mutual concerns of law and rhetoric. Even the study of *topoi* will throw light on "the continuing

---

[25]Norman L. Jones, "Usury in the Elizabethan Exchequer," *The Political Context of Law* (1987) 87–102. (See fn. 19).

mutual influence between rhetoric and law." Thus, as Vickers noted, the "modesty formula" (or humility *topos*) was originally derived, as in Quintilian (IV.i.8), from judicial oratory; and there is need to inquire into the continuing role of that *topos* among lawyers, as well as characteristic employments by them of other *topoi*.[26] There is the quite complex question of *status*, where there is a difference of more than emphasis between the usages of lawyers and those of rhetoricians. One final note involves the interpretation of texts, and in the 16th century we find commentators like Edmund Plowden reaching into the techniques of Scriptural exegesis to discover tools for explicating and interpreting English statutes. Recently, Ian Maclean has most searchingly compared differences between interpretation theory and praxis among the common and the civil lawyers during the 16th century.[27] And finally there is the vast area of equity, for the continuing development of which common lawyers who followed Christopher St. Germain went back to Aquinas, then to Cicero, and finally to Aristotle; and the more scholarly lawyers explored the layers of commentaries on questions of equity— even Erasmus (who early on had a spurning of common lawyers) became interested in the maxim *summum ius summa iniuria* and influenced the Basel school of jurisprudential thought.[28]

Tudor lawyers needed and valued their rhetoric. We 20th-century scholars who wish to understand more fully the manifold role of rhetoric in Tudor society, government, thought, and letters must give fuller account of these lawyers and their part in the continuing development of rhetoric.

---

[26]Ian Maclean, *Interpretation and Meaning in the Renaissance: The Case of Law* (Cambridge: Cambridge University Press, 1992). Compare Brian Vickers' valuable discussion in *Sir Francis Bacon and Renaissance Prose* (Cambridge: Cambridge University Press, 1968) 272. There is also a valuable, though brief, discussion of the humility topos ("affected modesty") by E. R. Curtius in *European Literature and the Latin Middle Ages* (Princeton: Princeton University Press, 1973) 83ff. One should also note the role of the legal maxim (studied by Peter Stein) in this area of the nurturing and shaping of legal thought by rhetorical or quasi-rhetorical forms. One should note the shrewd comments of Ann Moss on the "extremely confused terminology of 'places' in Renaissance dialectic and rhetoric": see Ann Moss, "Printed Commonplace Books in the Renaissance," *Acta Conventus Neo-Latini Torontonensis 1988*, ed. A. Dalzell, C. Fantazzi, and R. J. Schoeck (Binghamton: MRTS, 1991) 509–518.

[27]Maclean, *Interpretation and Meaning*, on which see my review forthcoming in *Renaissance Studies*.

[28]The adage *summum ius summa iniuria* was studied by Guido Kisch in *Erasmus und die Jurisprudenz seiner Zeit: Studien zum humanistischen Rechsdenken* (Basel and Stuttgart: Helbing and Lichtenhahn, 1960); and Erasmus' influence was studied in Guido Kisch, *Humanismus und Jurisprudenz: Der Kampf zwischen mos italicus und mos gallicus an der Universität Basel* Basler Studien zur Rechtswissenshaft, Haft 42 (Basel: Helbing and Lichtenhahn, 1955). See, further, G. Kisch *Gestalten und Probleme aus Humanismus und Jurisprudenz* Neue Studien und Texte (Berlin: Walter de Gruyter & Co., 1969). See Schoeck, "Humanism and Jurisprudence," for an introduction to these issues, and J. R. Schoeck, *Erasmus of Europe: Vol. 2. The Prince of Humanists 1501–1536* (Edinburgh: Edinburgh University Press, 1993) for a placement of Erasmus' thought in a biographical and historical context.

CONCLUSION

I have argued for the importance of law and rhetoric—two of our Borromeo rings—in the reading and interpretation of much literature of Renaissance England. I trust that my presentation of the case has produced a favorable verdict; and I further argue that this case would be reinforced by an appeal to the collateral examples of Rabelais, Montaigne, Bodin, and other lawyers in 16th-century France, and to Grotius and others in 17th-century Holland—all scholars and writers of *acutoritas*.

Let me underscore the fact that the lawyers whose writings I have been calling attention to all shared a sense not only of the importance of the law but also of the urgency of so many key issues of the 16th century (so many of which were legal, directly or indirectly). For Thomas More 1516 was such a moment of crisis; and I have argued elsewhere[29] that the *Utopia* addressed the perceived crisis both in English society and government and in the Christian church, by means of a unique putting together of humanistic dialogue (book 1) and rhetorical *declamatio* (book 2), with justice a powerful theme connecting these two books, and with the *parerga* of the early editions extending the discussion still farther. Next, in the 1560s, during the major decade of the Inns of Court plays, there was another such period of urgency: for a young queen had ascended the throne, and she and her nation faced grave constitutional, ecclesiastic, and legal problems. It is scarcely to be wondered that in the hammering out of a new government and a new political concept, as well as in the forging of the Church of England, young lawyers in the Inns should offer their thinking in a range of works from plays to *The Mirror for Magistrates*. And then in the late 1580s and 1590s there was a multiple sense of the imminent end of a regime with an aging queen and the uncertainty of her successor, of questions and disillusionments because of a new philosophy that called in doubt, and of the need to provide foundations for an emerging church under attack from Puritans and Papists. The fifth book of the *Faerie Queene*—published in 1596 and thus contemporaneous with the *Merchant of Venice*—is like Shakespeare's *Merchant* and the later *Measure for Measure*, an imaginative work of the first order that explored the moral depths of a troubled society and looked deeply and prismatically at problems of order. It was not only the lawyers who played with the three rings of law, rhetoric, and literature, but they were among the ringleaders.[30]

Yet another kind of argument for studying these three interrelated activities is that such a concern for law and rhetoric by those of us who are primarily teachers of literature may provide connections within the humanities so badly

---

[29]On *Utopia* see footnote 22.

[30]It may be germane to call attention to what I called the practical tradition of rhetoric, in R. J. Schoeck, "The Practical Tradition of Classical Rhetoric," *Rhetoric and Praxis: The Contribution of Classical Rhetoric to Practical Reasoning*, ed. Jean D. Moss (Washington: Catholic University of America Press, 1986) 23–42.

needed in our own time of urgency, in which overspecialization is a real and pressing problem, and we have largely failed to convince the general public, the administrators, and our own colleagues within the academy of the meaning and importance of our own humanistic enterprise. Further, such an approach can provide a bridge with the study of the law. Lawyers—especially in the United States—are even more grievously specialized than are teachers of literature; they need such a bridge, and I think that on the literary side we can make good use of more knowledge of the law and its ideas and institutions in the Renaissance world. For those of us who are primarily teachers of rhetoric, the history of rhetoric cannot be ignored (as the writings of James J. Murphy, George A. Kennedy, and others have been stressing in recent years); and one must appreciate that the intimate relationship of law and rhetoric has been repeated several times since the classical era in which so many of our culture's legal and rhetorical traditions were born: the world of the Italian universities that witnessed the renascence of legal and rhetorical studies together in the 12th century, and the immensely fruitful interrelationships of law and rhetoric in the 16th.

I leave you then with an image of three rings which should be put back into their original interconnected state—at least at some moments of study—and I leave you with a range of arguments and examples to plead the case that during the Renaissance that interconnectedness produced a complex literature that can best be understood and illuminated by a tripled approach. But the approach is more than tripartite, for that term recognizes and accepts a division into three parts, a division potentially as disastrous as Lear's division of his kingdom. It is more like a tripod, which needs all three legs of approximately equal length in order to function without embarrassment—or a triptych, which requires our viewing all three of its panels in order to complete the meaning. *The Borromeo Rings*, if you will.

ACKNOWLEDGMENTS

This chapter was first presented, in a somewhat reduced form, at the International Association for University Professors of English Congress at Lausanne (August 1989), and it still bears some references to the special audience.

Chapter 17

The Discourse of Cure: Rhetoric and Medicine in the Late Renaissance

Nancy Struever
Johns Hopkins University

All history is contemporary history, Benedetto Croce claimed. And historians' motives are present motives, often enough. The historians of rhetoric of my acquaintance, historians who have been at least slightly ill and have had some slight experience with the medical profession, have a firm conviction that medical rhetoric simply begs for analysis. But the past presents its own demands. The historian of the Renaissance finds not only doctors' rhetoric to be analyzed but also some very sharp rhetorical critiques of physicians' words. And he finds deeper, more fundamental connections between medicine and rhetoric as disciplines. Both, I argue, are rather shaky empirical sciences. Both rest their claims to certainty on control of certain methods; but both are beset by the uncertainties of empirical observation: by inadequate methods of reading and reacting to multiple and diffuse, manifest or occult signs. Beset by uncertainty, both are obliged to be interventionist, and the interventionist discourse of both attracts opprobrium. Most intriguing, they share a difficult topic: the recalcitrant, fractious domain of the passions, for appeal to the passions is the special competence of the rhetorician, while the passions are central to holistic cure in premodern medicine. I focus here on medical rhetoric, the problems with this rhetoric, the shared interests of rhetoric and medicine, and the Renaissance changes in the notions of rhetorical and medical interventions, changes that mark modernity still.

The first and simplest project is to analyze doctors' rhetoric. Here an exemplary Renaissance account precedes us. Michel de Montaigne, by virtue of his kidney stones, took the task of critique of medicine seriously. In the essay "Of the Resemblance of Children to Fathers" (vol. 2, 37), the resemblance lay, of course,

STRUEVER

in the kidney stones.[1] The long gestation of the disease in both the father and Montaigne inspires an account of disease, but also a demystification of the discourse of cure, the "sentences, threats, and consequences" of the doctors. But although he may deplore those "who know Galen well, but not sickness" (vol. 1, 25:139), the essay turns on Galenic points; its purpose is to report the "course of my humors." Indeed, the notions of Galenic humors, of the "complexion" or integral balance—physical and emotional—of individuals, pervade the essays. Galenic inquiry, however, is much more intellectually pretentious; where Galen would claim an alliance of medicine with a rigorous geometry, Montaigne undoubtedly sees medicine as functioning in the domain shared with rhetoric: the domain of probability, of beliefs rather than exact knowledge.[2]

Yet medicine is obviously the area where desire for certainty is greatest, and where the possibility of certainty is very small. In this intolerable situation, Montaigne opts for shared probabilities. In the essay "On Experience," he maintains that in cures, custom and customary beliefs are to be preferred to the unpersuasive, if authoritative, assertions of the medical profession, (vol. 2, 13:1080). His fascination with the untidy discipline of medicine and its verbal allures and his eschewal of the certitudes purveyed by medical authority define a limiting case of the possibilities of belief and develop a case for patient incredulity. It is a kind of democratization of the politics of cure, a program for talking back.

Now contrast this acerbic Renaissance critique of doctors' rhetoric with a modern analytic effort that claims that the late Renaissance provides the proper models for modern diagnostic arguments. A. R. Jonsen and S. Toulmin's *The Abuse of Casuistry* (the title refers to the wrongful attacks on casuistry rather than to its endemic faults) is a splendid illustration of Croce's dictum that all history is contemporary history. The authors, serving on a presidential medical ethics committee, found the physicians' testimony intriguing; they begin their defense of 17th-century casuistic moral argument by asserting modern clinical medicine is casuistry.[3] This immense casuistic literature, developed in great part

---

[1]M. Montaigne, *Essais*, ed. P. Villey, 2 vols. (Paris: Presses Universitaires de France, 1978); references are to essay volume and number, and page number of this edition. Two articles in K. Cameron, ed., *Montaigne and His Age* (Exeter: University of Exeter Press, 1981) describe the medical background: V. Nutton, "Medicine in the Age of Montaigne" 15–25; and M. Brunyate, "Montaigne and Medicine" 27–38.

[2]Brunyate, "Montaigne and Medicine," emphasizes the importance of "complexion" (cf. II,2:552;II,37:738; II,17:624–625), of Galenic humors, and of the intrication of body and spirit (III,5:821). On Galen's linkage of medicine and geometry see Galen, *On the Passions and Errors of the Soul*, trans. P. W. Harkins (Columbus: Ohio State University Press, 1963) 95f. Aristotle defines rhetoric as functioning in the domain of beliefs, as the "methodos peri tas pisteis," in *Rhetorica* 1355a3.

Rabelais, of course, must be considered as in the background of Montaignian initiatives; see R. Antonioli, *Rabelais et la medicine*, *Études Rabelaisiennes* 12 (Geneva: Droz, 1976), especially in regard to the intrication of mind and body in health and disease.

[3]A. R. Jonsen and S. Toulmin, *The Abuse of Casuistry; A History of Moral Reasoning* (Berkeley: University of California Press, 1988) 36f.

between 1556 and 1656, was the product of an effort to confront and dispose of the difficulties of the confessional trade: difficulties rooted in confessional confrontations over the moral economics of colonization and trade and in the vagaries of social customs such as dueling. The casuistic texts are modeled on case morality, available in and popular since Cicero, a morality that is controlled by the rhetorical principle of decorum: All argument must be appropriate to the specific occasion; general principles must be fit to the individual moral actions.[4]

Just so, they argue, and it is a rather piquant argument, the modern clinician deals with the relations of general principles of science to the individual cases for cure, because disease, like morality, resides in the realm of practice, not theory. Instead of an invidious comparison of 17th-century medical argument with modern, we have an approving connection of modern clinical work with an abused 17th-century mode, which is most surely a rhetorical mode. There are five elements of clinical (or casuist) argument: (a) there are lengthy, indirect, tangled chains of argument between case decision and general principle, either biochemistry or theology; (b) the grasp of taxonomy is essential (the depictions of genera and species of sins are very like the discriminations of syndromes, genera of symptoms); (c) analogical reasoning is used; (d) inferences are presumptive, rebuttable (no one wants to be stuck with a bad cure); (e) arguments leave room for difference.[5] Then, in both case morality—and, recall, Cicero is the model they invoke—and medicine, the whole argumentative structure is invested by an obligation to confess or cure; connections must be responsible—that is to say, appropriate—connections.[6] In other words, if the modern patient is lucky, his clinician argues in a baroque fashion. If the late Renaissance patient was lucky, his physician was a casuist.

Jonsen and Toulmin, of course, cannot elide the difficulties of casuistical or clinical argument, its susceptibility to attack, especially attacks in the name of an absolute certainty as a necessary element of religious faith or cure. This is the nature of Pascal's attack on the casuists. But casuistry as abused, as contested, points to persistent problems in the traditions of both rhetoric and medicine. To be sure, the rhetorician is more, the physician, less comfortable with the uncertainty of the belief domain; but the orator's audience, the confessee or the patient, share discomfort.

[4]Jonsen and Toulmin, *The Abuse of Casuistry* 155.

[5]Jonsen and Toulmin, *The Abuse of Casuistry* 42f.

[6]Jonsen and Toulmin, indeed, are insisting on the hegemony of the rhetorical canon of decorum in the connection of ethical obligation and the consideration of the specific case: clinical medicine is a "prototypically moral enterprise"; actions are not merely effective but also appropriate; "they fulfill his duty as physician" (42). Compare B. Croce, *History as the Story of Liberty*, trans. S. Sprigge (London: Allen and Unwin, 1941). Croce commends Montaigne's attack on book knowledge as asserting that one does not "truly know anything until under the stimulus of events . . . that [book] knowledge loses its deadly rigidity" (33). Croce points out that the medical experts "must by intuition and understanding diagnose the sickness of that patient, and that patient alone, in that way and under those conditions, and he grapples not with the formation of the illness but with its concrete and individual reality" (34).

The orator, the casuistic confessor as well as the clinician, combines upsetting power claims with a tendency to weak or confusing arguments. And in the traditions of both rhetoric and medicine there is a tentativeness, a self-questioning that invests both disciplines in their self-evaluation and, in particular, in their peculiar ambivalence about their commanding discourse.

In the long history of these ambivalences and self-questionings, the rhetoricians' own misgivings, and their attempts to repel others' misgivings, form large sections of rhetorical texts. But, to consider the rhetoric of medicine, let us begin with the classical ambivalences, for example, of Aristotle. On the one hand, he maintains that there is an easy distinction between common sense and disciplined statement: The example he invokes is the difference between a health proverb and the advice of a doctor (*Topica* 110a). Medical discourse is neat, tidy. On the other hand, Aristotle notes in his discussion of choice that agency in both politics and medicine is problematic: In both cases, deliberation is about things that occur as a result of our efforts, "though not always the same way" (*Ethics* 1112b3).[7] The control is not necessarily control of results; medicine and politics are untidy. And modern scholarship has emphasized that in the discourse of the *Corpus Hippocraticum* itself, the metaphors do not support an easy command, a simple medical control. The metaphors for bodily function are not those of a cheerful, reliable good politics and thus rational political competence; the metaphors are Homeric and depict the body as a place of conflict, where dominance is a dominance of force, violence.[8]

But the untoward politics infect the discourse of practice, of the classical doctor-patient relation. The *Corpus Hippocraticum* contains many injunctions to patients for silence, indeed, for doctor's silence. P.-J. Ottonson's description of classical and medieval semiology as one of silent observation of signs—very useful for a patient in a coma—underlines an essential element of scholastic medicine, as it is essential to the control of data: repelling the intrusion of the patients' discourse enables tidiness in systemic accounts of disease.[9]

To be sure, Rufus of Ephesus (late 1st and early 2nd century A.D.) took issue with this semiology. Relating the anecdote, in which Hippocrates praises a physician who discovered the disease profile of a city "without asking any of the inhabitants, but by his own observation," Rufus asserts that he "admires the

---

[7]Aristotle, *Topica*, ed. W. D. Ross (Oxford: Clarendon Press, 1928); also *Aristotelis topica*, ed. W. D. Ross (Oxford: Clarendon Press, 1958); when stipulating "whether the object before us tends to produce health or not" we should use not the words of *hoi polloi* but those of the *iatros*. *Ethica Nicomachea* (Oxford: Clarendon Press, 1925); also *Aristotelis ethica nicomachea*, ed. I. Bywater (Oxford: Clarendon Press, 1894); compare *Ethica* 1104a5: "Matters concerned with conduct and questions of what is good for us have no fixity, any more than questions of health."

[8]M. Vegetti, "Metaphora politica e immagine del corpo negli scritti ippocratici," *Formes de pensée dans la collection Hippocratique*, ed. F. Lasserre and P. Mudry (Geneva: Droz, 1983) 459–469; and G. Cambiano, "Pathologie et analogie politique," *Formes de Pensée* 441–458. See also J. Jovanna, "Politique et medicine," *Hippocratica*; *Actes du Colloque Hippocratique de Paris*, ed. M. D. Grmek (Paris: Éditions du Centre National tela Recherche Scientifique, 1980) 299–315.

[9]P.-G. Ottonson, *Scholastic Medicine and Philosophy* (Naples: Bibliopolis, 1984) 195–246.

man's wisdom and his excellent discoveries, but I urge anyone who is going to get full and accurate knowledge not to neglect interrogation."[10]

The ambivalence about the nature of medical discourse continues in the Western revival of the classical and Arabic traditions. On the one hand, Peter of Abano, a prominent medieval physician and author of the school text *Conciliator*, insists on the necessity of rhetoric for the doctor. He must be able to persuade the patient to take the cure; this is the textbook that claims that the doctor who persuades better, heals more. Confidence is vital.[11] On the other hand, of course, Petrarch deplores the involvement of doctors with rhetoric; they use eloquence to disguise their own defects and to blame the disease: "You are able to kill, and—*mirabile dictu*—to accuse those you kill." Petrarch attacks the "murderous" word systems, the heady abstractions of the physician removed from observation, from the semiology of symptom, the *signum*. Virgil is right, he said, in calling medicine mute: It is a mute, mechanical art; here silence connotes both efficacy and limit.[12] And certainly it is the case that professional motives in the late Middle Ages and Renaissance reinforce the discursive habits Petrarch deplores: They condone the allure of abstraction. The university physician, benefiting by an early professional elitism, defined himself as engaged in theory, although, of course, the bulk of the population was treated by practical apothecaries and barber-surgeons. V. L. Bullough reports that the status of the late medieval surgeon depends on his nonpractice, on speculation, not on manual qualification. Higher status stems from what one can learn without practice; lower status, from what one can learn in and requiring apprenticeship and "menial" work.[13] Prestige

---

[10]*Questiones medicinales*, ed. H. Gartner, *Corpus medicorum graecorum* 4, *Supplementum* (Berlin: Akademie-Verlag, 1962) s.72–73. Wesley Smith, *The Hippocratic Tradition*, (Ithaca: Cornell University Press, 1979), cites this passage on p. 241.

[11]P. Kibre, "Arts and Medicine in the Later Middle Ages," *Studies in Medieval Science* (London: Hambledon Press, 1984) 213–227. This is the most pithy maxim in Peter of Abano, *Conciliator* (Venice, 1496) Diff. 135: "Qui bene persuasus medicus magis sanat" (V2v).

[12]Petrarch, *Invective contra medicum, III*, ed. P. G. Ricci, *Prose*, ed. G. Martellotti, P. G. Ricci, E. Carrara, and E. Blanchi (Milan: Ricciardi, 1955) 648–693. The full passage where he laments the physician's use of rhetoric as not helping but injuring his art is: "Accusare, excusare, consolari, irritare, placare animos, movere lacrimas atque comprimere, accendere iras et extinguere, colorare factum, avertere infamiam, transferre culpam, suscitare suspiciones: oratorum propria hec; medicorum esse non noveram. Sed si rethorica tibi servit, quicquid vero ancille tue est, tum esse conceditur. Omnia hec, igitur, tua sunt, et quecunque alia oratoribus assignantur. Plusquam tibi permittitur, quam putabam. Potes enim occidere—mirum dictu!—et quem occideris accusare" (688). He cites Virgil, *Aeneid* XII, 397, on 690.

K. Park, *Doctors and Medicine in Early Renaissance Florence* (Princeton: Princeton University Press, 1985) 224, fn.116 cites an analogous passage from Petrarch's *Familiari* V, 19; 11.43–46. See my "Petrarch's *Invective contra medicum*: An Early Confrontation of Rhetoric and Medicine," *MLN* 108 (1993), 659–679.

[13]V. L. Bullough, *The Development of Medicine as a Profession* (New York: Hafner, 1966) 82, 93f, 110. Bullough cites some hilarious advice of late medieval medical texts for rhetorical efficacy; thus Henri de Mondeville, *Chirurgie*, trans. into French by E. Nicause (Paris: Alcan, 1893) 109, exhorts the physician to improve the mental state of the patient "by music of viols and ten-stringed psaltery, or by forged letters describing the death of his enemies, or if he is a churchman by telling him that he has been elected to a bishopric" (93).

is associated with command of the murderous word systems. Recall N. Siraisi's wry comment: The study of medieval and Renaissance university medicine at least instructs us in the difficulty of replacing entrenched systems of thought.[14]

The Renaissance and early modernity, then, are still dealing with a traditional set of aporia; indeed, a mental set that is at the very least ambivalent about words still invests modern clinical discourse with its commitment to tentative, silent *pronuntiatio*. In a recent centennial observation of Johns Hopkins Medical School, an article cites admiringly a Hopkins founding father's advice: Dr. William Osler commended his students to "look wise, say nothing, and grunt."[15] The clinician is not even monologic.

But there is a second, more intriguing level of rhetorical/medical relations. The intrications here are not simply those of the medical use of or rejection of discursive instruments, of argumentative techniques and persuasive effects. Rather, rhetoric and medicine as disciplines share difficulties, and the difficulties are structural, built into the inquiry, and affecting investigative premise and procedure in some significant way. First, bemusement with verbal conflict invested the entire history of medical learning. Thus, in the classical period the Hippocratic notion that silence is golden did not render the physicians mute. On the contrary: Wesley Smith, a historian of Hippocrates and Galen, insists that we must see Galenic theory, and especially Galen's account of Hippocrates, as shaped in the rhetoric of extreme confrontation of Roman medicine. Indeed, Smith queries "whether, and to what extent, his use of Hippocrates is simply a rhetorically applied antique patina on a strictly Hellenistic science . . ."; Hippocrates was a metaphor.[16] Galen tended to divide the traditional authorities into either "friends" or "enemies" of Hippocrates, a division that established good as opposed to bad medicine but that certainly doubled as a psychomachy of Galen and his opponents. But the adversarial tendency antedated Galen: A peculiar classical medical genre was *hamartography*, that is, the catalogue of one's predecessors' "murderous" mistakes.[17] In this genre, quarrelsomeness is an almost pathological trait, with its dominant motive the subversion of other authorities as the means of establishing one's own. And the wild success of the large corpus of Galenic texts in late antique, Arabic, and Western traditions simply embalmed for 1,500 years the confrontational rhetoric, the furious debates.

Both rhetoric and medicine stand accused of nourishing contention, verbal violence. But there are other, more fundamental thematic problems and temptations that rhetoric and medicine share. For a very long period, the parallels have been tempting. In the *Gorgias*, Plato ranks the physician's concern with health with the philosopher's concern with justice and ranks medicine above rhetorical

---

[14]N. Siraisi, *Avicenna in Renaissance Italy* (Princeton: Princeton University Press, 1987) 13.

[15]J. F. Worthington, "Osler's Sermon at the Bedside," *The Medical Centennial, Johns Hopkins Magazine* June 1989:81.

[16]Smith, *The Hippocratic Tradition* 97; compare 96, 175.

[17]Smith, *The Hippocratic Tradition* 224.

cookbookery.[18] In the *Phaedrus*, Plato asserts that both medicine and rhetoric may be practiced as mere empirical routine, *tribe* and *empeiria*, inferior to and needing "science" and a fundamental knowledge of the whole, of the nature of the body and of the soul.[19] L. Edelstein, the historian of ancient medicine, argued (according to O. Temkin) that Hippocratic empirical science did not nourish philosophy; the only contribution of medicine to philosophy was a metaphor: "the tantalising rule of the physician over man's body," a rule that seduced the philosopher into emulation.[20] What Edelstein remarks is an unsettling combination of power, instrumentality, and responsibility. A Platonic philosopher, perhaps, is unsettled by the way in which both medicine and rhetoric are interventionist: The doctor is obliged to cure, an obligation that forces casuistic argument; persuasion is a public office, a communitarian obligation of the orator that may oblige appeal to the passions. And, of course, the literatures of both disciplines share a tentativeness, an uneasiness about the goals, efficacy, and morality of their interventions. Recall that Jonsen and Toulmin point out that an essential trait of casuistic argument, for moralist or clinician, is that it must allow for rebuttal, change of diagnosis, change of cure. And surely Quintilian realizes that he is arguing against the grain when he stipulates that control of the emotions (*adfectus*) is the central capacity of the orator, indeed, that at times his duty is to draw the mind of the judge away from the truth by this control.[21]

I now argue that the most important issue confronting the historian of medicine and rhetoric in the late Renaissance is the peculiar and innovative involvement of both disciplines in the redefinition of the passions. The redefinitions not only change the possibilities of eloquence and cure but also serve as the submerged but powerful context of the attitudes toward physical and moral interventions in modernity. In the late Renaissance and in early modernity there is an exemplary expression of this disturbingly vital issue. The text of Descartes' *Les Passions de l'âme* (1649) is of extreme interest because Descartes attempts to address the

---

[18]Plato, *The Collected Dialogues*, ed. E. Hamilton and H. Cairns (Princeton: Princeton University Press, 1963); the analogy that rhetoric is to justice as cookery is to medicine can be found in 463b, 464d, 465c, 500b; medicine ranks higher because it has "investigated the nature of the subject it treats and the cause of its actions and can give a rational account of each" (501a); he contrasts (knowing) medical persuasion with (ignorant) rhetorical persuasion in matters of health (456b, 459a).

[19]*Phaedrus* 269, 270b–d; also *Platonis Opera* II, ed. J. Burnet, (Oxford: Oxford University Press, 1901). Smith regards the account of Hippocratean science in 270d as an authentic relation of Hippocrates, *The Hippocratic Tradition* 46f.

[20]O. Temkin, "Introduction," *Ancient Medicine: Selected Papers of Ludwig Edelstein* (Baltimore: Johns Hopkins University Press, 1967) xi.

[21]Quintilian, *Institutio oratoria*, trans. H. E. Butler (Cambridge, MA: Harvard University Press, 1960) VI,ii,5: "Ubi vero animis iudicum vis adferenda est ab ipsa veri contemplatione abducenda mens, ibi proprium oratoris opus est." See also VI,ii,7: "adeo velut spiritus operis huius atque animus est in adfectibus." See P. H. Schryvers, "Invention, imagination, et théorie des emotions chez Ciceron et Quintilian," *Rhetoric Revalued*, ed. B. Vickers (Binghamton: Medieval and Renaissance Texts and Studies, 1982) 47–58.

most fundamental metaphysical issues of mind/body relations by definition of the passions. And in his prefatory letter, Descartes claims he speaks as a physician; it is precisely the medical perspective that is needed.[22]

Behind the Cartesian text, however, is not simply the work of Harvey and the new anatomists, but also classical rhetoric as well as classical medicine: accounts that have many resemblances and shared points of view. An archetypical rhetorical account of the passions can be found in Quintilian's *Institutio oratoria*, books 6 and 11. Quintilian states flatly that the rhetorician's capacity to "move" depends on the capacity to imitate, represent the passions.[23] In the transition between books 5 and 6, the transition between argument and passionate appeal, Quintilian claims that although the philosophers would prefer not to deal with the passions, to deal only with reason, this is not an option in the legal practice of the courts.[24] Moreover, Quintilian's distinction between *ethos* as mild, gentle feelings and *pathos* as violent feelings exacerbates the point: The rhetor must use violence, force; he must perturb the audience.[25] To be sure, although his stipulation that the orator must first experience the passions himself demands a kind of symmetry that can pass for sincerity; the rhetor self-consciously functions in the domain of fiction, of fantasy and vivid imagination as the sources of feeling. Vividness, vitality, "fire" are the things he must communicate to the judge.[26]

But the mention of fire invokes the Hippocratic elements, humors, temperaments; the discussion turns on the physical as well as the imaginative. The strong connection in book 11 is between the task of moving the passions as object and the body as domain. It is to the delivery, *pronuntiatio*, that the audience responds: "Ut audit, movetur" (XI, iii, 2). Our voice is dependent on the strength, robustness, moisture of our lungs; our memory is dependent also on our physical condi-

---

[22]Descartes, *Les Passions de l'âme, Oeuvres*, ed. C. Adam and P. Tannery (Paris: Vrin, 1967) XI, 326: "Mon dessein n'a pas este d'expliquer les Passions en Orateur, ny mesme en Philosophe moral, mais seulement en Physicien." Montaigne, of course, uses the expression "passions de l'âme," as in I,42:263, II,12:596; and there were many linkages of "soul" and "passions": I,4:32; I,38:234; II,2:345; II,11:427; II,12:491,519,551,567; II,33:729. See my "Rhetoric and Medicine in Descartes' *Passions de l'âme*; The Issue of Intervention," in *Renaissance-Rhetorik; Renaissance Rhetoric*, ed. Heinrich Plett (Berlin: Walter de Gruyter, 1993) 196–212.

[23]Quintilian, *Institutio oratorio* XI,iii,156–157: "Movendi autem ratio aut in repraesentandis est aut imitandis adfectibus"; it is the control of "phantasia" that is essential; compare VI,ii,29f.

[24]Quintilian, *Institutio oratorio* VI,i,7: Quintilian acknowledges that "philosophers" see appeal to emotions as immoral, yet "necessarios tamen adfectus fatebuntur, si aliter obtineri vera et iusta et in commune profutura non possint." Or: "Nobis ad aliorum iudicia componenda est oratio, et saepius apud omnino imperitos atque illarum certe ignaros litterarum loquendum est . . ." (V,xiv,29).

[25]The passage concludes: "quos, nisi et delectatione allicimus et viribus trahimus et nonnumquam turbamus adfectibus, ipsa, quae iusta et vera sunt, tenere non possumus" (cf. VI,ii,24). The distinction between *ethos* and *pathos* is an important argument; see VI,ii,8f.

[26]On the necessity of the orator's first feeling passions (VI,ii,26f): "Primum est igitur, ut apud nos valeant ea quae valere apud iudicem volumus, adficiamurque antequam adficere conemur"; compare XI,iii,61–62. On the need for "real" fire and moisture, see VI,ii,28.

tion.[27] Quintilian recalls that gesture, *actio*, is most important to Cicero; in his own treatment, Quintilian goes into extremely fine detail about gesture and deportment as communicating—or not—passion and fire.[28] He appeals to the case of the actors to demonstrate the enormous difference between poetry heard and poetry read.[29] But the overarching rhetorical criterion, missing in drama, is decorum, appropriateness: Voice, gesture, argument all must be entirely suited to the nature of the defendant, and the orator's capacity is itself dependent on his own nature—a personal decorum that supports his strategies of decorum.[30]

The parallel account in classical medical texts is Galen's *On the Passions and Errors of the Soul*. The intertwining of moral wisdom and *bene dicendi* is a *topos* of Quintilian; the intertwining of moral philosophical instruction and medical cure is a Galenic *topos*. Passion, as an internal, violent force acting in the body, can be the source of error. Pervasive in his account is the metaphor of disease; both passion and error are described as operable or inoperable cancers, needing surgery or beyond surgery.[31]

The goals of cure are embedded in this view of the functionality of every part of body and spirit in regard to the whole. This telic notion embeds in turn the rules of "complexion," harmony, natural bent, balance; his doctrine integrates the four elements with the four humors with the four temperaments.[32] Suggestively rhetorical is the Galenic stipulation of decorum as canon; complexion, harmony, balance are a physical appropriateness. Each individual is to attempt correction and cure according to his own natural propensities: one must achieve one's own proper complexion.[33] And error in Galen's account represents another doubling of interest and investment. The domain of rhetoric is the domain of beliefs. Errors of the soul, for Galen, are inadequate believing practices: not simply false and

---

[27]"Adfectus omnes languescant necesse est, nisi voce, vultu, totius prope habitu corpis inardescunt" (XI,iii,2). XI,iii,19, emphasizes the importance of "firmitas corporis"; compare XI,iii, 20f, 40f, 78.

[28]XI,iii,1f is a discussion of *pronuntiatio* or *actio*; *pronuntiatio* was important to Demosthenes as well (XI,iii,6); on *ignis*, 'fire', see XI,iii,3.

[29]"Documento sunt vel scenici actores, qui et optimis poetarum tantum adiiciunt gratiae, ut nos infinito magis eadem illa audita quam lecta delectent . . ." (XI,iii,4).

[30]XI,i; XI,iii,177,181; indeed, the whole of book 11 is an exposition of the importance of decorum as canon.

[31]Galen, *On the Passions and Errors of the Soul*, trans. P. W. Harkins, (Columbus: Ohio State University Press, 1963); the text is in *Corpus medicorum graecorum* V, ed. W. de Boer, (Leipzig: Teubner, 1937): "Can you not take and tame this thing which is not some beast from outside yourself but an irrational power within your soul, a dwelling it shares at every moment with your power of reason?" (46); the metaphors of ill-health are pervasive, as on 37, 43, 53, 54, and 86.

[32]On the doctrines of the four humors, elements, and temperaments, and on the telic notion of body and function, see O. Temkin, *Galenism: Rise and Decline of a Medical Philosophy* (Ithaca: Cornell University Press, 1973) 17f; and Smith, "From Hippocrates to Galen," *The Hippocratic Tradition*.

[33]"Decorum" is a matter of paying attention to the nature, complexion, and balance of a patient; see Galen, *On the Passions* 54–56; compare Smith, *The Hippocratic Tradition* 96f.

reckless assent but weak assent, a failure to affirm what one's training authenticates, as in the failure of an elderly geometer to assent to Euclid's theorems.[34]

Then, in his discussion of cure, Galen connects moral-philosophical, medical, and discursive moments: the primary resource for the ordinary, self-loving individual is the counsel of others. Galen insists on the necessity of a mentor and the mentor's interventionist discourse in enabling both diagnosis and cure.[35] Indeed, Galen's positive account of the mentor is not all that different from Quintilian's praise of the mature orator.

In the classical program, the diagnosis of passions by the mentor is central to cure, and the representations of the passions constituted the core of the orator's power. In the Renaissance texts that provide the context of Descartes' *Passions of the Soul*, the intrication of passions and errors, cure and correction, is pervasive. Again, health becomes a moral choice, error is like disease, and discourse is the instrument of cure. For example, a very simple rhetorical and poetical expression of the program is the *topos* of poetry as a sweetener of bitter moral medicine (Sir Philip Sidney uses Montaigne's rhubarb as an example) or the *topos* of eloquence itself as medicine for the soul.[36]

And certainly, the continuities between classical program and Cartesian are many. Descartes' descriptions of the passions recall classical literary and dramatic usages. They recall, indeed, the rhetorical injunctions of *pronuntiatio*; his accounts are standard, derived. His passions are literary but locatable, physical. The Cartesian insistence on the door-like or valve-like function of the pineal gland to connect body and spirit is very like the stipulation in medieval Arabic texts of the function of the *vermis*, a worm-like door or valve that gave or denied access to the various ventricles of the brain. The point in both accounts is to concretize, to render physical, the initiation of mental acts.[37] Descartes' passions are truly locatable: they are the "perceptions, sentiments and emotions of the soul" that manifest themselves in flushing, heat, cold, trembling, contractions of the heart. Descartes certainly speaks as a physician, but his descriptions are those of the orator's *actio* and of the defendants' feelings that the orator must imaginatively present in his *actio*.[38]

Yet I also argue that the Cartesian formulations show signs of strain, of a sharp discontinuity with the classical, an intervening episode of great revisionary

---

[34]On false and reckless beliefs, see Galen, *On the Passions* 74; on weak assent, 74–75.

[35]Galen, *On the Passions* 32f, 78–79, 107.

[36]Heinrich Plett, *Rhetorik der Affekte* (Tubingen: Niemeyer, 1975) cites Sidney's *Apology for Poetry* on 134 and Harrington's *Brief Apologie of Poetrie* on 128.

[37]E. Ruth Harvey, *The Inward Wits; Psychological Theory in the Middle Ages and the Renaissance* (London: Warburg, 1975) 15; describes the *vermis* from Haly Abbas, *Royal Book*, trans. Stephen the Philosopher (Venice, 1492).

[38]*Passions de l'âme*, Art. 27; in Art. 1, Descartes recalls specifically a strategy of a Renaissance rhetorician, Lorenzo Valla, when he claims that action and passion are two names for the same thing; Valla also collapsed *pati* and *actio*; *Repastinatio dialectice et philosophie*, ed. G. Zippel (Padua: Anetenore, 1982) I,154; II,445.

force. We must not forget that there is no simple, direct link between classical medicine and rhetoric and Descartes' eloquent applications of early modern anatomical discoveries; we must confront the interventions of Christian anxiety. Peter Brown, in *The Body and Society; Men, Women, and Sexual Renunciation in Early Christianity*, remarks the "metaphysical ferocity" of the late antique Christian intellectual. Horrified by the pervasive decay and death of the world around them, the Christian theorists make the Paulinian assertion of the opposition of flesh and spirit into the basis for a radical program of metaphysical transformation. The Stoic sage, surely the model for Galen's mentor, is warped, distorted in their spiritualist mirror. But at the same time, the Christian elite, intrigued, like the non-Christian intelligentsia, by doctoring and medical speculation, specify the body as the site of conflict. The notion of the error of the passions is radicalized, and sexual purity and continence becomes the key strategy of liberation from the dying world and decaying flesh.[39]

The subtext of Brown's book is that the survival and triumph of the Christian sect owes in great part to its deliberate selection of the body as the domain for the strategies of radical differentiation of Christian identity and truth. Although I would not claim that virginity is a metaphysical gesture for Descartes, it is the case that, exacerbated by another episode of Christian metaphysical ferocity, the almost intractable mind/body issue became the site of major metaphysical confrontation in the late Renaissance and early modernity. The debate pushes the implications of mind/body linkages to an almost vertiginous edge, drives the debate to the articulation of "metaphysical horror." The thesis of L. Kolakowski's stimulating essay on this horror is that the strenuous search for an ultimate ground and an absolute meaning for the physical universe is simply the obverse side of an intense experience of human fragility. He also notes that desperate metaphysics enables science; certainly the contemplation of the relation of material to spiritual raises the issue of cure in a fundamental way.[40] And, of course, the description of the passions is a means of confronting the mind/body problem. In Descartes' text on the passions there are very troubling boundaries, very questionable limits assigned to body and soul. Perhaps Gilbert Ryle's metaphor of the Cartesian model—"the ghost in the machine"—should be revised as "the ghost trapped in the machine," or "the ghost caught in the gears of the machine." Descartes' premise of the indivisibility of the soul entails that the soul is truly joined to all the body (30, 68). And, in a peculiar phrase, he claims that there is "no subject" that acts more immediately against our soul than the body to which it is joined (2). Further, the machine is dominated by two very different kinds of moving

---

[39]Peter Brown, *The Body and Society* (New York: Columbia University Press, 1988); a continuous strategy of Brown is to footnote the involvement of spiritual interests and bodily preoccupations by means of intermingled references to medical and devotional texts. He also describes Tertullian as "a Stoic, and like so many of his contemporaries, a voracious reader of medical literature" (77); Gnosticism is, of course, a "cure" (108).

[40]L. Kolakowski, *Metaphysical Horror* (Oxford: Basil Blackwell, 1987) 13, 15.

parts. The passions and the spirits are intricated with each other, and their normal functioning can create untoward as well as toward effects in morality and health. The "passions of the soul" are the perceptions, sentiments, or emotions that, although they relate particularly to the soul, are caused, entertained, and fortifed by movements of the "spirits" (27) defined as "air" or "wind," the most live and subtle parts of the blood (7, 10). The passions are thus invested in the whole body, and they are given to the soul primarily to incite the soul to consent and contribute to actions in the interest of the body (40, 47, 137). The will, the only *actio* of the soul, does not have the power to incite the passions. The passions are absolutely dependent on the body (41); thus the soul is not entirely in control of the passions (46). The confusion is compounded in that the actions of the soul can cause movements of the very spirits that, in turn, cause, entertain, and fortify the passions of the soul. Descartes' passages on the evocation, dissimulation, and the uses of the passions for health or illness could be taken straight from any rhetorical text; but the rhetorical descriptions are embedded in accounts of involuntary physical actions. It is a moral Moebius strip, a continuous loop of reversible relations of body and soul, the physical and the moral.

Descartes, then, attempts simplification and tidiness but produces difficulties. The new anatomy, especially Harvey's contribution, lends precision and detail to the account of bodily process. But the contributions of rhetoric remain very strong; the orators, in claiming the passions as their peculiar competence, had made the case, the case Descartes uses, for the centrality of the passions in the economy of action. The new medical material provides a bizarre, distorting environment; Harvey lends credence to a physical isolation totally subversive of the old, interpersonal Galenic and rhetorical moments. Descartes' struggle to describe the sources of passion and his particular emphasis on "interior" moments simply underline his difficulty in articulating introspective evidence; the accounts produce a heavily textured solipsism, a solipsism that serves to question and diminish communication and communitarian issues. In modernity, community medicine and communitarian rhetoric struggle for identity in this damaging environment.[41]

For ascertaining the limits of spirit and body, of course, ascertains the limits of spiritual/bodily intervention. The holistic assumptions that had funded both

---

[41]Compare Vico's critique of Descartes in the *Autobiography*, trans. M. Fisch and T. Bergin (Ithaca: Cornell University Press, 1944). Although Descartes' text is more useful to medicine than to ethics, it is not *particularly* useful, for the anatomists did not find the Cartesian man in nature (130). See G. Cantelli, *Mente, corpo, linguaggio* (Florence: Sansoni, 1986) on Vico's intrication of body into his new science of society; and recall the important thesis of the *New Science*, trans. M. Fisch and T. Bergin (Ithaca: Cornell University Press, 1968) 1045, that language is the bridge between mind and body.

C. Gallotti argues that dualism is not Cartesian, but an invention of his followers; she presents a much more complicated notion of union/distinction. Union—the experiential rapport of the subject with reality—is combined with distinction—an analytic category for philosophy: C. Gallotti, "Un capitolo del confronto Ragione-Passioni; Il Dibattito sul Teatro," *Teorie delle passioni*, ed. E. Pulcini (Dordrecht: Kluwer, 1989) 83 n.1.

Galen's and Quintilian's programs continue to invest the Renaissance dialogue. Granted the presumptions of holistic medicine, the adjustments then define cure; briefly, the greater the interest in the spiritual, the psychic, the greater the faith in psychotherapy and, in particular, in discourse as cure and therapeutic counsel. But again, the most troublesome Cartesian legacy is perhaps, the pervasive solipsism. The moral/physical scenarios are irrevocably private. Civility seems to be defined as a simple extension of egoist, solitary interests to "someone else" (64f, 154f, 194f). Cure addresses a lonely combat, inside the skin. Medical cure is intensely personal, a cure of the self; it must include or be thwarted by the intimate relations of passions and body. And think of the Cartesian obsession with the "reality" of dreams—"so interior, so close, so remarkable" (26); the obsession is a significant piece of the deep background of Freudian cure, for example. For the rhetorician, the model produces no interesting arguments for civility, no basis for civil interventions; and rhetorical eloquence may call itself the medicine of the soul, but its verbal effects must play themselves out in a machine. Thus the mind/body issue shaped not only the medical debate, but the very notion of debate or counsel itself. Rhetorical as well as medical capacity is at stake.

Descartes' *Passions of the Soul* represents a concatenation of ill-sorted elements: Christian metaphysical anxiety, the new medicine, the old classical rhetoric and medicine. This revisionary work on the passions provides not simply notions of intervention, of medical and rhetorical cure, but also the context for cure: a difficult context, a pickle. But there are useful as well as disturbing results of these 16th- and 17th-century debates. First, the skepticism that is both cause and manifestation of Cartesian horror subverted a Renaissance piety toward the classics, a piety that cheerful scholars of humanism tend to regard as the most solid achievements of Renaissance rhetoric. In the 16th century, for example, an important contribution of rhetorical skills to medical doctrine was the development of humanistic medicine; rhetorical analysis of texts was vital to the philological recuperation of Galen and other classical medical texts. But Hippocratists such as Sydenham (1624–1689), dismayed by the counterproductivity of scholastic medicine, regretted the recapture of Galenic systemic doctrine and advocated a return to experience and observation, to Hippocrates' way.[42] Medical philology, no matter how sophisticated rhetorically, was beside the point.

Crucial to Ian Hacking's account of the "emergence of probability" in the 17th century, then, is the anti-textual moment. "The concept of internal evidence of things," he argues, "is primarily a legacy of what I shall call the low sciences, alchemy, geology, astrology, and in particular medicine. By default they could deal only in opinion. They could achieve no demonstrations and so had to resort to some other mode of proof."[43] Medicine is, therefore, part of a domain where

---

[42]Smith, *The Hippocratic Tradition* 20; Temkin, *Galenism* chap. 4, "Hippocratists vs. Galenists."

[43]Ian Hacking, *The Emergence of Probability* (Cambridge: Cambridge University Press, 1975) 35; compare Ottonson's discussion of *signum, Scholastic Medicine* 195f.

a new notion of and approach to the evidence of signs is worked out; and a new relation between the "ordinariness" of experience retailed in these signs is tied to the "probability" of mathematical rules. One could perhaps argue that this is a deeper kind of rhetorical commitment: to ordinary usage and to the domain of the probable, two Quintilianesque allegiances, to be sure. But the low sciences developed a sense of sign as not authorial testimony, not textual authority; and this liberates inquiry from Renaissance obsessions with textuality. The fragmentary, disinterring use by the new collectors and *curieux* of the signs to be found in the classical texts dismantles authoritative classical schools.[44] Instead of a philology that nurses the text's authority and the authorial identity, instead of staging a series of intertextual confrontations as personal confrontations of great personages, the investigator deals in vestiges, traces of experiments, experiences. Although the low sciences prejudice the unitary authority of the text, they prejudice as well the use of texts to maintain boundaries of schools, disciplinary begged questions. Medicine as a low science undermines the rhetoricians' naive antiquarian zeal and sponsors rhetoric's liberation from textuality. Philology counts; orthodox results, the perpetuation of classical schools, do not.

Exemplary of Hacking's thesis is the work of the Neapolitan Lionardo Di Capoa. His *Il Parere* (1681), a history of medicine functioning as a history of philosophy, is anti-text and anti-authority.[45] The humanistic recuperation of classical medical texts was of little importance, he claims, for the loss was no great loss. He does not lament their destruction by the barbarians, for if the lost texts were like the ones recovered, they are eminently forgettable. Further, part of the loss of ancient texts was due to the ancients' own failings: early Greek brilliance was suffocated in the weed-like growth of Hellenistic scholasticism, a decline into mere sophistry.[46] Di Capoa gloomily notes that in the 17th century only medicine, of all the arts, still suffers under the yoke of Aristotle and Galen.[47] He deplores Galen's enchantment with the "frivolous toys of Logic"; certainly philosophy does not gain at the expense of rhetoric.[48]

---

[44]K. Pomian, *Collectionneurs, amateurs, et curieux; Paris, Venise: xvie–xviiie siècle* (Paris: Gallimard, 1987).

[45]Lionardo Di Capoa, *Il Parere del Signor Lionardo di Capoa Divisato in otto ragionamenti ne quali partitamente narrandosi l'origine, e l progresso della medicina, chiaramente l'incertezza della medesima si fa manifesta* (Naples: Bulifon, 1681). Ragionamento 1 is translated by N. Lancaster as *The Uncertainty of Physick* (London: 1684). See M. Rak, "Una teoria dell'incertezza (Note sulla cultura Napoletana del sec. xvii)," *Filologia e letteratura* 5 (1969): 233–297. It should be remembered that the *Parere* was written in response to a demand for a political program for control of physicians' practice.

[46]Di Capoa, *Parere* Rag. 1, 35; Rag. 4, 240f.

[47]Di Capoa, *Parere* Rag. 6, 397. It is intriguing that Di Capoa recognizes the Renaissance rhetorician Lorenzo Valla as the first to liberate philosophy from a blind and miserable servitude to Aristotle (Rag. 8, 633). And, to be sure, this is an insight of Vico's as well (*Autobiography* 119).

[48]The phrase is from Di Capoa, *The Uncertainty of Physick* 78.

And it has always been observed, that as men have been more or less addicted to philosophy, proportionably more or less frequent have been the contests and wranglings of the Physicians: which is a manifest sign that these controversies proceeded from men's more or less examining the defects of their art.[49]

Di Capoa, indeed, develops a chronology of skepticism. Medicine's ineluctable uncertainty, dubiety, and inconstancy gives rise to sects, envy, slander, high contention, and this produces skepticism. Skepticism in turn nourishes quarrel, contest without pause or end. Still, he asserts that the physician is obliged to overcome uncertainty; the quarrels eventually foster a hope of progress, a zeal for advance. The history of painting, for Lionardo, demonstrates the possibility of progress, of surpassing the ancients. To be sure, progress generates different quarrels; he notes the mixed reception of Renaissance progress: of Paracelsian chemistry, of Vesalian anatomy.[50]

Skepticism was recognized as imperiling intervention. Giambattista Vico, writing shortly after Di Capoa, registers the burden of skepticism when he claims that "medicine had declined into skepticism. . . . Galenic medicine, which, when started in the light of Greek philosophy, and in the Greek language had produced so many incomparable doctors, had now, because of the vast ignorance of its followers, fallen beneath contempt." What he deplores is the failure to practice; the physicians, concluding "the impossibility of comprehending the truth about the nature of diseases . . . suspend judgement, withhold assent, withhold cure."[51] Indeed, the revival of Hippocrates in the 17th century took place in the context of "expectative therapy," the therapy of "observe, wait, and see"; just so, the revival of Hippocrates in the 19th century took place in the context of therapeutic nihilism. Splendid results in diminishing morbidity in early 19th-century hospitals were achieved by eschewing clinical interventions, eliminating the cures of doctors—and this nourished Hippocratean caution.[52]

The rejection of Galen in the 17th century was a rejection of an academic, dysfunctional discourse. At the same time, the stakes were never higher in the debates of learned men; Vico dubs the academic rejection of Galen as immoral in result. The mind/body issue readjusts, as we have seen, the terms that define the status and role of learning in physical intervention, of learned discourse as therapy, cure. The very ground shifts beneath the feet of orator and physician. Yet even though the nature and necessity of their interventions are questioned, a strong effect of the metaphysical crisis is to rethink the efficacy of counsel, of discursive interventions for the sake of health—moral and physical—against disease—moral and physical. We have, in short, early versions of the modern materialist confrontations with psychoanalysis. It is of interest that Descartes'

---

[49]Di Capoa, *Parere* Rag. 1, 35–36.
[50]Di Capoa, *Parere* Rag. 1, 48–49, 51, 58, 65.
[51]Vico, *Autobiography* 132.
[52]Smith, *The Hippocratic Tradition* part 1.

Passions of the Soul manages to pursue both materialist and psychic arguments at once. The 17th-century consideration is not simply the relation of language, mind, and reality, an epistemological issue, but the relation of language, mind, and the body as experienced reality. The vector pursued is succinctly indicated in Digby's aphorism: "Where philosophy leaves off, medicine begins."[53]

CONCLUSION

This chapter has been merely suggestive; it makes the claim that combining accounts of the careers of rhetoric and medicine in the radically changing context of Renaissance and early modernity would be useful. The rewards of such an inquiry are embedded, it seems to me, in that intriguing text, Robert Burton's *Anatomy of Melancholy*.[54] Burton's eccentric recapitulation of classical and contemporary medical material transpires in an atmosphere of genteel but mildly hair-raising crisis. He takes account of scholastic system and skeptical critique without favor. And he succeeds in posing, in a most recessive way, the major issues of the discourse of cure.

There are, minimally, three kinds of problems. First, there is the problem of the words of the healer. Di Capoa remarks, or laments, medical persuasion as the most forceful of all: "O forza, dell'arte del persuadere medicinale, alla quale ogni altra forza d'eloquenza convien che ceda!"[55] Surely, although the 17th-century rhetorical/philological recuperation of Galen may have been a fool's errand, there is something engaging and even charming about the *consilia*, the collections of actual medical advice to patients, of Cardanus (1501–1576), Di Capoa's favorite physician. His lengthy diagnosis and suggested therapy addressed to Archbishop Hamilton are familiar in tone, egalitarian in pose, and full of the kind of holistic advice we now associate with New Age medicine; Cardanus would have great vogue in Santa Fe. But the *consilia* were humanistic in a strict historical sense; they represented a recuperation of a piece of the classical past, of Galen's notion of healing as the gentle, psychiatric interference of a counselor, of the discourse of a mentor. Much of the specific advice has to do with the diets, airs, waters, places of Hippocratic interest; it is commonsensical, not only in its Renaissance context of medical ineptitude, but even to us.[56] Burton's accounts of *consilia* in all their vast profusion argue a similar and charming reduction, a unified strategy accosting all medical rhetoric.

---

[53]Everard Digby, *Theoria analytica* (London: Bynneman, 1579) 374: "Illa medicinam informat ubi namque desinit Philosophus ibi incipit Medicus."

[54]Robert Burton, *Anatomy of Melancholy*, 2 vols. (Oxford: Oxford University Press, 1989–90). Of particular interest to the rhetorician are the sections on cure by persuasion, good counsel; for instance, partition 3, section 2, member 5, subsection 3; section 3, member 4, subsection 1; section 4, member 2, subsection 6.

[55]Di Capoa, *Parere* 32.

[56]See M. Fierz, *Girolamo Cardano, 1501–1576* (Basel: Birkhauser, 1983) 41f.

Second, there is the problem of words to the healer: Foucault, in his formulation of knowledge as power, insisted on the patient's knowledge as a naive, low-ranking knowledge, as a disqualified, subjugated discourse.[57] Burton requires of the patient "obedience, constancy, willingness, patience, confidence, bounty etc., not to practice on himself."[58] Yet although Burton may be bemused by the "tantalising power of the physician over the body," the overwhelming detail of the erudition he proffers simply encircles, neutralizes that power. And Burton also suggests a different but quintessentially Renaissance perspective. Montaigne's valetudinarianism, one could argue, is a discursive tactic for the patient, a defense against the subjugating tactics of the physician. Burton's effort, as well as Montaigne's, was a bid for autonomy. Valetudinarianism is a strong initiative in Western literature, a strategy to counter the powerful semiology of silence of the physician.

Third, there is the problem of words accounting for disease: Therapeutic nihilism merely acknowledges the fact that medicine transpires in an uncertain domain of opinion and beliefs. Jonsen and Toulmin's casuistic description of clinicians' argument stresses the complicated and responsible nature of proper diagnostic practice. Their identification of 17th-century moral discourse and 20th-century clinical discourse was a strong tactic in the recognition of medical discourse as not merely amenable to rhetorical analysis, but strongly imbued with rhetorical values. As a final *exemplum*, consider the current statements on cancer: Leukemia is not a disease, but a range of diseases; recognizing the heterogeneity of disease stipulates a multitude of cures. Thus the obligation to cure, to intervene, is governed, as Burton exhaustively and encyclopedically demonstrated, by the rhetorical canon of decorum, by the need to discover the appropriate cure for a specific occasion. Cures have policies. As long as rhetoric and medicine dare to intervene, just so long they must argue the reasons for intervention.

---

[57]M. Foucault, "Two Lectures," *Power/Knowledge*, ed. C. Gordon (New York: Pantheon, 1980) 82.

[58]Burton, *Anatomy* partition 2, "synopsis," member 4, subsection 2.

Chapter 18

Deconstruction's Designs on Rhetoric

Brian Vickers
Eidgenössische Technische Hochschule, Zurich

Throughout its long career, rhetoric has been put to the most diverse uses. Originally called on to codify speeches in legal disputes, adapted by the Greeks and Romans for both legal and civic uses, moving from the law court to the forum and thence to the schoolroom, it permeated many areas of medieval culture and experienced a full-scale revival in the Renaissance.[1] In the four centuries since then it has been applied to all literary genres, to architecture, painting, music, and dance, to acting and singing, and to such unlikely practices as double-entry

---

[1]For the history of rhetoric see, for instance, G. Kennedy, *The Art of Persuasion in Greece* (London: Routledge and Kegan Paul, 1963); G. Kennedy, *The Art of Persuasion in the Roman World (300 BC–AD 300)* (Princeton, NJ: Princeton University Press, 1972); G. Kennedy, *Classical Rhetoric and Its Christian and Secular Tradition from Ancient to Modern Times* (Chapel Hill, NC: University of North Carolina Press, 1980); G. Kennedy, *Greek Rhetoric Under Christian Emperors* (Princeton, NJ: Princeton University Press, 1983); J. J. Murphy, *Rhetoric in the Middle Ages. A History of Rhetorical Theory from St. Augustine to the Renaissance* (Berkeley: University of California Press, 1974); J. J. Murphy, ed., *Medieval Eloquence. Studies in the Theory and Practice of Medieval Rhetoric* (Berkeley: University of California Press, 1978); J. J. Murphy, ed., *Renaissance Eloquence. Studies in the Theory and Practice of Renaissance Rhetoric* (Berkeley: University of California Press, 1983); M. Fumaroli, *L'Age de l'éloquence. Rhétorique et "res literaria" de la Renaissance au seuil de l'époque classique* (Geneva: Droz, 1980); P. France, *Rhetoric and Truth in France. Descartes to Diderot* (Oxford: Oxford University Press, 1972); J. Dyck, *Ticht-Kunst. Deutsche Barockrhetorik und rhetorische Tradition* (Bad Homburg: Gehlen, 1966); H. Schanze, ed., *Rhetorik. Beiträge zu ihrer Geschichte in Deutschland vom 16.–20. Jahrhundert* (Frankfurt: Athenaion, 1974); P. W. K. Stone, *The Art of Poetry 1750–1820. Theories of Poetic Composition and Style in the Late Neo-Classic and Early Romantic Periods* (London: Routledge and Kegan Paul, 1967).

bookkeeping.[2] It has worked with, and on occasion been rejected by, neoclassicism, romanticism, and realism, and no doubt naturalism, surrealism, and modernism. Every age, every school, it almost seems, has adapted rhetoric to its own ends, remade it in its own image. Rhetoric is the chameleon of the human sciences.

Yet even rhetoric has its boundaries, limits beyond which it cannot go, forms that it cannot adopt without destroying its own essential nature. In the recent approaches by that modern brand of skeptical philosophy known as deconstruction, I argue, the attempt to appropriate rhetoric merely brings out the fundamental incompatibility between two systems.

PART ONE

The word *deconstruction* was coined in the 1960s by Jacques Derrida to translate the term *Destruktion*, used by Heidegger in *Sein und Zeit* (1922), and was originally meant to be understood not "in a negative sense (to demolish) but in a positive sense (to circumscribe)," so that "the aim of a 'deconstruction' in philosophy would be to show how philosophical discourses are constructed."[3] Yet this neutral orientation gradually gave way to a critical, indeed polemical, approach as Derrida evolved a more extreme theory of language. Several constituent ideas were brought together to create a theory that in effect denied language the power to communicate determinate meaning. First Derrida acquired, only in order to undermine, Edmund Husserl's notion of presence, according to which the signified object must be present in order to fulfill the signifying intention. Vincent Descombes judges this requirement "unjustifiable" but notes that Derrida's opposed claim, " 'total absence of the subject and object of a statement,' " is equally unjustified.[4] Raymond Tallis has also commented on the violent opposed reaction in Derrida, by which "the impossibility of Husserlian *metaphysical* presence" is taken to imply "the impossibility of presence *tout court*," that is, "ordinary presence meant in the ordinary sense."[5] In a typically extreme inversion, Derrida concludes that "since presence is an unachievable absolute, it must be nothing."[6]

The second idea that Derrida takes over in his denial of language's ability to convey determinate meaning is the notion of the linguistic sign as formulated by Saussure in his *Cours de linguistique générale* (1916).[7] Saussure defined the

---

[2]For the application of rhetoric to other arts see, for instance, B. Vickers, *In Defence of Rhetoric* (Oxford: Oxford University Press, 1989). For its adoption in accountancy see J. A. Aho, "Rhetoric and the Invention of Double Entry Bookkeeping," *Rhetorica* 3 (1985): 21–44.

[3]V. Descombes, *Modern French Philosophy* (Cambridge: Cambridge University Press, 1981) 79.

[4]V. Descombes, *Objects of All Sorts. A Philosophical Grammar* (Oxford: Blackwell, 1986) 63–65.

[5]R. Tallis, *Not Saussure. A Critique of Post-Saussurean Literary Theory* (London: Macmillan, 1988) 205.

[6]Tallis, *Not Saussure* 208.

[7]For the complicated publishing history of this text, and for evaluations of Saussure, see L.-J. Calvet, *Pour et contre Saussure* (Paris: Payot, 1975); R. Harris, *Reading Saussure. A Critical Commentary on the 'Cours de linguistique générale'* (Oxford: Blackwell, 1987); and D. Holdcroft, *Saussure, Signs, System, and Arbitrariness* (Cambridge: Cambridge University Press, 1991).

linguistic sign (or word, roughly translated), as the unique fusion of an idea or concept with an acoustic image, terms that he subsequently replaced with the notions *signified* and *signifier*, which constitute two mutually defining parts:

concept	signified
acoustic image	signifier

Saussure constantly stressed that the two halves were inseparable, like the front and back sides of a piece of paper.[8] However, starting with Lévi-Strauss in 1950, it became general practice to split up the sign into two separable parts and to then designate a "floating signifier" (Lévi-Strauss, Lacan, Barthes), or assert "the primacy of the signifier" (Lacan), or celebrate "the free play of the signifier" (Barthes, Foucault).[9] Derrida was entirely traditional in taking over this fragmented notion of the sign and the related idea of a desirable "free play" or exemption from signification. Third, Derrida took over from Heidegger the notion of the *trace*, the vestige or relic of meaning that language can leave behind.[10]

In addition to other borrowings from Plato, Rousseau, Nietzsche and Mallarmé, summed up in specially coined phrases or neologisms, Derrida evolved a concept of his own, *différance*, a coinage intended to unite the two senses *différer* can have in French, 'to differ' and 'to defer'. Misquoting and misinterpreting what Saussure meant by *différence*, Derrida combined these various borrowings to propose a view of language marked by failure or at least indeterminacy, as in these typical assertions:

> The sign represents the present in its absence.... When we cannot grasp or show the thing, . . . when the present cannot be presented, we signify, we go through the detour of the sign.... The sign, in this sense, is deferred presence.... [The] circulation of signs defers the moment in which we can encounter the thing itself, . . . intuit its presence.[11]

> The signified concept is never present in and of itself, in a sufficient presence that would refer only to itself.... Every concept is inscribed in a chain or in a system within which it refers to the other, to other concepts.[12]

---

[8]Ferdinand de Saussure, *Cours de linguistique générale*, ed. T. de Mauro (Paris: Payot, 1972) 97–100, 155–157; translated by W. Baskin as *Course in General Linguistics* (New York: The Philosophical Library, 1959) 65–67, 111–113.

[9]See Descombes, *Modern French Philosophy* 96; Descombes, *Objects*; M. Angenot, "Structuralism and Syncretism: Institutional Distortions of Saussure," *The Structural Allegory. Reconstructive Encounters with the New French Thought*, ed. J. Fekete (Manchester: Manchester University Press, 1984) 150–163.

[10]On Derrida's debt to Heidegger see, for instance, P. Dews, *Logics of Disintegration. Post-Structuralist Thought and the Claims of Critical Theory* (London: Verso, 1987); M. Frank, *What Is Neostructuralism?*, trans. S. Wilke and R. Gray (Minneapolis: University of Minnesota Press, 1989) [orig. *Was ist Neostrukturalimus?* (Frankfurt: Suhrkamp, 1984)]; L. Ferry and A. Renaut, *La pensée 68. Essai sur l'anti-humanisme contemporain* (Paris: Gallimard, 1985).

[11]J. Derrida, "Différance," *Margins of Philosophy*, trans. A. Bass (Chicago: Chicago University Press, 1982) 9.

[12]Derrida, "Différance" 11.

Every process of signification [is] a formal play of differences. That is, of traces.
... The play of differences [means that] ... no element can function as a sign
without referring to another element which itself is not simply present. This
interweaving results in each "element"— phoneme or grapheme—being constituted
on the basis of the trace within it of the other elements of the chain or system. . . .
Nothing, neither among the elements nor within the system, is anywhere ever
simply present or absent. There are only, everywhere, differences and traces of
traces.[13]

I have chosen relatively simple and straightforward Derridian pronouncements,
avoiding the repetitions, inflations, and tergiversations that seem designed to
exhaust the reader, to make him or her lose all powers of independent judgment
and forget that there is a world outside. Derrida's categorical assertions, his
argument via metaphor, his begging all important questions, and his other viola-
tions of logical and rational canons of discourse have been often enough objected
to, and a substantial literature already exists challenging his account of language.[14]

I do not need to make yet another refutation, so I will simply take it as
axiomatic that any such conception of the infinite postponement of meaning or
the indeterminate nature of reference would mean the death of rhetoric. If language could not be reliably understood, whether instantly (as in the great majority
of communication acts), or after further reflection (as when reading poetry or
philosophy of considerable density), then there would be no point in developing
powers of eloquence or argument. No rhetorician I have heard of was ever so
foolish as to think that language could make things actually present; but everyone
who uses and understands a natural language knows what it means to make
things, people, landscape, states of mind, and even abstract concepts like justice
or mercy present to the mind's eye, as we say. Anyone with a smattering of
knowledge of classical rhetoric can recall a whole group of figures that describe
various ways of achieving visual presence: *hypotyposis, prosopographia,
prosopopoeia, evidentia, enargeia*, and many more. If language could neither
denote nor refer reliably, then it could neither describe nor be used to arouse
emotions in the service of judgment. It would become a useless, pointless tool.

Anyone reading these lines who is not familiar with deconstruction is already
wondering how, if language is truly so unreliable, its critics can convey their
own case reliably. That is indeed a fundamental objection, which Derrida tried
to meet by affirming that of course his discourse partakes of the weakness of
the system it sets out to attack. This apparently generous acknowledgment is in
fact an attempt to beg the question further, for nothing in Derrida's voluminous
utterances has ever managed to call language in question. Although he and his

---

[13]J. Derrida, *Positions*, trans. A. Bass (Chicago: Chicago University Press, 1981) 26.

[14]See, for instance, J. R. Searle, "Reiterating the Differences: A Reply to Derrida," *Glyph* 1
(1977): 198–208; and J. R. Searle, "The World Turned Upside Down," *New York Review of Books*
27 October 1983: 74–79.

followers have claimed that deconstruction has questioned "the whole of Western metaphysics" (or "Western philosophy," in some even more grandiose formulations), a historian of philosophy has shown that it has managed to challenge only a small part of phenomenology, namely, Husserlian descriptions.[15] The technique used to perform these mighty feats relies on finding words in philosophical texts that have what Derrida calls " 'a double, contradictory, undecidable value.' "[16] If philosophers have done their work properly, the common reader might well believe, there cannot be many such words, or else the structure of the whole work would be insecure. But, as Edward Said points out, Derrida is trying to reveal "the *entame*—tear, incision" in philosophy deriving from the "*entame* already inscribed in written language itself by its persistent desire to point outside itself. . . ."[17] Derrida's whole system rests on the denial that language could ever reliably refer to reality.

Finding the *entame*, however, involves Derrida in a curiously artificial process that actually calls in question the system he himself has expounded. As M. H. Abrams shows in two classic essays,[18] Derrida first assumes that language works in the normal way, construes passages in his chosen author as conveying determinate meanings, but then finds " 'strands' " in the text "which, when read determinately, turn out to be mutually contradictory."[19] Where other readers might see this as a sign of incoherence in the author or pursue the issue by contextual analysis to establish whether the contradiction is profound or merely superficial, Derrida takes the discrepancy as simply proving his point about the endless play of differences, the infinitely deferred closure of meaning along the chain of signs until it reaches the "transcendental signifier," and so forth. But, as Abrams shows, Derrida depends on a strangely "deliberate anomaly," namely, that:

> He cannot demonstrate the impossibility of a standard reading except by going through the stage of manifesting its possibility; a text must be read determinately in order to be disseminated [fragmented, divided] into an undecidability that never strikes completely free of its initial determination; deconstruction can only subvert the meanings of a text that has always already been construed.[20]

---

[15]Descombes, *Objects* 61–62.

[16]Cited by E. W. Said, *The World, the Text, and the Critic* (London: Faber and Faber, 1983) 206.

[17]Said, *The World* 207.

[18]M. H. Abrams, "The Deconstructive Angel," *Critical Inquiry* 3 (1977): 423–438; and "How to Do Things With Texts," *Partisan Review* 46 (1979): 566–588; both reprinted and quoted from Abrams, *Doing Things With Texts. Essays in Criticism and Critical Theory*, ed. M. Fischer (New York: W. W. Norton, 1989) 237–256 and 269–296, respectively.

[19]M. H. Abrams, "Construing and Deconstructing," *Romanticism and Contemporary Criticism* (Ithaca, NY: Cornell University Press, 1986) 127–157; reprinted in and quoted from Abrams, *Doing Things* 277, 304–306.

[20]Abrams, "Construing" 310.

That is an acute diagnosis of the inherent weakness of deconstruction, that it is parasitic on a system that it violently assaults yet never transcends. Indeed, as John Ellis has shown in his penetrating analysis, deconstruction is highly unsatisfactory in attacking things as they are without ever offering an alternative or superior system.[21] The Derridians' counter would be that the critic has no need to offer a replacement. But what if Derrida's position were misguided in the first place?

PART TWO

Whatever the notionally constructive possibilities of deconstruction, in practice it has turned out to be a polemical, destructive, unsettling critical practice. The thesis from which it begins, that language is inherently unreliable, can mean only that the critic seeks out darkness not light, fissures or cracks rather than solid structures. To quote only two of the dozens (hundreds?) of programmatic statements now in circulation describing this desire to obscure or undermine, we could attend to Paul de Man, in *Allegories of Reading*,[22] affirming that: "Deconstructions of figural texts engender lucid narratives which produce, in their own turn and as it were within their own texture, a darkness more redoubtable than the error they dispel" (217). Or, to vary the metaphor, consider J. Hillis Miller's description of how a critic should dismantle the structure of a literary work:

> The deconstructive critic seeks to find, by this process of retracing [each textual labyrinth], the element in the system studied which is alogical, the thread in the text in question which will unravel it all, or the loose stone which will pull down the whole building. The deconstruction, rather, annihilates the ground on which the building stands by showing that the text has already annihilated that ground, knowingly or unknowingly. Deconstruction is not a dismantling of the structure of a text but a demonstration that it has already dismantled itself.[23]

Given this orientation toward finding the flaw or fissure in a system, it is not surprising that deconstruction should have tried to fissurize rhetoric, in what I shall describe as the first phase of their relationship. So in his essay "Semiology and Rhetoric" (1973), reprinted in *Allegories of Reading*, de Man opposed grammar and rhetoric, semiology and deconstruction, inasmuch as semiology identifies grammatical features of a text, whereas, he claimed, deconstruction identifies

---

[21] J. M. Ellis, *Against Deconstruction* (Princeton, NJ: Princeton University Press, 1989) 69–82, 88–89.

[22] Paul de Man, *Allegories of Reading* (New Haven: Yale University Press, 1979); page references incorporated in the text.

[23] J. H. Miller, "Stevens' Rock and Criticism as Cure: II," *Georgia Review* 30 (1976): 330–348, quotation from 341.

rhetorical features. Having created this fundamental divide, de Man was understandably irritated with a number of contemporary critics for "letting grammar and rhetoric function in perfect continuity, and in passing from grammatical to rhetorical structures without difficulty or interruption" (6). Anyone familiar with the history of education in the West, from the Greeks to the 19th century, knowing that grammar, rhetoric, and logic formed the *trivium* that dominated two thirds of any student's school and university career in this period, will congratulate Barthes, Genette, and the others for getting the relationship between grammar and rhetoric right. To de Man, however, "the continuity . . . between grammar and rhetoric is not borne out by theoretical and philosophical speculation" (8). This vast assertion, which attempted to overturn more than two thousand years of humane studies, was supported with a paragraph referring in the most general terms to Kenneth Burke and C. S. Peirce (8–9: giving neither quotations nor references). De Man then illustrated "the tension between grammar and rhetoric" through "the so-called rhetorical question," citing an incident from the American television series "All in the Family" in which Archie Bunker, "asked by his wife whether he wants to have his bowling shoes laced over or laced under," answered, "with a question: 'What's the difference?' " Credit must be given to de Man for seeing that this remark can mean " 'I don't give a damn what the difference is' "; yet he used it to drive Archie into the deconstructionist's impasse: "The same grammatical pattern engenders two meanings that are mutually exclusive: the literal meaning asks for the concept (difference) whose existence is denied by the figurative meaning" (9). But, clever though this seems, de Man simply confused the two implications of the question, namely, difference to me and difference between, making a conflict between literal and figural meanings out of the question's unstated predicate.

This is only the beginning of a whole series of fateful deductions about rhetoric and its sister disciplines made by de Man from this banal anecdote. Archie Bunker's question was said to address the nature of "the difference between grammar and rhetoric"—seldom has so massive an issue hung on so slender a thread!—without resolving it: "grammar allows us to ask the question, but the sentence by means of which we ask it may deny the very possibility of asking" (10). Ordinary readers may by now be wondering why de Man should have so perversely missed the obvious point, but more experienced ones will recognize him straining to prove, yet again, from his own humble instances, the founding theses of deconstruction. Archie's question was now said to reveal "his despair when confronted with a structure of linguistic meaning that he cannot control and that holds the discouraging prospect of an infinity of similar future confusions, all of them potentially catastrophic in their consequences" (10). As a description of this fictional television character's state of mind, this is patently absurd; but as a *profession de foi déconstructionniste* it was obviously important to de Man. In fact, as I have shown elsewhere, de Man regularly leaped from quoting a potentially negative or nihilistic remark by a writer he was studying (Rousseau, say, or Mallarmé) to erecting it as a general statement about language, or literature, or life itself.[24] So, within nine lines of the last passage quoted, de Man made this remarkable assertion: "Rhetoric radically suspends logic and opens up vertiginous possibilities of referential aberration." That remark might score eight points on the Derrida scale, but reference to de Man's text does not reveal any coherent relationship between it and the preceding argument.[25] It is, then, the kind of remark that the deconstructionist needs to make just to prove that his system is working and the others are not.

Having tried to locate fissures between grammar and rhetoric,[26] and rhetoric and logic, de Man also offered to make one in rhetoric itself, which he understood in the sense of "the study of tropes and of figures, . . . and not in the derived sense of comment or of eloquence or of persuasion" (6). But this turns rhetoric upside down, or inside out: The tropes and figures were, precisely, means of persuasion, not separable from it; and ability in persuasion or eloquence was the prime goal of a rhetorical training, not "the derived sense." De Man complained that a recent critic, having conceived rhetoric "exclusively as persuasion, as actual action upon others (and not as an intralinguistic figure or trope)," was able to show a continuity between grammar and rhetoric (8). It never occurred to him that that critic had things the right way up, and that he had them upside down. De Man attempted to generalize or legitimize his practice by claiming in his preface that his view exemplified a "shift from historical definition to the problematics of reading . . . which is typical of my generation" (ix). (De Man was born in 1919.) This shift could "lead to a rhetoric of reading," he remarked (as if no one else had ever done this); and he described his work on Rousseau, Proust, and Rilke as exemplifying a "rhetorical scheme" or a "process of reading in which rhetoric is a disruptive intertwining of trope and persuasion . . ." (ix). Let it be said quite clearly that the disruption was all de Man's work, and that the intertwining of trope and persuasion in rhetoric is otherwise entirely harmonious and functional, uniting to bring about a successful act of communication and (it is hoped) persuasion.

---

[24]See Brian Vickers, *Appropriating Shakespeare* (New Haven: Yale University Press, 1993) 165–213.

[25]S. M. Olsen also commented on this "completely unwarranted conclusion . . . (or maybe . . . not unwarranted but simply nonsensical)": S. M. Olsen, *The End of Literary Theory* (Cambridge: Cambridge University Press, 1987) 205. As he notes, the general trend of this argument is to claim that deconstruction "is inclusive where semiology is exclusive," because it deals with "every conceivable" feature of a text (205–206).

[26]Denis Donoghue also asked "why does de Man present a strict choice between grammar and rhetoric, since he has already granted that one does not exclude the other," and since one of de Man's acknowledged authorities, C. S. Peirce, argued that "the laws studied by pure grammar, logic, and pure rhetoric do not contradict one another; they apply simultaneously": Denis Donoghue, *Ferocious Alphabets* (London: Faber and Faber, 1981) 175. The answer must be that de Man was really interested in finding "incompatible readings" (174), such as those he diagnosed in Proust between metaphor and metonymy, a claim that Donoghue has subjected to a courteous but devastating analysis (175–184).

Perhaps because he believed that such acts are impossible—an example given by Rousseau is said to be "textually ambiguous, as all situations involving categorical relationships between man and language have to be" (151)—de Man's relationship with rhetoric was deeply divided. He was obviously fascinated by it, used rhetorical figures in his own writing, and often referred to them by name (albeit inaccurately). However, he also attributed to rhetoric, or projected onto it, deep fissures, structural incompatibilities such as this between trope and persuasion. So in an essay called "Rhetoric of Persuasion (Nietzsche)," after a rather wandering discussion of some of the late fragments grouped together by Nietzsche's sister and posthumously published under the inadequate and misleading title, *The Will to Power*, de Man offered, with very little preparation, this extraordinary judgment on rhetoric:

> Considered as persuasion, rhetoric is performative but when considered as a system of tropes, it deconstructs its own performance. Rhetoric is a *text* in that it allows for two incompatible, mutually self-destructive points of view, and therefore puts an insurmountable obstacle in the way of any reading or understanding. The aporia between performative and constative language is merely a version of the aporia between trope and persuasion that both generates and paralyzes rhetoric and thus gives it the appearance of a history. (131)

I have commented elsewhere on the illogicalities in that passage,[27] its travesty of rhetoric, considered as a judgment. Here I cite it as an example of the deconstructive mode of criticism which, as used by de Man, emerges as a full-blast negation with very little connection to the analysis or argument that precedes or follows. In fact, one has to wait until the last paragraph of the book to find de Man reverting to what he claimed to be the fundamental fissure that he discovered, or created, when he comments on Rousseau's *Confessions* that "performative rhetoric and cognitive rhetoric, the rhetoric of tropes, fail to converge" (300). That judgment was reiterated with some of the favorite recurring terms in this book: "disruption . . . discontinuity . . . undoing . . . aberration" (300–301). That belated addition gave no support to the diagnosis.

The organizing thread of de Man's work was just such acts of inversion, reversal, negation, often pulling authors and readers toward a nothingness or void. In this mode he used or invoked rhetoric freely, now a valuable tool in his deconstruction kit. In the chapter called "Tropes (Rilke)" de Man spent much time analyzing *chiasmus* (a figure, of course), which he found abundantly in Rilke as image of a general "reversal of the figural order . . . that crosses the attributes of inside and outside and leads to the annihilation of the conscious subject . . ." (37). Explaining that he found it "preferable to reverse the perspective," echoing Foucault and others by not conceiving "the poem's rhetoric as the

---

[27]Brian Vickers, *In Defence of Rhetoric* 464; also Brian Vickers, "The Atrophy of Rhetoric, Vico to de Man," *Rhetorica* 6 (1988): 21–56.

instrument of the subject" but rather seeing the subject as serving "the language that has produced" it (37), de Man declared that in Rilke's poetry "the determining figure" was "chiasmus, the crossing that reverses the attributes of words and of things" (38). That would be a remarkable achievement in the first place, one may feel, to be able to distinguish attributes separately assignable to *res* and *verba*, let alone to reverse them. How could one make such a separation? Not deigning to clarify his point, de Man subsequently suggested that the reader of Rilke's *Neue Gedichte* could "isolate the poles around which the rotation of the chiasma takes place," identify "a reversal of their categorical properties" that is so total that the reader could then "conceive of properties that would normally be incompatible (such as inside/outside, before/after, death/life, fiction/reality, silence/sound) as complementary. They engender an entity, . . . which is also a closed totality" (40). I cannot disguise my disbelief that any of these pairs of opposites can be compatible, such that both parts—silence and sound, death and life—could apply simultaneously, or that they could form "a closed totality." It seems to me that de Man was playing with the spatialized metaphor of poles and rotations, making a purely verbal manipulation that could find no empirical grounding either in reality or in the texts cited. What this claim really reveals is the extent to which de Man was possessed by the processes of opposition and reversal. Within three pages all these supposedly "closed totalities" in Rilke were said to suffer many forms of "reversals: reversal of . . . inside and outside, of death and life" and so on (43). This swing from one pole to another is much more typical of de Man's restless running forward and back on the continuum he had set himself. Having itemized in detail patterns of reversal in Rilke (43–49), de Man attained the climax toward which so much of his writing strove, the void: "Chiasmus . . . can only come into being as the result of a void, of a lack that allows for the rotating motion of the polarities" (49). That is, the "experiences, like the figural objects" that Rilke chooses as figures "must contain a void or a lack if they are to be converted into figures. It follows that only negative experiences can be poetically useful" (50). Once again the argument is perfectly coherent at the level of deconstructionist expectations (reversal: incompatibility: reversal: lack: void: negation), only it is in no way borne out either by the analysis of Rilke's poems or by the nature of this rhetorical figure. Chiasmus, we may counter, never comes into being as the result of a void, into which its opposed terms might sink. Rather, it presupposes a plenum artificially limited to polar opposites that can be interchanged in order to make a specific point, often ironical.

De Man appropriated rhetoric in these essays to fulfill characteristic deconstructionist goals. A certain repetition can be traced in his work, a certain monotony, as writers in very different genres, in different historical periods and languages, are judged to be using the same figures for the same goals. So in Proust, de Man found "two apparently incompatible chains of connotations," opposing light/dark and inside/outside, "so frequent that they could be said to make up the entire novel"—a grotesque exaggeration—and once again he put them into an exchange relationship that seemed to reconcile incompatibilities (60 and note). Yet de Man promptly went on to discover "numberless" instances of a "failure" to unite the oppositions (71), a constant "disjunction" that "undoes the pseudo-synthesis"—his "pseudo-synthesis," we remember—"of inside and outside, . . . container and content, . . . metaphor and metonymy, that the text has constructed" (72).[28] A specific rhetorical figure, *synecdoche*, was even said to be "one of the borderline figures that create an ambivalent zone between metaphor and metonymy and that, by its spatial nature, creates the illusion of a synthesis by totalization" (63n.). But it was only in de Man's scheme of things, riven by reversibility, striving toward impossible syntheses in the knowledge of their unattainability, that synecdoche had such a role.

The essay on Proust went through a whole series of reversals, first repeatedly emphasizing the "complementarity" between his categories of literal and figurative, inside and outside (68–70) but then introducing "another set of binary themes, those of 'love' and 'voyage,' " which represented "the irresistible motion that forces any text beyond its limits and projects it towards an exterior referent." But the text also asserted "the impossibility for any consciousness to get outside itself," paradoxically wishing but unable to "remain . . . esconced," so that, "like so many objects and so many moments in Proust's novel, it has to turn itself out and become the outer enveloping surface" (70). This "disturbing movement, a vibration between truth and error," de Man claimed, "functions like an oxymoron," but "is in fact an aporia" (the rhetorical figure expressing doubt or uncertainty), describing "at least two mutually exclusive readings" (70). In Proust, de Man claimed, the two meanings, literal and allegorical, "fight each other with the blind power of stupidity," while the "polarity of truth and falsehood" led to "the confrontation of incompatible meanings between which it is necessary but impossible to decide," an impasse in which one can no longer "allegorize the crossing, or chiasmus, of two modes of reading" (76–77). As ever, rhetoric for de Man was in the service of division and irreconcilability.

---

[28]De Man followed Roman Jakobson's influential but schematic and impoverishing opposing of metaphor and metonymy. See Vickers, *In Defence of Rhetoric* 442–453 for critical comment on Jakobson's theory, including the penetrating objections by Gérard Genette. De Man made another idiosyncratic division, identifying metaphor with necessity and totalization, metonymy with mere chance and contingency (*Allegories of Reading* 13–18, 62–63) and then set out to challenge the superiority usually accorded to metaphor (14ff, 67ff). Several critics have objected that the two figures cannot be separated so clearly, nor judged "epistemologically incompatible." Christopher Butler argues that "the metonymic implications of metaphor, far from being epistemologically 'incompatible' with it, are simply the interpretation by which it becomes intelligible to the reader": Christopher Butler, *Interpretation, Deconstruction, and Ideology. An Introduction to Some Current Issues in Literary Theory* (Oxford: Oxford University Press, 1984) 69–70. Fredric Jameson argues that "the concepts of metaphor and metonymy cannot be isolated from each other": Fredric Jameson, *The Prison-House of Language. A Critical Account of Structuralism and Russian Formalism* (Princeton, NJ: Princeton University Press, 1972) 123. See also Donoghue, *Ferocious Alphabets* 181–183.

In Nietzsche, too, de Man found the polarity "Appearance/Thing," the division "between figural and proper meanings in a metaphor" (90). Commenting on Nietzsche's own lectures on rhetoric (which he grievously misrepresented[29]), de Man found here, too, a striking "property of language" as having "the possibility of substituting binary polarities such as before for after, early for late, outside for inside, cause for effect, without regard for the truth-value of these structures" (108). Certainly that comment applies to de Man's own use of these polarities in his essays on Rilke and Proust, where the "truth-value" seems highly doubtful. It is more appropriate to find such reversals in Nietzsche, the great master of the ironical recoil on the self that undermines the preceding argument (a trick that makes him fascinating to read but a terrible model for philosophy). Yet, having detected in Nietzsche not only reversed patterns but even "the reversal of the categories of good and evil" (112), de Man went on to claim that Nietzsche's "original pairing of rhetoric with error"—original to de Man, that is, and never justified—"was based on the cross-shaped reversal of properties that rhetoricians call chiasmus." The "very process of deconstruction," as practiced by Nietzsche, turned out to be "one more such reversal that repeats the selfsame rhetorical structure." Indeed, de Man affirmed, "all rhetorical structures, whether we call them metaphor, metonymy, chiasmus, metalepsis, hypallagus, or whatever, are based on substitutive reversals . . ." (113). The lumping of "all rhetorical structures" under this description shows how much de Man had become obsessed by patterns of reversal, and why rhetoric was so useful to him.

This monotonous, all-embracing experience of reversal and substitution was later said to typify not only Rilke, Proust, and Nietzsche, but also Rousseau, who used "a binary system" in which various terms stood "in polar opposition to each other" (145). Actually, Rousseau is said to oppose not just specific terms but—a development that made him a guinea pig for deconstructionist linguistics—two attitudes to language, "on the one hand, figurative, connotative, and metaphorical language and, on the other, denominative, referential and literal language" (146). The first type, metaphorical, is said to "correspond exactly" to what de Man defined as the basic human process of "conceptualization, conceived as an exchange or substitution of properties on the basis of resemblance" (146), a new and (to me at least) hopelessly idiosyncratic idea. Predictably, de Man saw Rousseau opposing "the two modes antithetically to each other," in order to allow "for a valorization that privileges one mode" (146). But, equally predictably, de Man immediately denied Rousseau competence in the "referential linguistic model," diagnosing in him a "failure . . . to 'name' the subject" of his

[29]See Vickers, *In Defence of Rhetoric* 459–466; Vickers, "Atrophy of Rhetoric" 46–53. For a more detailed study of how de Man perverted Nietzsche's rhetoric see Brian Vickers, "Nietzsche im Zerrspiegel de Mans: Rhetorik gegen die Rhetorik," *Nietzsche oder "Die Sprache ist Rhetorik,"* ed. J. Kopperschmidt and H. Schanze (Munich: Wilhelm Fink, 1994) 219–240, in English as "De Man's Schismatizing of Rhetoric," ed. S. IJsseling and G. Vervaecke (Louvain: Leuven University Press, 1994) 193–247.

autobiography (this point was simply taken over from another critic and taken by de Man to be so self-evident as to need neither argument nor citation of texts), a failure that then "undercuts the authority of Rousseau's own language" and made his text "truly incoherent" (147). Because one of Rousseau's texts started by considering the metaphor of the "state of nature," de Man asserted that it therefore "reverses the priority of denomination over connotation that it advocates" (147). There was no extended analysis of the text's argument, no discussion of just how and why this metaphor was used, no demonstration that it did indeed oppose those de Manian categories, merely a categorical assertion enacting the making and collapsing of distinctions that became an obsessive feature of de Man's thought. That this process of reversing or destroying categories lay deeper than the overt argument[30] is, I think, clear from this passage discussing metaphor:

> Paradoxically, the figure [metaphor] literalizes its referent and deprives it of its para-figural status.... Metaphor overlooks the fictional, textual element in the nature of the entity it connotes. It assumes a world in which intra- and extra-textual events, literal and figural forms of language, can be distinguished, a world in which the literal and the figural are properties that can be isolated and, consequently, exchanged and substituted for each other. This is an error, although it can be said that no language would be possible without this error. (151–152)

Any distinction between language and reality has to be abandoned, according to de Man, for "language . . . speaks about language and not about things" (152–153). All notion of reference, then, must be abandoned as an "aberration" (160, 161, 162, 169, 170, 182, 185, 186, 187, etc.).

At this point I end the discussion, although my account of de Man's compulsion toward reversal is not complete, because it is clear by now that such a view

---

[30]Having completed this analysis I followed up Stanley Corngold's essay, "Error in Paul de Man," *Critical Inquiry* 8 (1982): 489–507, which includes a discussion of the "extreme degree of repetitiveness" in de Man's work, especially the "simple, even mechanical inversion" of traditional categories (500). De Man's "procedure," Corngold observed, "is invariably, first to call attention to, establish, or otherwise mark a difference, a line distinguishing an inside from an outside—between, for example . . . metaphor and metonymy," or grammar and rhetoric. "This refined distinction, however, is no sooner formulated than it is taken away, the opposition tampered with and effaced." The couple grammar/rhetoric is now " 'certainly not a binary opposition since they in no way exclude each other,' " whereas claims "made on behalf of metaphor . . . to the same extent belong—and do not belong—to metonymy" (501). Corngold acutely noted that "the effacement of specific differences points . . . to universal indetermination," what de Man called " 'a suspended uncertainty,' " or " 'suspended ignorance' " (502). As Corngold showed, "more and more radically, de Man registers the principal undoableness of all distinctions . . . because the grammatical and rhetorical, the performative and constative, dimensions of such utterances are *a priori* at odds" (503), pronounced as such by de Man. Corngold judged de Man's principle of "omnipotent disjunction" an "arbitrary dictum," pointing to "a universal void of indetermination" (503 and note). In that sense one could say that de Man used rhetoric in order to define or dramatize his world view and in this way assigned a functionality and a representative linguistic role to it, that his explicit theory of language would deny. Such contradictions are, of course, proof to deconstructionists that their system really works.

of language as a self-contained entity is wholly antipathetic to rhetoric. Quintilian was able to create his famous metaphor of eloquence as a sword, copied by innumerable other writers on rhetoric, because he could confidently invoke the literal, referential attributes of a weapon to describe the conquering power of rhetoric. Deny language the ability to refer to the world, and rhetoric becomes pointless. De Man's fascination with language led him toward rhetoric; and his own writing certainly used figures of antithesis or reversal to perform the self-canceling, self-undermining skeptical critique beloved of deconstruction. Only he never seemed to have realized that his ideology and methodology canceled out rhetoric too.

PART THREE

The other prominent figure in the deconstruction movement who showed a strong but also ambivalent attitude to rhetoric was J. Hillis Miller. A great admirer of de Man, Miller (perhaps fortunately) lacked de Man's fascination with the void. For him deconstruction was a critical method that he practiced and preached with conviction, in no way introverted but turned to the outside world in a consistently political awareness. By *political* I mean that Miller was always conscious of the status of deconstruction within the academy or republic of letters. When it was an exciting new method, fighting to make itself known, Miller would set deconstruction aggressively against rhetoric. Once it had succeeded and even seemed on the wane, Miller could claim that deconstruction and rhetoric were essentially engaged in the same activity.

For the early phase we might take Miller's essay on a poem by Wallace Stevens ("The Rock"), in which he diagnosed "a repetition of the act of manifestation" in various scenes, but also a "deconstruction of that structure." Miller turned to rhetoric to define this process:

> The rhetorical name for this is catachresis. Catachresis is the violent, forced, or abusive use of a word to name something which has no literal name. . . . Catachresis explodes the distinction between literal and figurative on which the analysis of tropes is based and so leads the "science" of rhetoric to destroy itself as science, as clear and distinct knowledge of truth.[31]

Impressively trenchant though this pronouncement seems, it creates more problems than it settles. It is hard to see how one trope, forming part of the arsenal of rhetoric, can possibly make the whole of rhetoric "destroy itself." (Under the deconstructionist onslaught, literary works, or indeed whole disciplines, willingly commit suicide, having had their weaknesses exposed. This is a proof of the

---

[31]J. H. Miller, "Stevens' Rock and Criticism as Cure," *Georgia Review* 30 (1976): 5–31, quotation on 28.

theoreticians' megapower.) Further, if catachresis depends on the distinction between literal and figurative (not every one would accept this definition), it can hardly explode that distinction. And I cannot think of many advocates who have claimed that rhetoric gave a "clear and distinct knowledge of truth": such claims have usually been made by philosophers attacking rhetoric. Beneath the trenchancy, then, we find a muddle, travestying rhetoric in order to defeat it as an art that has no choice but to rely on language. For Miller also believed that "all referentiality in language is a fiction," that "all words are initially catachreses," and that "all poetry and all language are *mises en abyme*, since all language is based on catachresis."[32] Such categorical assertions allow the reader no response but monosyllabic exclamations, such as "Great!", or "Rubbish!" Either way, the rejection of reference leaves no role for rhetoric.

In the second part of this essay Miller made a specifically political survey of the current state of literary criticism, in the breakup of structuralism into "warring sects" that nevertheless shared a common "focus on language as the central problematic of literary study."[33] Under this rubric Miller was prepared to countenance "a return to the explicit study of rhetoric," but he instantly added a caution evidently inspired by de Man (then his colleague at Yale): "Rhetoric means in this case the investigation of figures of speech rather than the study of persuasion, though the notion of persuasion is still present in a more ambiguous, displaced form, as the idea of production, or of function, or of performance."[34] Once again, though, we must deny this splitting of the figures of speech, tools of persuasion, from the persuasive faculty itself. And again note that the proponent of deconstruction sees no incompatibility in appropriating rhetoric for a system that believes, inter alia that "the critic cannot by any means get outside the text, escape from the blind alleys of language,"[35] that "the text performs on itself" a deconstruction of the ground on which it stands, including "the solid, extra-linguistic world of 'objects'. . . ."[36]

The tension between deconstruction and rhetoric, set aside here, emerged with full clarity toward the end of the essay, as Miller charted what he saw as some striking total "reversals" in contemporary criticism. One of these, he claimed, was the way in which the "rational and reassuringly 'scientific' study of tropes by present-day rhetoricians"—the scare quotes are another cheap slur, because no one studying rhetoric confuses it with science—depends on a distinction between literal and figurative uses of language and "ends by putting these distinctions in question and so undermines its own ground."[37] That typical decon-

[32]Miller, "Stevens' Rock" 29.

[33]J. H. Miller, "Stevens' Rock and Criticism as Cure: II," *Georgia Review* 30 (1976): 330–348, quotation on 332.

[34]Miller, "Steven's Rock II" 333.

[35]Miller, "Steven's Rock II" 331.

[36]Miller, "Steven's Rock II" 333–334.

[37]Miller, "Steven's Rock II" 343–344.

structionist ploy (Kt to Q4) was a judgment on Gérard Genette's essay on "Métonymie chez Proust" (in *Figures III*), where Miller loyally sided with his friend de Man. I do not think he gave a fair account of Genette, who seemed to me in every way a more interesting and stimulating writer than de Man; but in any case this critique of rhetoric was just a buildup to the total deconstruction of it that followed on the next page, along with another rival, structuralism, which was also said to have committed its "self-subversion" (another instance of "the deconstructionists' *hara-kiri*") by its

> discovery that language is not a base. This is the moment of the self-destruction of rhetoric. The study of tropes looks at first like a safely scientific, rational, or logical discipline, but it still leads to the abyss, as it did for the old rhetoricians in the endless baroque, though entirely justifiable, proliferation of names for different figures of speech. More fundamentally, the study of rhetoric leads to the abyss by destroying, through its own theoretical procedures, its own basic axiom. Broadening itself imperialistically to take in other disciplines (philosophy, anthropology, literary criticism, psychology), rhetoric ultimately encounters, within itself, the problems it was meant to solve.[38]

Miller thought it enough to buttress this judgment with a quotation from Nietzsche's *Death of Tragedy* (in the awful translation by Oscar Levy), and to end by ringing the changes on his school's value terms ("deconstructed—abyss—expresses its own aporia—underlying chaos—illusions—self-subversion—destroys its own terminology—*mise en abyme*—the abyss itself"). Non-deconstructionists might feel that any argument has yet to be made.

Miller's demolition of rhetoric in 1976 was so total that the innocent reader might well think, "Hector is dead: There is no more to say." But in his later writings, Miller's political awareness had changed, and with it his attitude toward rhetoric. Deconstruction had established itself in many university departments and publishers' catalogues; Miller himself had become a senior figure in the profession and was frequently called on to address meetings of English teachers or preside over professional bodies. Addressing a summer conference of the Association of Departments of English in 1979, Miller chose as his topic "The Function of Rhetorical Study at the Present Time."[39] Having surveyed some recent changes in society and education, and having urged the importance of critical theory in "disabling the power of the works read to go on proliferating the ideology that traditional canonical or thematic readings of it have blindly asserted" (89)—not exactly a model sentence to utter in the presence of composition teachers—Miller recommended to the teachers present: "a form of literary

---

[38]Miller, "Steven's Rock II" 345–346.
[39]I quote from the revised text, reprinted in J. Engell and D. Perkins, eds., *Teaching Literature. What Is Needed Now* (Cambridge, MA: Harvard University Press, 1988) 87–109; page references incorporated in the text.

study that concentrates on the rhetoric of literary texts, taking rhetoric in the sense of the investigation of the role of figurative language in literature. This method is sometimes called 'deconstruction' . . ." (93). There, calmly and coolly, having earlier officiated at the "self-deconstruction of rhetoric," Miller now appropriated it as an allied discipline, by reference to which deconstruction could be recommended as an essential part of both undergraduate and graduate curricula.

Miller's new advocacy for rhetoric was carefully cut from the cloth available, the expectations of assembled teachers of English, divided between those who taught expository writing and those who taught literature. Miller told his audience of his belief in the need to develop "integrated programs in reading well and in writing well" and announced that " 'rhetorical study' is the key to this integration" (95). Yet he outlined a precondition, namely, that both groups of teachers must become aware of the "transformation" in their subject created by "developments in modern linguistics." Not referring to Chomsky, Lyons, Austin, Grice, Searle, Labov, Bernstein, or any of the other leading linguists and philosophers of language in our time, Miller alluded vaguely but confidently to "what is sometimes called the 'paradigm shift' from a referential or mimetic view of language to an active or performative one" (95–96). Like any good salesman, Miller praised the product he represented, describing those people "involved at the frontier of this exciting new branch of the broader discipline of English" (who have abandoned the concept of language as being able to refer to reality) as having "the air of persons doing something justifiable and good, while teachers of literature sometimes seem to me to have a furtive and guilty air, as though they were doing something not altogether justifiable in the present context" (96). But an audience of experienced English teachers was surely unlikely to succumb to such simple tricks. Using the metaphor of paradigm shift, to begin with, Miller tried to present the development that he asserted to have taken place as a decisive, widely shared change of attitude, whereas it was no such thing. Those who have really abandoned the notion that language can refer to reality are a small group of avant-gardistes who, if they truly practice what they preach, must be having great difficulties negotiating the world they live in. Far from doing "something justifiable and good," they are actually destroying language as a fundamental medium of human existence. The linguists and philosophers of many different persuasions who hold this belief are not noticeably "furtive and guilty" either, just going about their normal lives.

A less obvious but equally false dichotomy that Miller advanced was that between a "referential" view of language and an "active or performative one." Actually, the one includes the other; in fact one could argue that it is precisely because language can refer reliably to the world we live in that people are able to use it for speech acts. What other function would these have if they did not mediate between human beings living in what we call the world, or society, or reality? Miller, echoing de Man, then tried to drive a wedge into the "two-branched discipline" of rhetoric, setting on one side "the study of persuasion," which he linked with "the teaching of expository writing"; and, on the other, "the study of the function of tropes, the whole panoply of figures," which he linked with "programs in literature" (96–97). It appears, he adumbrated, that some of the people teaching composition "are still . . . inhibited to some degree by the mirage of straightforward referential language" and believe that "good writing . . . is calling a spade a spade." (This is called travestying the opposition, using the figure *meiosis*.) Their more enlightened colleagues in literary study, however, know that the crucial ability in reading "is expertise in handling figurative language" and have duly recognized "that all language, even language that seems purely referential or conceptual, is figurative language" (97). But this dichotomy must be rejected, too: Even when we use tropes, our language is still referential. The literal and the figurative levels in language can be distinguished, even though it is not always easy to say how we are able to do so;[40] and both levels can be used to refer to real worlds, possible worlds, or fantastic and impossible worlds. Language, being reflexive, as everybody knows, can also refer to itself.

Miller, however, as a loyal deconstructionist, was still unaware of the gulf separating rhetoric and deconstruction and believed that the linguistic skepticism of deconstruction somehow preempted rhetoric by asserting "the irreducibly fig-urative nature of language"—whereas the whole rationale of this branch of rheto-ric was that rhetorical figures and tropes should be used for effects of contrast or emphasis on specific occasions, for clearly defined ends. Miller therefore thought it legitimate to claim that deconstruction supplanted rhetoric, since it attempted "to interpret as exactly as possible the oscillations in meaning" pro-duced by figurality (97). The term "oscillation," one of several scientistic meta-phors that Miller favored, seems innocuous, as if deconstruction were not the aggressive, undermining, questioning mode he had earlier celebrated. More typi-cal of the real thrust of his argument was the reference in his final paragraph to "the decisive function of figurative language in making meaning heterogeneous or undecidable" (108). Miller was now trying to harness rhetoric to the more radical goals of deconstruction. But if, as he claimed, all language was figurative, why should that make meaning "undecidable"? Metaphor, irony, allegory—all tropes have the function of illuminating meaning or making it more memorable. Although lacking de Man's daemonic nihilism, the fear of falling that attracts one to the abyss, Miller was just as prone to asserting sections of the decon-structionist credo without satisfactory argument. The way ahead, though, was clear, for "what is the teaching of reading but the teaching of the interpretation of tropes?" (97). If "the center of literary interpretation is the study of tropes" (97), then "the key to understanding . . . a good work of literature . . . is a sophistication in the interpretation of figures," always bearing in mind that the work's function is "more performative than mimetic" (109).

Some teachers of rhetoric might feel flattered to be included in the decon-structionist fold, with a great future behind them. If so, it would be under false pretenses. The study of literature is much more than the study of tropes and

---

[40]See, for instance, Christopher Butler, *Interpretation, Deconstruction, and Ideology. An Introduction to Some Current Issues in Literary Theory* 8–25.

figures! I write that sentence as one who has frequently advocated, and practiced, rhetorical analyses of literary works; yet the point of departure and return in my work has always been the function of rhetorical devices in representing thoughts, experiences, arguments, feelings, whether as self-discovery, as self-reflection, or as attempts to persuade others. Language is a specifically human mode of communication, a symbol system that depends on interpretation by both the speaker and the listener. It is not a mechanically perfect system of encoding and decoding, as philosophers and rhetoricians know full well. Yet it works, for it has other resources that can overcome ambiguity and misunderstanding, most of the time, and it permits its users remarkable creativity within a system of rules. The deconstructionists' paradox—superficial and increasingly empty—that they have to assume determinate meaning in order to indict language of indeterminacy, induces in its believers a state of passive acceptance that seems to prevent them from thinking about language, or rhetoric, in any other terms.

Thus J. Hillis Miller, when delivering the Presidential Address to the Modern Language Association in 1986,[41] still believed that the great breakthrough of modern literary theory was its "focus on referentiality as a problem" and that this was "the theory of rhetorical reading or of deconstruction" (283). Miller's task on that occasion was to defend what he insisted on calling "text-orientated rhetorical theories of reading" (286), namely, deconstruction, against Marxism and versions of historicism that, Miller feared, had gained the ascendancy in American universities and had displaced theory. (Whether that had actually happened, or whether Miller simply feigned defeat in order to strike back all the harder, I am unable to say.) Miller's strategy was to attack Marxist terminology, bringing in rhetoric for this purpose. The term "materiality," he claimed, was nothing more than "a catachrestic trope . . . for what can never be approached, named, perceived, felt," and so on. This term, any term (even deconstruction?) is an unreliable key to reality, for "the word materiality gives us possession of what it names but only by erasing the named object," for "what materiality names can never be encountered as such because it is always mediated by language . . ." (289). Members of the MLA gathered in the Marriott Marquis Hotel of New York in December 1986 would have instantly recognized the ideas of Derrida and de Man, deconstructionists typically taking a dichotomy to a one-sided extreme and concluding that because we can talk about rifles or bombs (Miller had earlier vaunted literary theory as a new American product, exported, "along with other American 'products', all over the world—as we do many of our scientific and technological inventions, for example, the atom bomb" [287]—regrettably, I can detect no irony), then these weapons have been "mediated by language" and are therefore, somehow, less material or not at all material, or . . . but where could this argument go? (One of de Man's notorious pronouncements

---

[41]J. Hillis Miller, "The Triumph of Theory, the Resistance to Reading, and the Question of the Material Base," (Publications of the Modern Language Association) *PMLA* 102 (1986): 281–291; page references incorporated in the text.

was to describe history as a linguistic event.) But whatever MLA delegates may have expected from a deconstructionist president, I doubt if either deconstructionists or Marxists could have predicted Miller's further reasoning: "The concept of the material base involves the area of rhetorical study where the tropes apostrophe, catachresis, and prosopopoeia overlap and diverge. Such mastery of the problem of materiality as is possible will be attained only through the study and understanding of these tropes—no easy task . . ." (289). Indeed, Miller could affirm that "our best hope" for "the future of literary studies" would be "a rhetorically sophisticated reading," namely, "that rhetorical reading which today is most commonly called 'deconstruction' " (289). This "real reading" would not only recognize how "the rhetorical or tropological dimension of language undermines straightforward grammatical and logical meaning"; it would also confront "the performative or positional power of language as inscription over what we catachrestically call the material" (291).

Students of contemporary history always run the risk of being too close to the topics they study, with all the dangers that implies. At a distance of only 5 years from Miller's lecture, it seems a clear case of deconstruction once again appropriating rhetoric in order to legitimize its own activities, with the added twist that rhetoric was then used as a tool to attack the Marxists, a rival school at that time. Although the Marxists cannot have been pleased to see the materialist base, their alpha and omega, reduced to a mere rhetorical figure, and an abusive one at that, rhetoricians cannot feel comfortable in being aligned with deconstruction on epistemological grounds, whatever its political ambitions. For it should now be clear that such claims—that figurative language makes meaning undecidable, or that figurative language is by definition anti-referential—fixed principles in deconstruction, are antipathetic to the whole tradition of rhetoric.

Contemporary historians can also have advantages that later students lack. Being so near to these events, we can understand them. A future generation may ask in puzzlement: We know what rhetoric is; but what was deconstruction?[42]

---

[42]As the century grows older, evaluations of deconstruction have become more severe. See, for instance, the works already cited (footnotes 10, 14, 18, 21) by M. H. Abrams, P. Drews, M. Frank, L. Ferry and A. Renaut, J. R. Searle, J. M. Ellis, C. Butler. See, in addition, A. D. Nuttall, *A New Mimesis* (London: Methuen, 1983); J. G. Merquior, *From Prague to Paris. A Critique of Structuralist and Post-Structuralist Thought* (London: Verso, 1986); Wendell V. Harris, *Interpretive Acts. In Search of Meaning* (Oxford: Oxford University Press, 1988); Thomas Pavel, *The Feud of Language. A History of Structuralist Thought* [originally *Le mirage linguistique*, Paris, 1988], trans. L. Jordan and T. Pavel (Oxford: Blackwell, 1989); Leonard Jackson, *The Poverty of Structuralism. Literature and Structuralist Theory* (London: Longman, 1991); David Lehman, *Signs of the Times. Deconstruction and the Fall of Paul de Man* (New York: Deutsch, 1991); Robert Alter, *The Pleasures of Reading in an Ideological Age* (New York: Simon and Schuster, 1992); Seán Burke, *The Death & Return of the Author, Criticism and Subjectivity in Barthes, Foucault, and Derrida* (Edinburgh: Edinburgh University Press); Valentine Cunningham, *In the Reading Goal, Postmodernity, Texts, and History* (Oxford: Blackwell, 1994); and Dwight Eddins, ed., *The Emperor Redressed. Critiquing Critical Theory* (Alabama University Press, forthcoming), especially the contributions by M. H. Abrams, "What Is a Humanistic Criticism?" and John Searle, "Literary Theory and Its Discontents."

PART FOUR

This evaluation of deconstructionist attempts to appropriate rhetoric (on the principle, perhaps, of "if you can't beat them, join them!") has been unavoidably negative. It may be that deconstruction needs rhetoric to legitimize itself, but it is hard to see that rhetoric needs deconstruction. I should like advocates of Derridian language games to fundamentally rethink their position, learn from rhetoric the actual power of language both in real and fictional worlds, and consider by an open-minded empirical study of language just how it is that people are able to communicate reliably with each other, not to speak of the ability of poets, dramatists, and novelists to create works of art in language. For a much richer alternative conception of language they could turn to the later Wittgenstein to Stuart Hampshire, John Searle, Paul Grice, John Lyons, to name just a few writers whose work is easily accessible and understandable.[43] To see how rhetoric can be reanimated by contemporary philosophy, they could turn to the work of Chaïm Perelman,[44] unknown to all the deconstructionists I have read. (He provides a powerful, and therefore threatening, reconstruction of the function of language in argumentation, from which they would undoubtedly benefit.) They could also follow out the links between rhetoric and a relatively new linguistic discipline, pragmatics, in the work of Geoffrey Leech, Dan Sperber, and Deirdre Wilson.[45] Or they could tackle the still-growing oeuvre of Jürgen Habermas, in which the notions of dialogue, a shared communication framework, and the centrality of speech to society and ethics are vital.[46]

Deconstructionists should break out of their self-contained mould and see rhetoric with fresh eyes. The fact that rhetoric has survived for so long and continues to contribute to the growth of many disciplines must mean that its view of language cannot be all that bad.

---

[43]See, for example, Stuart Hampshire, *Thought and Action* (New York: Viking Press, 1959); John Searle, *Speech Acts. An Essay in the Philosophy of Language* (Cambridge: Cambridge University Press, 1969); John Lyons, *Semantics*, 2 vols. (Cambridge: Cambridge University Press, 1977); Paul Grice, *Studies in the Way of Words* (Cambridge, MA: Harvard University Press, 1989); and Simon Blackburn, *Spreading the Word. Groundings in the Philosophy of Language* (Oxford: Oxford University Press, 1984).

[44]Chaïm Perelman (with L. Olbrechts-Tyteca), *Traité de l'argumentation. La nouvelle rhétorique*, 3rd ed. (1958; Brussels: Editions de l'Université de Bruxelles, 1976); trans. J. Wilkinson and P. Weaver as *The New Rhetoric. A Treatise of Argumentation* (Notre Dame, IN: University of Notre Dame Press, 1969).

[45]Geoffrey Leech, *Principles of Pragmatics* (London: Longman, 1983); Dan Sperber and Deirdre Wilson, *Relevance. Communication and Cognition* (Oxford: Blackwell, 1986).

[46]See, for instance, J. Habermas, *Communication of the Evolution of Society*, trans. T. McCarthy (London: Heinemann Educational, 1979); J. Habermas, *Theory of Communicative Action, I; Reason and the Rationalisation of Society*, trans. T. McCarthy (Boston: Beacon Press, 1984); T. McCarthy, *The Critical Theory of Jürgen Habermas* (Cambridge, MA: MIT Press, 1978); M. Pusey, *Jürgen Habermas* (London: E. Horwood: International Thompson Publishing Service, 1987). The concluding chapter of Thomas M. Conley's admirable survey, *Rhetoric in the European Tradition*, 2nd ed. (Chicago: Chicago University Press, 1994), "Philosophers Turn to Rhetoric" (285–310), contains brief evaluations of Perelman and Habermas.

Index of Persons

Subject Index